BÊTES NOIRES

BÊTES NOIRES

NOIRES

LAUREN DERBY

SORCERY AS HISTORY

IN THE HAITIAN-DOMINICAN BORDERLANDS

DUKE UNIVERSITY PRESS | DURHAM AND LONDON | 2025

Project Editor: Livia Tenzer
Designed by Matthew Tauch
Typeset in Merlo Tx and Anybody Expanded by
Westchester Publishing Services

Library of Congress Cataloging-in-Publication Data
Names: Derby, Lauren author
Title: Bêtes noires : sorcery as history in the Haitian-Dominican
borderlands / Lauren Derby.
Other titles: Sorcery as history in the Haitian-Dominican borderlands
Description: Durham : Duke University Press, 2025. | Includes
bibliographical references and index.
Identifiers: LCCN 2025009458 (print)
LCCN 2025009459 (ebook)
ISBN 9781478032786 paperback
ISBN 9781478029359 hardcover
ISBN 9781478061564 ebook
ISBN 9781478094401 ebook other
Subjects: LCSH: Santeria—Haiti—Customs and practices | Oral
tradition—Haiti | Witchcraft—Haiti | Vodou—Haiti | Superstition—
Haiti | Santeria—Dominican Republic—Customs and practices | Oral
tradition—Dominican Republic | Witchcraft—Dominican Republic |
Vodou—Dominican Republic | Superstition—Dominican Republic |
Spirits—Folklore
Classification: LCC BL2566.H2 D473 2025 (print) | LCC BL2566.H2
(ebook) | DDC 299.6/433097293—dc23/eng/20250509
LC record available at https://lccn.loc.gov/2025009458
LC ebook record available at https://lccn.loc.gov/2025009459

Cover art: Leah Gordon, *Lansè Kòd I (Rope Throwers I)*, 2000.
Courtesy of the artist.

This book is freely available in an open access edition thanks to
TOME (Toward an Open Monograph Ecosystem)—a collaboration
of the Association of American Universities, the Association of
University Presses, and the Association of Research Libraries—
and the generous support of Arcadia, a charitable fund of Lisbet
Rausing and Peter Baldwin, and the UCLA Library. Learn more at
the TOME website, available at: openmonographs.org.

FOR ALEC, JAMES, JULIAN, AND ANDREW

CONTENTS

ACKNOWLEDGMENTS

I am grateful for the generous support for this project I have received from the American Council of Learned Societies, the National Endowment for the Humanities, the University of California Humanities Research Institute, and a LASA Special Projects Grant, as well as research grants from the University of California, Los Angeles, for twelve research trips to Haiti and the Dominican Republic, and the Center for Gender Studies at UCLA for a research grant as well as a manuscript review, which was immensely helpful in clarifying the organization and arguments of the draft. UCLA's Institute of the Americas and the Center for the Study of Women also funded research trips to the Dominican Republic, and some of the revisions were made while I was a fellow at the University of California Humanities Research Institute and benefited from discussions with Aaron James and the other fellows in the seminar on truth. I will be eternally grateful to Lizabeth Paravisini-Gebert, Elizabeth DeLoughrey, Katherine Smith, Carla Pestana, April Mayes, and Randol Contreras, who gave me incredibly helpful feedback during the manuscript review and saw beyond the disorder to help me clarify the core arguments of the work.

One's second monograph offers its own particular challenges, but I am immensely grateful to the community that nurtured my ideas as they have developed over the years and who guided this manuscript in critical ways. Marcy Norton, with whom this research commenced at the Huntington Library, has been a key friend and colleague who pushed me to see Indigenous traces on Hispaniola and has deeply shaped how I understand relations between human and nonhuman animals on the island and beyond. Marcy and Carla Pestana introduced me to the early colonial Caribbean. I am so lucky to have the enduring friendship of Caribbeanist colleagues Elizabeth DeLoughrey, Katherine Smith, Judith Bettelheim, and Lizabeth Paravisini-Gebert, who went way beyond the call of duty reading multiple drafts of these chapters and provided critical support and feedback over the years. Colleagues, friends, and fellow travelers in the journey that this research and write-up have entailed who have improved the book in important ways include Raúl Fernández, whom I relied upon frequently to clarify queries and provide research materials, as well as Rodrigo Bulamah, Pablo Gómez, Anne Eller, Patrick Polk, Marion Traub-Werner, Sara Johnson, Paul Christopher Johnson, Martha Few, Leah Gordon, Zeb Tortorici, Tony Lucero, Judy Carney, Sophie Mariñez, Sarah Stein, Toni Monnin, Kristen Block, Aaron James, Diana Schwartz Francisco, Jenna Gibbs, María Elena García, Charles Walker, Andrea Goldman, Elizabeth McAlister, Karen Richman, Chip Carey, Vikram Tamboli, Maria Cristina Fumagalli, Reinaldo Román, Ginetta Candelario, David Sartorius, Kyrstin Mallon Andrews, Jean Daniel Lafontant, Julie Franks, Peter Pels, Frantz Voltaire, Ada Ferrer, Ra'anan Boustan, Allen Wells, Tracey Dewart, Michel and Brier Eckersley, Bill Gannett, Josefine Wallace, David Sutton, Frank Polyak, Louis Pérez, Lázara Menendez, Reinaldo Funes Monzote, Bill Beezley, Teresa Barnett, Gabriel Rosenberg, Jim Scott, Amy Wilentz, and Sara Melzer. Thanks to Hélène Cardona for translation assistance and to Bob Dannin, who introduced me to Marxist theory. I am deeply indebted to Martha Ellen Davis, who has taught me so much over the years about Dominican popular religiosity and first brought me to the central frontier town of Bánica, Elías Piña, which became my central field site. I am grateful to Rachel Afi Quinn and Rubén Durán for their images of Dominican Carnival. In Santo Domingo, Raymundo González, Frank Moya Pons, César Zapata, José Frias, Giovanni Saviño, Alicia Sangro Blasco, Alicia Landestoy, Tess Kulstad, Víctor Camilo, Julio César Santana, Samuel Gregoire, and Austria Alcántara have provided support and insights over the years, as has Toño Arias Pelaez, whom I met several times on pilgrimage to the sacred cave of San Francisco. Thanks to the two anonymous readers for Duke University Press for their deep read and thoughtful, incisive, and meticulous insights. My title gives homage to Michael Taussig, whose work has long inspired me, and I am equally indebted to trailblazers Martha Ellen Davis on Dominican folk Catholicism, Carlos Esteban Deive on the history of Dominican *vodú*, and Raymundo González on the *montero*. Thanks to Sharon Farb and the Young Research Library for their support of the digital edition, and to Edward Trujillo for solving some seemingly intractable image issues.

After years of visits to Bánica, I feel as if I have found my place in the town, especially when Sija Moreta requested a photograph of my twins for her altar through which she told fortunes for her clients on

Fridays. Doña Pico Mora, leader of the St. Francisco cofradia, with whom I stayed during many visits to Bánica, also said that she foresaw my arrival through a vision of one of my twin boys. As in Haiti, in Bánica twins are considered particularly numinous as well as potentially dangerous, and they are said to have powers of magic and divination since they are the "original dead"; I was admonished never to feed them vegetables so that they would not lose their special powers, a taboo they appreciated even if I did not. And during one of my visits I was sent home with a yucca seedling to plant in my garden, which was intended to make me a true Baniquera (alas, it did not thrive, since I lack gardening skills). Special thanks to Doña Pico Mora for her hospitality over the years as well as Martín Alcántara Fragoso (Bubú) and his wife, Reyes; Hécfredes Gómez, from whom I have learned so much about religious matters; Irio Ramírez; Edwin Pérez in San Juan de la Maguana; Jennifer Severe in Elías Piña; Fernando Alcántara, Héctor Alcántara Fragoso, Mello, Riderson, Judy Mora, and Sabia who fed me macaroni and cheese on many occasions; and countless others who have spoken with me at length during my many visits. I am grateful to Father O'Hare, Mari Ramírez, Johnathan, Carlito, Flor, Elvis and Carmen, Arsenio and Bienvenido, and other friends who have made Bánica such a wonderful place to visit; Niccolo in Biassou, just across the Artibonite River, with whom I shared *kleren* (bathtub rum) on many occasions; and in Port-au-Prince, Watson Denis, Kendy Vérilus, Ronald Edmond, Zidor Sophonie, Fred Lagrandeur, and the students in our seminar on oral history at the Université d'état d'Haiti who taught me so much. Román Alcántara and his wife, Beba, in particular were exceedingly hospitable, offering me many cups of coffee and stewed guinea fowl when one could be had. Abercio (Abel) Alcántara has been an exceptional research assistant in Bánica, just as Georges René has been an extraordinary assistant in Port-au-Prince, Haiti; I never could have collected or deciphered this material without them.

I am deeply grateful to Pauline Kulstad, Mandie Nuanes, Alyssa Goodstein, Elizabeth Landers, and Karen Li, who provided crucial assistance and support at precisely the right moments when my enthusiasm was sagging. Erik Peña traveled to Bánica with me and contributed to the research. A special thanks to my family for supporting me through this project on what they jokingly called "Santa Bánica": to Julian, James, and Alec, who visited the Easter masquerade Las Máscaras with me and grew up amid stories about the wily *bacá*, and to Andrew Apter, who spent more than a decade listening to me puzzling over this material and helping me think through it. Thanks to Gisela Fosado for her faith in this project. And thanks to Livia Tenzer, Sue Warga, and David Prout for their meticulous editorial assistance.

Unless otherwise noted the translations are my own. Most names have been changed to anonymize my interlocutors.

PREFACE
FROM THE MOUTH OF THE GOAT

The *baka* (*bacá* in Spanish) has been furtively trailing me for a very long time.[1] The seeds of this study were sown when Richard Turits and I were collecting oral histories about the 1937 massacre of Dominicans of Haitian descent in the Haitian-Dominican frontier and I first heard mention of the baka. Someone made a joke about stories that a car in Ouanaminthe, Haiti, had been taken to be a baka. Later I was told that the poultry, mules, and pigs left behind by Dominicans of Haitian descent fleeing the killing fields around Dajabón and Loma de Cabrera in 1937 were accursed baka that no one should touch.[2] I then heard stories that the brutal dictator Rafael Trujillo had a bacá that identified his enemies so he could have them eliminated, and that this accounted for his longevity in office.[3] And later I was told about a bacá that was responsible for several untimely deaths and blood in the toilets at a Dockers assembly plant in Santiago in the early 2000s.[4] But it was in the central frontier town of Bánica that I first heard about bacás in the form of uncanny dogs, pigs, cattle, and horses (and occasionally goats), which raised the thorny question of why only these particular beasts have become spirit demons today. My grandmother, who was haunted by a family member's revenant, eventually requiring that her apartment be subjected to an exorcism by a priest, prepared me to listen to these tales. (I use the Spanish spelling *bacá* when referring to a Dominican *bacá* reference and the Haitian Creole spelling *baka* when referring to a Haitian one.)

Although its name bears some resemblance to the Spanish word *vaca*, "cow," the term *bacá* is ultimately untranslatable; it accords with the names of other, very similar nonhuman spirit entities throughout the West Indies, *bakoo*, *buck*, and *bakru*. All of these provide their owner spiritual power to gain wealth and are often associated with ethnoracial others.[5] Like the indigenous Taíno spirits of the dead, they are open secrets lurking in the shadows, widely recognized but generally not publicly discussed.[6] They are also shape-shifting creatures that can morph from a little black humanoid figure in urban contexts to an animal host in rural settings. As *campesino* (rural smallholder) Domingo Bautista put it, "The bacá is a natural being that is made with an animal, into which the spirit of a dead person is introduced."[7] This specific fusion of a moneymaking male spirit and a being that can shape-shift into an animal is unique to Hispaniola and is a manifestation of what Dominicans call the *fukú de Colón*, or curse of Columbus, since it is only the types of animals brought by Columbus that have become spirit demons.[8] Perhaps the most diabolical of all these creatures is the goat, as evidenced by the fact that repressive dictator Rafael Trujillo was nicknamed "the Goat"; those who loathed him had a feast of goat meat upon his death, and Dominican popular speech includes dozens of vernacular sayings about goats.[9] But as we shall see, bacá spirit demons most often appear as dogs, cattle, horses, and feral pigs—the animals that enabled the dispossession of the indigenous Taíno.[10] I argue here that the bacá is first and foremost a "commodity familiar," a sign of ill-gotten wealth associated with predatory capitalism.

Yet in animal form, the baka also conveys a *longue durée* history of environmental despoilage that accompanied extractivism and had devastating human, faunal, and environmental costs. I propose that baka narratives are signs of what philosopher Paul Ricoeur has called the "space of experience," which includes the inchoate emotional traces left behind by past events—latent desires and fears, vestiges of which cannot often be found in written archives.[11] An avatar from the past with a distinctively disquieting frisson, the baka is a visceral conveyor of strong emotions such as sorrow, jealousy, and anger. Even if late-nineteenth-century travelers noted the abundance of forests (mahogany, pine, and other fine log woods) and birds, over time deforestation has taken its toll, even if it took longer and was not as extensive as in neighboring Cuba, since sugar's arrival in the Dominican Republic as a large-scale monocrop economy was delayed until the twentieth century, and even then sugar did not define the economy as it did in Cuba, Jamaica, or Puerto Rico.[12] These stories of spirit animal predation are polyvalent but may in part represent a defiant refusal to let go of the free-range hunting ecosystem called *montería*, notwithstanding the fact that the teeming animal commons of yesteryear that took refuge in the extensive forests has given way to domesticated animals grazing on parched and eroded savannas today. Thus baka revenants might be seen as a form of "environmentalism of the poor," since in refusing to go away, they seem to decry the violence and ecological damage wrought by industrial agriculture on the island; these "spirited things" appear to want to wish back into existence the feral animal commons now long gone.[13]

I have been fascinated by the biculturality of the "center-island" borderlands since traveling there in 1989 (see map 1).[14] Located on the banks of the Artibonite River, which serves as the dividing line between Haiti and the Dominican Republic, Bánica, Elías Piña, is one of the oldest towns on the island and has been called the Macondo of the Dominican Republic, a reference to the fictional town made famous by Colombian novelist Gabriel García Márquez, a master of the Latin American literary genre *lo real maravilloso* (magical realism), in which magic is cast as real and the forces of capitalism are presented as inscrutable and even supernatural.[15] Founded in 1504 and named for its abundance of ebony, Banique, as it was called during the colonial period, originally formed part of the Taíno Maguana *cacicazgo* or chiefdom. The past is palpably present in this town, where one can still see crossing the river canoes fashioned out of single logs (a technique passed down from the Taíno indigenous population, which is now long gone) (fig. P.1), and one can see atop mules that transport produce to market saddles fashioned out of intricately woven straw (a craft that dates from the early sixteenth century). I argue that, like these historical vestiges, the bacá in animal form is a historical artifact of the imagination, a searing "point of memory" of the mass death that commenced with the indigenous Taíno and continued through successive waves of brutal Indigenous and African slavery (the Spanish colony known as Santo Domingo was where the first African slaves arrived in the Americas and became the central depot for Indigenous slavery routed from New Spain and Amazonia in the sixteenth century).[16] The northern border later became the theater of the 1937 slaughter that took the lives of some fifteen thousand Dominicans of Haitian descent who were viciously killed by machete by the Trujillo regime (1930–61), a regime that was supported by the United States during the Cold War.[17] The bacá thus could also be seen as the "rot remains" of the "tangible effects of ruination" left behind by *longue durée* imperial histories of extractivism on the island.[18]

Haiti and the Dominican Republic are often cast as dramatically opposed nations and cultures, and these states have clashed at times.[19] Through sugar plantation agriculture, Haiti became the wealthiest of France's colonies in the eighteenth century, while the Dominican Republic languished as a colonial backwater dependent on extensive cattle ranching. But the baka/bacá is a poignant reminder that within the realm

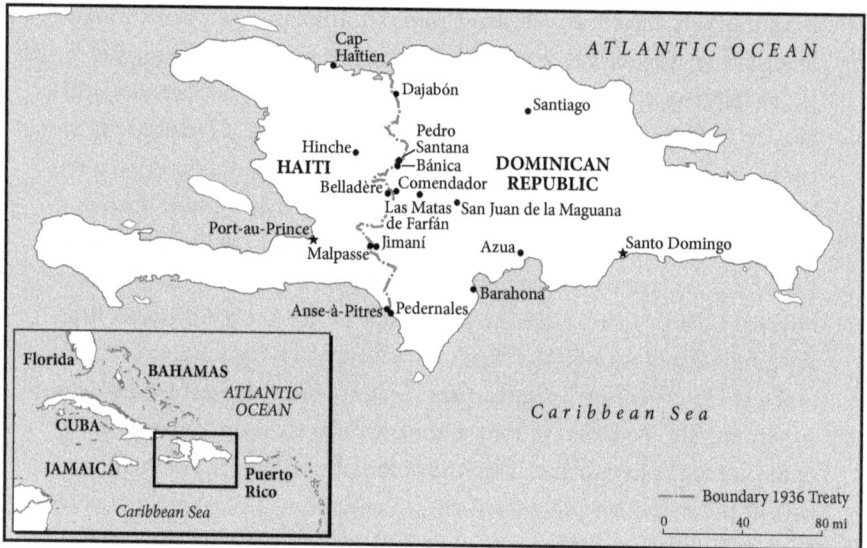

MAP 1 The Haitian-Dominican border and borderlands. Map by Emily Vogt, Committee on Geographical Studies, University of Chicago.

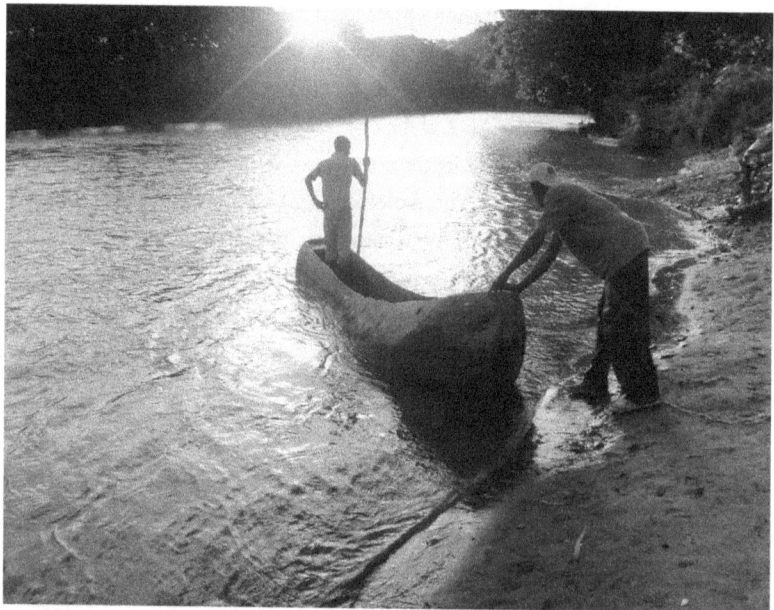

P.1 An example of the canoes used to cross the Artibonite River, which forms part of the border between Haiti and the Dominican Republic. Haiti, 2012. Photo by the author.

of popular culture, there is much on the island that is shared, since the stories told about its powers of predation are eerily similar, and Dominicans and Haitians share the same visceral reaction to signs of its presence. Of course, the island as a whole was ruled as a Spanish colony during the formative buccaneering period until the French colony of Saint-Domingue was founded in 1669.

Even if I primarily narrate the bacá's predations from the Dominican side of the island in this account, these stories exuberantly cross the border and serve to pit Haitians and Dominicans against one another as well as knit them together, just as the bacá transgresses other antinomies such as life and death, nature and culture, and human and animal.[20] This study offers an entangled view of the island, one in which Haitians and Dominicans are intertwined in "complex relations of dependency and interdependence" with spirits and animals as well as each other.[21] It is significant that in Port-au-Prince, Haiti, a pathway to the spirit world may be opened through Dominican red wine, while in the border province of Elías Piña, Dominican Republic, this may be done through Barbancourt, a Haitian rum.[22] These ties of codependence are conveyed through what anthropologist Birgit Meyer has termed "sensational form," since spirits and their animal hosts cannot speak and their presence is registered in and through the body.[23] Animals figure prominently as hosts for the divine and the diabolical in this context, and have long formed an integral part of everyday life and labor. In this rural community with a long-standing dependence upon livestock, animal sounds fill the air. The soundscape is replete with the distant sounds of cocks, cattle, goats, dogs, and donkeys. On market days, there are more burros carrying produce to market than trucks. Farmers contend that they can smell when it is going to rain, and the spirits make themselves known through dreams as well as sensations such as a gust of wind.[24]

The central frontier today is perceived by those living in the Dominican capital city, Santo Domingo, as a remote hinterland, but in the eighteenth century it became the centerpiece of the national economy as cattle and oxen poured across the border into the sugar plantation economy of Saint-Domingue when it became the world's largest sugar producer. The illicit cattle trade long knitted together Dominican ranchers and Saint-Domingue's sugar producers; not surprisingly, this was the region where the flag for a United Spanish Hayti—a unified island—was first raised in the nineteenth century.[25] As it expanded rapidly over the course of the eighteenth century, Bánica served as a bridge between the major township of San Juan de la Maguana, Dominican Republic, with its ample grazing savannas, and Hinche, Haiti, en route to the Artibonite Valley, where the sugar plantations formed that fueled Saint-Domingue's eighteenth-century sugar boom. Yet the population diminished at the turn of the century, when the sugar economy receded and it became a theater of war during and after the Haitian Revolution (1791–1804).[26] Bánica today is still dominated by descendants of the four principal cattle clans that founded the town, including the powerful cattle baron and political broker Wenceslao Ramírez of San Juan, whose grazing lands straddled the border, even if ranching is no longer a central feature of this area today (fig. P.2).[27]

This study is based on extensive oral histories with members of the founding ranching families, especially the extensive Alcántara clan and their field hands, descendants of General Victoriano Alcántara, who was said to have survived on the run from authorities through miraculous protection from bullets.[28] A member of the Alcántara family I spoke with had a sugar mill in Thomassique, Haiti, speaks Haitian Creole, and holds on to the pre-1937 border view of Haiti as grander and more cosmopolitan than the Dominican Republic due to its majestic architecture, ample imported goods, and formidable elite, harking back to a time when the Dominican border currency was the Haitian gourde. As he put it, "Haitians were very, very, very rich."[29] Nor are the Alcántaras the only family whose lives and kin have traversed the border. Renowned Haitian leader Charlemagne Péralte, who led the Caco uprising against the US occupation of Haiti (1915–34), actually hailed from the Peralta family, which was originally from Restauración, Dominican Republic, and his brother-in-law was Dominican. When Dominican legislation was passed in 2013 aimed at expelling Haitian-Dominicans born on Dominican soil after 1929, I was told that it did not have an appreciable impact on everyday life in Bánica.[30] Today the dance hall in Bánica plays Haitian *konpa* dance music alongside Dominican bachata.

The region's reputation for fierce independence is also due to the fact that it was long a refuge for maroons, or runaways from slavery. It was there that the Taíno chieftain Enriquillo stood up to the brutal Spanish colonizers, establishing a "locus of defiance" of runaway Indian and African slaves for nearly a decade.[31] Through the eighteenth century the southern Bahoruco Mountains were an outpost of insurgent runaway slaves who refused to submit to Spanish authorities and established what

P.2 Cow at rest outside Biassou, Haiti, 2014. Photo by the author.

historian Charlton Yingling has called a "realpolitik of evasiveness."[32] So in collective memory this area has long been a locus of fierce resistance to authorities. Even today the frontier identity as a "society against the state" remains palpable.[33] When border trade was officially shut down due to a cholera outbreak in Haiti in the 2010s, Dominicans in Bánica resisted by setting up a night market in the cemetery, where they surreptitiously traded with Haitians.[34]

While this study examines narratives of spirit demons in animal form, this region has also long been seen as a holy land due to its reputation for miraculous healing—in the eighteenth century its mineral springs were said by the French to be curative.[35] Its hallowed reputation was later burnished by the fact that faith healer Díos Olivorio Mateo took refuge in the area while on the run from authorities and that it was where he was eventually killed by US Marines in 1922, during the military occupation (fig. P.3).[36] It is said that Bánica's patron saint, San Francisco (St. Francis—appropriately, the patron saint of animals), has appeared in the sacred grotto there, which is a site of national pilgrimage, just as the national patron saint, the Virgin of Altagracia, appeared on a water tank.[37]

P.3 Irio Ramírez's altar with images of faith healer Dios Olivorio Mateo alive and slain. San Juan de la Maguana, Dominican Republic, 2015. Photo by the author.

The sacred cave of San Francisco is located on a mountain above Bánica and is the oldest pilgrimage site in the Caribbean, dating from precolonial times.[38] This may help explain why the largest town in the central frontier, San Juan de la Maguana, is seen as a center of potent sorcery on the island.[39]

I have long used oral history as a primary source in my work, but one particular challenge of this project has been centering a disorderly corpus of narratives of ghostly encounter episodes as my primary archive; perhaps this is necessary if we are to come to terms effectively with what it means to live "in the wake" of slavery in the Black Atlantic.[40] I commence each chapter with an anecdote about a personal encounter with a bacá, but this material should not be taken as folklore—that is, as something located in the past. These were related to me as contemporary historical events, even if there is at times a presumption that as the border has modernized these monstrous apparitions have lessened over time. This was made patently clear to me during an oral history class I co-taught at the State University of Haiti: I was presenting on the history of scholarly approaches to folklore, and the students responded by relating their own personal encounters with baka, which I interpreted as a repudiation of the framing of this material as traditional folklore and thus part of a distant past.[41]

My interviews were generally conducted as life narratives with follow-up questions about bacá sightings and encounters, but given the taboo nature of these phenomena, I had to approach the topic indirectly. In one case, I heard one particular version from one interlocutor and then very different versions from others (see chapter 5), but since my fieldwork was conducted in a series of short visits to the region over the span of over a decade commencing in 2008, it was rare that I was able to collect various perspectives on one particular incident. Some Catholics and most evangelicals object to even uttering the baka's name, which could conjure it, and instead describe it through a euphemism such as *pájaro malo* (evil creature).[42] Since bacá stories are male drinking tales, women play a role in transmitting them but tend not to discuss them in public, which required me to conduct my research with a male research assistant, even if, as a foreigner, I was granted access to male spaces. While oftentimes oral history is portrayed as a straightforward process of storage and retrieval, in this case deciphering these "anecdotal authority stories" and perceiving their patterns required interpretation.[43]

Walter Benjamin once claimed that storytelling was a declining art, but clearly it lives on robustly in Haiti and the Dominican Republic, where one might even say there is an excess of memory.[44] Perhaps, as Paul Ricoeur has said, storytelling and "critical history can contribute to the healing of collective memory."[45] In this case, as we shall see, this would involve healing the cultural trauma wrought by colonial conquest, as the seed animals brought by Christopher Columbus became technologies of famine and terror and today have been converted into spirit demons stalking the central frontier.[46] This popular vision of Columbus's *fukú* or curse is, of course, completely at odds with a state that has long sought to define the Dominican population as descended from Columbus via rooting a mythic Hispanic identity in his remains.[47] The interface between trauma and the spirit world has been noted by Cathy Caruth, since to be traumatized is to be "possessed by an image or event," which is also a way to describe being seized by a spirit. She also recognized posttraumatic stress to be not just a symptom of mind but also a "symptom of history."[48] Christopher Columbus himself noted the absence of monsters on Hispaniola, which is more than a little ironic, since if I am right, he actually unleashed them there.[49]

SPIRITS, HISTORY, & POWER

A day for the hunter,
a day for the prey.
BOUKMAN EKSPERYANS | "Ganga."

If you eat the meat, you have to pay for the meat.
AVADRA GRAND CHEMIN THROUGH ERNST NELSON

In June 2015 in Port-au-Prince, I went to speak with Avadra Grand Chemin, through his "horse" (spirit host) Ernst Nelson, about the shape-shifting skills of Haitian secret society members, since Nelson is a member of the Sanpwèl (fig. I.1).[1] The conversation touched on many themes, including mobility, eating, theft, and vital matter:

> EN: A secret society member can turn into an *asson* [a sacred rattle to call the spirits], a *kalbas* [gourd], a wheelbarrow, a lamp—they can turn into anything on earth.[2] They can turn into animals too: cattle, goat, pig. If they turn into a pig you cannot eat them. They can turn into a dog. You join the society [*inscrit*] when you enter the Sanpwèl. You lose a lot of things when you join. If you have a wife or a child, they might die—they might get eaten.[3] The

Sanpwèl eat meat. If you eat the meat, you have to pay for the meat. If you want to enter the society, someone has to present you. Both women and men can enter the Sanpwèl. In Sanpwèl, the girls fly higher than men. They can fly. When the Sanpwèl make a ceremony they have a special bottle. It is through the bottle that they become an animal. They can go anywhere—they may arrive in Aux Cayes or Jérémie as an animal. In one night, the Sanpwèl can visit all of Haiti.

LD: Could you ever by mistake eat a pig that was actually a Sanpwèl?

EN: No, because they only become animals at night. If someone becomes a pig, they are bad (*malfetè*); he is a *lougawou*. The lougawou can turn into an animal—a large pig or cow. If you try to sell that one in the market it will die. If someone eats that animal in the market, they are eating human meat.[4]

This study considers the spirit demons called baka/bacá on Hispaniola from the perspective of its Dominican victims who found themselves becoming its prey. Such was the case for Juan Alcántara, who was on sentry duty at a remote border post on the Dominican frontier when he was attacked by a phantom in the form of a rabid dog, which he eventually fought off, but only after a violent exchange of blows that left him very shaken up. Or the case of Hegel, who recounted to me that for years his house was haunted by a wild dog that would repeatedly scratch at his door, and which continually evaded him until someone suggested that he install a protective charm that eventually kept the beast at bay.

Here I want to consider this phenomenon for a moment from the perspective of its assailants, those skilled in the arts of sorcery who have been tasked with sending spirits as a form of supernatural assault. One of these is Ernst Nelson, who worked as a *bòcò* (sorcerer) in Martissant, Port-au-Prince, Haiti.[5] I will then explore how the baka might be seen as a "commodity familiar."[6] As a member of the Sanpwèl secret society, Nelson commands a virtual battalion of *mò* or spirits of the "*vagabon* dead," which he converts into *zonbi* and sends on expeditions to do specific things—for example, secure a straying wife, obtain a favorable legal outcome, or get vengeance on someone.[7] Working with the skull of a former *ougan* (vodou priest) who was his mentor in the arts of sorcery, Ernst has several squadrons of spiritual mercenaries at his disposal.[8] One group is represented by a cluster of small wooden chairs bound together

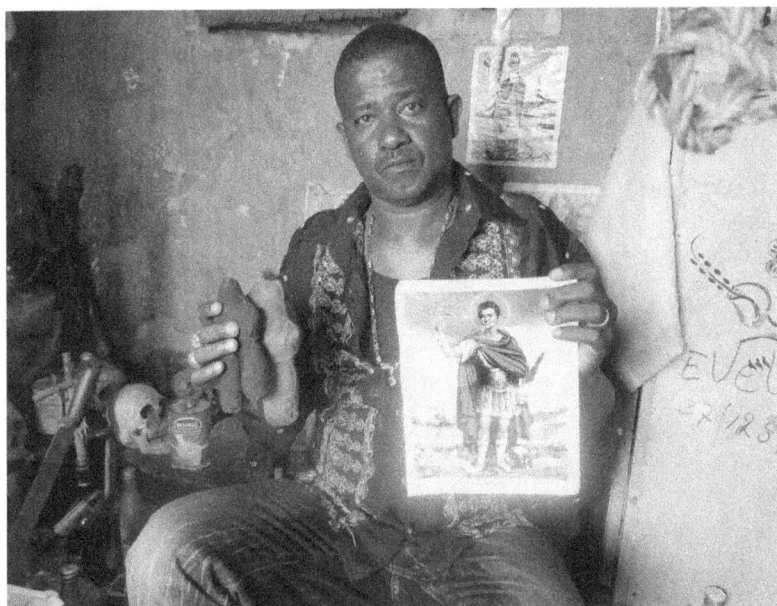

I.1 Vodou priest Ernst Nelson with his *zonbi*-making paraphernalia, including an image of St. Expeditus, the patron saint of urgent causes and desperate situations. Martissant, Port-au-Prince, Haiti, 2018. Photo by the author.

and hung upside down with twisted ropes from the ceiling of his *atelier* (fig. I.2); at the center of his workspace there is a skull with a lit candle in an ornate candelabra. He also works with small red and black cloth dolls and the skulls of several other former ougan, which can be used to send spirits on *zonbi expedisyon* (zonbi expeditions). As a member of the Sanpwèl, Ernst can change form as well, becoming (among other things) an animal, which confirms the observation that shape-shifting is centrally about experimenting with forms of power.[9]

Said to be the "first modern monster," the zonbi has received considerable attention as an allegory for the dispossession of labor under slavery—as literary critic Colin Dayan expressively put it, "the most powerful emblem of apathy, anonymity, and loss." It expresses the human cost of slavery, which produced "soulless husks deprived of freedom."[10] The zonbi presents "the animated corpse as allegory of the slave's disempowerment," alienated from kinship and community; the depleted slave who survived against all odds but is socially dead.[11] But this monstrous presence may have another, more visceral source as well. Since slaves

I.2 Detail of Nelson's altar. Photo by the author.

often lacked proper ritual mortuary care, their death was deprived of ritual recognition, which meant that "the border between the dead and the living is not properly sealed." For this reason, the suffering and angry dead became a menace threatening the living. As Valérie Loichot has put it, the deceased deprived of ritual strike "back at the system responsible for [their unmarked death] in the first place."[12] This confirms Haitian medium Georges René's interpretation that the baka are slave souls seeking revenge on the living for their distress. As one *curandero* (popular or folk healer) put it, "The baka isn't real, because it hasn't got a body by itself, but it has a reality."[13]

In the wake of slavery, forms of spirit work emerged in which the living work with the dead through "mystical labor."[14] Ritual specialists like Ernst Nelson channel these disembodied spirits and put them to use. On their own, these spirits can wreak tremendous havoc. This was the case after the 1937 massacre, when Haitian victims of the slaughter became vengeful spirits that hovered over the land they had lost when they fled.[15] Or after the 2010 Haitian earthquake, thousands of unburied dead victims were said to have become lougawou, causing furniture to fly out

I.3 Sign for Sosyete Dyab (Djab), a Haitian secret society, with Creole sayings. Port-au-Prince, Haiti, 2010. Photo by the author.

of second-story windows as far afield as Little Haiti in Santo Domingo, an area where Haitian traveling merchants reside.[16] Like the *pwen*, the baka, and the *djab*, the zonbi is a "manufactured, unnaturally vitalized power," a spirit of the dead that is trapped and conveyed by the invisible hand of an agent (fig. I.3).[17] The baka that shape-shift into animal form are specific to Hispaniola, but they bear a strong resemblance to morally ambivalent minor spirits with the power to both heal and harm, such as the buck of Trinidad, the *baccoo* of Guyana, the *bakru* of Surinam, and Amazonian practices that anthropologist Neil Whitehead has described as "dark shamanism" and which have become a feature of political power in the circum-Caribbean.[18] Thus the baka should be seen as part of a multispecies story of imperial violence and of spiritual power likely deployed as weapons of the weak during slavery, and may share a common etymology in *buck* or *bokjs*, the derogatory Dutch term for Amerindian, which derives from the word for "he-goat."[19] Another possible source is *mbakára*, which is an Ibo/Efik term for white man.[20] This lineage would also connect with the contraband trade in slaves and mules that long linked Hispaniola to Venezuela and the eastern Caribbean through Curaçao.

I.4 Sign for Piedra Imán (lodestar) and zonbi for sale. Elias Piña, Dominican Republic, 2016. Photo by the author.

The zombie has long been represented in Hollywood film as the depleted husk of a person who has had their soul removed, but that is not necessarily the primary way in which it functions in Haiti and the Dominican Republic.[21] The term *zonbi* derives from the Central African Kikongo word for "spirit" (fig. I.4), and Haitian talk about zombies is more centrally concerned with the work done with the disembodied souls rather than the soulless bodies. Ethnomusicologist Martha Ellen Davis has noted that in the Dominican Republic there is no real distinction between the dead and the living; the dead are merely invisible "vibrant matter," which make their presence known through the sensory realm since, like animals, they cannot speak.[22]

One source for zonbi practice is indigenous Arawak beliefs that spirits can be conveyed into stones or animals such as the sacred *zemi* power object, which itself had agency since it could speak, make things, grow, and roam on its own. Archaeologist José Oliver has described this as an expression of the "partible character of persons," since the zemi could extract, contain, and neutralize illness as well as shape-shift, taking different forms.[23] As in Nelson's testimony, the bottle as spirit container is a root metaphor and a "perspectivist shifter like Clark Kent's phone booth" since it can trap a spirit and empower a spell, just as spirits can be sent to reside in other containers. The bottle (*bouteille, botella*) is also a container for herbal medicine.[24]

The zonbi also has roots in Central and West African beliefs about embedding spirits in power objects such as *minkisi* (pl.; sing., *nkisi*), which accords the spirits personhood, as well as in male secret societies like the leopard-men of Nigeria or the Tabwa lions of the Democratic Republic of the Congo, which have the ability to shape-shift at night and were the basis for the secret maroon associations of colonial Saint-Domingue (fig. I.5).[25] The uncanny personhood of the zonbi bears a strong resemblance to West and Central African and Amazonian practices in which animals and objects have agency and animating spirits can be transferred from one vessel to another; thus the body is seen as an "envelope."[26] Shape-shifting was also a feature of Iberian witchcraft during the seventeenth century, when women in particular were said to be able to transform into goats, fowl, and rats.[27] In historian Caroline Bynum's categorization, these diabolical entities are hybrid creatures and do not represent true metamorphosis.[28]

Zonbi (*zonbi astral*) can be harnessed and sent as supernatural assistants to do things such as secure child support, enact vengeance against a wayward spouse, or steal another's crops. Zonbi are errant spirits that can also afflict a person who incites jealousy. Georges René, for example, was plagued by a zonbi that affixed to his leg, causing it to become swollen and painfully inflamed until he could see a specialist who could remove it; he attributed his affliction to *jalouzi*.[29] Ethnomusicologist Elizabeth McAlister has written that during the Easter carnivalesque rite called Rara in Haiti, secret society members carry brooms with which they sweep up zonbi to "heat up" and energize their troupes; after the procession, they return the zonbi to the cemetery.[30] Ethnobotanist Wade Davis discovered that bones and thunderstones (celts) are key ingredients in zonbi preparation alongside puffer fish toxin, and that the ingredients are placed in a jar and buried in the coffin of a dead infant before use.[31] Similar to Hollywood depictions, the zonbi is an emblem of horror.

I.5 *Baka* sculpture by André Eugene of a boy turning into a pig. Atis Rezistans studio, Port-au-Prince, Haiti, 2012. Photo by the author.

While they represent a single genre, baka stories appear in three distinct narrative idioms of tales of self and other.[32] The first represents fugitivity, in which a person transforms into an animal or something else—often to escape from authorities. This idiom was canonized during the Haitian Revolution when runaway slave and conjurer François Makandal bragged that he had escaped from jail by turning into a mosquito.[33] Baka stories can form masculine encounter narratives in which the eyewitness comes across these wily spirits in animal form at night, as we shall see in chapter 6. Baka can also be cast as supernatural assistants, engaged in surreptitious protection or thievery, or as covert profit generators. All of these variants appear in this study, but I focus here on the baka's appearance via an animal host.

PHANTOM CAPITALISM

As in Michael Taussig's classic formulation in *The Devil and Commodity Fetishism*, baka stories would be classed as devil pact tales; alternatively, I characterize baka as "commodity familiars," an analytic that reduces them to one singular defining motif of the stories—profit as theft—since the elusive creature enables the stealth acquisition of wealth, albeit at a grave cost.[34] Thus clandestine ownership of a baka often emerges as an explanation for otherwise inexplicable wealth acquisition. Secrecy is a key aspect of this phenomenon, which one might say is actually a characteristic feature of Latin American capitalism, since the motor of capitalist investment and its profits has long been invisible to locals on the ground.[35] This folk view of capitalism in the Caribbean makes sense, since from the start capitalism was an alien process—investment capital, technology, labor, managerial staff, and profit were all exogenous to the island, and the product itself was shipped overseas. Yet while these narratives clearly critique excessive and exogenous profit (baka, djab, pwen, and zonbi are all moneymaking *maji*, in Haitian parlance), there is much more going on in these stories than just a popular commentary on inequality.

The baka shares with other Latin American commodity familiars such as the zonbi an "essential foreignness," or telltale signs of whiteness. For example, zonbi beef turns deathly pale, and the bakru and Trinidadian buck crave bananas and milk—a breakfast popularized by the global fruit monopoly firm United Fruit.[36] More examples are the siren spirit, which prefers whiskey; blond mermaids who dole out cash; and stories in St. Lucia of a sea demon in the form of a huge white man astride an enormous steed that drags a chain behind it.[37] The spirit that guards the Oruru mine in Bolivia, El Tío (the uncle), has a large phallus and a cowboy hat. And industrial steel water tanks and jeeps are often said to be telltale signs of the dreaded Andean *pishtaco*.[38] These demons are specters of a long history of foreign extractivism and surreptitious flows of profit; rumors course that the dreaded *ñaqak* of Peru seek human fat to pay off the foreign debt.[39] Anthropologist Mary Weismantel has focused on how these stories convey *longue durée* patterns of exploitation. As she has said of the Andean *kharisiri*, "It is this pregnant narrative of social and material history, made visible in the pishtaco, that makes his body an object of fascination and disgust. Embedded in its possessions and its flesh is the record of what it has done to Indians in the past, and the threat of what it is about to do again."[40] These apparitions resonate with the Ibo etymology of *bukra* as "white man."[41] Unlike Taussig, I avoid the term *devil* here because of the way this flattens these spirits into a Christian model of demonology when, as Haitian sculptor André Eugene told me, from the perspective of believers they are *puissants* (powerful), but not necessarily evil.[42]

The fact that these phantasms are fetishes of the foreign also relates to the fact that they represent a particularly modern form of labor, commodity production—which, as Karl Marx has said, is a "social hieroglyphic" of concealed labor time investment, a fact that renders every commodity a public secret. Commodities are mysterious since they "conceal rather than disclose" the social character of labor; thus, like the baka, they reek of "magic and necromancy."[43] These conditions of labor "superexploitation" first associated with slavery later accompanied the rise of industrial agriculture in the post-emancipation period. This type of agriculture created intensive work conditions so harsh they demanded new forms of labor servitude, such as debt peonage and long-distance labor migration, to staff them; West Indians and above all Haitians were brought in as contract labor to cut cane on US-owned plantations in the Dominican Republic and Cuba.[44] No wonder baka rumor panics have coalesced around foreign-owned sugar plantations (such as the Haitian sugar firm HASCO, in the 1920s, and the sugar producer Gulf and Western, which operated in the Dominican Republic in the 1970s with Haitian labor receiving the paltry wages of 34 cents an hour; laborers' encampments were described as "slave labor camp[s]," and efforts at organizing there would be met with jail time or torture) and industrial free trade zones (where all inputs, capital, and products are foreign-owned).[45]

Baka narratives are not traditional folklore but rather popular commentary on the particular forms of surreptitious wealth generation that expanded in the twentieth century but have been a central component of Caribbean labor regimes since Christopher Columbus's arrival. These labor forms have a long and dark history in the Caribbean, where indentured servants were spirited away through a toxic combination of debt coercion, "'trick' and 'cheat' . . . [and] 'allurements and deluding falsities,'" and where slavery ruled through the nineteenth century.[46] As ground zero of Spanish colonization, Hispaniola experienced massive violence, famine, and epidemics that wiped out 90 percent of the Indigenous population, eliminating its existence as a corporate community within thirty years. With steel weapons and attack dogs, Europeans overcame Indians and then worked them to death. As the Taíno population receded, Santo Domingo became the central hub of Amerindian slavery, as upward of 650,000 Indigenous people were enslaved, uprooted, and shipped around the Atlantic, although mortality was very high.[47] Santo Domingo was also the first site of African slavery in the New World, as some twenty thousand enslaved people arrived by the 1550s to staff mining camps and sugar plantations until Spanish attention shifted to the mainland.[48] Death was a central point of intersection and shared experience between Amerindian and African slaves.

The annihilation caused by Latin American colonialism commenced with gold mining and the repartimiento system of forced labor drafts, which led, as Marcy Norton has put it, to "the dispossession of Indigenous labor, land, and, often, life."[49] Conditions were so dire that Indians often chose suicide over working for the Spanish.[50] Indigenous slaves and West Africans quickly took over Hispaniola placer gold mining after the rapid demise of the Taíno; some of the Africans likely brought with them mining skills that located them as "intermediaries between nature and culture," and they were rumored to be sorcerers with command over the supernatural, such as the earth spirits that guarded the ore.[51] Indeed, a possible linguistic leftover from the early mining economy may be the fact that the notion of being ravaged by malevolent spirits is often conveyed through the idiom of eating. And the devil pact logic presumed that minerals could be acquired only through sacrificial exchange relations between humans and underground spirits—which were not respected by the Spanish, of course.[52] West African miners, who like marabouts were "masters of secret things," were also said to be able to transform into animals. Similar rumors of shape-shifting continue to be whispered today on the island about the clandestine secret societies of Haiti.[53]

Narratives about spirit demons such as the baka condemn the new system of profit and human expenditure that first gold mining and later slavery and plantation agriculture brought to the Americas; thus they represent a folk vision of capitalism from the perspective of labor that highlights the violence required to produce profit for social outsiders. These stories denounce the terrible human cost of the "plantation machine" that made Saint-Domingue the richest French colony in the eighteenth century.[54] But this is not just a generic rejection of capitalism by a partially uncaptured peasantry, as Taussig would have it.[55] It is a wholesale rejection of a new form of brutal industrial technology that created invisible profit through the violent expenditure of unfree labor. These stories condemn what Marx termed the "'monstrous' world of commodities [generated] by one of capitalism's most blatantly violent appropriative mechanisms, slavery."[56] As devil pact tales, baka narratives give voice to a popular excoriation of the particular form of capitalism brought to Latin America, which consumed people to produce phantom profits, which accrued to foreigners and elites. In the Caribbean, this type of capitalism deployed industrial technology on the plantations, which have been described as "factories in the field."[57] Anthropologist Karen Richman has said that the pwen mimics the alienation of labor power. As she puts it, through the pwen, "peasants symbolically control and make sense of their incorporation as producers of alienated wage laborers."[58] Baka narratives are a genre of "occult cosmology" with formulaic signature elements such as industrial technology, clandestine cash, and signs of Haiti (long a symbol of capitalist profit to Dominicans, due to its history of colonial grandeur); they express moral indignation at flows of illicit wealth that do not trickle down and are not shared.[59] This helps explain why Dominican assembly plants have had bacá sightings that so terrified workers that the plants had to be shut down.[60] As Richman has put it, maji's "illicit powers descend from the above and the outside"— thus from exogenous powers.[61]

No wonder the very words for "work" in Haiti (*travay*) and in the Dominican Republic (*trabajo*) have a diabolical cast to them, since they are also the terms used for sorcery.[62] This folk view yokes debt as a nexus of social obligations to violent death as part and parcel of capitalist production. Profit is here cast as dependent upon blood sacrifice, which corresponds to the proposition that ritual human sacrifice may have accelerated in West Africa when Caribbean plantations expanded the slave trade, as West African leaders sought to expiate their sin of being complicit in that trade.[63] In Haitian and Dominican popular parlance, the blood sacrifice requisite to capital accumulation is conveyed through idioms connoting voracious eating—a figure of speech that resounds with slave rumors concerning fears they would be consumed by the human "butchers" who were their enslavers.[64] Perhaps this history helps explain why the term for cultural outsiders among the maroons of Suriname is *bakaa*.[65] Correspondingly, when the *mystère* (spirit) Grand Chemin arrives and puts Ernst to work, Ernst puts on a cowboy hat—a gesture that marks the arrival of a powerful outsider (fig. I.6).

If the baka/bacá first emerged as a sign of now-traditional forms of stealth profit such as foreign-owned sugar mills and lottery vendors, it has also been repurposed for novel "mysterious modes of accumulation" and dark money, such as political graft and narcotrafficking, which came to light under neoliberalism.[66] In the postcolonial period, bacá narratives have continued to express moral condemnation of new forms of surreptitious wealth generation, which in the twentieth century have

I.6 Avadra Grand Chemin at work, 2018. Photo by the author.

increasingly flowed through the state. This occurred during the crony capitalism of the regimes of Rafael Trujillo (1930–61), in which profitable monopolies were doled out to family members and his henchmen, and during the regimes of Joaquín Balaguer (1960–62, 1966–78, 1986–96), which sanctioned bribery and corruption on the part of the police and civil servants and which were sustained through flows of US economic and military assistance.[67] These regimes were propped up by clandestine military support as the United States sought to keep communism out of the hemisphere since it could threaten US economic interests.[68] Balaguer's time in office also saw the decline of sugar, the traditional staple crop, and IMF structural adjustment policies such as currency devaluation were imposed in response to the growing debt crisis. The state then promoted tourism as a revenue generator. The Dominican Republic has since become the most-visited island in the Caribbean, yet this has not generated growth in jobs and has only accelerated the expansion of underemployment and the informal sector.[69] These forms of clandestine wealth continued under the Partido de la Liberación Dominicana (PLD), which developed ironclad control over state and party finances upon Leonel Fernández's rise to power in 1996, which came about through an alliance with Balaguer's Reformista party and continued a patronage regime in which party members were allotted *botella* (sinecure) positions as clientelistic rewards from 2004 to 2016.[70] The PLD imposed a lucrative tourist tax in 2018, but flows of surreptitious wealth increased dramatically as the Dominican Republic became a major money-laundering hub for drug profits using shell companies; the amount of money that had its origins concealed in this way reached $260 million in just three years, generating cash for bribes to police and government officials.[71] All this took place during a period of economic decline, including a massive banking crash in 2003, that resulted in most Dominicans today being forced to rely on informal-sector work and relations of trust through *fiao* (credit) at the *colmado* (corner grocery) to get by.[72] Baka/bacá are not just signs of hidden wealth; they can also be emblems of covert state violence, an element that links the secret police of strongmen Trujillo and Balaguer in the Dominican Republic to François and Jean-Claude Duvalier's paramilitary force in Haiti, the Tonton Macoute.[73] This helps explain why the animals left behind by the ethnic Haitians fleeing the 1937 massacre were said to be baka and should not be touched.[74]

Anthropologists Jean and John Comaroff have proposed that across the globe "occult economies"—"magical means to material ends"—have surged since the 1990s as a result of a volatile combination of scarcity and deregulation.[75] Because my archive of popular baka narratives is oral, I am not often able to historicize these rumors, even if some of my informants indicated that bacá visitations were more frequent during their youth (during the years of the Balaguer regime) than they are today. But beyond the actual ebbs and flows of surreptitious wealth and violence, a key factor driving sorcery accusations today, I would argue, is the rise of evangelical Protestantism, which has seen the number of its adherents increase tenfold since 1960.[76] Pentecostalism in the Caribbean has staked its claim on the grounds that it can stamp out "Satanism" (unlike Catholicism, which is perceived as coterminous with African-identified practices such as vodou/*vodú*), and its increasingly martial imagery has fueled a militant zealousness and a call to "spiritual warfare."[77] Adepts see conversion to Protestantism as a defense against malignant forces such as zonbi and baka.[78] Evangelical Protestantism defines vodou as a form of witchcraft, a view that has instigated periodic moral panics, such as after the 2010 earthquake in Haiti when vodou temples were attacked by Pentecostals as rumors surged that the temblor had resulted from a *vodouisant* devil pact.[79] Richman has argued that Protestant discourse makes *lwa, wanga,* and djab (vodou deities, charms, and malevolent spirits, respectively) "hyper-real"; they are reified so that they can be ritually extirpated.[80] The role of Pentecostalism in fomenting rumors about shape-shifting is not always apparent, but it certainly has served to amplify and spread baka/bacá rumors, especially when those rumors are picked up by television and digital media.[81]

It has been said that sorcery discourse persuades through the power of metaphor. Anthropologist Michael Jackson has written about how metaphors mediate between the body and social environments; they are not just a means of saying things but also a way of doing things.[82] Sorcery practice, however, is also reflective of the precarious agency of the poor, for whom there are many constraints on their field of action. This was the case for a woman I met in San Juan de la Maguana, Ángela, who sought out a mystical "work" when she was running for a local-level political office against a powerful contender. But her rival managed to usurp the spell to his own advantage, winning the post through her device. Of course, sorcery discourse is also a means of empowerment, through enacting the "persuasive force of . . . articulated visions."[83] Anthropologist Jeffrey Kahn thus argues that stories of djab must be seen as an alternative form of reality, since they have the power to shape social events.[84] Baka are also fundamentally a way of thinking through questions of power and the ethics of its deployment. As Charlotte Otten has put it, lycanthropy narrative "is not escapist: it is realistic."[85]

This study homes in on the question of the animal host within these sorcery narratives and practice and how, as "cultural objects," baka phantoms convey the past.[86] Drawing upon Pierre Bourdieu, one might say that these spirits convert history into the supernatural.[87] Chapter 1 explains why the invasive species brought by Columbus became spirit demons, conveying the horror of conquest from the Indigenous people to the African slaves who arrived in their wake. Chapter 2 explores a mysterious suicide said to be caused by demonic cattle specters surging across the border, invoking ties of interdependency that have long bound Dominican cattle to Haitian markets; but this particular episode also articulated Dominican political rivalry and rumors of ill-gotten illicit wealth. Chapter 3 treats stories of baka in the form of fearsome black dogs, a version that resonates with the history of canines as technologies of terror used to force the rebellious into submission—first the indigenes and later African slaves during the Haitian Revolution. Chapter 4 analyzes bacá narratives as haunting tales of loss and longing in stories about the creole pig in the aftermath of the military's pork slaughter across the island in 1979. Women formed a large percentage of the small pig farmers in the Dominican central frontier who recounted to me their despair at the loss of the creole pig in the aftermath of the army slaughter, since female heads of households have long relied on the family pig to pay for school fees and cover domestic emergencies. Chapter 5 examines bacá rumors that swarmed around La Manicera, a vegetable oil processing plant associated with one of Trujillo's henchmen and a man whose nickname was "Colón" (the Spanish version of the name Columbus).

The final chapters shift from history to performance to consider the meaning of bacá storytelling and representations of animals within popular culture. Chapter 6 discusses the semantics of bacá stories as vehicles of masculine bravado that transform the narrators into trickster heroes. Chapter 7 shifts to the genre of the grotesque, focusing on the figure of the animal in Carnival masquerade as well as its role as masculine partner, foil, and rival and the pleasures of artful braggadocio and popular humor; it thus celebrates the bawdy verbal arts that embrace the animal and the history of free-range beasts and the men they long sustained on Hispaniola.

CHAPTER ONE

PRETER- NATURALIA

OF TALKING COWS

The monster is difference made flesh, come to dwell among us.
JEFFREY JEROME COHEN

It is a rare breed of fabulist who transcribes and records
—rather than invents—a reality invisible to most of us.
GUILLERMO DEL TORO

It has been said that the Caribbean is a crucible of modernity, since plantation slavery fueled European industrialization and the *ingenio* or sugar mill was the precursor to the modern factory.[1] Many have acknowledged the mass death of indigenes and African slaves that accompanied Spanish colonization, but the role of nonhuman animals in this process has received less attention.[2] Yet it should not surprise that from Indigenous peoples and Africans to sea turtles and manatees, the Caribbean was also ground zero of species extinction: More fauna have vanished there in the last century than anywhere else, and Hispaniola was ground zero, of course, for the Spanish colonial project.[3] As one writer dramatically put it, "The Caribbean is the world's largest laboratory of extinction."[4] Mammal diversity in the Caribbean began to erode with the first arrival of humans, with large sloths and monkeys as well as a variety of rodents vanishing.[5]

But Columbus's arrival on Hispaniola caused a veritable scourge of animal death, as manatees, hutias, solenodons, turtles, and many bird species disappeared as victims of non-native species introductions as well as human predation; out of 130 species, today only 13 non-bat mammal species and 60 bat species remain. Indeed, the Natural History Museum of Havana today has the feel of a morgue.[6] Cuban literary critic Antonio Benítez-Rojo has noted that much of Caribbean cultural memory resides in the environment, which has been brutally assaulted by the plantation system, a precocious paradigm of industrial engineering.[7]

No wonder the countryside of Haiti and the Dominican Republic is haunted today by animal specters. In Bánica, I was told stories about animal revenants, in particular phantasmic stray livestock engaging in strange behavior such as flying, crying, or talking. I also heard about people who have been able to accumulate vast amounts of wealth in this context of primarily subsistence agriculture and who stand accused of controlling large clandestine herds of feral cattle minded by no one. As Hegel explained to me, "What people say is that there are lots and lots of animals, lots and lots and lots of animals—steers, dairy cattle, goats, pigs, horses—and no one takes care of them. No one minds these animals. Understand? Nono, for example, has something that takes care of his things; he has a bacá that takes care of them. No one steals them. No one watches them. They don't get lost; they don't stray. They are not fenced in, yet they don't stray. And how many trucks does he have? Today Nono has one, but before he had so much more money compared to everyone else at that time in the Dominican Republic. He had millions of pesos. For the 1990s, he had way too much money and no one knew where it came from."

The bacá can be a manifestation of occult illicit wealth; it can also be a clandestine form of agency. Colón, who served as manager of La Manicera, a vegetable oil processing plant, in the 1980s, elaborated further on the use of bacá as a supernatural assistant: "In those days, people had these creatures [*pájaros malos*] to protect their livestock; people would have them around the house and they would do what they wanted them to; they would also go to the farm and they would bring the animals to their owners. A bacá can become a person or a cow or a goat or a dog. They come from Haiti, but Dominicans have them too—especially people with money. They would often be sent to steal livestock; this happened a lot. They can also be sent to steal fruit. These are people who wanted to acquire wealth without working." These tales are alarming reminders that "evil is never dormant; it gestates."[8] In their presumption that there is an "invisible hand" enabling profit to accrue to some and not others, these stories also indicate a profoundly suspicious view of wealth acquisition.[9]

In Hegel's and Colón's stories these animals were located at a comfortable distance, but I spoke with many people who had fraught encounters with these creatures, which are often predatory. Indeed, Hegel's home had been haunted by a canine specter, which he heard incessantly scratching, growling, and barking at his door for weeks, until he found someone who could remove it. As Juan Ramón told me:

> JR: The dogs here come from Haiti as *galipotes*. Every night and every day. Every night and every day. All the time. People from over there would do this to do bad things over here.
>
> LD: And how could you tell those dogs were not dogs?
>
> JR: If they are too big, they are galipotes.
>
> LD: But how did you know they were people [turned into dogs]?
>
> JR: Because they turned back into people. Dogs don't eat dogs. They were killed and eaten. Dogs don't eat dogs. Emilio, during the day, in the morning, when he went to El Caracol, he would shoot them and take them out. A dog much bigger than he was. Up there, we did everything. We bushwhacked, we killed. Every night, every night. We saw some crazy things. There once was a female dog in a rocking chair, rocking herself in the chair. That was a galipote also. Yes, I remember that time. I was going down the same road when I said, "There's a galipote!" I went into my house and grabbed a machete and ran out fast, but it had gone. Then in the road at El Cebe we bumped into it again. I felt it was there, but in a flash it was gone; it had disappeared toward the canyon. It jumped away and we did not see it again. Back then it was a festival of those creatures every day. Not one, not two—they were everywhere.[10]

Like in Sigmund Freud's classic work on the uncanny, these animal revenants are described as everyday creatures made strange that create a sensation of dread.[11] As spirit animals, they are redolent of death and evoke a visceral kind of "morbid anxiety," which is why children first learn about the bacá as a frightening demon that will come after them if they step out of line.[12] I want to argue that these popular bacá stories of animal phantoms can be seen as a form of popular witnessing, forming visceral archives of terror, since quadrupeds were the storm troopers of colonialism and dogs ensured that slaves could be worked to death without any chance of escape.[13]

This study explores narratives of encounter with this particularly feared genre of shape-shifting phenomena called bacá—spirit beings that are deployed to steal or protect farm animals, harvests, and cash in Haiti and the Dominican Republic. Bacá are spirit demons created by sorcerers; they can help amass wealth. Butchers told me about sheep that meowed, goats with pigs' tails, and bulls that cried like a baby—creatures that were really bacá or spirit animals. They are pigs sold at market with human fingernails, or cows that talk or cry. Most often they present as dogs, pigs, or cattle with eyes that glow red.[14] I heard haunting stories about invisible visitations (and how they were eradicated), struggles in the bush by virile men who fought off these beasts, ranchers' and butchers' tales about bacá that eviscerated their herds and drained their cash; a *curandera* (healer) boasted that she could make one for me. Workers resisted cruel employers by secretly stealing their crops via bacá, just as heroic men protect their families and the nation from feral packs of baka streaming over the border from Haiti. I spoke with Haitian secret society members whose special skills include shape-shifting and who can turn into canines, among other things. As a spirit demon in animal form, the baka conjoins the specter of mass death brought on by colonialism in the Caribbean with the animals that enabled the subjugation of first Native American and then African slaves and that later went on to provide sustenance for freedmen on the island. These narratives raise many questions, but the first conundrum is why the bacá almost invariably appears as the seed animals first brought to Hispaniola by Columbus: the dogs, cattle, pigs, horses, and goats that were the first line of attack during the conquest.[15]

Alfred Crosby's pioneering work on the Columbian exchange charted the biotic impact of the flora and fauna brought by Columbus to the New World.[16] But in seeking to explain the visceral horror engendered by these ghostly "creatures of empire" today, I have had to search for answers elsewhere.[17] Witchcraft studies have not taken into consideration the significance of the host on the grounds that in the Anglo-American model, whether the beast was an ass, ox, ram, or black horse, it was a manifestation of the singular embodiment of evil, Lucifer.[18] However, the semantics of animals in bacá apparitions are not arbitrary or contingent. I want to make the case that these narratives can be a source for what historian Ranajit Guha has termed the "small voices of history," but this requires taking stock of the historical animal traces in these stories.[19] I argue that these narratives of animal demons are related to the phenomenology of interspecies contact and labor in an environment in which animals have long been a constant sensorial and affective presence in everyday life. This study considers these animal hosts as repositories of popular memory derived from a *longue durée* history of multispecies entanglements on Hispaniola that carry sensory, aesthetic, and ontological meanings. The many meanings of nonhuman animals in this case are far more than just symbolic; animals have long played leading roles as technologies of domination and terror, material sustenance, codependent laboring partners, sacrificial beasts, and companion animals, as well as the inspiration for animal metaphors used as "identity assertions" and mimetic alter egos in pseudonyms, fables, nicknames, jokes, storytelling, and Carnival masquerade; they even provide a language of ludic sexual innuendo in everyday speech.[20] In anthropologist A. R. Radcliffe-Brown's terms, the particular animals invoked in these narratives have ritual value because of the acute emotive resonance they invoke, whether despised (vicious attack dogs that hunted slaves) or adored (pigs that enabled the privilege of autonomy at a time when slavery was the rule for people of color).[21] If animals long served as Other in Europe, this was not the case within contexts of slavery, in which slaves were classed with and often lived and worked intimately with farm animals in circumstances in which those animals likely provided a modicum of solace under brutal conditions, or within post-emancipation societies, in which subsistence peasants unattached to plantations could be demeaned as just as lowly as free-range pigs.[22] The final historical layer of these narratives is one of mourning, since the narratives conjure feral animals such as the long-tusked *jabalí* boar (*Sus scrofa*), which is now a rarity; over time the animal commons was eviscerated by a series of challenges, from fencing laws and population growth to pesticides in the twentieth century. Yet these phantasmic sightings also indicate an element of African American trickster heroism's defiant "refusal to mourn," as popular storytelling and playful speech acts in the idiom of the carnivalesque refuse the elegiac and instead insist on ribald humor and brash audaciousness in the face of harsh challenges.[23]

Sigmund Freud explored how trauma could affix itself within the psyche, emerging unconsciously in jokes, dreams, and slips of the tongue, but he was less attuned to nondiscursive forms of affect and memory such as forms of embodied knowledge that are not cognized but rather prediscursively sensed "at a level beneath awareness" and which can manifest in ritual and other privileged domains of social life.[24] Anthropologists have considered how sorcery and witchcraft can be media in which "implicit social knowledge" such as popular memories can be glimpsed, and how demons can be studied as "cultural objects."[25] Rosalind Shaw, for example, has explored how fragmented memories of slavery have sedimented like palimpsests that accumulate historical layers over time.[26] Memory here is not consciously recalled but tacitly apprehended, forgotten as history but embedded in images and practices in ritual and other forms of cultural expression.[27] Freud termed this "involuntary memory," which is registered through shocks and can result in a kind of traumatic neurosis in which the patient repeatedly returns to the initial catastrophe.[28]

Bacá stories are cultural performances of "haunted landscapes, where assemblages of the dead gather together with the living"; thus they convey the experience of being haunted and hunted by predatory spirits in animal form that conjure the experience of terror wrought by colonialism and beyond in conditions of domination and precarity.[29] These emotionally dense animals serve as charged mnemonics apprehended somatically in tales of everyday furtive encounters with frightening beastly demons, as well as more playful forms such as roasting and eating them in patron saint festivals, masquerading as them in Carnival, and joking about them as sex objects in carnal humor. As Holland, Ochoa, and Tompkins have put it, "We see viscerality as a phenomenological index for the logics of desire, consumption, disgust, health, disease, belonging, and displacement that are implicit in colonial and postcolonial relations."[30] I argue that bacá stories reveal that the trauma of conquest lives on unresolved in implicit social knowledge, as these apparitions of spectral animal demons force a never-ending revisiting of the animal terror that created the "lingering trouble" in the first place. The visceral dread evoked by these animal demons is a material manifestation of what Dominicans call the *fukú de Colón* (curse of Columbus), a popular taboo that extends even to uttering the name of Columbus due to the scourge he unleashed. (*Fukú* is a Kikongo term for "night" that connotes illicitness and subterfuge.)[31]

The appearance of a bacá, an errant spirit, is a sign of clear and present danger, but one which is conveyed through rumor or unsanctioned speech and thus operates clandestinely, as if obscured by a fog; there is an "interpretive ambiguity" that is part and parcel of bacá storytelling.[32] Thus I am unnaturally casting a spotlight on the bacá here when it would otherwise be lurking in the shadows; its natural habitat is the penumbra of darkness, a space of "reasonable conjecture" and "epistemic murk."[33] But as historian Luise White has argued, these narratives of shape-shifting can provide evidence for the experience wrought by colonial processes—evidence unavailable elsewhere—as key motifs, images, and idioms evince the emotions triggered by new forms of technology and labor and forms of unspeakable terror.[34] French historian Alain Corbin has demonstrated how rumors can reveal collective anxieties and hopes grounded in local experience, particularly during moments of social unrest.[35] I hope to demonstrate that spirit animal accounts can offer a window into deep-time temporalities that revisit the violence of conquest and have forged a "mutilated historicity" that has become embedded in the landscape like dregs.[36]

MAN AND BEAST ON LA ESPAÑOLA

Christopher Columbus arrived on the north coast of La Española in 1492, commencing the colonial economy, which initiated the dramatic demise of the largest Amerindian population in the Caribbean.[37] But his arrival had an important animal component to it as well, a story of human-animal codependence accompanied by massive violence and death. In 1493, on Columbus's second voyage to the Caribbean, he arrived with 17 ships, 1,200 men, 6 mares, 6 cows, pigs, donkeys, poultry, 1,600 sheep, and various cats and dogs as seed animals to provision the new colonists. La Española became the "vestibule to the Americas," as the colonists went on to spread ranching extensively in New Spain, Venezuela, and beyond.[38] The North American colonists brought livestock to service agriculture, and in sharp contrast to the Iberian model, in North America animals were located on the periphery, not at the center.[39] Subsequent vessels brought more pigs, as they were easier to transport across the sea than cattle and horses, which were difficult to load onto the ships and required massive amounts of feed. European cows, horses, dogs, and pigs thrived in their new environment, as the Andalusian culture of extensive cattle production took root amid Caribbean tropical forests and grasslands.[40] As nineteenth-century Dominican statesman and essayist Pedro Francisco Bonó put it, La Española became a pastoral society like its Iberian predecessor, but patently without the bucolic associations of the term *pastoral*. The feral animal commons that formed there over time became the basis of a violent extractivist economy founded on mass human and nonhuman animal death, although later that animal commons came to sustain an independent peasantry, enabling it to remain outside of slavery and the harsh sugar plantation regime.[41] This may be why, as symbols of power, these animals—like dangerous twins—flip from being signs of doom and abjection to being signs of sustenance and conviviality.[42]

Christina Sharpe has written eloquently about how living "in the wake" means grounding "the history and present of terror" at the core of Black existence, a method of "encountering a past which is not past."[43] The account I offer in this book is a poignant reminder that Caribbean settler colonialism brought mass death not only to Indigenous and African slaves but also to the nonhuman animals originally brought as seed animals. Thus bacá apparitions must also be seen as acts of witnessing and mourning, with several layered meanings: first in response to the horror of mass death of Amerindians and slaves, later becoming extinction narratives mourning a feral animal commons that long sustained freedmen outside of slavery. Freud observed the sensory emotional charge conveyed by taboo phenomena, which he described as like "an electrical charge; they are the seat of tremendous power which is transmissible by contact."[44] If at times traumatic events are silenced as the result of a taboo, by contrast bacá sightings seem to obsessively revisit the violence wrought by the Columbian exchange, as these cursed animals shadow, hunt, and terrorize contemporary residents of the island in a carnivalesque inversion of the hunting economy that defined rural life for centuries, with the animals now hunting the humans.

The animal herds that formed over the course of the sixteenth century consisted not only of animals for food, breeding stock, and pack animals; some of the cats, dogs, guinea fowl, and goats brought on Columbus's ships were "rewilded"—that is to say, they returned to a free-ranging wild existence from a domesticated state. Other animals did not succeed in the Caribbean; as in Barbados, even camels were brought initially, but they did not thrive.[45] The forest, "so dense even a rabbit could not penetrate it," provided shelter to a constant stream of runaway Indigenous and African runaway slaves as well as stray livestock.[46] Cattle proliferated extravagantly, with reports of a tenfold increase in three or four years.[47] Gonzalo Fernández de Oviedo y Valdés in 1650 reported that there were people with as many as twenty thousand head of cattle—herds of a size that claimed vast areas of land.[48] In Cuba, Diego Velásquez de Cuellar reported that their seed animals expanded exponentially; there were "more pigs than I had ever seen before in my life," thriving on the abundant forage.[49] Pigs have the unique characteristic that they rapidly revert to boars in the wild, with an extended back and long tusks.

The feral pigs and dogs in particular became ferocious predators. The canines brought to hunt and subjugate the Indigenous population over time formed vicious packs that were such a menace, even to the boar population, that the governor of La Tortuga island eventually called for poison to cull them.[50] Feeding on rats and lizards, dogs took to the forest; packs of fifty to sixty canines became savage predators, with a contemporary observer reporting that they were found "preying on calves and fo[w]ls and were so fierce that they would assault an entire herd of wild boars and worry them until they take down 2 or 3."[51] Fernández de Oviedo y Valdés said the wild dogs are "worse than wolves and do more damage"; of course, the wolf in the European imagination has long been an emblem of the "dangerous and threatening qualities of the wild."[52] Feral swine have been described as "the most invasive animal on the planet" and "an ecological train wreck."[53]

These feral beasts that "multiplied marvelously" were actually invasive species that wrought havoc on the ecosystem and contributed to the rapid demise of the Taíno population. With only the alligator serving as a natural predator, the packs of wild dogs and boars became fearsome predators preying on young calves. By the time Gonzalo Fernández de Oviedo de Valdés and Bartolomé de Las Casas arrived in 1650, roaming swine had decimated the local rodent population, which had been a major protein source for the Indigenous population, and they likely raided hunting grounds, chasing away game. In the seventeenth century, cattle took over as the largest species of "vertebrate immigrant."[54] Traveling in herds, these ungulates surely compacted the soil and ravaged ground cover, likely contributing to the semi-arid vegetation in certain areas such as Azua that became centers of cattle grazing. They also spread seeds of the guayaba (guava) fruit tree, to the point that in some areas forest growth was choking out pasture.[55] Moreover, animals were vectors of disease, spreading it into the interior where runaways had taken refuge. Due to their omnivorous nature, huge appetite, and rooting skills, the wild boars raided Indigenous gardens of tuber staple crops such as manioc (cassava), *batata* (sweet potato), and *ñame* (yam) and ate their guayaba and zapote, contributing to famine.[56] The ecological impact was localized, however, since five forested mountain ranges, including the highest in the Caribbean, prevented erosion from occurring outside of the savannas.

Given this scenario of ecological devastation as the Indigenous population died off and the animals expanded into immense feral herds, a messianic prophet in New Spain believed that the Spanish were turning people into cattle and exhorted people not to eat the Spaniards' meat.[57] No wonder there was a sighting of a Taíno spirit demon who returned as a goat (fig. 1.1).[58]

Looming far larger than all the other quadrupeds on the island, horses were agents of terror—a fact the conquistadores deployed to their advantage, making the horse (as well as the dog) a central player in the domination of the Taíno indigenous population.[59] Contemporaries noted the look of astonishment on the part of the Amerindians when horses first arrived, and later in an effort to render these quadrupeds even more frightening, the Spanish laced strings of bells across their mounts in battle so as to augment their otherworldly aura. But surely it was the fact that the indigenes were hunted with dogs and lanced en masse from atop these martial steeds that rendered them terrifying, as horses, men, and canines worked together in lethal squads.[60] There are reports that the horse and rider in their military garb were perceived as single beings by the indigenes—as monstrous centaurs—and the Spanish sought to augment these terrifying rumors of their own supernatural immortality by carefully hiding the corpses of horses that died.[61] Indeed, it is significant that the first Indigenous image painted after the arrival of the Spanish did not represent the powerful technology that they brought with them, the battleships and guns; rather, it sketched the dreadful sight of a man on horseback.[62]

Over time the new sights, sounds, and smells came to convey the horror of these animals, forming a sensory memory in which these beastly traces conjured up a visceral reaction of dread.[63] Dogs were trained as attack animals to hunt escaped Indians and Africans and disembowel their victims, and were fed their flesh as a reward. As Bartolomé de Las Casas graphically reminds us, Native American infants were tossed to canines to eat, and the body parts of indigenes, who were seen as nonhuman, were even sold as dog food in markets.[64] Indeed, it was on La Española that barking at fugitive Indians paralyzed with terror came to be called "dogging" (*aperreamiento*), as siccing attack canines on Amerindians became a verb.[65] The heft of the cattle on La Española had an impact as well; there they grew considerably larger than in Europe, developing over

1.1 A Taíno monster lurking in the forest. From the manuscript *Histoire Naturelle des Indes*, ca. 1586, fol. 111r, "How the indians usually have visions of the evil spirit." Morgan Library and Museum, New York, MA 3900, bequest of Clara S. Peck, 1983.

time into enormous 1,600-pound creatures (with extremely large hides, eleven to thirteen feet long, that were particularly coveted in Europe).[66] In addition to the new sounds and smells of gunfire, the soundscape of these introduced beasts snorting, barking, snarling, braying, and stampeding must have been particularly frightening given the quietness of the previous landscape, with its softly shuffling hutias, silent lizards, and dogs that didn't bark—an observation made by Fernández de Oviedo y Valdés.[67] Since the Taíno hunted at night, they surely collided with feral boars. The fact that boars are nocturnal predators must have contributed to their image as a "harbinger of death," as did their capacity for violence, which was comparable only to that of the feral dogs.[68] As the leather trade to Europe expanded, the stench of death added to this ambiance of dread, as the noxious smell of rotting carcasses filled the air.[69] This history helps explain later uses of these animal icons as signs of power, such as the use of a horse tail as a power object, a zonbi that appears in the form of a steer, a dog skull used as a wanga, or a fetish called *chien des buissons* (bush dog), used to protect against jackals. As subalterns sought to acquire some of the Iberians' ferocious might, horse-and-rider zemis (power objects) made out of cotton—white being the color of death—began to appear in caves where Indigenous people took refuge, hid their ritual paraphernalia, and died.[70] This history helps explain why the dog and the horse serve as the primordial gateways to the spirit world in Haitian and Dominican vodou/vodú.[71]

Yet over time the meaning of the feral animal commons gradually changed as it came to sustain the free peasantry and enable its autonomy.[72] Hispaniola's rural society was forged during the buccaneering economy of the sixteenth and seventeenth centuries, in which masterless men could make a living on their own in the contraband trade of hides and tallow and later as subsistence hunters or *monteros* (hunters) in the Dominican interior. By the seventeenth century Santo Domingo had become an important stop on the mule trade circuit, as interior creoles expanded from the leather trade into mule contraband networks that reached as far as Venezuela.[73] Livestock—first hunting and later extensive ranching—lay at the center of Hispaniola's agrarian history, even if Haiti took a different path, becoming the world's largest sugar producer by 1750.[74] But the rise of sugar and coffee in Haiti actually deepened the reliance on animals in the Dominican Republic, since the entire eastern portion of the island came to provide cattle and oxen to the plantations of Saint-Domingue, much of this livestock pouring across the central frontier into the Artibonite Valley in order to evade authorities. Just as anthropologist E. E. Evans-Pritchard noted for the Nuer, on Hispaniola cattle long formed the organizational core of daily life and was "the medium through which social and mystical relations are expressed," especially in the eastern side of the island, which became the seat of the cattle ranching economy.[75] And even as Saint-Domingue turned toward sugar, it consumed the cattle and oxen of the east. Cattle thus became a common currency that knitted the two sides of the island together.

If Haiti and the Dominican Republic share a common popular cultural affinity for animals and shape-shifting beliefs, I argue that it has to do with the importance of, proximity to, and reliance upon animals created by this feral animal economy. From the seventeenth century onward, the meaning of the animal commons shifted from a menace to a means of subsistence, as it enabled the poor to remain outside of slavery; in the nineteenth century, it helped make the island a refuge for freedmen while slavery raged in neighboring Puerto Rico and Cuba.[76]

BEASTS OF MEMORY

Clearly bacá are "good to think with," as Claude Lévi-Strauss would say, but what can they tell us? Phantasmic figures of the mass death that was a feature of Caribbean history for the Native Americans and Africans who toiled in the mines and plantations, bacá also are evidence of a culture of proximity to death characteristic of West and Central African and Arawak cultures in which the portal between this world and the other world is always slightly ajar.[77] In between the familiar dead of the ancestors and the legendary dead of the saints or lwa (spirit pantheon), as anthropologist Victor Turner has theorized them, these liminal entities are associated with death, darkness, and the wilderness and often disguise themselves as monsters.[78] Part of a class of shape-shifting spirit demons, the baka, galipote, *garadiablo*, and lougawou are constituents of the extended family of the "ambient dead," which are invisible but omnipresent—ephemeral trickster spirits that become manifest in multiple forms and unpredictable ways, and form part of "the darker side of faith," as horror enthusiast Guillermo del Toro has aptly put it.[79] These beliefs are shared by Protestants, Catholics, and *vodouisants*, so they transcend religious denomination, yet they occupy a very particular semantic space and moral location and can serve as a push factor for religious affiliation, since fear can drive a need for protection from these spirits.[80] Portents of the unseen, they can appear in one's dreams and prophesy—for example, indicating where hidden treasure is located or who is next in line to die.[81] The bacá can be glimpsed, but it remains defiantly covert. This was made clear to me when an interlocutor recounted that he had written a long email to me describing his encounter with a bacá, but the email mysteriously vanished before it was sent; this proved to him that bacá are, as a rule, inherently clandestine and ephemeral. This anecdote seems to confirm sociologist George Simmel's observation that "secrecy is, among other things, also the sociological expression of moral badness."[82]

These wicked creatures are also implicitly gendered. Baka are bearded little men or feral beasts whose incessant ravenousness and thirst for violence render them "aggressively masculine"; their infernal sisters the lougawou are women who turn into birds and devour children.[83] Because they are vectors of the "dark arts" of sorcery, these spirits are seen as part of what literary critic Sylvia Wynter has termed the "demonic ground," because they "reside in the liminal precincts of the current governing configurations of the human."[84] The racial politics of the island—Haiti's embrace of its slave past in stark contrast to the Dominican Republic's *mestizaje*, which tilts toward whiteness—accounts for the fact that these spirits are perceived as Haitian, even if Dominicans use them and are abused by them just as frequently.[85] Baka are classed as Haitian in part, I think, because in being able to become invisible they are most famously associated with escape through camouflage, a signature technique of the runaway slave (though they may likely also have roots in the Indigenous "fleeing gods" that could change into animal form).[86] As Georges René put it, "Baka are slave spirits who were killed and return for revenge." The baka should be seen as complex assemblages since they "channel-surf" between logics of animism and those of totemism.[87]

The Haitian wanga, the Kikongo *ndoki*, and the Yoruba *àalè* are assemblages with the power to make things happen because they are seen.[88] By contrast, this study explores something that exerts its force covertly.[89] Bacá narratives are clearly a product of the world of fugitive slave resistance and the island's martial past, as the baka is frequently a mercenary demon used as protection in warfare as well as a clandestine agent of predation.[90] Baka shape-shifting served as the inspiration for the literary genre Cuban writer Alejo Carpentier described as *lo real maravilloso*, which was born of maroon leader Makandal hiding from authorities during the Haitian

Revolution by shape-shifting (indeed, the protective talismans deployed in battle came to be called *makandal*).[91] Baka are thus figures of fugitivity that celebrate marronage, the escaped slave being a culture hero of particular significance in the Caribbean, a region forged through the violence of plantation slavery.[92] The bacá can be seen as a materialization of a popular genre of storytelling about *cimarrones* (runaway slaves)—evidenced in songs, for example, about black birds (furtive underclass men, or *choncholi*) going to the *monte* (bush), where they become invisible from authority.[93] Freud made a case for the value of studying not just what is spoken but also what is left unsaid—not just one's public face but also what is concealed.

Above all, baka are terrifying. Anthropologist Karen McCarthy Brown described them as "evil incarnate," since they can literally scare people to death, but such a characterization is problematic because it renders these phenomena abstract when the reaction they invoke is far more visceral.[94] Freud studied dreams, but the baka take us into the realm of nightmares and the social ecology of fear.[95] Similar to the pishtaco fat-stealers of the Andes, baka are rumored to be cannibals, although anthropologist Laënnec Hurbon explains that this is because the Haitian expression "to eat someone" (*mange moun*) can mean to capture someone's spirit through sorcery or can refer to the human sacrifice necessary for the angajman, the implicit cash pact requisite to generating a baka.[96]

I wish to propose something else: that the loathsome bacá is not just a figure of wondrous nature but also a figure of race.[97] The bacá is black in more ways than one; it can appear as a little black dwarf, but it also channels the idea of blackness as a stealthy "latent and nascent power" that is feared and must be controlled.[98] It thus invokes the very mestizo idea of blackness as not necessarily self-evident but latent.[99] There is something black about the sense of threat posed by the baka; it is the barely discernible baka lurking in the shadows "ready to pounce" that represents an "unconsummated surplus of danger." Similarly, the image of the baka channeling the "wild French negroes" forms part of a Gothic narrative of Haiti that commenced with the Haitian Revolution.[100]

At times, allegations of shape-shifting may be deployed as a figure of speech, an expressive metaphor for rule-breaking violence, as in the comment that the late nineteenth-century Dominican strongman Lilís (Ulises Heureaux) was satanic, a wizard (a galipote, a close cousin of the bacá) who could turn into a dog or a pig.[101] Indeed, perhaps due to the way slavery cast Black men as virtual beasts—as eighteenth-century

Jamaican jurist Edward Long put it, "Africans, first imported, were wild and savage in the extreme"—turning into an animal is cast as a technique of blackness.[102] Gothic literature became popular in Britain just as emancipated slaves were arriving on British shores in the late eighteenth century, and the werewolves of that literature became powerful vectors of racialization, conjuring the inner beast and purported "super bodies" of Black men, meanings that also course through baka stories in their evocation of the stealthy and purportedly diabolical powers of Haitian magic.[103] Drawing upon the imagery of blood, soil, sex, and violence, the baka is a discourse of Gothic cultural alterity that renders Haitians vectors of covert violence as well as of powerful magical protection throughout the Caribbean.[104] Yet it also represents an idiom of popular martial masculinity that some Haitians have come to embrace, as in the vodou deity Lwa Criminel or the Carnival figure Lansè-Kòd, both daring street toughs who threaten to do the unthinkable.[105]

We have now strayed from the topic of anti-Haitianism and moved toward the topic of "racial assemblage."[106] The latter is not unique to Dominicans. It is a local variant of a colonial racial order disseminated throughout Latin America, one that forged a certain "racialist revulsion and spiritual awe of latent and nascent power," with the presumption that the darker the skin the blacker the magic. It is also a composite, or what linguist Michael Silverstein would call a "text-artifact." Rather than essentialize this assemblage, we seek to uncover the various dialogical threads implicit within it.[107] Colonial diabolism imposed a racial order within which African-derived practices were cast as a stealthy threat redolent of Satan; in the Caribbean, Haiti came to substitute for Dahomey, the source of many slaves, and it also became the target of an immense European rumor mill about purported African cannibalism and witchcraft.[108] As anthropologist Laura Lewis has explained in her study of the Mexican Inquisition, witchcraft hierarchy was closely correlated with caste, hence race; in that hierarchy, greater social distance is seen to be correlated with greater invisible powers.[109] Tales Dominicans tell about Haitians who can walk on burning coals and transform into packs of ferocious dogs that stream over the border, stories of "fantastic credibility," conjure up images of Haitian wildness and its attendant marvels; they also convey what Zakiyyah Jackson has called "the animalization of blackness."[110]

Anthropologist Mary Weismantel has written that the Andean pishtaco, which sucks the fat of Indians and accumulates wealth, is actually a figure of whiteness that serves as a visual metaphor for a long history of colonial predation and accumulation.[111] Similarly, the baka, a spirit which has been turned into an animal—a pig, dog, or cow—requires the conjuring skills of a very powerful priest—usually, in the view of Dominicans, a Haitian, since Dominican magic is insufficiently potent. Like the pishtaco, the baka is raced not only by its color but also through its association with wildness. Like a newly arrived African slave (*bozal*), it is seen as feral and impossible to entirely control. It is important to note, however, that this aspect of Haitian identity is an "open secret" that is not easily articulated.[112] It hovers in the shadows, in fugitive speech forms such as gossip and rumor, and in stories that do not necessarily name Haiti but invoke, as Alfred Métraux has written, an unspoken colonial heritage of "the witchcraft of remote and mysterious Africa which troubled the sleep of the people in 'the big house.'"[113] Indeed, in spite of pervasive cultural entanglement—or perhaps because of it—the borderline between Haitians and Dominicans becomes visible through stories in which Haiti is cast as a locus of demons. As literary critic A. James Arnold has put it, "The monster occupies a necessary, liminal position at the edges of any culture's conceptual field."[114]

Lest we blame Dominicans alone for these rumors, it should be noted that Haitians themselves have long burnished rumors of their enhanced sorcery skills. Many Haitians themselves fear the notorious Sanpwèl and Bizango, secret societies whose members boast they can shape-shift. As Taussig reminds us, this malevolent and mystical vision of power has been incorporated into Haitian sorcery practices.[115] Indeed, the presence of bones and particularly skulls on Haitian altars fueled rumors of Haitian cannibalism during the US occupation, rumors spread by marines who were uninterested in the particular function of bones as spiritual circuitry in Haitian altars.[116] As a bundle of stigmatized attributes, the idea of the Haitian Other most frequently appears in the border region through stories of Haitian spiritual potency, a view that is in accord with a long history of racialization dating from colonialism, slavery, and the Haitian Revolution, a story of "the power of blackness . . . that is to be feared and controlled."[117]

Haiti and the Dominican Republic are coded within their respective national identities as culturally opposed—as vodou/Catholic and Black/mixed—but the material presented here recounts another story.[118] It is a poignant reminder that Hispaniola had nearly two hundred years of shared history as a *terre mêlée* before French colonialism arrived, splitting the island in two, and before the rise of the sugar industry, which differentiated the two sides of the island in the early eighteenth century, as Saint-Domingue became the world's largest sugar producer with a slave majority and the eastern side of the island deepened its reliance on cattle managed by freedmen. Yet notwithstanding the divergent national histories and foundational narratives of identity, baka narratives share the same structural logic on both sides of the island. Given this, they invite us to take seriously historian Prasenjit Duara's call to reveal the "rhetorical strategies [that] conceal the aporias and repressions necessitated by the imposition of a master narrative" of intra-island difference.[119] Popular religion as well as sorcery practices in the central frontier traverse the dividing line between the two nations. Haitians and Dominicans have long shared pilgrimage networks, with Haitians traveling to the Dominican festival for the patron saint the Virgin of Altagracia in the eastern town of Higüey, and Dominicans frequenting the healing pool and waterfall at Saut D'Eau (Sodo), which is the locus of the Virgin Mary of Mount Carmel.[120] And folk Catholicism and vodou/vodú in Haiti and the Dominican Republic share features common to Afro-Atlantic religions, such as spirit possession, which binds the living to the spirit world.[121]

The baka transgresses the border while simultaneously relying upon it, as circuits of harming and healing rely upon its opposed yet complementary meanings. As "composite fabrications," fetishes seem to thrive in contact zones where, as anthropologist Patricia Spyer has said, they mark and negotiate forms of difference.[122] Indeed, the very concept of *fetissio* (fetish) emerged as a term for incommensurable value within the first zone of contact between Europeans and Africans in the sixteenth century.[123] So when a Dominican curandero in Elías Piña found his powers of clairvoyance through a miraculous cure when he was an infant in Arcahaie, Haiti (which Dominicans consider to be the central zonbi depot), or a Haitian *bòcò* is needed to discharge a pesky baka or heal a "sent illness," or a Dominican prostitute requires a Haitian zonbi to protect herself from AIDS, an inter-island codependence is revealed that is occluded in official narratives of nationhood.[124] While baka stories trace binational entanglement and a shared cultural unconscious occluded in official narratives, there is one crucial difference in the narration of subject position or point of view within this corpus of stories: In my experience only Haitians boast that they can actually become animals. This dark art is considered the sole province of the shadowy members of secret societies such as Sanpwèl or Bizango, who burnish their fearsome reputations as larger-than-life virtual predators, making them man-gods with strong parallels to the *nahualli* witch of Mexico.[125] For Dominicans, the baka is, in the end, an index of alterity, hovering within that "primal space between fear [of] and attraction" to the Other.[126] Since Dominicans perceive these spirit demons as Haitian creations that only Haitian magic can get rid of, the baka relies upon the antinomies of Haitian and Dominican identity and might well be described as a "mediator" that channels anxieties about money (cast as alien) into morally charged ethnic boundaries that "inculpate ethnic others in local suffering" and that convey a latent threat perception. But they are not solely negative, because they also provide a proscenium for Dominicans to cast themselves as valiant heroes.[127]

If these narratives cast capitalism as exogenous and Haiti as the font of money magic, it is relevant that the Dominican Republic had a slightly different trajectory compared to much of the rest of Latin America, since it was long a backwater and its economy grew parasitically as a result of the prosperity of Saint-Domingue. After Santo Domingo was no longer the colonial *audiencia* and trade shifted to the mainland, settlers had to purchase their French cloth, silk stockings, hats, gunpowder, and shot from filibusters, whom they paid with smoked meat and *mantegne* (pig's lard).[128] As Saint-Domingue developed into a massive engine of industrial sugar profit in the late eighteenth century, cattle became the primary protocurrency through which Dominicans acquired slaves and manufactured goods such as rum, cloth, and rope.[129] These trade relations rendered Saint-Domingue the motor of capitalist profit on the island, and the east could only siphon off some of that through proffering their asses, mules, horses, oxen, and cattle. This was more than a "secular meat dependency," since these animals fueled the energy for the Jamaica Train (the sugar refinery) as well as providing hauling and transport; they also provided critical ingredients—bovine blood and bone char—needed for sugar refining.[130] These relations of exchange cast Haiti as a sign of the mysteries of capitalist profit to Dominicans who lived in a natural economy of use value and who participated in global capitalist flows only vicariously. The perceived unbridled danger of Haitian sorcery and money magic also can fuel popular anti-Haitianism and may have contributed to popular understandings of why the 1937 massacre took place.[131]

This accounts for why Haiti is rendered a surreptitious cash machine in these popular narratives. Héctor Alcántara Fragoso, for example, told me the story of Feliz de los Santos Alcántara, alias Felito, who became a

> multimillionaire although he wasn't a professional and didn't own a factory. Native to this region, he met a girl and got married and she ended up having to leave him because at night a little animal would place bags of money under the bed. She was so scared that she ended up leaving him and going home. She saw a little black man and they could not figure out how it got in there to deposit money under the bed. The little man placed the money there but she could not take the money—only the owner could. Felito sold lottery tickets. He was from La Cañita, Rincón Grande, and he first came on a burro and then he was able to buy a bicycle with twenty-eight-inch wheels on which he sold lottery tickets and his business grew in part through said animal, the bacá. A brother of mine was his driver. Felito sent him to the capital and wouldn't let anyone drive with him, but [Héctor's brother] could feel the evil that was present in the *guagua* [car], which was a Datsun. It had this intense smell but he couldn't see anything. And when he tried to sell the vehicle—that was when the strange person who traveled along with him on his side disappeared. So the smell came from the bacá, which rode in the car.

Héctor also related a story about a native creature, a snake—which, notwithstanding its satanic associations in the Bible, served as a spirit double for his father, Nicolo Fragoso, known as Negro, who was having a tough time with this snake, which ate his chickens and even a small goat.[132] So one day he shot the creature, and it returned to its cave to heal—and Negro spent two months in bed recuperating as well. They finally killed the snake, but on that day Negro could not get out of bed. As Héctor put it, "They say that when someone dies, the snake looks for its partner."

ANIMAL ENTANGLEMENTS

I argue that baka stories, taken as an archive, chart a *longue durée* culture and history of interspecies contact and reliance upon animals among the rural poor. Sugar plantations required livestock, since mills were driven by cattle, mules, or oxen until the twentieth century; as historian Linda

Rupert notes, mules were preferred for Caribbean sugar mills yet required constant inputs because they are sterile.[133] Mules and cattle were important draft animals, and manure was used as fertilizer until petrochemical inputs were developed in the twentieth century. Humans and animals were the core labor power for the plantation; as one planter put it, "slaves and stock . . . are the sinews of a plantation."[134] Both branded, slaves and livestock were classed together in plantation registries; the term *maroon*, which later came to mean an escaped slave who lived in a settlement with other escaped slaves, initially was used to refer to a hunter of wild cattle.[135] From moving the herds and carrying grass to searching for strays, mending fences, and building chicken coops, much slave labor was expended in animal care. Outside of the plantation context, donkeys have long been the most important form of transport in the interior.[136] Proximity and contact, which continued within mule contraband networks, forged a sense of "kinesthetic empathy" and even identification between slaves and their animal charges. Livestock also could become surrogates for vicious owners, as slaves lashed out at them when they could.[137] Enslaved people were also used to frame spectacles of subjugation through animal props, as in Jamaica, where enslaved footmen were forced to run behind whites when they went out riding.[138] Anthropologist Clifford Geertz stressed that practices, not just words, play a key role in generating cultural meanings, yet the study of human-animal relations has been slow to link linguistic evidence to interspecies contact and everyday interactions.[139]

Compared to the backbreaking work of cane cutting with its industrial regimentation and systems of surveillance and punishment, cattle work was lighter, the labor force was smaller, the work entailed less supervision and far more autonomy for slaves, and it required mobility, which was a privilege.[140] This was the case for Iberian pastoralism, as well as the system of pen-keeping in the British West Indies.[141] As historian of Barbados Verene Shepherd has demonstrated, pen-keeping forged a non-sugar elite that tended to be free, mixed-race, and creole. Through what was termed the "happy coalition of interests between master and slave," since it was cheaper to allow slaves to grow their own food, provision grounds called *conucos* gave birth to creole culture, as anthropologist Sidney Mintz has argued. Yet the family chicken and hog were crucial components of farming, and not only because they provided much-needed protein when slaves were allocated rotten or scrap meat and bones.[142] In the post-emancipation period, livestock

1.2 A Dominican farmer plowing with oxen. Hato Major, Elias Piña, Dominican Republic, 2014. Photo by the author.

could also provide a bargaining chip for a sharecropping arrangement, and could serve as collateral for loans.[143] As a result, codependence was forged between slaves and freedmen and their animal charges. A strong sense of togetherness is apparent in the treatment of companion animals, especially mules and oxen, which worked in tandem with their human charges and were not eaten (fig. 1.2).[144] Fed, their feet checked, stroked, trimmed, and spoken to, they were individuated through names. Further evidence of the social value of livestock was when the Haitian Revolution broke out and the insurgents attacked frontier ranchers' cattle, or when a red mule was sold adorned with "French braids"; and when their slave caretakers often protected and took refuge with their animal charges.[145] No wonder the independent lifestyles enabled by freedmen owning horses, goats, and pigs engendered a crackdown from authorities throughout the Caribbean in the post-emancipation period.[146]

A freedman subculture that was born in the sixteenth century over time became a sizable force engaging in tasks such as logging of precious woods in combination with hunting and itinerant sales.[147] Despised by elites, these freedmen led a lewd and licentious lifestyle that in a time of slavery was extravagantly mobile and frequently involved animals.

Freedmen typically engaged in a multiplicity of activities to complement subsistence farming: They hunted feral cattle, boars, and game; butchered and sold meat at market; carted water via donkey; drove horse-drawn carriages; tilled the soil with oxen; managed the oxen at the sugar mill; raised chicken and guinea fowl for sale; and roamed the interior on horseback or on burros, depending on their class circumstances. Long-standing elite anxieties about freedmen who were said to be prone to violence or (with the late nineteenth-century rise of liberalism) were cast as indolent solidified into certain negative stereotypes that accrued to certain occupations. The *longue durée* genealogy of Dominican freedmen should commence with the *vaquero* or stockman, descriptions of which emerge as early as the sixteenth century. Luis José Peguero in a *décima* (ten-stanza poem) lists the characteristics of these rustic backcountry travelers armed with lances, who traversed the interior *"montes y sabanas"* (woodlands and plains) looking for wild cattle and who were known to be cocky and saucy womanizers. As Peguero put it in this décima:

> I would like to ask
> everyone in the whole world
> if there were no cowboy,
> Who would practice herding cattle?
> To the weapons, it would be roasting [dangerous];
> to the sciences, audacity;
> to the arts, mischief,
> with which in walks, and others,
> either the women would herd cattle,
> or there would be no cowboy.[148]

Horse-drawn carriage drivers had a bad reputation even in Spain, where they were seen as "fiendish and insolent" and were subject to a constant stream of abuse casting them as greedy and irritable; they were "scoffed at, disrespected but always searched out."[149] The *cochero* (driver) of the *volanta* (carriage) was a principal character of urban life, as noted in the classic Cuban *charanga* song "Pare Cochero" about a "delicate boy" who is ill and needs a ride to the doctor.[150] They were likely mistrusted because they overheard small talk and could relay damaging gossip.

The fact that beliefs about shape-shifting are a feature of societies centrally reliant upon animals may indicate that it is the everyday practices involving animals, and especially people's proximity to animals, that engender cross-species affinity and respect, as we see this combination in the Sami people, who are pastoralists; in Amazonian hunting cultures; and in Jamaica, Nicaragua, and the Dominican Republic, where hunting gave way to extensive ranching. Evans-Pritchard observed how Nuer pastoralists exhibit a "dominant interest in their herds," imitating their horns in rituals, and Mary Douglas's theorization of animal classification was based upon the Lele, who are hunters.[151] As Marcy Norton has said, predation forged mimesis, which "was an intersubjective practice that transcended the species divide."[152]

This may surprise, since cattle on Hispaniola have not always been companion species, so these forms of copresence are more detached than those of pets, of course.[153] Yet transspecies entanglement over time breeds intimacy, attachment, identification, and a shared habitus, especially among beasts that are individuated through labor, such as the ox, which works in tandem with a human while plowing; significantly, oxen and mules are the only livestock that are individuated on Dominican farms, receiving names.[154] An ethos of commensality is evident in the fact that in the Dominican Republic, the same charismatic healing practices of laying on hands and saying prayers are used for both people and animals.[155] As James Frazier argued in his discussion of sympathetic magic, the "palpable, sensuous contact between the very body of the perceiver and the perceived" can endow the object with an aura.[156] This helps explain the curative properties of goat milk and even more so burro milk. In a story linking *leche de burra* (burro milk) with the magical properties of twins and faith-healings lineage, I was told about a woman who gave birth to twins and died, so her *comadrona* (midwife) took them over, nursing them with burro milk, which is said to have strong medicinal properties (as does *batata de burro*, or burro sweet potato, which is said to cure gonorrhea).[157] Yet this was a very special burro; it was provided by the grandson of Juan de la Cruz Alcántara, a *sabio* or persecuted faith healer who evaded authorities by turning into a tree stump and who was known to have brought people back from the dead. This narrative seamlessly braids together human and animal genealogies, with one becoming a substitute for the other.[158]

There are other popular cultural signs of interspecies co-identification, especially with charismatic megafauna such as the horse.[159] For example, as in the popular phrase *saber de qué pata cojea uno* (to know someone's Achilles' heel), personality defects and tics are said to be able to pass from a horse to its rider. A second example concerns the purported magical properties of the blood of a cow or black horse (used in talismans to increase the yield of a fishing expedition) or the magical properties of horse excrement (used to fumigate spirits).[160] The *djablesse* shape-shifter demon has a cloven hoof. Individuals tasked with castrating animals refrained from sexual relations the night before, otherwise the beast could die. And both people and their animal charges can be "boarded" by a lougawou spirit.

As anthropologist Eduardo Kohn has argued, transspecies boundary overlaps can also create discomfort.[161] In a passage eerily similar to Derrida's musings about the discomfiting experience of being the object of an animal gaze, Víctor Garrido Puello, whose family was one of the largest ranchers in San Juan de la Maguana in the early twentieth century, wrote about how livestock were a constant presence when he was growing up. In the evening, cows and goats would invade the town to sleep in the streets and in the plaza. His family had cattle and three horses, and every night he and his brother would take them to the river for a drink. He wrote that as a child "I was terrified of cows with their deathly blank stare and their constant rumination, and often I told my mother this cow is staring at me and talking."[162] In Jamaica, "talking cows" are an omen of death, indicating that the beast is not what it appears to be but is actually a messenger from the spirit world.[163] In Juan Bosch's novel *La Mañosa*, the narrator grew up hearing stories of talking mules from his father, who was a rancher and merchant from San Juan. Afro-Cuban myths of origin also note a time "when animals could speak."[164]

What are we to make of these allegations of talking cows? Since the early modern period, as evidenced in the writings of philosopher René Descartes, speech has long been a sign of "real specific difference between men and dumb animals," so this is a strong violation of the deep divide between nature and culture that is fundamental to the Western canon.[165] I would argue that it is evidence of a culture of proximity to animals and of human-animal boundary crossing specific to countries with a robust history of animal-based economies such as pastoralism and hunting, as in the Dominican Republic.[166] In Europe and the United States, hunting was part of a colonial project of dominion over nature, but the phenomenology of slaves' and freedmen's relationship to animals was, of course, quite different due to their close proximity to the animals as their caretakers and shared role as beasts of burden.[167]

The phenomena of talking cows may also result from the ontological mimesis between human and nonhuman animals that is characteristic of hunting cultures. From Amazonia to Siberia, hunting involves a kind of mirroring or "mimetic encounter" in which humans imitate the movements and sound of their prey at times, to attract them, and at others are silent like a beast, so as not to disturb them.[168] As anthropologist Rane Willerslev puts it, "Hunting is anchored in a skilled 'dehumanization,' the reshaping of the qualities of one's human body into those of the prey."[169] Or as anthropologist Neil Whitehead wrote, "Hunting itself is always a mimesis of prey—what they do you must do in order to find and kill them. Killing by being an animal gives rise to affinity."[170] Hunters view their prey as equals, a relationship that shifts dramatically with the advent of domestication.[171]

As the feral animal commons receded in the Dominican Republic, the everyday labor of animal husbandry replaced it, but I argue that a deep affinity and identification with these feral mascots has remained, as seen in the ubiquity of animals in Hispaniola's popular culture: nicknames in everyday Dominican banter; Carnival characters; the case of Enercido Matos, who was tried in court for raping a neighbor's burro; or the opposition between free-ranging dogs and yoked oxen as metaphors of freedom and its obverse.[172] Scholarly literature has long separated the economic and symbolic roles of animals, but the case of Hispaniola indicates that these two aspects are inextricably bound together.[173] While certainly the hunting commons lasted longer in the sparsely populated mountainous eastern regions of Santo Domingo than in the western portion of the island, which became Haiti, shape-shifting is prominent in Haitian Carnival—for example, in the Lansè-Kòd, which turns people into cattle, as we shall see in chapter 2. And figures of speech derived from hunting have also become root metaphors in Haiti (where, notwithstanding the pig massacre of 1979, creole pigs remain highly prized), as in the popular adage "A day for the hunter, a day for the prey."[174] No wonder one of the first things the slaves of Saint-Domingue did upon joining the rebellion was to open the aviaries to free the birds.[175]

CHAPTER TWO

THE MYSTERIOUS MURDER OF JAVIER

In October 2010, during one of my visits to Bánica, Javier killed himself early one morning with a shotgun. This was a particularly shocking event because no one in the town could recall another suicide; suicides are extremely rare in these tightly knit rural communities. As a crowd of neighbors formed around the house to console his wife and son, who were left to clean up the carnage, a discussion ensued over what must have caused this tragedy. Javier's wife had many friends who were nurses, and they wondered why she had not previously sought psychological treatment for him, since he must have suffered from depression. But a parallel and quite distinct conversation emerged among some of the men, many of whom descend from the four clans of herdsmen who founded the town.[1] A story commenced that Javier's first cousin Rafael, the *síndico* (rural councilman), was responsible on the grounds that he had a large herd of phantom cattle across the border in Haiti, one that mysteriously grew just as everyone else's was diminishing. Some reported a portent that something was amiss—that Javier had been seen in Haiti, where he vanished, reappearing as an animal in the herd; the implication was that his spirit had been sold to the *vende-gente* (people-sellers) in Arcahaie, Haiti, in a form of nefarious border commerce that accrued wealth to Rafael. These stories also indicated that these cattle were not actually livestock but rather bacá or spirit demons presenting in animal form.

As they were mulling over the event, several people mentioned that they had seen black clouds in their dreams, reflective of a nocturnal malevolent presence. The night before, I had been awakened by footsteps in Doña Pico Mora's cavernous house on Avenida Duarte, which was taken as further evidence of a demonic visitation. This was construed as evidence that Javier's death was actually not a suicide but rather a murder, and that Rafael was to blame. This rendered Javier's death the result of mystical assault caused by Rafael's malignant emotions.[2] The issue was complicated by the fact that Javier and Rafael were both first cousins, as noted earlier, and political rivals from opposed political parties. Nor did it help that Rafael was widely despised for his ineptitude and rumored corruption, for which he had been given the sobriquet "El Burro," which appeared in graffiti all over town. By contrast, Javier was youthful and vigorous and many hoped he would soon unseat his incompetent cousin as mayor; thus his death was taken as a case of sorcery spurred by *envidia* (jealousy), that "ominous, tiresome, and unpleasant fact of nature" that produces evil effects on the body and sometimes can even engender a violent death.[3]

This chapter considers the story of Javier's murder via sorcery in relation to several apparently minor clues in the narrative, especially the fact that Rafael was said to have conducted his illicit work via demonic cattle. Rooted in the sixteenth-century buccaneer economy, the criollo breed of cattle holds a special significance on Hispaniola, since the cattle trade formed the backbone of the contraband economy that knitted together the French colony Saint-Domingue and its poorer eastern neighbor Santo Domingo until the Haitian Revolution (1791–1804). As historian Juan Guisti-Cordero has noted, work animals were a key component of the sugar plantation economy, and by the eighteenth century the economy of Santo Domingo was defined by the *hato* or extensive cattle ranch, the entire product of which flowed west to the French colony of Saint-Domingue.[4] For centuries, the leather trade was the basis of an illicit but extensive commerce across the border that formed the basis of island-wide collaboration, irrespective of official opprobrium. Part of the historic resonance of cattle today stems from the fact that for centuries it formed a popular protocurrency that knitted together subalterns and authorities on the island, at a time when commerce between the two parts of the island was prohibited.[5] The cross-island traffic in animals is often overlooked in models that privilege metropolitan export trade and treat the border as a hard dividing line, as a result failing to home in on the frontier, which was transformed from the periphery to the center of the economy of the Spanish colony Santo Domingo in the late eighteenth century because of the cattle trade. Indeed, due to the flourishing cattle trade, in 1784 Bánica was far larger in population than even San Juan de la Maguana, which is today the third-largest city of the country, after Santo Domingo and Santiago. In the eighteenth century a traveler said Bánica was "denser and better built than San Juan."[6]

This essay deploys historian Carlo Ginzburg's methodology of following seemingly minor details that may reveal otherwise unseen underlying logics.[7] As Freud has demonstrated in his analysis of humor, such minutiae can offer traces of submerged meanings—in this case, the protean emotions generated by past events that linger in the present.[8] This chapter thus focuses on dreams, specters, and rumors as forms of historical evidence that may reveal unspoken forms of affect unavailable to historians working with transparent historical records. As historian Reinhart Koselleck has said, in moments when "language is struck dumb," dreams and visions may afford a window into "worlds of experience" and the preconscious domain of sentiment and sensibility related to the past before they were edited out of the record.[9]

Bacá conjure very different threat perceptions depending upon whether they present as dogs, pigs, or cattle. While in all such cases the bacá are shape-shifters, dogs, and, in the case of Javier and Rafael, cattle, are more akin to vampires than to werewolves, due to the prevalence of blood imagery that accompanies them. Indeed, the very term *bacá* resonates with *vaca*, the Spanish term for "cow," since *b* and *v* are often interchangeable in spoken Spanish. These stories of spirit demons that graphically slaughter their prey convey what anthropologist Neil Whitehead has termed the "poetics of violent death," the cultural expression of violent bloodshed and mutilation here imaged through a surrogate beast.[10] Historian Luise White has read vampire rumors as "an epistemological category" through which people "described their worlds, both as beliefs and metaphors."[11] I propose that these bovine bacá stories express the danger and vulnerability inherent in the experience of those who formed part of the eighteenth-century hunting and contraband economy of the border. These rumors thus may be read as "visceral indicators" of the "potent threat" that was part and parcel of a lifestyle based on hunting and selling feral cattle as contraband, and the particular kind of harrowing human/beast encounters it involved, particularly for freedmen who were vulnerable to being swept up again as slaves.[12] These stories of surreptitious predation via cattle are also popular memories of slavery, since it was through cattle that slaves were acquired due to a shortage of specie in the Spanish colony; thus the "mysterious character" of this manifestation of the bacá is also due to its role as a commodity fetish.[13]

The fear and loathing conjured by these beasts thus conveys historical memories of the illicit cattle economy that articulated the Dominican and Haitian economies in the eighteenth century as the French plantation economy expanded and came to rely on Dominican cattle as a source of meat and energy and as a surrogate currency. These popular narratives also offer a lens through which we can examine the meanings generated by interspecies interactions at a time and in a place when nonhuman species were still dominant. Thus such accounts provide a means of excavating a preanthropomorphic historical moment. I propose that these tales of changeling cattle are reflective of a particular phenomenology of interspecies relations characteristic of cattle economies, and channel a fusion of human and beast that is characteristic of hunting cultures.[14] They also reflect contemporary popular anxieties about clandestine human and drug trafficking in the border region, as we shall see.

ISLE OF BACÁ

The horse was the core technology of conquest that enabled the Spanish to subdue large groups of Native Americans, but Spain also had a unique cattle culture that it transferred to the New World.[15] The extensive peninsular ranching system based on a dual system of corralled and feral cattle was characteristic of Andalusia, the province in which Seville is located, and reinforced by the high proportion of Canary Islanders and Galicians—both pastoralists—who migrated to the colonies. It was perfectly adapted to the semi-arid conditions of parts of the San Juan Valley, where forage was minimal and the grazing area had to be large.[16] The first colonial administrators were all large cattle ranchers, but cattle really developed as the backbone of the economy of La Española after the decline of placer mining and as emigration to the mainland increased in 1520 as the newly conquered lands filled with extensive cattle herds; the suitability of ranching was enhanced by the fact that it required minimal labor. Cattle was also used to support new immigrants, who were loaned oxen until their first harvest.[17] The leather trade developed into a major industry along the coast and principal rivers, but meat was not exported, which left behind an abundance of beef for feral dogs and, unusually, even some for the burgeoning slave population. The official trade in hides involved primarily corralled cattle, leaving the *ganado bravo* (feral cattle) of the interior to contrabandists.

Food access is often a tool of colonialism, and in this case meat provisioning was more than a merely utilitarian project. Given the centrality of meat-eating to the Iberian diet, and the fact that wild game in Europe was mostly reserved for elites, bingeing on meat seems to have been the colonists' reward, as the conquistadores' hunger for riches was matched only by their "chronic hunger" for animal protein, though they refused to countenance the indigenes' diet, which included snakes, lizards, spiders, and worms—animals that these unrepentant carnivores did not consider food.[18] In the 1550s, for a population of six hundred, fifty cows, fifty-five sheep, and twelve pigs were slaughtered each day.[19] In fact, the indigenous Taínos' lack of a hearty red-meat diet was in part due to the fact that the Spanish only gave them "grasses," particularly during the years of famine; this may help explain the fact that the Indian was seen as "weak and effeminate," as opposed to the manly conquistadores.[20] Columbus himself blamed illness among his men on the "lack of fresh meat" in missives calling for animals to provide protein and portage.[21] The Indigenous community was horrified at the ravenous appetite of the conquistadores, who it was said ate in one day more than an entire Taíno family in a month.[22] Indeed, it was the overreliance upon meat—characteristic of southern Spain—that in part caused the neglect of agriculture and resulted in famine.[23] Extractivist hunting also had a major impact on fragile ecosystems, as sea turtle eggs, for example, were ravaged to near extinction alongside indigenous rodents and barkless dogs, which had been raised as a protein source by the Taíno.[24]

This "sugarless" society that developed along the *banda norte* (northern coast) offered unusual upward mobility for a select group of mixed-race mestizos who formed the first creole society on the island. Illicit trade networks linked them with eastern Cuba and other secluded ports such as Jamaica, where they provisioned ships, replacing the rations of "putrid salt beef and rotten biscuit" that were the norm.[25] In this "freebooter" economy they sold smoked meat and hides as well as tallow, the last of which was critical to industrialization.[26]

By the sixteenth century, the feral pigs, dogs, and cattle brought by Columbus had formed vast herds in the interior that sustained an ever-expanding community of maroons and other fugitives from the law. Ungulate populations can contribute to deforestation and erosion, but these large herds appear to have actually spread vegetation, as observers noted the dense woods that provided a major obstacle to the British when they invaded in 1655.[27] This community of masterless people consisted of a motley crew of European indentured servants such as Alexandre Exquemelin, who provided one of our best eyewitness testimonies, alongside other plebian castaways including escaped African and Indigenous slaves.[28] The word *boucan*, which referred to a rack for smoking meat and eventually was anglicized as *buccaneer*, was originally an Indigenous term, a reminder that the smoking process originated among Amerindians and was reinforced by runaway slaves, but Europeans were incorporated into this lifestyle. Governor Antonio de Osorio tried to combat this contraband scourge by forcing the removal of the northern settlements in 1605 in what is remembered as the "devastations," but ended up actually expanding it by creating a vast no-man's-zone of fugitive animals, hunters, and escaped slaves as well as enabling the establishment of large cattle ranches without a community of agriculturalists to challenge them.[29] France's recognition of the buccaneers commenced the division of the island into distinct colonial communities, one French and one Spanish, but the cattle trade was already well established when the Treaty of Ryswick, which ended the Nine Years' War in Europe and ceded the western third of Hispaniola from Spain to France, was signed in 1697.[30]

Pigs and cattle adapted very rapidly, soon becoming the primary protein source for early settlers, and the immense herds of the densely wooded interior formed an important component of what historian Michael Jarvis in the context of Bermuda has termed an "Atlantic commons" for the poor, an "extraimperial frontier zone" where social outcasts from bondsmen to runaway slaves could subsist on extracting resources such as wood, salt, pearls, and turtles and thus maintain a subsistence base outside of the core settlements where mining and later sugar and slavery ruled. Jarvis has stressed how this economy of seafaring men was a vital part of Atlantic maritime trade, providing essential raw materials upon which other industries relied.[31] On Hispaniola, cattle and pigs formed the basis of a thriving hunting economy, one that sustained freedmen in the interior to the detriment of agriculture. This frontier society held appeal for its autonomy from forced labor, and must have been rein-forced by the Andalusians' and Canary Islanders' preference for livestock raising over farming. The Iberian land tenure system that provided col-lective lands for grazing (which later became *tierras del estado*, which enabled the poor squatters to claim rights) and the right to hunt feral boars over time gave rise to a sense of collective hunting rights, especially for feral pigs.[32]

By the mid-seventeenth century, the hunters of Hispaniola (called *monteros* for the forest [*monte*] where they worked) had emerged as a social category and had split into two groups, those hunting cattle and those hunting boars. The two groups swapped smoked meat and hides to the corsairs and planters for tobacco. A portrait of the Hispaniolan hunter emerges in these accounts. Armed with hunting dogs and the ubiquitous machete and knife, these men wore simple attire of trou-sers and shirt, with a sheath for the machete that was essential to their trade. Animal bones were even used as furnishings and tableware. But with their belt and *gargoussier* (tote bag) fashioned of bull's hide, shoes of leather slabs, and their faces smeared with hog's grease, their attire rendered them mimetic apparitions of the very animals they hunted.[33] Due to the dense forest undergrowth, the monteros usually hunted on foot. This was very difficult work, and these hunters were highly skilled; they were also fearless. As one observer put it, "It was a brave man who could confront a wild bull with sharp horns and the terrible boar with those sharp, penetrating tusks."[34] Into the eighteenth century, observers were surprised to see no evidence of agricultural cultivation or animal husbandry in the interior.[35] Monteros were often sought out by authori-ties for their knowledge of local terrain, distances between points, water sources, and animal locations, but they were patently not treated with respect.[36] As Archbishop Carvajal y Rivera put it, they "lived in the bush like savages," and Fernando Araújo y Rivera manifested his "horror" at these men who could stand up to wild beasts.[37] Of course, in a slavehold-ing society, these men of color without slaves who worked with their own hands were considered nonpeople.

Oliver Cromwell's military incursion into Santo Domingo in 1654 was fended off very effectively by these "cow-killers" (including some women dressed as men), who fought the British with only lances, using surprise tactics such as ambush and attacking from the rear (which is similar to how wild dogs brought down feral boars, by attacking their testicles); using these guerrilla tactics, only four hundred people were able to put down an invasion force of seven thousand.[38] In addition, the British were unable to locate and bring down feral animals, and they starved as a result, eating horse, dog, or boiled shoe leather for lack of anything more appealing.[39] Certainly the "shameful" defeat "by a few cow killers" was all the more ignominious due to the tawny complexion of this motley crew of mulattos and *alcatraces*, or people with both Indian and African heritage. An indication of how impressive these hunters must have been is that traders called their guns *boucaniers* after these hunters, who were clearly esteemed for their martial skills.[40]

A vibrant commercial trade in hides arose in tandem with this subsistence peasantry, which lived a nomadic life in the interior and only sporadically articulated with the market economy. Indeed, Santo Domingo provided a whopping one-fourth of all hides imported into Spain in the late sixteenth century.[41] At this time Seville became the main entrepot for leather, which was exported to the Low Countries and beyond. This *cuir de Cordoue* was manufactured into luxury goods, such as leather furniture, tapestries, wallpaper, decorative screens, trunks, and other gilt furnishings.[42]

BOVINE CAPITAL

Yet the balance between the interior backwoods montero peasantry and the extensive cattle ranchers tipped in favor of the latter with the dramatic expansion of cattle production that occurred as a result of the rise of Saint-Domingue, which with its rapidly expanding sugar economy became the jewel in the crown of the French Empire by the 1740s. By the eve of the Haitian Revolution, the "centerpiece of the Atlantic slave system" was the world's leading producer of coffee and sugar, exporting as much sugar as Brazil, Cuba, and Jamaica put together.[43] At that time, sugar production required livestock for hauling and transport and as a protein source for workers, but most importantly oxen were the motor of the animal-driven trapiche (sugar mill). But cattle blood or bone char was also used in the refinery process for the better-capitalized mills that could afford the technology to refine on-site, a process that expanded rapidly between 1750 and 1790.[44]

Over the course of the eighteenth century the entire eastern Spanish portion of the island redirected its trade toward commerce in cattle with Saint-Domingue. The price differential between hides sold legally and illegally in Saint-Domingue was considerable, and this incentivized contraband.[45] This shift also probably redirected the proceeds from the merchants to the ranchers themselves. Even though the majority of trade was conducted over land to Saint-Domingue, commerce with British, Danish, and Dutch ships continued to be important, as flour, wine, butter, salt cod, cheese, and porcelain were swapped for wood, hides, and tobacco.[46] In the latter half of the eighteenth century, cattle became, as historian Antonio Gutiérrez Escudero put it, "the true wealth of the island," which at this time had far more cattle than the more expansive cattle regions of New Spain such as Guadalara and Sonora. Cattle fueled a golden age for the backward colony of Santo Domingo, as municipalities were for the first time flush with cash and imported goods flowed eastward.[47] But this also set in motion political conflict, as state authorities sought to garner as much taxation as possible from the illicit cattle trade, just as ranchers resorted to various schemes to keep the revenue to themselves, from accusations of cattle sickness and theft to paying off border guards.[48]

As cattle became a highly profitable resource, large clans in the central frontier region, such as the Alcántaras, sought to expand and monopolize the gains while evading taxes. One way they did this was by expanding into townships such as Hinche and Las Caobas that were proximate to the Artibonite Valley, where many plantations were located. Hinche was behind only Bánica in terms of numbers of cattle by 1774, since Hinche and Bánica were exempt from the *pesa*, a tax on the illicit livestock trade imposed to incentivize legal sales of meat to Santo Domingo.[49] Theft, especially along the border, became a problem, but there were also middlemen (*metedores*) hired to move the livestock who at times falsely declared theft to avoid taxation.[50] But since extensive ranching required little in the way of capital inputs such as slaves, and given the system of *terrenos comuneros* with its differentiated usufruct system, freedmen and people with few resources were also able to enter the trade, and eventually were able to convert their stock into land ownership.[51] During this period, the identity of the two sides of the island became differentiated through trade, as Saint-Domingue became a sugar plantation economy while Santo Domingo provided the livestock it relied upon. Yet the importance of the cattle trade also forged extensive cross-border family ties; one-quarter of all the major clans of Santiago, for example, came to include a French relative.[52] Cattle enabled the acquisition of luxury goods in the Spanish colony which had been out of reach previously, as cattle, horses, and mules were swapped for rum, cloth, and clothing.[53]

The late eighteenth-century slave insurrection in Saint-Domingue brought a range of travelers to the island who traversed the interior, leaving us rich documentation of the landscape. For example, the engineer Daniel Lescallier spent four months traveling around Santo Domingo in 1764 and wrote a memoir of his travels, and what is striking is the way he moves across the land from hato to hato; the hatos provided the principal place markers and were far more significant than towns at that time. As he writes, "Leaving the Hato of San José or del Piñón and following the skirt of Piñón mountain, we arrived at the Hato de Buenavista, to the right of the road, and two leguas and a half from the mountain."[54] Since he kept to known routes, he did not encounter the areas where feral cattle ranged, but one gets glimpses of them—for example, in the important cattle town of San Juan de la Maguana, "where everywhere we encounter savannas where there is an immense quantity of cattle . . . and there are huge herds of oxen and horses." Even into the nineteenth century, the free-range cows and goats would return to the town at night to sleep.[55] He notes how many townships such as Dajabón, Bánica, and Azua developed out of the transient *bohíos* (huts) ranchers camped at while moving their livestock; many were either founded due to the eighteenth-century cattle trade to Saint-Domingue or expanded in size because of it.[56] Lescallier does not describe his own entourage, but clearly he was on horseback, given the way he maps rivers and whether they dry up or not, plains for grazing, and impassable areas such as mountains and forests. In many towns, animals were more numerous than people. Azua, an important stop-off point between Santo Domingo and Port-au-Prince, had 3,600 people, a number dwarfed by 18,000 cattle and 10,000 horses.[57] The French travel accounts often note the extensiveness of cattle ranching in relation to the relative absence of agriculture, which they saw as an indication of lassitude.[58] Indeed, Martiniquan jurist M. L. Moreau de Saint-Méry exclaimed in horror that the Spanish colony would be better off recolonized by France and suffused with pedigreed cattle, insinuating that the mongrel populations of both humans and nonhumans were to blame for the colony's backwardness.[59]

The value of the hides and the difficulties of transporting the meat created a frenzy of extractivist animal slaughter that by the mid-eighteenth century reduced the herds significantly. A "great decrease in wild cattle" was noted by observers, and conservation measures were put into place,

such as prohibitions on the use of dogs for hunting boars, lest they be decimated.[60] One indicator that cattle were diminishing is the fact that the
local diet, which once had been centered on beef, by this time had shifted
to pork, as noted by the Franciscan Jean-Baptiste Labat who was offered
fresh pork by hunters in exchange for wine and brandy and who noted that
the price of pork had risen due to declining access.[61] Indeed, as cattle became a highly valued commodity, hateros (ranchers) avoided slaughtering
their own cattle as a meat source, seeking out wild cattle for that purpose.[62]

Antonio Sánchez Valverde, a creole priest writing in 1780, classified
the cattle subcultures into three distinct groups. Hateros depended upon
state lands for grazing. Ranchers had *agregados* or *corraleras*, which were
kept by the dozens and maintained close to home. There were also *man-
sas*, cattle that were castrated and left free outside the township.[63] But
most of the cattle resided in sparsely inhabited wooded areas in mountainous terrain. Although the first two forms of ranching required only a
few field hands, who were given unusual autonomy since they followed
the grazing herds and were alone for weeks at a time, the feral animals
called *extravagantes* demanded a very different set of techniques. A group
of men on horseback, armed with *jarreteras* (lances), was assembled,
and a pack of dogs was formed. Working together, the men and dogs
would corral a group of animals into a *rodeo* or roundup, and then the
men would down the cattle by grabbing their tails. They would "stop the
horse, get off quickly and throw themselves on the animal before it can
get up, twist the nape of the neck, grabbing the horns the tips of which
they try to stick in the ground when they can, and this way they keep
them muzzled as long as they need."[64] This was a highly labor-intensive
operation; and most often it ended in the death of the beast, although
occasionally one or two could be tied up and transported. Once trade
had shifted from primarily exports of hides to live cattle sales to Saint-
Domingue, this method was not preferred.

This last type, the feral extravangantes, *montaraces* or *bravias*, lived
deep in the woods, rarely saw people, and would flee on sight. They
would be located with dogs, then subdued with a whip; finally the
hunter would assault the furious animal "body to body with the lance."[65]
As Sánchez Valverde notes, the profit for this was small given the dangerous and exhausting nature of the work. The hatero had to be vigorous,
strong, and agile, and have an intimate knowledge of the terrain. But he
worked mounted, which afforded him a higher status than the montero
who routed out boars and small game on foot.[66]

Sánchez Valverde's elaborate description of the hatero was intended as a critique of the feral cattle complex, since hateros did not pay *diezmo* (tithe) to the state, consumed valuable pastureland, and seeded guayabo and xicaco trees everywhere.[67] He was also unhappy with the hato labor regime, since he claimed there was no shared interest between the slave *mayoral* (overseer), who grazed the herd willy-nilly, and the owner, as the slave mayoral's sole objective was to gain his freedom. Given the availability of grazing lands, no landscaping was done to cut back undergrowth, and no benefits accrued to either owners or the state. Neither the slaves nor the cattle were subjected to any kind of vigilance given the impossibility of surveying the vast expanse of terrain.[68]

While Sánchez Valverde's objections were in keeping with the ideas of liberal reformers concerned with harnessing the rural sector for state formation and development, his contemporary Edward Long of Jamaica had another set of objections. Long was worried about the avenues for upward mobility posed by this freewheeling subculture, which facilitated forming one's own herd—or, worse, "flagrant robbery."[69] His discussion of the related freebooter economy, provisioning small maritime vessels, shares a highly disparaging view of the audacity of freedmen who had "stolen" their own manumission. By sharp contrast, Sánchez Valverde, himself a descendent of freedmen, reveals a certain veiled pride in the bold antics of African-descended privateers such as Lorenzo Daniel (Lorencín), the most important corsair of the second half of the eighteenth century, who worked with a group of creoles and Canary Islanders who brought much-needed imported goods and contraband slaves to Hispaniola during a period when a full two years could pass without a Spanish ship stopping at a local port. At a time when the city of Santo Domingo had become the central theater of the freebooter economy, these maritime vessels also served as a coast guard, and even penetrated the local elite.[70] Sánchez Valverde defended the leather trade on the grounds that it supplied labor, which was key to growth and prosperity (Lorencín is said to have introduced at least 1,313 slaves between 1729 and 1750).[71] As he says, "nobody is more courageous than the poor," and these creole pirates "were highly respected for their vigor and nautical skills," and though "their bounty was enormous . . . [y]ou can already see how they relieved the suffering of a miserable island."[72] And courageous they were. In one example, in which a filibuster ship attacked a British ship near Barbados, French clergyman Jean-Baptiste Labat comments how he could not fathom how a small frigate with six cannons could have attacked the huge vessel it did; in that attack the British lost fifteen people, while the filibusters lost only four. But there were no complaints from him, since they endeared themselves to him with elaborate gifts, including six bottles, twelve crystal goblets, and two cheeses from the seized ship.[73]

Certainly Long's disgust was related to the fact that in a sugar plantation economy, cattle and slaves were the most significant capital outlays for cane farmers, as can be seen in the property registries Long produces for each province.[74] And for ranchers given free access to state lands, cattle and slaves were the basis of capital accumulation.[75] "Cattle and negroes" are consistently listed in parallel columns, as both were taxed, and the two were linked, since, as Long reminds us, for cane farmers owning slaves was requisite to owning cattle. Cattle were necessary for transporting product, just as oxen were needed for grinding cane before the invention of mechanized mills. The appeal of cattle for former slaves thus may have transcended the role of cattle as an asset that could be converted to cash and goods; it also probably had to do with the way cattle could become a bargaining chip in negotiating other objectives, from land to credit.[76]

Given the demographic preponderance of Wolof, Fulani, and Mandingo slaves among the *vaqueros* (cowboys) of the interior, historian John Thornton has proposed that African-derived ranching practices were the norm on Hispaniola.[77] Given the lack of available labor after the demise of Amerindians, a system of cattle management developed using just a few herders working with long sharp instruments called *desjarretadera*. On horseback the *lanceros* (lancers) would sever the feral animals' hamstrings, disabling them; after the animals were killed, they would remove the hide and tallow, leaving behind much of the meat, which sustained packs of feral dogs in the interior.[78] Certainly the technology and techniques used in cattle rustling were derived from West African practices.[79] However, the enormous wild herds of Hispaniola presented a very different kind of challenge than was the case in the Senegambian context, where a combination of castration, water scarcity, and some nocturnal penning partially tamed the animals. The Wolof were highly skilled pastoralists, and were intimately codependent upon their cattle, which provided milk, their single most important protein source. André Alvares reported that the Jalofos (Wolof)

> make excellent cavalrymen, being fine riders and fierce warriors. Their horses are so well trained, so much so that we might say that they are ruled more by habit and reason than by the rein; for if

one . . . tells his horse to lie down, it lies down; to get up, it gets up, to bow it bows. The black leaps down like a bird [from his horse's back], and runs off without laying a hand on their horse, but it follows him like a dog.[80]

It is true that the Hispaniolan monteros deployed the Wolof lance, worked on horseback like the Wolof, and had milk products as an essential component of their diet like the Wolof. However, the close pacific codependence between the Wolof and both their cattle and their horses starkly differentiates the West African precedent from the hunters of Hispaniola. The montero worked in a group, but felling the cow required engaging in a man-to-beast tussle with the animal, a highly dangerous operation in which the man risked his life and was often left covered in blood and sometimes injured by the sharp horns.

There are parallels between how the montero worked and the Spanish bullfight, which also is a theater of man versus beast and a stage where concepts of honor and masculine valor are showcased.[81] During the eighteenth century, the *toreo* (bullfight) on horseback was replaced by the *capea* (bull running) on foot; the bullfight was also transformed from an elite event to a popular festival. As Ortega y Gasset has said, the capea reveals some of the best-kept secrets of Spanish national life.[82] Originating in the transhumant cattle complex, *torradas* or herds of wild bulls were plentiful in Spain, and those from western Andalusia were said to have special *bravura* (aggressiveness). The aristocracy delighted in taking down these animals with packs of dogs; the lancers who could fell the wildest charging bulls were accorded the greatest respect, and bravura was cultivated through selective breeding practices.[83] Indeed, as historian Timothy Mitchell has stated, "today's *toro bravo* [Spanish fighting bull] is not a natural but a cultural product, the result of a conscientious process of cultivation," ironically to enhance savage behavior.[84]

In rural New England, where the chief predators of livestock on farms were wolf packs, killing wolves was never merely a "pragmatic act of destroying livestock-devouring predators"; it was celebrated in a series of bloody and dramatic rites and oral legends about canid savagery, through which wolf-hating was institutionalized.[85] Similarly, the bullfight elaborates and celebrates the bloody contest; it does so through elaborate "disembowelings" which represent the viscera when the death is neat.[86]

HARNESSING THE WILDERNESS

There is ample evidence that this long history of hunting and extensive pastoralism has made its mark on the popular culture of Hispaniola. For one, elements from them have made their way into figures of speech, such as when an eighteenth-century priest complained that his flock lacked *"pasto espiritual"* (referring to spiritual nourishment through the metaphor of pasture) since there were insufficient priests in most interior towns.[87] And the phrase *"comer burro"* (eat burro) is a revoltingly absurd colloquial term for abject sacrifice due to the fact that the burro is a tried and true member of the family that works hard without complaining and which, like a pet, should absolutely not be eaten.[88] Donkeys may have a special significance as well due to their biblical resonance.[89]

Yet while a rancher might classify all of his quadrupeds (cattle, pigs, goats, oxen, and mules) as "livestock," popular taxonomies resist this kind of bundling. Indeed, likely due to the close engagement between human and beast in ox-driven plowing, oxen are the only livestock on a Dominican farm that are named, and they are often given women's names such as Rosita, connoting familial tenderness and intimacy.[90] There is also a Haitian Bouki and Ti Malice *conte créole* (creole tale) in which, due to his rapacious appetite, the lazy Bouki ends up killing the family cow, much to everyone's dismay; the story intends to enforce the point that one must not be controlled by base hunger and the family cow as a rule should not be eaten.[91] And elsewhere in the African diaspora cow's milk is a panacea used in sympathetic magic to calm agitated farm animals.[92]

Pastoralism's reverence of animals is evidenced as well in creole forms of magic. In the sixteenth century, a slave woman accused of witchcraft in Puerto Plata prepared baths from animal fat, which she mixed with imported herbs, and she broke a spell on a woman using the water from a scalded dog.[93] And in Haiti, protective "work" lamps used in slavery (using fire, which is associated with the dangerous, hot *petwo* spirits) are today animated via oils combined with animal body parts depending upon the spirit in question that is invoked.[94] Invoking the forest that used to shelter these feral beasts, these lamps are supposed to be placed in trees.[95] Activating ingredients include *piment-chien* (dog pepper) and soot or ashes from a decomposed corpse.[96] Others use the gallbladder of an ox, a sheep's brain, cowhide, or a pierced beef heart.[97] Cattle are thus used as actants in agentive magic, but they required protection as well, since they were often the object of sorcery via attacks on property.[98]

Spirits of beloved kin can return in the form of cattle, making themselves known by tramping and snorting.[99] The fact that these animal parts were coupled with items such as dirt and gunpowder indicates that they are classed as part of the dangerous petwo side of vodou, which is associated with the powers of the foreign.[100] This may reflect the fact that livestock hailed from the east, as did Don Pedro, who is said to be the eponymous founder of the petwo line of spirits within Haitian vodou. For slaves, of course, free-range animals held appeal, since they offered the promise of life beyond confinement.[101]

The use of the bull as a power object resonates with the bull's history as the largest and most powerful of the charismatic megafauna that Columbus brought to Hispaniola. Due to their size, strength, and aggressive behavior, bulls have been seen in many cultures as "the supreme example of masculine strength and ferocity in nature, the epitome of fertility and virility."[102] Correspondingly, the bull is a popular representation in the spirit world as part of the iconography of Haitian *lwa* or *mistère*, with Bosou Twa Kon, Kalfou Mapaka, and Toro Pikant used for grave problems (fig. 2.1).[103] The *djablesse*, for example, has one cow foot, and a wanga may be wrapped in cowhide.[104]

Bosou Twa Kon has three horns, which may be a function of the power of triplism in the Celtic world; as Miranda Green states, "the unnatural extra horn serves to remove the image from nature and give it a supernatural, supranormal status," rendering it "unequivocally sacred." Donald Cosentino has proposed that this melded with the "*tohosu*, a sacred monster of the [Fon] royal family, especially associated with Akadja who was said to rule over a kingdom where humans mated with goats and so gave birth to the *tohosu*."[105] Horns provide a visual metaphor for power and force, indexing a brave spirit who will fight for his own, and appear with frequency in vodou imagery, from sacred *vèvè* drawings drawn on the ground to invoke the spirit world to power objects and Carnival figures such as Yahweh, which has horns and masks its face with an animal skin (figs. 2.2 and 2.3).[106] Horns also figure predominantly in West Indian Carnival masquerade figures such as Jonkonnu, which could be clad in "an entire bullock's hide, horns, tail and . . . skull" as well as ox horns and boar tusks to achieve a fearsome profile. And the Cocorícamo mask found in Sabana Alta, a rural commune of San Juan de la Maguana, sports an ox head and horse tail (incidentally, San Juan has long been the site of the Dominican national meat market).[107] When the Ashanti of Ghana wanted to bedazzle the British trader Bowditch in 1817, they

2.1 Fausto, a Haitian sorcerer who works with the spirit Toro, also known as Toro Lisa, who is the head of the petwo division. Pedro Santana, Dominican Republic, 2016. Photo by the author.

2.2 Fausto's altar with red and white cloths covering a large horn and chain; (*below altar*) chromo-lithographs of St. Jacques, St. Miguel, and Mami Wata, among others. Pedro Santana, Dominican Republic, 2016. Photo by the author.

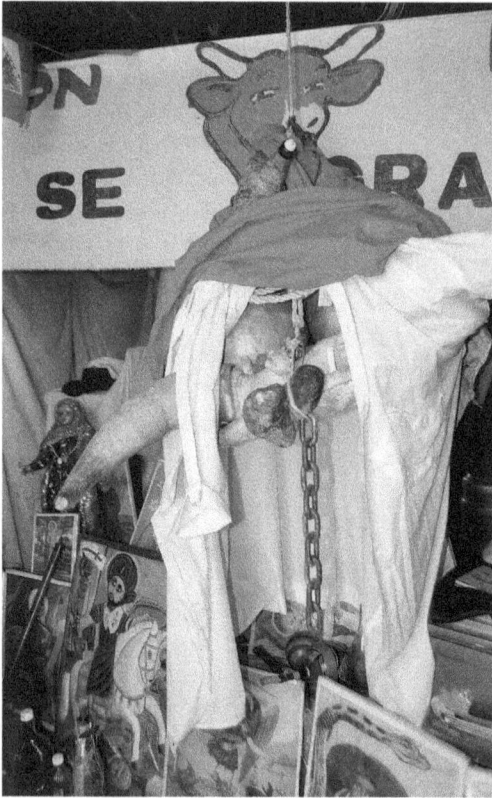

2.3 Detail of Fausto's altar. Note the incorporation of bovine imagery from the popular snack cheese *La Vache qui rit*, 2016. Photo by the author.

similarly paraded bedecked with horns and tails of animals in order to achieve a weighty but "unnatural materiality" to create a terrifying monstrous animal-human hybrid.[108]

In anthropologist Edmund Leach's classification, in the ritual pantheon the bull is the distant stranger, one who is "known to exist but with whom no social relations of any kind are possible."[109] The bull figures in many forms of popular performance precisely because it is a symbol of maximal power, which can render it a portal between the natural and the supernatural realms. Within Cuban Santería, horns are sometimes said to invoke Elegua, the liminal trickster.[110] Animals are objects of sacrifice in Haitian and Dominican vodou rites, but these are most often poultry or pigs. Today cows are sacrificial beasts only at major public ritual feasts that hundreds of spectators attend, such as Haiti's Souvenance (on Easter), which receives political patronage.[111] The preferred sacrificial beast in the Dominican *campo* (countryside) today is a chicken, goat, or large pig. As noted by anthropologist E. E. Evans-Pritchard, it is through animal sacrifice that representations of the human and the beast are fused.[112]

The extensive cattle ranching economy incorporated these figures of the wilderness into a regime of hunting, production, and consumption that enabled a rare affluence for plebian men. In this context, the figure of the bull came to signify both remoteness and nearness, a combination of distance and intimacy that Leach characterizes as "tabooed ambiguity" and which can give rise to "supernatural monsters which are half man/half beast."[113] Significantly, the term *capital* originally derived from *capitale*, the Middle English term for stock, since livestock were a property form that predated currency, and came to specify cows and bulls in the sixteenth century.[114] This helps explain why cattle are often cast as demonic and as a sign of hidden wealth in Latin America.[115] As we have seen, cattle have long had a special significance on Hispaniola because they became a money form; thus they are "natural symbols" that are also enigmatic because, as Karl Marx reminds us, they are fetishized objects that reveal their hidden value only in the act of exchange. As he put it, "There is a definite social relation between men, that assumes, in their eyes, the fantastic form of a relation between things. . . . This fetishism of commodities . . . is [from] the peculiar social character of the labour that produces them."[116] Like the parrot in Brazil, it could be said that cattle on Hispaniola are totemic, providing what Claude Lévi-Strauss has called a foundational *mythe de référence* (reference myth).[117]

There are striking correspondences between certain horned Haitian and Dominican Carnival figures such as the pig, for example, which appears in Haiti as well as in the Dominican form of Lechón in Santiago's carnival.[118] But there is a particularly entangled mimetic relationship between the "monstrous doubles" of two of the most popular figures in Dominican and Haitian Carnival—the Dominican "limping devil," *diablo cojuelo*, and the Haitian *lanceurs de corde*, in Creole the Lansè-Kòd—which, as René Girard argues, seem to represent an "unrecognized reciprocity."[119] The Diablo Cojuelo is a devil with bull horns that carries a bladder or a whip with which he strikes at children (fig. 2.4). He is the wildest spirit of the underworld and descends from medieval Spain.[120] The Lansè-Kòd djab is associated with the feared Bizango secret societies of Haiti and appear in troupes. They mask their faces, wear bull horns, blacken their skin with cane syrup and soot, and carry whips with which they are said to change people into cattle; these whips are said to be made out of the umbilical cord and intestines of an infant

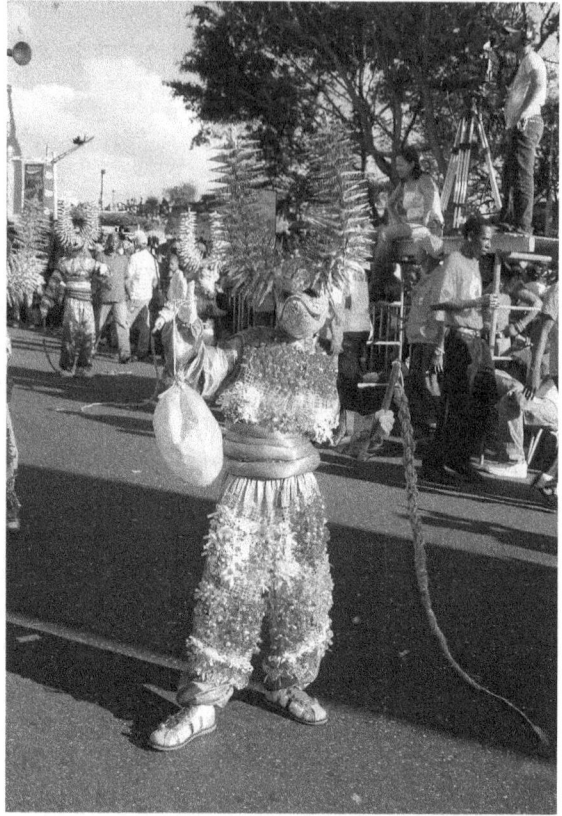

2.4 The Dominican Carnival character Diablo Cojuelo displays its characteristic swagger in a porcine mask with large horns, holding a bladder. Photo by Rubén Durán, Carnival in the Dominican Republic, 2009–10. Courtesy of Artstor.

(fig. 2.5). As art historian Katherine Smith explains, the Lansè-Kòd are diabolical minions or "spiritual mercenaries" sent by the Bizango or Sanpwèl secret society to transform people into animals.[121] But they do not create just any animals; they create bulls, which they cannot eat since they themselves are cattle, so these are traded at the market or sacrificed. As she writes, both the whips and the terrifying transformation into cattle are "spectres of history" that evoke the terror of slavery and the transformation of people into chattel. The umbilical cord whips may also reference the infamous case of Rosalie, a slave midwife in colonial Saint-Domingue who killed infants to provide them an escape from slavery and who made knots out of their umbilical cords, which she wore around her waist.[122]

But the vectors of the whips of these two carnival figures trace the pathways of the intra-island cattle trade. In the Dominican Easter masquerade Los Toros, for example, men dress as bulls and whip each other, thus

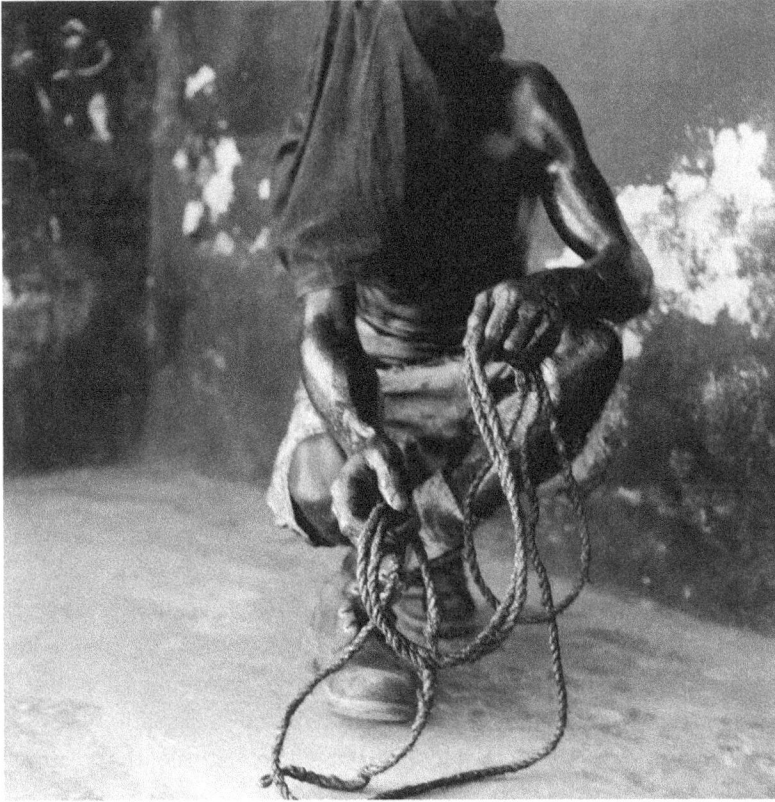

2.5 A participant in the Lansè-Kòd (Rope Throwers). Jacmel, Haiti, 2000. Photo by Leah Gordon.

demonstrating a deep identification with these beasts, which sustained them for centuries.[123] By contrast, the Lansè-Kòd's whip turns others into cattle, which corresponds to the fact that in the eighteenth century cattle were purchased from the eastern Spanish colonists, who then used the revenue generated to purchase slaves and thus turned people into beasts.[124] Like twins, these figures represent a wondrous hybrid of human, spirit, and animal and thus mediate between "animality and deity."[125] Indeed, if people are said to turn into cattle after death, this may be why. It is notable that the Nuer, another pastoralist culture, access the spirit world through their cattle. When the Nuer rub ashes along the backs of cattle, the bovines become agents of divination, and it is through their cattle that the Nuer establish contact with the ghosts of their ancestors. During rituals people call out their cows' names and imitate horns with their hands. In addition, a bull is considered the tutelary spirit of its owner.[126]

Historian Samuel Kinser has argued that Carnival is not a surface-level "playful fantasy"; rather, it has a deeper meaning since it is centrally about revealing secrets.[127] Carnival plays along the seams of the most symbolically important social oppositions, such as human and nonhuman animal (an opposition that is always vexed in former slave societies), use value and exchange value, people and things, life and death, and the identities of the French and Spanish colonies, Saint-Domingue and Santo Domingo.[128] These codependent diabolical twin Carnival figures represent cattle as the "dominant metaphor of value," while positioning Dominicans themselves as the cattle they long produced and Haitians as the wizards who transform people into cattle and cattle into slaves (thus men into beasts), which corresponds to the fact that cattle were a currency with which slaves were purchased on the island.[129] As anthropologist Stephan Palmié has argued, these Carnival figures revisit the "phantasmic object [of slavery,] the human being who is . . . 'a thing possessed' by an alien power—a body seized and transformed into what must be the most uncanny commodity of all, viz. a slave," thus revealing the fiction of the classic liberal doctrine of possessive individualism.[130] And both figures brandish the whip, which, of course, during slavery was fashioned from the very skins of the creatures that bound both sides of the island together.

PUBLIC SECRETS OF STATE

There is another layer to the story of Javier's murder, however. Narratives of stealth cattle as a sign of hidden profit may also channel unease about Rafael's illicit profiteering in his role as mayor, since he was apparently making money but it was not at all clear where it was coming from.[131] In this face-to-face context, however, Rafael could only be accused indirectly. Such accusations took the form of graffiti that appeared all over town: "*Rafael el burro*" (Rafael the burro)—perhaps because the burro carries things of value but is so lowly and ubiquitous it is barely noticed. Still, everyone knew something was wrong.

The mayor stood accused of profiting from illicit human trafficking. It was said that he was ferrying Haitians seeking safe passage across the border through Bánica to the interior towns in his official cars, which were able to bypass the military checkpoints.[132] This was credible because the Dominican Republic today has one of the highest rates of human trafficking in the Caribbean, and human trafficking has now become the third-largest international crime enterprise in the region. Safe transport typically is provided for $50 a head, generally for youths who work in construction, in agriculture, or as beggars. One study reported that 3,300 victims were reported in one month, generally in the north, but the central frontier area is preferred due to the laxity of official border control there. Just as during the colonial economy, when contraband cattle fueled the illicit acquisition of slaves, cattle spirit demons may be a sign of the surreptitious acquisition of Haitian day labor for construction, domestic service, and agricultural work. These laborers, like zombie stealth workers, produce value but are unseen.[133]

Rafael was also accused of profiteering from construction kickbacks, drug running, and political payola from his party, the Partido de la Liberación Dominicana (PLD), which developed a decades-long stranglehold on the presidency. This accusation too is credible, since around that time the Dominican Republic became mired in the Odebrecht corruption scandal, in which some $90 million flowed to Dominican officials through public works projects, much of it coursing through the ruling PLD, which until recently had an ironclad grip on the state.[134] A public park inaugurated in Bánica under Rafael's tenure and paid for by the state cost 23,000 million pesos, a sum some said was simply way too high.

The Dominican Republic has long been a major transshipment location for drugs, in particular cocaine, heroin, and fentanyl moving from South America to the United States, but this peaked during the PLD presidencies, as drug money was laundered through nightclubs, the whole enterprise earning the nefarious title of "the most important drug trafficking structure in the region."[135] Twenty-four pounds of cocaine found in cosmetics vials were confiscated from someone traveling from the Dominican Republic at Boston's Logan Airport in 2014.[136] In 2010 José Figueroa, a major drug baron from Puerto Rico, was abducted by the police in the Dominican border town of San Juan de la Maguana, as was later his Dominican girlfriend, and both were jailed in the nearby town of Azua.[137] Stories of his profligate womanizing and his efforts to alter his physical appearance via plastic surgery provided popular entertainment for Dominicans for years.[138] Finally, suspicions linking Rafael to drugs may have been piqued when he was temporarily seized by authorities, notwithstanding his eventual release due to insufficient evidence.[139] Stories of stealth cattle are thus isomorphic with narratives of hidden wealth as a form of "occult cosmology" that represents a profound suspicion of state power.[140]

Anthropologist Rosalind Shaw would argue that contemporary rumors in this case of illicit flows of wealth can have a deeper historical reach, via what she calls "palimpsest memories" invoking the foundational experience of slavery.[141] In Bánica, today a peripheral backwater not far from the northern Artibonite Plains, where the battles of the Haitian Revolution took place, during colonial times slaves were primarily obtained via cattle; contemporary rumors may thus be layering events into a longer historical trajectory.[142] Moreover, during the Haitian Revolution, some revolutionary chieftains became entrepreneurs, "liberating" slaves from the French only to turn around and sell them to the Spanish to fund their cause—a stark reminder of how the exigencies of war can force one into morally dubious actions. Georges Biassou was one such revolutionary commander who found himself compelled to traffic in slaves to raise funds when he switched his allegiance to the Spanish crown, and in fact the Haitian hamlet across the Artibonite River—Bánica's sister town—is named after him.[143] Biassou's cause of liberty required that he seek funding through nefarious predations that may be implicitly recalled in local collective memory. As in West Africa, in the Haitian-Dominican border region contemporary politicians' hidden accumulation is a sign of sinister occult predation with a long historical trajectory, and rumors of trafficking in bacá locate such activity within a "moral discourse of witchcraft."[144] Ritual and fugitive speech forms such as rumor recount a story of unspeakable violation that otherwise could not easily be uttered.[145] Here fugitive speech represents discourses of suspicion that are actually popular truth claims that call out for testimonial justice on the part of those without power.[146]

CONCLUSION

This chapter has argued that in the central frontier zone of Hispaniola, cattle have become a palimpsest of historical memory, with several embedded layers of meaning: the extensive cattle economy of the seventeenth century, which turned feral cattle into hides; the eighteenth-century cross-border trade from east to west in live cattle, which enabled the purchase of slaves; and allegations of a contemporary illicit trade in Haitian labor from west to east. Originally a "creature of empire" brought by the Spanish that caused terror, death, and dislocation for the Amerindian population, the bull has since been creolized, empowering magic that is dangerous precisely because it is associated with power, strength, courage, individual gain, and the cash nexus, as well as *rescate*, the colonial term for the dangerous and often violent business of contraband.[147] The story of cattle in the Haitian-Dominican border region was a local by-product of global capitalist articulation fueled by sugar and slavery in the French colony of Saint-Domingue, an articulation that assumed a particularly predatory form, so it should not surprise that this story has long been associated with blood and violence. Cattle were imported as a means of transport, as a source of power for the sugar mills, and for meat, tallow, and leather; furthermore, cattle blood was actually a key ingredient in eighteenth-century sugar refining, used alongside "animal charcoal" or bone char to remove impurities and produce refined white sugar.[148] These narratives cast stealth cattle as conjuring a Gothic assemblage of blood, soil, and violence that was born with the Haitian Revolution, rendering these as a kind of vampire in bovine form.[149] No wonder it has been rumored in Cuba that the state surreptitiously imports bulls from abroad to provide meat for tourist hotels and that in the past those bulls fed an *nganga* (power object) that Fidel Castro used to protect himself from his enemies.[150]

As we have seen, the story of cattle on Hispaniola commenced with a shared culture of hunting feral beasts that ended up being channeled into a "vision of excess" that today animates powerful and dangerous sorcery on both sides of the border.[151] Following Marx, the ambivalence of cattle may well lie in the fact that cattle were part of a "natural" economy in the east with very little labor investment, becoming a commodity when the animals were swapped for slaves and manufactured goods such as cloth and porcelain by French traders in the frontier. Marx has said that the "mystical character of commodities" results from the fact that their labor power is occluded from view; they assume a "fantastic form" upon becoming objects of exchange. This insight helps explain why in this context these phantom cattle have become demonic shape-shifters.[152] Yet this is also a logic that inverts history, since cattle were once a currency that turned humans into slaves, and blood into white sugar, yet today the Lansè-Kòd turns people into cattle, just as the Bosou Twa Kon enables people today to solve the most intractable of problems. As Shaw has said, this theory of memory suggests a different way of remembering the past, one in which violent processes are "(literally) incorporated into people and social and cultural practices."[153]

CHAPTER THREE

THE INSCRUTABLE JAILBREAK OF CLÉMENT BARBOT

I'm going, I'm going to the mountain!
Slave driver, release the dogs!
He's not going to get me!
Let the dogs loose on the runaway slave!
PALO SONG, HAVANA, CUBA

In 2010, former Haitian ambassador to the United States Raymond Joseph told me a story about dogs in Haiti. Born into a Haitian family, he grew up on a sugar plantation in San Pedro de Macorís, Dominican Republic, where his father was an accountant. When he first traveled to Haiti during the regime of ruthless dictator François "Papa Doc" Duvalier (1957–71), he was told that the dogs that wandered the streets of Port-au-Prince were actually spies for the regime; that is to say, the dogs were actually people who had been shape-shifted into animal form, becoming baka—a phenomenon called *dedoubleman* in Haitian Creole.[1] This rumor must have emerged from the notorious case of Clément Barbot, longtime

3.1 Clément Barbot (*right*), previously the chief of Haiti's Tonton Macoutes paramilitary force, in hiding with his brother Harry after his falling out with President François "Papa Doc" Duvalier, 1963. Courtesy of AP Images.

henchman, intimate friend, and loyalist of Papa Doc's who was known for his savage brutality.

When Duvalier faced mounting challenges to his rule in the early 1960s, he turned on Barbot and had him thrown in jail. But Barbot infuriated Duvalier by absconding and, worse still, taunting him with the threat that he would kidnap his children (fig. 3.1). Barbot was said to have escaped from prison by turning into a black dog. As a result, as part of the rampage that followed the Barbot insurgency, Duvalier was so livid that he ordered all black dogs of Port-au-Prince slaughtered on sight.[2] Joseph told me that this story haunted him for years, and he interpreted it as reflective of the depths of paranoia that the repressive dictator had forged through the myriad invasive and barbarous acts of terror perpetrated by his secret police, the vicious Tonton Macoutes. Thus the paramilitary forces were seen as the personal attack dogs of the dictator—his virtual eyes and ears—with their depredations not just a reflection of his power but an extension of it.[3]

There is another layer to these stories, however, in which these numinous canines are more than merely metaphors of Duvalier's preternatural power; they are a result of the particular history of dogs on Hispaniola, where dogs were long used as slave-catching tools.[4] In this chapter I consider the symbolic and material traces this history of canines has left behind in Haiti, as well as the emotional residue left behind after the actual events of the past have washed away with time. Thus I am arguing that these popular narratives about dogs have become what Sara Ahmed has termed "objects of emotion" that conjure the panic generated by historical events and thus enable us to reclaim the emotions that were part of the experience of the past.[5] I wish to approach the dogs of Hispaniola as avatars of historical memory that convey not the actual history of the canines but rather the "poetics of predation," conjuring the terror they evoked through their role as tools of war against slaves on the island during several historical phases.[6] I contend that we must relocate these popular narratives from the domain of myth to that of history, and thus treat history and myth as "comparative cultural categories," in anthropologist Terry Turner's phrase, that must be woven together as we craft historical narratives, so as to capture the experiences of those who lived them.[7]

As the animals most proximate to humans, dogs are anomalous boundary crossers that traverse the lines between wildness and domesticity, culture and nature, home and yard, life and death, myth and history. If they have become "lingering phantoms" on Hispaniola, I will argue, it is because dogs were the shock troops of empire that enabled the dispossession and subjugation of first Indigenous and later African slaves.[8] Dogs are an "emotional trigger" in former slave societies due to the fact that canines were used to terrorize Black populations throughout the Americas, a history that actually commenced on Hispaniola, where dogs were first used as attack animals against the indigenes by Christopher Columbus and his men.[9] If freedom for African-descended freedmen in the US slave south was associated with escape from slave-catching dogs, we need to ask what it means that these spectral dogs refuse to go away.[10] The "unresolved social violence" that the dog embodies has become not a passive, evanescent ghost but rather a virulent monster, one that has come to occupy a strange space in between fear and desire, as we shall see.[11]

In Haiti, dogs are far afield from the domesticated human surrogates found in the United States. By sharp contrast, scavenging the streets looking for food, they are perceived as wild beasts. Even when they are kept as guard animals, they are often not domesticated as pets, allowed to enter the house, or given veterinary attention. Indeed, the treatment of dogs in Haiti has given rise to foreign calls for intervention and rescue, even though, as one US observer put it, the Haitian canine is not really a dog, since it is not considered a pet. Cats and dogs often figure in traditional tales as contrastive beasts, the dog frequently being the abject loser in contrast to the clever trickster cat, as in the classic Bouki and Ti Malice tales of Haiti.[12] And in contemporary Haitian literature, the dog is frequently invoked as part of the atmospherics of terror, not seen but rather heard, their distant bark a threatening omen portending the worst. The escaped slave in Patrick Chamoiseau's *Slave Old Man* who is mercilessly hunted by a mastiff describes its growl as "something astringent and acid and irresolvably evil"; as he states, "the dog is the Master's rudderless soul. It is the slave's suffering double." In a short story by Madison Smartt Bell a character observes that "a number of starved dogs quarreled in the dark streets ... he felt sure they would devour him if they could."[13] Or in another short story, of a kidnapping, the sound of dogs barking makes the victim worry whether the kidnappers might turn the hungry dogs upon her as a means of torture.[14] Dogs have a dreadful reputation elsewhere as well. In Costa Rica, a black dog in chains makes nocturnal appearances, and in England the howling of a dog is an omen of death.[15] In Mayan culture, dogs served as spirit guides that guided the dead to the underworld. Elsewhere, dogs' esteemed hunting skills associated them with preternatural powers; for example, the Bakongo of Central Africa use the term "smelling out" to convey divination.[16]

Our opening story of baka appearing in the form of dogs links the practice of shape-shifting to the Tonton Macoutes, the paramilitary force formed by Duvalier as a counterweight to the army, which he feared could become a threat to his authority. Of course, Barbot was actually the chief architect of the force of armed, ragtag *noir* loyalists who beat, raped, pillaged, and extorted. In rural areas, the Tonton Macoutes frequently drew upon regional notables such as *chefs de section* and ougan (vodou priests), and in some cases they might have been captains of secret *sosyete* such as Sanpwèl and Bizango, members of which are rumored to have special mystical powers such as shape-shifting skills and the ability to instantly change location.[17] Shape-shifting as a technique can be used for protective purposes, as it was during the Haitian Revolution, when maroons hid through sorcery, but it can also be deployed as assault sorcery, with bakas sent out as mystical minions to do ill works. In these narratives the black dog is a harbinger of doom; as Neil Whitehead put it, they evoke the "taste of death."[18]

One issue concerning these narratives of Tonton Macoutes shape-shifting into canines is how a technique canonized as a "weapon of the weak" during the Haitian Revolution could be repurposed to assist Duvalier's dreaded henchmen. As in all forms of sorcery, of course, this skill set is morally neutral and can be deployed for either healing or harming.[19] Moreover, the Tonton Macoutes (formally called the Volontaires de la Sécurité Nationale) actually originated as a means of defense for the rural population, which sought to protect itself from state depredation through taxation and anti-vagrancy legislation that had been vigorously enforced by the new national army created during the 1915–34 US occupation.[20] As historian Marvin Chocotte has argued, the Haitian peasantry saw participation in the *milisyen* as a means of defending itself from the repressive practices of the military-police structure created during the US occupation and the overbearing authority of the rural police chiefs. Thus even in this case, shape-shifting could be seen as a form of what political scientist James Scott has called "infrapolitics"—the "disguised resistance" of political struggle, which has been deployed by slaves in revolt and fugitives on the run ever since.[21] Benoît Batraville, the rural Caco guerilla fighter who resisted US Marine depredations, was said to have spells that enabled him to escape authorities through becoming invisible, just as did maroon leader François Makandal and African soldiers during the Haitian Revolution.[22] But underdog political outsiders also resorted to "occult idioms of power," as was the case with Dominican dictator Rafael Trujillo, who was said to have a supernatural assistant that protected him.[23] Some have alleged that such techniques are a part of all warfare; as one Mozambican soldier put it, shape-shifting is not witchcraft but "power, pure and simple," since all warfare deploys "dark matter" or forms of occult predation of various kinds.[24]

Baka narratives of shape-shifting into canine form have one point of origin in traditional French *loup-garou* (lycanthrope) tales dating back to medieval Europe. Formulaic features such as the nocturnal setting and the wolf as invariably black or gray—the colors of evil in Europe—are shared with baka shape-shifting stories, notwithstanding the fact that the loup-garou was called a *chien de dieu*, dog of God, not dog of the devil, and the fact that *loup-garou* became a generic term for sorcery in the early modern period.[25] The evil beast was contrasted with the innocent women and girls, serving as shepherds, who were frequently its victims. In these narratives of shape-shifting as resolving sublimated desire, men who were *moniteurs* who spent a decade in jail without trial turned into wolves, or the husbands of women who craved the meat they never had access to would turn into wolves to hunt for it. These stories centrally concerned the plight of the poor, their rage and frustrated desires, and must have spoken to the conditions of the precarious "oceanic proletariat" that made its way to Hispaniola in the seventeenth century as *engagé* bondsmen forced to work off their debt.[26]

Shape-shifting was also an Amerindian and African practice of subterfuge as well as a form of assault sorcery. Members of secret male sodalities such as the leopard-men of Nigeria or the *kanaimà* of Guyana developed totemic associations with charismatic megafauna such as leopards, lions, or jaguars through hunting, tribute, and consumption practices and came to have the reputation of sharing some of their characteristics.[27] This form of totemic identification did make its way to the New World, as in the Abakúa secret society members in Cuba who were rumored to turn into leopards, and was thus a motif of predatory masculinity and male braggadocio not dissimilar to French tales of men turning into wolves through military initiation.[28] By contrast, women such as Juana Isabel, a Nahua in colonial Mexico during the Inquisition, deployed shape-shifting as a form of stealth agency. She was said to change into her Indian dress, transform into a dog, and pass through a door without opening it.[29]

But I argue that the canine baka draws upon another form of human-animal entanglement as well. These spectral dogs are derived not from the role of canines as companion animals, or as "natural symbols" and hence signs of social relations, but rather from the way that dogs become tools or extensions of the body in hunting practices.[30] The north coast of La Española became the site of the seventeenth-century buccaneering economy, in which plebian French and runaway slaves hunted feral pigs and cattle and sold the smoked meat to ships engaged in contraband trade, and a backwoods hunting economy continued there into the twentieth century. Yet the dogs used in those two historical contexts were creole dogs, not slave-catching mastiffs.[31] The baka in canine form is a technique not of the self but of the Other; it is thus a logic not of identification but of predation, as a history of the use of canine violence has transmuted into a landscape embedded with spectral adversaries and "lurking assassins."[32]

Aristotle insisted that those able to live outside the city beyond the rule of law had to be either animals or gods.[33] If dogs tend to have a diabolical cast in these popular narratives, this cannot be traced to Africa, where dogs in many contexts are sacred, at times becoming objects of sacrifice. One of the most striking images in African cinema is the opening scene of French filmmaker and anthropologist Jean Rouch's *Les maîtres fous*, which treats the Hauka spirit cult of Niger, West Africa, in which possessed men became rabid "dogs" thrusting their arms into vats of boiled dog meat and eating it.[34] A religious sect, the Hauka were rural migrants arriving at mines, docks, and lumber mills in the 1950s who when possessed became colonial officers—figures of power, the strength of which was manifest by their violation of the strong taboo on consuming dog meat. In Nigeria, Yoruba hunters who are simultaneously feared, honored, and disdained as polluted (because they enter the bush at night, when one should stay home, and take life in order to sustain it) are said to control their hunting canines through incantations; this indicates that they have a very special spiritual contiguity with their hounds, which they rely upon for hunting and which they reward with the head of the prey.[35]

Anthropologist Alma Gottlieb has argued that dogs are creatures of ambiguity that play a role as alter egos to humans in the mythology of the Beng, a people of Ivory Coast. There they are the only creatures that receive names in the animal kingdom; however, in popular lore they are also blamed for human mortality, even though they help enable life as well.[36] This special status as both protectors and destroyers of the human race accounts for the ban on dog sacrifice since, as she states, there is "not . . . the right mix of conceptual distance and identity [between man and dog] for the one to serve as a sacrificial substitute for the other."[37] Nor do the Beng eat dogs. Dogs are objects of sacrifice for the West African deity Ogun, due to the fact that he is the paradigmatic hunter and thus heavily reliant upon them. The dog is also a key figure in Central African Kongo minkisi (power objects), the prototype for the Haitian wanga, which are fashioned for spells and protection.[38] Charms fashioned in the form of dogs embody the mediating role of minkisi; as "seers extraordinaire," dogs hover between the worlds of the dead and the living, and it is their status as powerful threshold creatures that animate minkisi and enable divination. Minkisi are embedded with forces harnessed from the underworld; for this reason dogs have been used in rituals to "return souls from the dead."[39] As art historian Robert Farris Thompson reports, "Between the village of the living and the village of the dead there is a village of dogs."[40]

WILD DOGS

If dogs have a sacred cast in the Old World, they were transformed into agents of the "impure sacred" with their arrival on Hispaniola.[41] Like a corpse, the impure sacred inspires dread and possible contagion, but as Émile Durkheim theorized, the sacred and the impure sacred are actually two manifestations of the same kind of power.[42] Indeed, in Hispaniola the dog became an agent of horror and dread, repulsion and distress, as in Freud's notion of the uncanny.[43] The uncanny is the emotional timbre generated when something familiar and taken for granted is transformed into something strange that evokes fear. An example is the central monster of the novel by Philippe Thoby-Marcelin and Pierre Marcelin, *The Beast of the Haitian Hills*, the *cigouave*. A gruesome beast that is hidden and which is the object of rumor because few have seen it, the cigouave is a beast that many hear growling, a sound that elicits a sensation of foreboding and uneasiness. It lives in the mountains, engaging in random attacks, in one case crushing the testicles of its victim—the signature act of attack dogs. No one knows what the beast is exactly, but the marks on its victims resemble the marks of fangs, which make some believe it is a mad dog.[44] Yet there are indications as well that it is not an animal but rather a spirit demon, a baka. For example, like a zonbi astral—a spirit captured and sent—the cigouave never comes of its own account; it seems to be sent by an invisible human agent. But it is not at all clear whether it is a common dog or a supernatural being. In the book, Morin Dutilleul armed himself with a loaded pistol and stayed up all night hoping to vanquish the beast, trying to quell his fear with rum. At one point he heard the horrifying shriek of a pig being ravaged by the creature. Then it appeared. The cigouave had the body of a dog and the head and feet of a man; its eyes glowed "intensely like a charcoal brazier," the red color a sign of clear and imminent danger.[45]

This account is similar to stories I heard in rural Haitian-Dominican border towns about spirit demons that appeared in the form of black dogs. In Bánica, Juan Ramón told me about how one night when he went to bathe, he felt something pass over him. In the old days, he continued, "it was very dangerous around here. When we were kids there were a lot of bad things around here. Every night galipotes came pouring across the border. Every night. They were people turned into dogs. Packs of them. Every single night. Once I saw a dog in a rocking chair. A galipote. It was a festival of galipotes back then! Every night. Bacas everywhere fought to kill. Today they are peaceful but not back then." When I asked how one knew they were galipotes, he said, "Only dogs eat dogs." And when I asked if these particular demons could appear as pigs or cows, he said they appeared only as dogs.[46]

CANINE HISTORIES

As noted earlier, dogs were deployed as hunting aids in the feral goat- and hog-hunting economy practiced by slaves and freedmen from the buccaneering period into the 1950s in the Dominican Republic, called *montería*.[47] Contemporary observers of hunting in Jamaica described the dogs as terriers, but these creole dogs were hounds used for stalking and trapping game. However, the dogs of war bred and trained in Cuba for slave-catching were another matter altogether. Although at times called "bouledogues," these were patently not your average domesticated pet.[48] Eighteenth-century British army officer Marcus Rainsford contended that the species was similar to the Irish wolfhound (known then as the Irish wolfdog), the largest dog breed in the world, which can weigh in at a whopping two hundred pounds.[49] Their extraordinary size—reaching six feet when standing on their hind legs—rendered them effective at tracking large game in Ireland, such as gigantic Irish elk, bears, and wild boars. For their grand and majestic profile they achieved such global fame in the eighteenth century, when they were known by the name *canis maximus*, that they were highly prized gifts, first to Roman consuls and then to kings of England, Scotland, Spain, France, Sweden, and Denmark, as well as the shah of Iran. As one contemporary observer said, "If there is a dog living that could capture and kill a wolf, single handed, it is, undoubtedly . . . the Irish wolfdog."[50]

But dog breeds were not yet codified at that time the way they are now, and there is more evidence concerning which breed may have been used for slave-catching in Cuba and was exported during the period of slavery.[51] What was called in the eighteenth century the "dogge Cubano" was said by some to be a type of Spanish bullmastiff used in dogfighting that had been introduced into Cuba to chase runaway slaves. A plantation staple, they were raised to guard coffee and sugar plantations. The first major breeder of these Cuban mastiffs appears to have been a Spaniard based in Bejucal, eastern Cuba, who started mixing Spanish mastiffs and greyhounds that had been previously used to "reduce" the Taíno population, capture maroons, and guard Spanish properties. The Spanish marquesa Doña María Ignacio de Contreras became famous for the bravery and training of her dogs, and her farm in Bejucal became the central exporter and producer of these prized hunting dogs, used by hunters and slave-catchers (known as *rancheadores* or *chasseurs*). She was so successful as a breeder that the dogs became a major Cuban export after their success during the Miskito uprising in Nicaragua and later during the second Jamaican Maroon War in 1795, which cemented the fame of what came to be known as the Bejuco dogs.[52]

As literary critic Sara Johnson has documented, these dogs were used principally as a tool of slave terror in the Caribbean.[53] Commencing with the first wave of plantation agriculture in the early sixteenth century and continuing through the Haitian Revolution, dogs brought in for protection were also found useful in overcoming Indigenous resistance and were trained as attack animals to rout out runaway Indians and slaves. Indeed, Christopher Columbus's men quickly discovered the efficiency of dogs in terrorizing the indigenes—what Norton describes as "lethal canine mauling"—to the point that "dogging" (aperreamiento) became a term for scaring the indigenes to death.[54] The first use of dogs on Hispaniola was at the Battle of Vega Real, in which twenty dogs were able to rip apart one hundred Indians per hour and the cacique Guarionex was defeated, the survivors fleeing to the interior.[55] Indeed, it was the crucial role of dogs that enabled the capture of Jamaica by the Spanish in 1494.[56] In what came to be called the "hellish hunt" (*montería infernal*), Colonial Governor Bobadilla trained dogs to "attack like wild beasts, to disembowel and devour ... and after the struggle was over, they gorged on the bodies of the victims." Dogs came to relish Indian flesh for its tender skin as compared to tough animal hide, and so Indians were fed to voracious hounds. In a macabre twist, after consuming all the native dogs and facing starvation, the Spaniards then proceeded to eat their own dogs as well.[57]

In the eighteenth century, Cuban chasseurs whipped, starved, and chained their bouledogues to render them supreme assailants. To maximize their effectiveness as "gruesome weapons," they were allowed to ravage and even devour their prey once located.[58] Indeed, Indigenous and slave body parts were even doled out as dog food. Rainsford stressed that domesticated dogs could never have behaved so savagely, and that the slave-catchers had to ravage the dogs to render them prone to vicious attack; the rancheadores mercilessly beat their slave-catching dogs with heavy muskets.[59] So although Hispaniola has a history of feral canines, in this case it was the domesticated dogs which were trained to be especially savage, and more likely it was they that forged the iconic image of the dreadful canine in popular culture.

Contemporary observers tended to naturalize the savagery of the dogs, arguing that brutality was needed given the viciousness of their animal opponents. An observer from eighteenth-century Jamaica said that a well-toothed boar was "a dangerous enemy to encounter" and required "a powerful and artful combatant."[60] Yet one wonders whether this might not be an exaggeration. In fact, creole hunting did not require such a violent use of dogs. Eighteenth-century Jamaican planter Sir Hans Sloane revealed that groups of dogs were used in Jamaica merely to locate the boars, keep them at bay, and tire them out, but the boars were actually felled with lances by the hunters, not their canines. Moreover, these very same "wild" boars slept in corrals placed in the forest and were trained to come to the hunters when they called them with a conch shell.[61] Indeed, an article on hog hunting in Cuba states that creole hogs—wild or tame—were nothing compared to the wild dogs that were the truly ferocious beasts of the interior.[62]

The ferocity of attack dogs was confirmed most forcefully during their role in the Maroon War of Jamaica in 1795, which was the testing ground for the Haitian Revolution. Four hundred chasseurs were brought in from Cuba along with more than a hundred dogs. It is noteworthy that just the rumors themselves of the savagery of these "extraordinary animals" played a critical role in quelling the maroon rebellion. The canines formed part of a theater of terror, which commenced with the fact that they used three dogs per group to rout out the maroons, when many said two would have sufficed.[63] The image of the fearsome dogs was also magnified and spread through puppet shows in which a naked Black man was chased by dogs.[64] In staging this performance of terror, the assailants tried to be secretive about the arrival and departure of the canines, but this was foiled by the loud, incessant barking of the packs of dogs.[65] Further evidence of the theatricality of the dogs' role as agents of terror is that while 104 canines were shipped, only 36 of them were properly trained, leaving a full 68 as a pure demonstration of force. That said, in Jamaica those deployed were those not yet broken in, and would fly at the victim's throat and fail to quit until the victim's head was severed from the body.[66] By all accounts, the spectacle of terror was highly successful.

It was said that wherever the chasseurs went, "terror flew before them." It was reported that "no time, therefore, was lost in landing the chasseurs and their dogs, the wild and formidable appearance of both spread terror through the place; the streets were cleared, the doors of the houses shut, and the windows closed. Not a negro ventured to stride out."[67] A writer from the Jamaican governor's office alleged that "it might be supposed that the Spaniards had obtained the ancient and genuine breed of Cerberus himself, the many-headed monster that guarded the infernal regions." He continued that "terror, humiliation and submission" were achieved via the rumors alone, without shedding a drop of blood.[68] He noted that the slaves "mention the Spanish dogs as objects of terror, from the wonderful representations of them, but that they had never suffered by, or even seen them."[69] Yet that was patently not the case. On the dogs' first day out, a woman's head was actually severed by the heinous creatures when they attacked her at a watering hole.[70]

After their success in Jamaica, these dogs of war were brought to Saint-Domingue during the last and most sanguinary phase of the Haitian Revolution, when Napoleon's brother-in-law General Leclerc was deployed with twenty thousand elite troops to retake the colony from the rebel forces. These were later backed up by eighty thousand more as the most savage phase of the war began. After Leclerc succumbed to yellow fever, the Vicomte de Rochambeau took over his post; he promptly sent to Cuba for twenty-eight dogs as a central tool in his campaign of terror in a last-ditch effort to retake the island and reinstitute slavery after most of the north and south had been lost to the rebels. As Johnson has noted, they brought no provisions for the dogs, since the slaves themselves were to serve as feed for the beasts. Upon their arrival, in a particularly opprobrious spectacle of terror, a servant of one of the French generals was sacrificed in a gruesome public execution in which the dogs were set upon him until they had eaten him alive, with only the bones and a few palpitating organs remaining behind.[71] So appalled was Rainsford by the barbarity of canine warfare that he devoted a special appendix in his account of the Haitian Revolution to a description of the training of the dogs as slave-catchers and how their savagery was induced (fig. 3.2).[72] They were fed sparingly on blood, and as they matured the confined animals were teased with a wicker figure the size and shape of a slave embedded with animal entrails inside; after repeated taunting, they were eventually "allowed to gorge themselves with the dreadful meat."

3.2 "Blood Hounds Attacking a Black Family in the Woods." From Marcus Rainsford, *Historical Account of the Black Empire of Hayti* (London: Cundee, 1805).

The chasseurs at times even saved the heads of the decapitated slaves as "monuments of their barbaric prowess."[73] Rainsford saw the chausseur of this era as the direct descendent of the barbarous buccaneer. As he stated, "Every part of their dress, their migratory life, power of forbearance, and savage habits in the woods all exhibit the modern buccaneer in the modern chasseur." But it was actually the Spaniards' purported civilizing mission—not the subaltern settlers—that gave rise to this cruel practice.[74]

OF MAD DOGS AND HAITIAN MEN

Up until now I have stressed the commonality of Haitian and Dominican popular narratives of ferocious canines. Indeed, they form part of a common discursive grammar in terms of plot structure and formulaic elements, and thus should be seen as part of a larger shared oral genre of shape-shifting tales with a strong point of origin in French loup-garou folklore.[75] However, these narratives can locate Dominicans and Haitians at different ends of the predatory trajectory. Thus when Juan Ramón described how in the old days there were packs of wild dogs crossing the border that valiant Dominican men fought off, he may be narrating a veiled story of Haitian immigration as it was cast by the Trujillo regime in the aftermath of the 1937 slaughter in an effort to exculpate its crimes.

As the regime sought to justify the slaughter of migrants of Haitian descent in 1937, anti-Haitianism became a central political motif of the Trujillo dictatorship (the Trujillato). In the 1940s a series of histories officialized by the regime sought to portray Haiti as a nation intent on a "pacific invasion" of the Dominican Republic. This narrative merged the idea of Haiti's superior military force with the fear of engulfment by Black people via stealth immigration.[76] Casting the spirit animals as black vermin emanating from the west draws upon the visual vocabulary of the Trujillo regime's official anti-Haitianism while translating it into a vernacular language of predation. These stories cast Haitians as wild dogs crossing the border in ferocious covert packs aimed at terrorizing Dominican homes and thus implicitly justified violence to keep this feral enemy out.[77] And in the border regions one need not explicitly spell out the horrifying bloodbath of 1937 in which Dominicans were forced to kill ethnic Haitian neighbors, relatives, and loved ones, with upward of fifteen thousand border residents of Haitian origin slaughtered gruesomely by machete; this is an open secret locals generally avoid discussing at all costs.[78]

When Dominicans narrate these stories of border-crossing feral canines, they may be conjuring another eighteenth-century history as well, one that pitted slaves and freedmen as implacable enemies on either side of the bayonet. As the revolutionary war unfolded in Saint-Domingue, slaves from the Spanish colony were hired into the free Black militia to hunt down escaped slaves, enticed by the fact that after one year in service they could earn their freedom as well as the status and honor conveyed by *fueros* (rights) such as the right to bear arms.[79] Slave-catchers required intimate knowledge of the land as well as survival skills in harsh conditions, which is why monteros were sought after for this dangerous work.[80] So many freedmen joined the militia in this way that this resulted in an enormously inflated colonial militia in Santo Domingo, four times the size of Cuba's or Chile's.[81] Slave-catchers carried a machete or *couteau*, but their most important tools, of course, were their hounds. Much of their time was spent caring for and preparing their dogs, which were trained not to kill but merely to corner their prey unless they encountered resistance—which, of course, was invariably the case.[82]

If Haitians cast their national identity as resulting from the defiant communities of rebellious maroons insistent on their independence, the fact that some Dominican hunters found their freedom as chasseurs locates these two peoples as being at odds.[83] In these narratives, the feral dogs could be a synecdoche for the wily Haitian maroons who claimed their freedom by crossing the border during the revolutionary war—or, alternatively, for the alleged silent migration of Haitians spilling across the border in the nineteenth century to escape a state bent on capturing their labor. Of course, it is also possible that these tales were a "supportive interchange"—an underhanded performance of ethnic superiority for my benefit as a white American.[84] As sociologist Margaret Somers has argued, social narratives are always fashioned in relation to particular audiences and settings.[85] Yet given the popularity and ubiquitousness of jocular animal nicknaming practices as emblems of underclass *hombría* (manhood) today in the Dominican Republic (with nicknames such as Tíguere, "tiger," or León, "lion"), it is disturbing that the first such moniker appears to have been given to Leoncillo (little lion), a warrior dog covered with battle scars from Indian arrows and "with a reputation for vicious accomplishments" in 1511.[86]

CONCLUSION

This chapter has sought to explain the terror invoked by dogs in popular narratives from Haiti and the Dominican Republic through the real history of canines on the island, from their origin as privileged hunting companions to their role in spectacles of ruthless violence during the conquest, the Jamaican Maroon War, and the Haitian Revolution, and finally their role as figures of dread under the Duvalier regime invoking the harrowing butchery of Duvalier's paramilitary forces, the Tonton Macoutes. As anthropologist Neil Whitehead reminds us, violence cannot be explained without reference to its expressive aspect. As he says, "Violent acts may embody complex acts of symbolism that relate to both order and disorder in a given social context, and it is these symbolic aspects that give violence its many potential meanings in the formation of the cultural imaginary."[87] This helps explain why the dogs imported to Jamaica during the Maroon War had to do little else besides arrive before their task was accomplished; so efficient was this beast and the singular history of brutality and panic it conveyed that the rumors were often enough to achieve the objective. For some, this history is best silenced. As Rainsford put it, "The picture becomes too dreadful for description even for the best of purposes," and even Rainsford, who spoke out against these practices, preferred to use engravings instead of words to tell a story that left him for all intents and purposes speechless.[88] Yet traces of these demonic canines remain on Hispaniola, since as Stephan Palmié reminds us, sometimes "spectral evidence" offers a form of "release of versions of history that . . . otherwise not just remain 'unevidenced' but are actively rendered invisible or unspeakable."[89]

I hope to have explained why the dog holds a singular position in the pantheon of fiendish creatures on Hispaniola as uniquely spectacular "memories of figures of savagery," to use Taussig's words.[90] Anthropologist and filmmaker Maya Deren has said that the forceful yet illegitimate "left hand" of vodou—the petwo line of spirits—were born of a slave's rage that was forced underground into a mode of occult aggression associated with "alienable labor power" and sorcery.[91] The dog first arrived as a lethal technology of predation that ensured the dispossession of first Indigenous and later African slaves, leaving them with a visceral bodily memory of terror.[92] Yet the dog has subsequently been appropriated as a singularly important figure within the spirit world, as the most secret, foreboding, dangerous, and powerful of all baka incarnations, one that is deployed in forms of assault sorcery similar to the way the zonbi is used.[93] These symbolic forms of aggression mimic occult warfare and are often used in military contexts. For example, Michel-Étienne Descourtilz, who visited Saint-Domingue in 1799 during the last phase of the Haitian Revolution, when Haitian troops faced off against regiments from France, Britain, and Spain, came across a group of former slaves working with a wanga (power object) that had a dog's head.[94] And today in Cuba, practitioners of Palo Monte refer to both their mediums and the spirits of the dead as "dogs" in a religious practice that includes "ritually stylized forms of social mimesis" that draw upon the principal logics of slavery—chase, capture, and mystical domination; in this context, the dog carries the load of the force of the spirit, yet in this case it is a sign of honor to do so.[95] In a perfect illustration of Simmel's argument that secrecy can be construed as the very embodiment of moral badness, a Haitian secret society has taken a canine as its emblem, calling itself Dubreus di Chien Move, or "bad dog society" (fig. 3.3).[96] Afro-Atlantic religions often draw upon imagery of force from slavery in spirit work, but the dog also is a sign of the dark corners where demons lurk, inspiring revulsion and fear.[97] Dog bone—in particular, shavings from the tibia of a rabid canine—is an activating ingredient in the poison used to make a zonbi. Zonbis have been sighted handling packs of vicious dogs with a whip.[98] And as the ultimate social transgression, the "ambient dead" of Palo Monte can request a dog as a sacrificial offering, as might the Mondongue spirit within vodou, whose icon is a canine and which has a particular hankering for the tip of the tail or the ears of a dog.[99]

Of course, the very term *Mondongue* invokes another kind of transgressive rule-breaking with a long history in the Caribbean—that of cannibalism. In the eighteenth century, several slave women said falsely to be of Mondongue ethnicity were accused of eating infants in Guadeloupe and Saint-Domingue.[100] Such cannibalism is a particularly heinous crime since feeding is, of course, the most important form of maternal care, and provisioning the gods with food incorporates the dead into the family lineage. If cannibalism is the epitome of "moral badness," the fact this label affixed itself to a group of slaves is particularly surprising, especially given the consumption behavior of the Spanish. It was they who first "grilled" Indians on fires like barbecues, fed the flesh of Indigenous people to their dogs, and then proceeded to eat those very dogs that had consumed Indigenous people's flesh after food supplies disappeared due to native resistance. By sharp contrast, Indigenous people kept dogs for

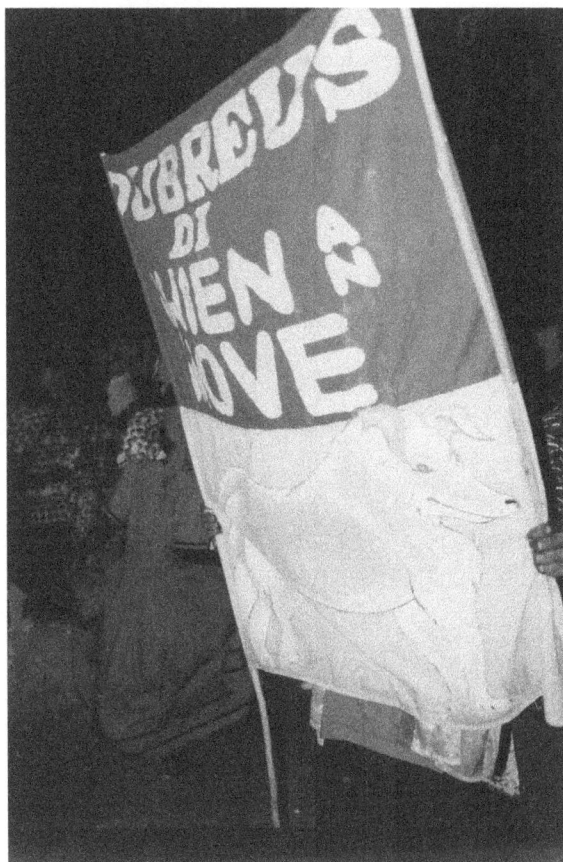

3.3 A banner for the Chien Move Haitian secret society. Jacmel, Haiti, 2005. Photo by Katherine Smith.

ritual exchange and as a reserve food source, akin to the Andean guinea pig. No wonder Haitians say that zonbi meat foams white, the color of the colonizers themselves and of the death they engendered in the colonies.[101]

Beyond the specific history of dogs on Hispaniola there is additionally the particularly acutely paradoxical combination of wild and tame that dogs embody. In a truly uncanny way, they seem to be one's faithful companion, yet they are capable of savage acts of violence. They appear as agents of nature, yet they are actually monstrous products of culture. In the Caribbean, they play the part of surrogate wolves, which in France gave rise initially to the shape-shifter lore of the loup-garou, which originated the werewolf narrative genre in the French imperial context. As anthropologist Garry Marvin has aptly put it, "Wolves are, or have been, revered in some cultures but feared and loathed in others, a sacred creature of the benign wilderness for some people but an abhorrent monster of dark forces for others, regarded as noble hunters or common criminals, admired as warriors or reviled as abject cowards, provoking terror as creatures into which humans can be transformed or wondered at as creatures that can nurture orphaned human children."[102] In this sense they resemble the birds in the classic Hitchcock thriller by that name, conveying a bleak history of ominous evil. However, in this case, the dread ultimately is not of nature, but of culture, since after all it was humans who invented slavery and trained the bloodhounds to keep slaves in their place.[103]

CHAPTER FOUR

CREOLE PIGS AS MEMENTO MORI

Gumercindo, whose nickname is "El Ranchero" (the rancher), recounted to me the story of a harrowing trip home on his motorcycle to the township of Bánica, where he lives. Like most residents, he is today a small-scale subsistence farmer who raises pigs, goats, and cattle for a living. I found him through his son Hegel, whom I met during my first extended trip when I had letters of recommendations to send, since at the time he was working at the town's computer center. Hegel told me a long story about how his house had been haunted by a bacá and his quest to get rid of it. When I asked him whom else I could speak to about these spirit demons, he recommended his father, who was a retired elementary school teacher who had named his children after his favorite philosophers, Socrates and Hegel. Indeed, Gumercindo's story of facing trials far from the metropole with a measure of skeptical irony—requiring a certain "suspension of belief" on the part of the audience, too—and the way his account showcases the "pleasures of waywardness" and the "impossibility of certainty" could class him as a modern-day *pícaro* (rogue).[1]

   One night Gumercindo was riding his motorcycle until he was forced to stop due to a very large tree—about four feet in diameter, perhaps a ceiba—that had fallen across the road, blocking his way. He got off his bike, confounded because the tree was a species that is not common in the region today, and looked around, only to be accosted by a beast he could not immediately recognize. He had trouble identifying the creature that jumped onto the tree trunk. It resembled a large dog or a pig, and he thought it must be a jabalí, a feral boar with long whiskers and tusks that was common in the area into the 1970s. Thinking, "Lo mato o me mata" (I kill it or it kills me), he grabbed his gun just as the animal disappeared, vanishing into the night as quickly as it had appeared. When he arrived home, he told his neighbor about the episode, and the neighbor asserted with confidence that it must have been a bacá, a mischievous spirit prepared by someone for purposes of sorcery.[2]

The perplexing thing about this testimony is that the jabalí is today all but extinct.[3] The jabalí, or *Sus scrofa fera*, was descended from the pigs brought by Columbus, which were called water pigs or *lapa*, were red with brown spots, and were a prized feast food for the Taíno and the Spanish.[4] Yet all the creole pigs on the island were slaughtered in a campaign sponsored by USAID, among others, between 1979 and 1982.[5] Moreover, why did the creole pig appear alongside a seriously endangered species of tree such as the ceiba, which, along with other slow-growing precious woods such as mahogany and ebony, was nearly wiped out due to logging in the nineteenth century? Was this boar a flesh-and-blood animal, or was it actually a "phantom of remembrance"—a memory that conjured a previous ecosystem of robust forests replete with hidden free-range *cochons marrons* (wild pigs)?[6]

Saidiya Hartman has described her own efforts to "reclaim the dead" in the Black Atlantic—to see beyond the ruins of violence and dispossession and thus "reckon with the lives undone and obliterated in the making of human commodities."[7] The pig is a perfect vehicle with which to do this, since it marks the boundary between human and animal, people and ancestors, sacred and the profane, life and death, wild and domestic. Until the pig slaughter, feral swine alongside cattle had long served as a free-range commons that sustained the poor from the sixteenth century onward. But the creole pig had a unique place within that feral animal commons. It was the backbone of the provision grounds system of subsistence agriculture.[8] The pig ate food garbage and pests, fertilized crops, and when sold provided cash for school fees, medicine, and other emergencies. But the pig was far more than this. Much like the Andean guinea pig, it lived in particularly intimate proximity to the family, consuming household remains

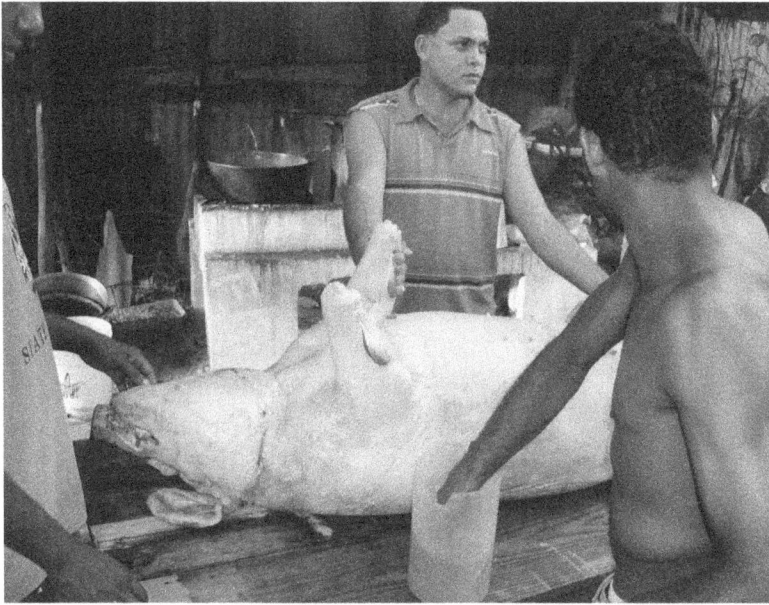

4.1 Sacrifice for the Feast of San Francisco, protector of animals and patron saint of Bánica. Bánica, Dominican Republic, October 4, 2010. Photo by the author.

(thus sharing human food) and being cared for largely by women.[9] In a world long structured by slavery, the free-range pig was also a sign of the possibility of a world without confinement.[10] No wonder *pork* is a term of endearment in Barbados and courting a woman demands the gift of a pork chop.[11]

The black creole pig also stood at the center of the ritual economy.[12] Just as it is the favorite sacrificial animal for the Haitian vodou deity Èzili Freda, pork is an "exceptional food" eaten at meals on Catholic holy days that constitute family and community, such as Noche Buena (Christmas Eve), and on patron saint feast days such as the feast of San Francisco, the patron saint of Bánica, on October 4 (fig. 4.1).[13] It is also what I would term a "resistant commodity," since it should not be sold. Like the Andean guinea pig, it was an *iegue*—a familiarized yet not domesticated animal that was central to the Amerindian gift economy and accorded personhood within a broader ecology of selves.[14] As such, these creatures offered an alternative to the paradigm of mastery and possession basic to processes of capitalist commodification, an alternative that featured free-range proximity and entanglement. When consumed, they are a marked sacred food served at feasts. Might these phantasms be both signs of melancholy as well as "acts of recovery" that seek to resist the *longue durée* history of interspecies "social death" of humans and the pigs that sustained them, a history that commenced with slavery and continued through the calamitous pig eradication program?[15] I wish to argue that these creole pig sightings might be seen as "critical interruptions" of popular desires to hold on to the beloved creole pig, a sign of home and the system of non-market exchange in which the gift is an extension of the person.[16] Like the Taíno zemi, these ghostly specters of porcine bacá lurk and roam furtively in forests and represent what art historian David Doris would call "wasteful spirits," which share suffering as a constitutive element because that is part of their historical legacy.[17]

FORESTS OF PIGS

When Jean Parmentier visited La Española in 1526, he was impressed by the immense tropical forest and the packs of feral animals he encountered there. Arriving from the eastern coast, he observed the mountains and the "palm trees, forest, boars, birds and rock all along the coast." In the interior he noted the orange and lemon trees and the sugar cane, as well as the abundance of wild cattle and dogs and horses "with savage force"; as we have seen, cattle were the basis of the leather trade, as hides were sold to corsairs and most of the remaining meat left in the forest, sustaining the scavenger animals. Feral animal packs thrived just outside the city of Santo Domingo. The long northern coast, between the northern coastal town of Puerto Plata and the Bay of Samaná, he described as particularly dangerous, because of the contraband trade that passed through there and because a group of runaway slaves had formed a community there.[18] The rapid decline of the Indigenous population, who were agriculturalists, made available vast areas for livestock. The predominance of wild cattle and pigs, which often mingled and bred with tame animals, forged a hybrid animal stock, in which temperament, not physical characteristics, determined how an animal was classified.[19] The ecology of feral animals was even inscribed in the landscape as place names such as Morne à Mantegue (Lard Mountain), Cau de Cabrón (Goat Cay), and Ile-à-Vache (Cow Island). Of course, pigs are deeply inscribed as signs of the forest even in Europe, where the size of a forest was long estimated in terms of the number of pigs it sustained.[20] Due to the late arrival of sugar in the eastern portion of the island, today the Dominican Republic, the forest there remained largely intact far later than in Haiti and Cuba, where intensive sugar plantation economies caused a dramatic erosion by the mid-nineteenth century.[21]

As noted in chapter 2, the feral hunting economy commenced in the sixteenth century to sell smoked meat to corsairs (fig. 4.2). Based upon feral cattle and pigs, the buccaneering economy declined with the Treaty of Ryswick in 1697, as authorities encouraged agricultural settlement in the Artibonite Valley of Saint-Domingue and promoted sugar plantations; however, extensive cattle ranching of semiferal herds later expanded in the Spanish eastern area, providing meat and oxen to the thriving plantation economy of the western French colony until the 1790s, when the Haitian Revolution commenced. The forest cover provided by five mountain ranges provided a free commons of wildlife and hardwoods into the twentieth century, important supplements to the subsistence economy that sustained the rural poor outside of unfree labor and the market economy for centuries, at a time when dark skin could be read as a sign of slave status. Sugar's late arrival saved the forest cover and the animal commons it protected in the Dominican Republic. Indeed, as late as 1922, an estimated 75 percent of the Dominican Republic was still forested.[22] For Francisco Puello, writing in the 1890s, the true locus of Dominican identity was the forest, home to boars and dogs. As he waxes lyrically, Monsieur Santo Domingo finds himself "at the foot of the mountain, contemplating the untouched virgin forest, where the birds have made their nests for centuries without being disturbed, where you sometimes hear the bark of a dog that hunts wild boars that drink from a spring and that produces the only sound in those awe-inspiring moments of solitude."[23] A black pig sacrifice in the forest of Bois Caiman also has been said to have commenced the Haitian Revolution, which freed the slaves and founded the independent nation of Haiti.[24] If the pig is a beloved synecdoche for the forest that housed it, signifying freedom, it is not hard to see why. Which is precisely why the USAID-directed slaughter of all creole pigs in 1979 on the island was such a calamity for the rural poor.

Yet getting at the affective significance of the backwoods world of *el monte* conjured up by the pig requires moving beyond tracing the contours of the feral livestock economy to consider popular storytelling as a popular archive. The broader cultural significance of the creole pig became apparent to me through stories I was told of phantasmic

4.2 The earliest depiction of wild boar hunting in Hispaniola, with buccaneer hunters. Nicolás de Fer, *Mapa de la isla la Española*, 1723, detail. Courtesy of Mapas antiguas, Archivo General de la Nación, Santo Domingo, Dominican Republic. Photo by Martha Ellen Davis.

pig sightings in which the *puerco criollo* (creole pig) was associated with other traces of this landscape of memory. Animal familiars, of course, are common in Africa also, and were present at the Salem witch trials.[25] And the presence of any unusual animal behavior creates suspicions of obeah practice in Jamaica.[26] But the pig stands out, since it is the only bacá host that is beloved, and the creole pig is the only animal besides the goat brought through the Columbian exchange that was indigenized.[27]

Minor spectral spirits such as spirit demons are often classed together as if their embodied host is entirely irrelevant. This is not the case here, and the baka/bacá may be located on a visceral continuum from the most terrifying apparition, which is the dog, to the most cherished, which is the creole pig. I wish to argue that bacá pig narratives are haunting tales that conjure a deep sense of melancholia, loss, and nostalgia for creole swine and that these narratives can help us discern a particular culture of intimacy with the pig and its associated emotional resonance.[28] The pig's rooting behavior is associated with the underworld, and this may explain its link to the spirit domain, rendering the creole pig bacá more like a spirit double or familiar than a demon, thus differentiating it from other bacá animal revenants.[29]

Drawing upon Ann Stoler's work, one might say that these porcine ghosts are "archives of the visionary and the expectant" that reveal "epistemic anxieties" and "affective tremors," traces of trauma and grief that found no ready outlet given the fact that the military forcibly carried out the pig slaughter at gunpoint.[30] If I am correct, these revenants should be seen as more than just static folklore; they are dynamic "mythic kernels" that get us closer to the lived experience of the creole pig slaughter on the island of Hispaniola, and the deep emotional attachment smallholders felt to the "patio pig," which was a junior member of the family and the bedrock of the subsistence economy until the pigs' demise at the hands of the army. I try to approach these stories as they are narrated, however, which portray the pig bacá as fleeting and inchoate entities that become apparent in a flash or viscerally sensed in a moment of contact only to vanish before they could be completely grasped, vanquished, or at times even fully identified.[31] These persistent pig apparitions should be seen as evidence of a deep-rooted affective economy of subsistence and as a mode of popular resistance to the erosion of everyday life for the rural poor.

As has been argued for African pastoralists whose livelihood is intimately bound up with their animals, the significance of livestock in this case is not merely economic; beasts can become a metaphor of the human community, a sign of the human condition.[32] Pigs were a constant live everyday presence around the household, fed and cared for by women and children, as well as the most prestigious food (which should be served at Christmas dinner and on religious feast days, or as pig's feet or roast pork on Sunday; it was invariably paired with cornmeal, *chenchen* or *mayi moulin*, a sign of indigeneity and autochthony, at religious feasts) and the primary object of sacrifice in certain Afro-Catholic rites and vodou/vodú. Creole pigs were indeed what anthropologist Marcel Mauss described as "total social phenomena," things that contained all the threads through which "the social fabric is woven."[33] No barnyard beast conveys home in the Caribbean like the pig does.[34] This is nicely summed up in the Dominican proverb "El puerco cimarrón sabe en el palo en que se rasca" (the wild pig knows where he belongs).[35] Unlike in Europe, where the pig has long been a sign of incivility connoting filth, lust, and excess, the Caribbean does not vilify pigs, and in jokes and songs they often appear as surrogate people, as we shall see in chapter 7.[36] Scholars have explored the significance of livestock in the African context, but the broader cultural meaning of animals has been largely left out of relevant historical research on Latin America.[37]

The scholarship on animals hinges on a wild/domestic binary in ways that are problematic for the case of Hispaniola. First of all, the creole pig descended from the domesticated pigs that were brought by Columbus but which reverted to a feral state on Hispaniola. The creole pig was not a "companion species" in Haraway's sense, nor was recognition of their "nonhuman personhood" cause for suckling them, as in Malawi or Melanesia. However, the fact that practices such as faith healing and "laying on hands" are used for both people and livestock indicates what anthropologist Eduardo Kohn has described as a "transspecies ecology of selves."[38] While there was human-pig codependence and intimacy, they were not socialized into the world of humans, as were Fulani cattle or Andean guinea pigs. While a pig or two was kept around the home to eat leftovers and food scraps, as the offspring accumulated, they were left to roam in the forest; yet, I have been told, even these feral mountain pigs came when called. Fighting cocks were also left to range in the forest on the grounds that the experience toughened them and made them braver warriors. Such practices involving the taming of wild animals, their conversion into iegue, may be a Taíno legacy of familiarization and as historian Marcy Norton has argued, evidence of a transspecies concept of personhood, which the Spanish adopted from the Indigenous population during the early conquest period.[39]

This essay seeks to excavate the history of multispecies engagement and entanglement that gave rise to this particular genre of ecological animism in Hispaniola.[40] I trace the history of pig raising on Hispaniola from its European predecessors through the slaughter of all creole pigs in 1979, an event that was cataclysmic for the rural poor of both Haiti and the Dominican Republic. This popular culture of animal practices and lore also traverses the wild/domestic divide in surprising ways, as we shall see.

CATTLE AND PIGS

In the backwoods hunting economy of Hispaniola, cattle and pigs became contrastive signs. During the seventeenth-century buccaneering period, these animals enjoyed the grassland savannas created by slash-and-burn agricultural practices. Hunters worked on foot with lances, using a technique that was likely Spanish in origin.[41] The cattle were hunted for meat and hides, the pigs solely for meat. Tame animals were marketed live, and packs of stray dogs, which were also a mix of domesticated and feral, frequently preyed on calves. Early on, it appears, there developed an occupational specialization, with the term *boucanier* applied to the mounted cattle hunter and *chasseur* to those who hunted hogs; the latter remained important in the interior after cattle hunting declined with the rise of sugar in Saint-Domingue. Over time the feral animal presence (including cats) diminished, and the French botanist Michel Étienne Descourtilz noted a dramatic decline in avian species by the 1780s, probably due to excessive hunting during the Haitian revolutionary war due to the availability of guns. However, feral cattle, hogs, horses, donkeys, dogs, goats, and guinea fowl remained present in the Spanish eastern region (Santo Domingo) due to the sparse population.[42]

Cattle became important transatlantic commodities that were traded internationally, first to regional corsairs and later to the *colons* (colonists) of Saint-Domingue, as we have seen. In Santo Domingo, where there was a shortage of specie, live cattle or hides were swapped for slaves, as was the case elsewhere in the West Indies as well. Because cattle and oxen were valuable commodities, there was some border theft involving these animals, but that was not the case for pigs. During slavery, pigs became a ubiquitous feature of the *conuco* or provision grounds, since slaves were rarely given meat and had to provide their own; in Barbados slaves were allotted two fish, and a cattle head and entrails if any cattle died by disease.[43] Thus livestock were a crucial component of the "protopeasant" subsistence economy that commenced within slavery and extended into the post-emancipation period (fig. 4.3).[44] For slaves, the extraordinary fertility of pigs enabled a steady protein source as well as ready cash in times of need. Historian Rebecca Scott has noted the importance of obtaining livestock as slaves transitioned to freedmen; pigs could serve as credit for loans.[45] Seventeenth-century Barbados planter Richard Ligon attested to the ubiquity of pig raising in Barbados, the animals' enormous size (they could reach four hundred pounds), and the meat's distinctively sweet taste (due to their diet of fruit, plantains, and locust nuts there; in Jamaica they were fed coco yams or taro).[46] While on the intensive sugar-producing islands all meat animals became commodities, on Hispaniola this was not the case. On Hispaniola, the family pig became a ubiquitous and highly prized exceptional food, its value stemming not from its exchange value but rather from its sustenance of hearth and home. While their offspring could be sold, the family pig should ideally remain what anthropologist Annette Weiner has described as an "inalienable possession," kept out of circulation, its path tracing the social networks of family and friends.[47]

Wild pigs became an emblem of the open-range free commons, which had provided subsistence to the poor for centuries. Swine cultivation on Hispaniola drew upon practices from France and Spain, where

4.3 "Hey, hey! That ham is not for you. I only wanted you to smell it!" The man with the cane, labeled "PD," represents Rafael Trujillo's Dominican Party, and the man running off with the "liberty ham" represents the people (*pueblo*). *Unión Cívica*, June 4, 1961. Courtesy of Archivo General de la Nación, Santo Domingo, Dominican Republic.

pig raising is a national tradition. In Spain, pigs were seasonally taken to the oak forests of Andalusia, where the black Iberian swine ate acorn mast during the winter months, giving rise to the famed *jamón ibérico*; in Alsace, the lucky pigs were a vital component of the dairy farm and dined on cream and potatoes.[48] Both Spain and France developed the ideal of a family pig, the slaughter of which was a festive family occasion; in Spain the annual slaughter resulted in the beloved *jamón serrano*, a cured meat that could be enjoyed for months.[49]

The Dominican Republic shared the Iberian tradition of common pasturage and separation of usufruct claims until the early twentieth century, when fencing laws were introduced.[50] Indeed, liberal reformers railed against itinerant pigs, which became a symbol of a land tenure system that favored free-range livestock. As Emiliano Tejera wrote in a screed that linked hunting to political tumult, "The revolutionary and the pig are the principal enemies of the country." The "enemy that is the free-range animal" and "ignorant ranchers," he wrote; governing nineteenth-century caudillos such as Pedro Santana had prioritized free-range livestock to the detriment of tobacco farmers and agricultur-alists. He continued, "He that is favored by the law is the rancher, though he spends most of the time in his hammock, plucking his guitar, or visit-ing his neighbor. . . . Reducing the free-range pigs will reduce the revo-lutionaries, because rarely is the revolutionary a working man who has interests to lose, and there will be more working men when there is no free-range grazing."[51] In this view pigs were a drain on national progress, perceived as a natural economy that escaped taxation and threatened ag-riculture, enabling hordes of idlers and vagrants and uppity caudillos. To colonial observers, for whom export agriculture was the paragon of activ-ity, the "hauteur and overbearing pride" of these vagrant freedmen who lived off the feral commons was noxious, since they lacked the requisite deference, which slaves had been obliged to offer.[52] To Dominican state-builders, pigs were a problem due to their itinerancy and the fact that they enabled an uncaptured protopeasantry to thrive without capital or wage labor.[53] Officials seeking to incorporate fugitive people and their pigs into the national economy even resorted to requiring passports in order to move hogs from one region to another in the early twentieth century; such documents had been required in Cuba in the eighteenth century and beyond.[54]

In England, a shift in the pig's habitat away from the black forests where it had developed its reputation as elusive, dark, and fearsome in the Middle Ages gave way to the more modern image of the pig as a wholesome, jolly domesticate.[55] But the feral pig stubbornly retained its mysterious, elusive cast in the Caribbean. It also preserved a strong link to the spirit world. One case in point is the djablesse creature, which lurks in forests; it is a siren with cloven hooves and is surrounded by piglets, which are the souls of women who died in childbirth and the spirits of aborted fetuses.[56] Beliefs about minor spirits that can serve as familiars, venturing outside the body and inhabiting animals or traveling to the underworld, are common to Mesoamerica, which was a source for Indian slaves arriving in Santo Domingo.[57] Songs in Jamaica link pigs with birds, which are also seen as celestial travelers and thus were associated with witchcraft.[58] Pigs' rooting behavior linked them to the earth and what lay within it—much as are snakes, which are often taken to be familiars or spirits of the dead.[59] Yet, interestingly, the pig does not conjure dread the way bacá in the form of cattle or dogs do. In the wake of the slaughter, the creole pig has become a sign of longing and nostalgia.

Early primary sources for the buccaneering period offer numerous glimpses of the elusive "hunters" in the outback. William Walton, for example, characterizes them as "a hardy warlike set of confederates." But they are rarely described in any detail.[60] The totemic prestige hierarchy ranked the mounted boucanier (later the *hatero* or extensive cattle rancher) and their cattle over the chasseurs and their pigs, but the two groups appear to have been different social groups initially as well. The former were considered more skilled and may have been primarily European former bondsmen initially. The latter appear to have been half-castes and former slaves, monteros who practiced swidden agriculture but sought out meat and lived reclusively in the mountains, only occasionally returning to urban centers for muskets, shot, and clothing. British geographer and botanist Robert Schomburgk noted that horticulture was a rarity in the Dominican Republic and that only in certain areas did one see small patches of plantation, or fruits intercropped with cacao, for domestic consumption in the mid-nineteenth century.[61] There were also sizable communities of maroons—for example, around Neyba, the population of which Walton estimated at six hundred in 1820; he said that a full one-third of them were a standing army, which "lived upon game and the abundant fruits of the earth," and dipped into town when they had tortoiseshell to sell or a "superabundance of cured game . . . principally wild hog and horned cattle," which they usually snared, and the meat of which they exchanged for gunpowder and clothes.[62]

We must wait until the twentieth century for a three-dimensional portrait of these hunters, who are mostly despised by contemporary observers as savage barbarians. Historian Emilio Rodríguez Demorizi demonstrates a rare glimmer of respect at least for the cattle-hunters, which is worth quoting at length:

> The *montero*, less than those who are *hateros*, was not the peasant dedicated to the cultivation of the land, but rather that which, half naked, machete in his hand, with his multi-hued team of dogs, walked on foot through the cattle plains, the outback [*montería*], through the scrub, chasing wild cattle; brave men who had to confront the wild bull with sharp horns and the terrible boar with its razor-sharp tusks, curved knives that stand out on each side of their destructive snout. A man of admirable restraint, who goes about the whole day in

pursuit of the elusive hunt with only a gulp of morning coffee. The montero was always the man who came from the troops of the hatero converted into a caudillo, his loyal and selfless soldier, because montería was heroic, akin to a harsh and permanent guerilla war against the cattle scattered along the intricate wilderness [*montes*].[63]

He maintained that the montero had to be superior to the average soldier: He had to ride well, be able to fell an animal from behind with a lance, swim and climb well, be able to rapidly scale a tree, and then cut the steed's or boar's throat. He also had to withstand hunger and be able to carry the harvested meat through torrential downpours.[64]

The original pigs of Hispaniola were later transferred to Florida and with them, certain features of their hunting practices. Swine were brought to Florida from Cuba in the De Soto expedition of 1539. Indians stole some, and others escaped into the forest; after some time, the southern feral woods hog or monstrous razorback emerged. The spare and rangy black Iberian hog with its large floppy ears and sparse bristles of Florida was technically not a wild boar, but its ferocious behavior made it seem a close cousin. Florida also had Texas peccaries, which were faster than a horse and were brave enough to attack hunters' dogs; they also were known for their anthropomorphic-sounding, terrifying scream.

Hunting and warfare have long had a symbiotic relationship in the circum-Caribbean. The privateer Henry Morgan created battalions from "the sharpshooting cow-slayers of Hispaniola," deploying them to conduct military raids on Panama; the Spanish responded by driving bulls against the marauding buccaneers.[65] Santo Domingo had four times the size of Chile and Cuba's standing army in the 1720s and most soldiers were not professional; they were unpaid militiamen.[66] In the nineteenth century, this relationship deepened. Hunting was necessary to provision the armies in the Dominican Republic and Cuba, where independence warfare lasted for decades. Dominican liberal Pedro Francisco Bonó visited an army camp at Bermejo in 1863, where he came upon ragtag troops smoking after dinner, their munitions perched atop a barbecue with a slab of bacon and plantains. Bonó inquired, "And what do we eat here?" The response was "That is not a concern . . . each soldier is a *montero*." The camp subsisted through foraging, which was easy for them because it was situated in the middle of a mountain hunting area.[67] Each army hut had its side of bacon, a butcher block, and a couple of pigs. Due to the scarcity of guns, most men fought with sabers, using knife skills honed through hunting.

In Cuba, hunting was considered excellent training for the military. It provided tactical skills, enhanced bravery, and helped develop "the physical attributes of manliness." As a 1909 hunting manual put it, "Hunting is the art and knowledge of fighting and winning."[68] This manual recognized three categories of game: wild, partially tamed, and tame.[69] In Spain *montería* was the term for the big-game hunting practiced recreationally by aristocrats, who hunted bear, deer, or jabalí. It was very popular around the time of Iberian expansion, becoming a motif of Christianity after the Reconquista.[70] However, in the Caribbean, hunting was more frequently the province of runaway slaves and freedmen seeking to supplement their diet and income.

But hunting came to hold more than merely utilitarian significance to some, becoming a badge of plebian male pride, particularly for men who lacked other benchmarks of male status. In Florida, for example, on a single shooting spree, two hunters at the St. Johns River bagged fifty alligators averaging twelve feet long. On another expedition they collected twenty deer, thirty turkeys, and three hundred pounds of trout. One famed backwoods hunter was said to have shot more bears, wolves, bobcats, panthers, alligators, and Indians than anyone else in the state.[71]

The casual mention of human prey here should not surprise, since in the Spanish Caribbean the best hunters were often enlisted as slave-catchers. In fact, in Florida bloodhounds were called "negro doges" and were used to track game, slaves, and Indians; it was hoped that they "would put a new face on the war [with the Seminoles] and lead to a speedy conclusion."[72] Living in quarters near the livestock, their labor used to care for it, slaves were seen as virtual swine; their skin was described as hide, their diet as salt pork and "Indian [corn] meal." This slippage between man and beast was not lost on contemporary observers, for whom the slave, as a nonperson, was "always already positioned in fraught proximity to animal life."[73] Jamaican planter Edward Long casually remarked that a slave named Sarah lay in a pool of blood on the floor "just like a hog had been killed." Long also mentions that in Jamaica slave children were fed pork lard so that their skin would gleam, and when visitors came to call, they were showed off, standing in a row with about the "same kind of pride in showing off a flock of good sheep or a lot of good hogs."[74] And of course slaves and pigs alike required passes to move from place to place. As Neil Whitehead has said, "Hunting and war are the primordial relationship through which humanity and animality are created," but slavery, of course, also made beasts out of humans.[75]

Given the absence of meat provisions during the colonial period, however, slaves were also eager hunters, and access to wild game came to be considered a customary right. In Florida, they trapped smaller game such as raccoon, turkey, and possum, since bear, panther, and bobcats required access to firearms. But not all animals were potential prey. Owls were spirit guardians and could not be hunted or eaten. Michel Étienne Descourtilz recounts how he came upon a dead owl in a cemetery in the Artibonite Valley (Saint-Domingue) and wanted to collect it as a specimen, but his slave assistant refused to touch it.[76] This special quality of owls, however, is due not to their personhood but rather to the fact that they are messengers from the underworld.[77]

Perhaps due to the fact that their natural home is in *el monte*, the forest, which is the locus of animal souls, pigs (like birds) provided a bridge to the domain of spirits. Pigs were clairvoyant, could "see the wind," and could sense when a storm is coming. A pig femur was commonly used as a good-luck charm.[78] Possibly because of dogs' crucial role in hunting as seers and seizers of game in the bush, dog parts were also used in sorcery. Such practices, in the words of anthropologist Todd Ochoa, aim at fixing "the protean flux of the dead so that it can be worked."[79] An obeah recipe in Antigua included dog's tongue alongside ground bones and wood ashes; even spells, it seems, need bay dogs, which locate prey, as spiritual messengers.[80]

Hunters were fond of keeping relics from their prey, mementos of conquest of particularly fearsome beasts that demonstrated their prowess. From the alligator teeth worn by a Cuban slave to the elaborate tattoos of snakes, iguanas, crocodiles, and owls etched upon former Dominican national guardsman and bandit Enrique Blanco—a creole version of heraldic use of animal iconography—the practice of taking "war trophies" was commonplace.[81] The question is, how are they to be interpreted? In William Pietz's formulation, *fetish* arose as a term to denote a value form that disavowed processes of commodification. Yet these images are drawn from the feral animal commons. Marcy Norton might see these as collecting practices through which the hunter "appropriat[ed] the courage, ferocity, and power of these apex predators."[82] Yet could these relics possibly evidence a shared experience between the hunter and the prey? Alternatively, in a context in which the stigma of slavery deprived free Black men of personhood, could these mementos also serve as insignia of power that located former slaves as human subjects and not beasts?[83] Being a hunter, of course, was *not* being prey, and thus enabled one to avoid the passive, feminine position of "prostrate other" which was dishonorable (indeed, *cochón*, French for "pig," is a term for "queer" in the Dominican Republic).[84] The animal turn in scholarly studies has attended to the construction of nonhuman persons, but not quite as much to the "animalization of humans," an important by-product of slavery.[85]

HOME IS WHERE THE HOGS ARE

Of all the members of the animal kingdom, pigs are physiologically the closest to humans. Pig heart valves are used in human heart valve replacements, and medicine is now harvesting pig organs for human transplants. Current xenotransplantation practices involve cloning and genetically modifying pigs to make them more compatible with the human immune system.[86] The close proximity of pigs and humans also makes them, like monkeys, potential transspecies disease transmitters. This may be one of the reasons for officials' panic after swine fever emerged in the United States in 1976, given the disease's resemblance to the 1918 pandemic, the most deadly flu outbreak in world history, and the fact that swine fever is endemic in several parts of the world and there is no vaccine to combat it. Another reason is that the US pork industry was facing financial difficulties in the late 1970s and likely wanted to curb competition.[87]

In 1979, to prevent the spread of African swine fever (hog cholera) to the United States, USAID coordinated and funded the slaughter of all creole pigs on the island of Hispaniola, a project that was carried out by the local militaries.[88] A hemorrhagic disease, swine fever has a long history on the island, having first erupted there on Columbus's second visit to the island, yet it is often asymptomatic among free-range pigs. In the twentieth century, the disease started in Villa Mella, a commune outside of Santo Domingo, where pigs were fed airline food that included contaminated Iberian sausage, and it spread from there.[89] Over the course of thirteen months, the armies of Haiti and the Dominican Republic ventured into the interior, where they butchered pigs en masse, countering immense popular resistance with arms. Observers lamented that it was "the worst calamity ever to befall the Haitian peasant," since the pig was the central axis of the subsistence economy.[90] This draconian remedy was considered necessary due to the free-range nature of hog production, which made other containment measures impossible.[91]

The pig slaughter signaled a shift away from rural development efforts and hence the beginnings of extreme food precarity in both countries. Due to a drop in the US sugar quota and the rise of high-fructose corn syrup as a sweetener in processed foods, both nations had to replace traditional export crops with development schemes such as export free trade zones; tourism was also promoted in the Dominican Republic. In Haiti, the pig slaughter was a tipping point, culminating in peasant suicides and an exodus of refugees to the United States.[92] In the Dominican Republic, things also went from bad to worse. In 1978 Antonio Guzmán was elected in a landslide but soon landed the nation in a major corruption scandal, which left the government bankrupt just as oil prices spiked and debt arrears forced a turn to the IMF for emergency loans.[93] Resulting stabilization measures sent food prices skyrocketing at a time when wages had sunk to some of the lowest in the Caribbean, in part as an effort to attract foreign investment. It should come as little surprise that bread riots eventually erupted in Santo Domingo in 1982.[94] The pig debacle affected the two countries differently, however, because in Haiti 70 percent of pig production was domestic and only 30 percent was commercial, while in the Dominican Republic those figures were reversed.

The pig slaughter catastrophe hit the central frontier especially hard, since this was the small pig farmer belt on the island and replacement pigs were not distributed there. Protests broke out in the southern Dominican border towns of Pedernales and Jimaní, while later protests occurred in Dajabón and the province of Elías Piña.[95] Worse still, the pig slaughter arrived after a series of droughts that had left the population even more dependent on livestock than previously.[96]

Until then, creole pigs had been the mainstay of the peasant subsistence economy. In addition, the black boar was a key ritual symbol in Haiti (it had been the chosen sacrificial object at Makandal's Bois Caiman vodun ceremony, the ceremony that sacralized the Haitian Revolution). The French term *marron*, which became *maroon*, the word for "runaway slave," came from the *puerco cimarrón* (wild pig) which was the primordial forest creature on both sides of the island.[97] Creole pigs were extremely well adapted to their environment, thriving on palm fronds, worms, and grubs. They disposed of household food remains such as yucca and plantain peels, their excrement provided fertilizer for the conuco or garden plot, and their rooting loosened the soil for planting. From an initial investment of less than $10 for a pig, the offspring could bring in as much as $250 due to pigs' high rate of fecundity.[98] For virtually no cost in maintenance, pigs were an ample and secure protein source; they also could be used as credit to secure a loan.

Although caring for the animals in the *monte* was a male pastime, the creole pig massacre became largely a women's issue (in part because, as some men reported to me, men concealed their pigs from authorities in the mountains, whereas the family pig, cared for by women and children, was harder to hide). French philosopher Simone de Beauvoir claimed that women's "animality is more manifest" than men's, which also might help explain why the pig slaughter mobilized irate women en masse.[99] Perhaps it is the pig's exuberant fertility that genders them female, or women's labor caring for the family pig that renders the sow contiguous with domesticity itself. The close proximity of pigs and humans can even extend to pollution taboos, such as beliefs in Portugal that menstruating women can spoil sausage prepared during the annual *matanza* (slaughter).[100] In Japan it is said that wild boars prefer a pregnant woman's fields, and a shape-shifting boar can turn into one's mother.[101] And in Haiti, it is the wrathful "goddess of love," Èzili Dantò, who, it has been said, has "exclusive title to that which distinguishes humans from all other forms"—and requires a creole pig for her sacrifice.[102] In Spanish the term *crianza* refers to the rearing of children or animals. Yet irrespective of the popular prohibition against killing sows, especially pregnant sows and their offspring (which are taboo to eat and said to make you sick), these were also killed in the 1979 slaughter, a fact that outraged owners, who railed that "this was the only thing to sustain a family."[103] Like the Andean guinea pig, the creole pig is gendered female along several axes since it is associated with fertility and reproduction, the ghosts of the ancestors, and the "spirit of the gift."[104]

Another reason the pig slaughter may have particularly enraged women is that they usually had fewer options for generating cash than men, and as matrifocal heads of families they were even more dependent on their pigs than their menfolk.[105] Women, of course, were also the primary caretakers for the family hogs, which resided near the house and lived off household leftovers, food that the women prepared. In their pitiful complaints to the authorities they wrote, "We are women who sustain our families from pig production," and pointed out that they were now destitute.[106] Some of the most strident resistance came from outraged women who preferred to kill and eat their own pigs rather than hand them over to the soldiers.[107] Incensed protesters sent in telegrams and petitions. In one letter signed by 102 claimants from a "humble section" of

Jimaní, fully a third were women, which is a very high percentage when you consider that women in the Dominican Republic historically have not played a leading role in civil society. A plaintiff wrote, "We are all poor people, and pig rearing helps us to solve some of our most basic needs."[108] A group of three signatories cried out, "We want justice to be done!"[109] Some believed that the pig slaughter was political persecution, since in the recent presidential elections the region had come out strongly in favor of Antonio Guzmán, who had forced out strongman Joaquín Balaguer after his notoriously repressive twelve years in office.[110] This is why the governmental campaign to explain the rationale of the slaughter was aired on the radio programs *Dimención Feminina* (Feminine Dimension) and *Nosotros en Su Hogar* (We at Home), as well as on Radio Guarocuya and on popular rural radio stations in border towns such as Barahona, Pedernales, Neyba, and Jimaní.[111] Interestingly, while official correspondence used the term *matanza* (massacre) for the slaughter, many officials themselves described it as a *sacrificio de cerdos* (ritual slaughter of pigs), a term that may have been intended to rationalize the violence, since such ritual killing is of course legitimate.[112]

The pig assault cut to the heart of the family, perhaps even more so since the rate of serial polygyny in the border pig zone is higher than elsewhere, so there were more women-headed households with a single income stream that were more dependent on their pigs. One woman from Villa Vasquez wrote that she had received a voucher for reimbursement for the loss of her pig, but when she went to the Agricultural Bank she was told there was no money left. She exclaimed, "Please pay as soon as possible, I am a poor widow with seven small children to take care of."[113] A majority of the aggrieved were *humildes* and *gente pobre* (the humble and poor) who owned one or two hogs.[114] To add insult to injury, in an act of colossal bad taste the secretary of agriculture hosted a seminar on swine fever at an elegant colonial hotel in Santo Domingo where imported whisky and Campari were served along with ham, cheese, and caviar canapés and bacon-wrapped meat tapas.[115]

PIGS AS ANCESTORS

The bacá is a spirit in animal guise. This dual identity corresponds to the close relationship between pigs and the spirit world in the Kongo culture of Central Africa, which was the origin of many slaves in both

Haiti and the Dominican Republic. In Central Africa, the Baka people were renowned for their skills in felling the most prestigious of game animals, the elephant, becoming central players in the nineteenth-century ivory trade, but they relied far more upon red bush hogs as an everyday protein source.[116] Hunters must have visionary powers, since they are said to "walk with the game spirits" when pursuing game. Indeed, hunters have privileged access to the spirit world, since the forest harbors both human and animal souls, and forager-band communities are said to be linked not only by family ties but also by coguardianship of the tutelary spirits of the dead, and the forest is seen as both a reciprocating parent and a reciprocating ancestor.[117] Spectral pigs also form a central part of ceremonies surrounding Central African male initiation, such as that of Bakongo men into secret societies, and their sacrifice is key to activating certain minkisi (power objects) that are embedded with white clay, a substance marking the threshold between the living and the dead.[118] In the Wiko masquerade of urban Zambia, initiates are accused of stealing a wild pig, an accusation they must contest by saying that someone else has concealed it; the initiates wear palm frond skirts, which conjure the bush.[119]

The family pig is anomalous because it is an animal that is part of the extended family; this, according to Mary Douglas, would render eating the beast taboo. But as a form for a spirit demon, the pig is quite the opposite; it is the very epitome of the "impure sacred," the marked composite that incessantly flips between angel and demon, beneficent holiness and evil, and thus is the very embodiment of impure transgression.[120] Of course, even in the barnyard context pigs are anomalous because they share the remains of human food, yet they also eat feces. They are associated with both life and death, a paragon of exuberant fertility while eating subterranean roots; they thus delve into the "underground realm of being" where the dead reside.[121] In Amazonia, ancestors return in the form of peccaries and offer themselves as food to their former kin.[122] As literary critic René Girard explained the paradox that is the essence of sacrifice: "Because the victim is sacred, it is criminal to kill him—but the victim is sacred only because he is to be killed." In acts of sacrifice, Girard continues, the animal is a surrogate for humans, because "from the animal realm were chosen as victims those who were . . . the most *human* in nature."[123] This may help explain the surprising fact that Bánica residents actually fashioned a cemetery for the pigs murdered at the hands of the army. It may also explain why many people insisted on killing their pigs themselves and eating them, rather than turning them over to the army. The slaughter in a way made people into pigs, as people gluttonously stuffed themselves with as much pork as they could, one man reportedly eating a whopping forty-five *tasos* or sides of pork.[124] Perhaps this is why pigs bear the brunt of so much "rough teasing," as in the "permitted disrespect" of classic joking relationships that A. R. Radcliffe-Brown described as marking intimacy, since the human-pig relationship is one in which the "conjunctive and disjunctive components . . . are maintained and combined."[125] Appropriately, then, the most popular character in Dominican Carnival is Lechón, today a beloved trickster figure with a porcine face that is clothed in colorful rags and carries a pig bladder that he uses to whip children and scare them away (fig. 4.4; see also fig. 2.2 for the related figure Diablo Cojuelo).[126]

But the spectral pig has not always been an innocent victim. Indeed, the djablesse is a demon who uses her feminine wiles to lure men and then cruelly mocks them. She is an alluring femme fatale with a secret porcine identity manifest in her telltale cloven hoof and the fact that in Carriacou she is surrounded by a halo of little putti in the form of piglets, which are the spirits of the infants she aborted while alive.[127] Interestingly, Hispaniolan hunters often left the pigs' feet behind, since the carcasses could be very large. However, in Sicily, pigs' feet link these creatures to the underworld, a reminder that, unlike other barnyard beasts, pigs travel between realms. St. Anthony's sign—appropriately, since Anthony is the patron saint of lost and stolen things—is a pig, which is why at his festival swineherds race their pigs.[128]

As spirit doubles, these bacá revenants may have emerged during the food crisis that developed in the 1980s, right after the creole pig slaughter, as Ronald Reagan's Caribbean Basin Initiative was intended to transform the rural Caribbean from a subsistence economy into one that produced nontraditional products for export—a vision of development in which cheap labor was the comparative advantage of Haiti and the Dominican Republic.[129] The swine fever eradication plan for the Americas had a preference for industrial pork production, allegedly because it made disease control easier compared to contexts where swine were raised free-range. Yet USAID knew the pig slaughter would cause tremendous rural-urban displacement, increasing urban populations by 75 percent, and would generate an ample reserve army of labor which would keep the price of labor down, thus benefiting the very assembly plants the plan encouraged.[130] Indeed, this was part of the plan. USAID promoted a vision of

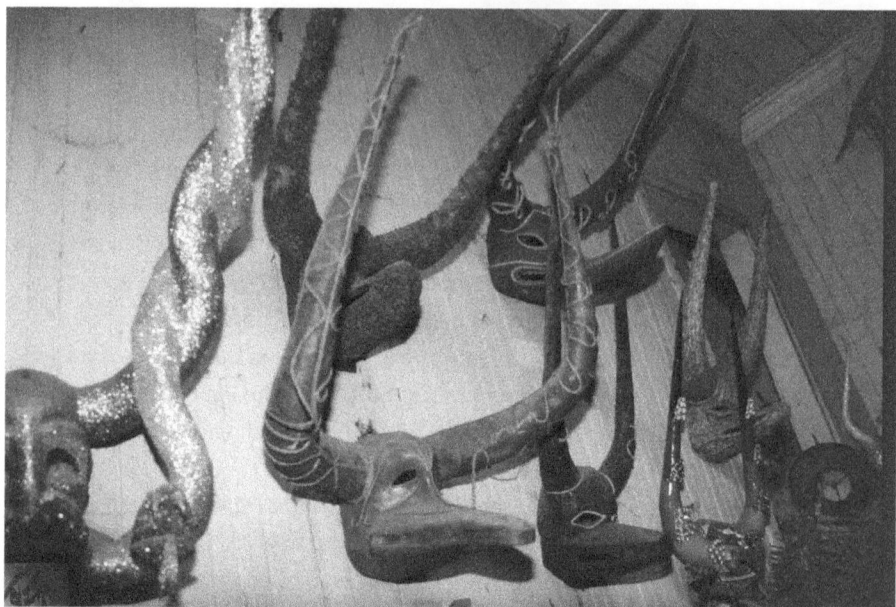

4.4 Dominican Lechón Carnival masks with porcine snouts and large pointed horns. Photo by Rubén Durán, Carnival in the Dominican Republic, 2009–10. Courtesy of Artstor.

Taiwan's "dependent industrialization," which prioritized export agriculture and freed up labor for export free trade zones.[131] As Haitian labor was intended to shift from subsistence agriculture to export free trade zones in the capital, lower tariffs that were imposed by the IMF eventually promoted imported food and displaced staple foods; as a result, Haiti—the poorest country in the Western Hemisphere—became the largest net food importer in Latin America, a trend that only deepened during Bill Clinton's trade liberalization policies of the 1990s and after the 2010 earthquake.[132] As of 2019, half of the fourteen Caribbean Community nations import 80 percent or more of their food, a trend that is accelerating as a result of climate change.[133]

Given the dramatic erosion in food security since 1982, it should not come as a surprise that the creole pig continues to haunt the border, a poignant reminder of better days for the *campesinado* (peasantry). I have not met one person in Bánica who would admit to purchasing a US replacement pig, and I have been told that these were paradoxically much more difficult to handle than the feral jabalí, which was said to be *mansa* or gentle.[134] Indeed, it is said that the viciousness of the gringo pigs meant that one had to watch them constantly; they were so ruthless, they would even eat a small child. Indeed, these tales of gringo pigs eating humans bear an uncanny resemblance to accounts of the vicious attack dogs brought to hunt down runaway slaves and ravage them during the Haitian Revolution—that dog being a very different animal than the beloved family sow, but also perceived as equally alien.[135] These tales of the bacá, as historian Luise White has said, uncover intimate layers of personal experience and emotions such as anger, betrayal, and grief, which are not always apparent in the cold historical archive.[136] They also reveal the central place that the pig has played in the social history of the central frontier, as a resistant commodity that formed the basis of the subsistence economy while maintaining the magic of the gift.[137] Given the prevalence of itinerant hunting in the Dominican Republic, it makes sense that the "hearth defines the home," and that bonds of family are indexed through where one eats, who feeds whom, and most of all, what's for dinner.[138] The pig slaughter was a particular kind of catastrophe because there was no public acknowledgment of the loss or public rituals available to contain the grief.[139] The creole pig phantasms might be seen as a labor of elegy, expressing a deep melancholy over the loss of this beloved beast. As Avery Gordon has said, haunting is "unresolved social violence making itself known," as the ghost reminds us what has gone missing.[140]

CONCLUSION

El monte is a highly charged ontological domain within Afro-Cuban culture and has great poetic density.[141] During the colonial period it was a space of fugitive freedom where maroons claimed autonomy in defiance of state authorities as Indigenous and African slaves escaped into the untamed mountains and woods.[142] But it is far more than that. The monte is also a space of danger, a "cosmological location" where the ancestors and deities reside and medicinal herbs and poisons can be foraged.[143] Deities such as Legba (Elegua), the god of the crossroads, reside there; fittingly, the offerings for this messenger deity are black hens, horse grass, and cow tongue.[144] Legba, which is the nexus between life and death, childhood and old age, and the "keeper of the secrets," is an apt messenger for this space of transformation, especially since he can also be called Gran

Bois, guardian of the forest, who guards access to Gede, the god of the dead, and Grand Chemin, who "opens the road" to the otherworld.[145] El monte is invoked in Cuban nganga cauldrons, which are charged with bones and sticks and serve as analogues to the *palenques* or maroon settlements and channel their "mercenary ethos."[146] But it was the wild cattle and hogs hidden in the monte that enabled the maroons to exist in this space of refuge; hence the very term *cimarrón* took on a double meaning that inextricably tied together "enslaved-turned-fugitive people and domesticated-turned-feral animals," as Gabriel Rocha has put it.[147] This may be why some Afro-Cuban insurgents during the independence insurgency carried protective devices in the form of cow horns embedded with medicines.

So we must now return to the vexatious question of why the creole pig continues to haunt the border, as recounted in tales of male bravado by men like El Ranchero, who heroically face off with these spirit demons and thus match the valor and courage of their beastly opponent.[148] Perhaps this vengeful revenant is bitter because there are no more creole pigs to appease the dangerous petwo spirits of the dead (creole pigs, of course, being their preferred sacrifice).[149] Like the man who, it is said, turned from a hearty cocoa color to ashen white during the US occupation in Haiti, the spectral pigs may have blanched to gray—the pallid color of disease—as they became symbols of imperial extraction; the United States, of course, was behind the creole pig slaughter, and Haiti and the Dominican Republic have a long and sordid history of US intervention.[150] Or perhaps it was the brutal mass slaughter at the hands of the army (which should have been instead a carefully executed ritual sacrifice for the gods) that morphed the hearty piebald creole pigs into human-eating, grave-robbing, spectral *cochons gris* (gray pigs).[151] The slaughter thus transformed what should have been an act of sharing and commensality into its obverse—an act of predation and violence.[152] And the child-eating genetically modified replacement pigs were said to be uniquely violent. While one should feed the spirits so that they in turn can offer protection, the porcine bacá was a zonbi animal that foams white when cooked and can actually eat you up (mange moun).[153]

Just as an act of ritual sacrifice transforms "the maleficent into the beneficent," this heinous creole pig slaughter did the exact obverse, as the surrogate victim met its death and became "the monstrous double."[154] The pig is used for more powerful sorcery than other animal sacrifices.[155] Anthropologist Zora Neale Hurston described her visit to the terrifying Cochon Gris secret society in Port-au-Prince, where instead of devotional chromolithographs and saintly images in the altar, she found an alarming large black stone secured with a heavy chain.[156] Reputed to be shape-shifting cannibals, the Cochon Gris have been seen at market in their pig form with human fingernails instead of pig's feet.[157] Since the creole pig slaughter turned a symbol of family, comfort, and nourishment into one of cruel death and destruction, no wonder these feral jabalís continue to haunt the border, returning with the rage and despair that is all too characteristic of the goddess Èzili Dantò who loves her *cochon kreyol* (creole pig) most of all; she is said to be "the divinity of the dream" and, apparently, the conjurer of nightmares too. As Maya Deren aptly put it, "Hence she must weep; it could not be otherwise."[158]

CHAPTER FIVE

SPECTERS OF COLUMBUS

In its first and simple "impurity," the history of
ghosts unfolds in several moments.

JACQUES DERRIDA | *Specters of Marx*

Property is theft!

PIERRE-JOSEPH PROUDHON

JA: There was a little goat climbing around the farm where I worked
one night around 7 p.m., and he walked all over that farm, from one
side to the other. And the farm had a little pathway, and the goat just
jumped from here to there, to over there where the chickens were kept,
and then it went over to the pigs. Some of the guys were there hanging
out and saw it; how could they lie to me? I was the night watchman,
so this was my responsibility. So that night they saw it and they called
me: "Watchman! Watchman! What's going on?" They said, "Get it and eat
it!" Then they said he was crazy and they went to the bathroom and went
to sleep. They did what they had to do at that time because when the
animal presented itself the three of them saw it flying around in the air
and they are not cowards.

LD: So that means that the goat was not an animal?

JA: It was the bacá of the owner of the property.

JUAN ALCÁNTARA | interview by the author

In 2008, I interviewed an elderly man in Bánica whose nickname was "Colón" (Christopher Columbus) (fig. 5.1).[1] At that time, Colón lived in a cavernous wooden shell of a home on the road leaving town toward Pedro Santana, the tall ceiling dwarfing his frail and diminished frame. Blind from age thirty, Colón was extremely solitary, especially for this context; he had occasional visits from a young Haitian caretaker who brought him his meals, and from a demented man who frequented Colón's home when he wasn't wandering around town. I started the interview by eliciting a life narrative about his family's past and work history. He recounted to me that for many years in the 1980s he had been manager of La Manicera, a large peanut oil processing plant in the town. When we discussed labor relations at the plant, he told me in no uncertain terms that when he was *gerente* (manager), one of the vexatious problems he faced was that workers at the plant sent scores of bacá spirit demons to engage in clandestine theft of peanuts and oil, to the point that there was a substantial drain on output. He also spoke of a veritable panic about livestock rustling as the bacá scourge also forced ranchers to sleep on site with their animals or face herd depletion through poaching. In Colón's view, these spirit demons were a "weapon of the weak," a popular tactic enabling the perfect anonymous crime for the poor. These unseen vigilantes observed the plant, engaging in stealth attacks when no one was present; however, Colón saw this as not so much a metaphysical issue as a problem of simple economics.[2]

This was a surprise to me since this was the first bacá narrative I had encountered that hinged on the trope of theft. I had mostly heard these stories of demonic encounters cast in a heroic mode, voiced in the first person by a protagonist who encountered these monsters on remote dirt roads or in isolated rural locations and mightily fought off these infernal creatures. Such stories stress the terror of an invisible threat encountered in remote locales by lone men with only their wits and their courage to protect them, as these beasts cannot be vanquished by conventional means alone; facing off against them requires exceptional valor. As one informant said emphatically of his encounter with a bacá while guarding a Haitian border sentry post overnight: "Yo no soy pendejo" (I am not a wimp).[3]

My surprise derived from the fact that I was developing an understanding of these bacá narratives as a form of subaltern resistance or "minority history," yet Colón's story did not fit that rubric.[4] Not only did Colón's story shift in voice from my other informants' tales, since

5.1 Portrait of Colón. Bánica, Dominican Republic, 2008. Photo by the author.

his events were cast in the third person, but it shifted dramatically in subject position as well. I came to realize that notwithstanding his feeble demeanor when I met him—blind, abandoned, accompanied only by a mentally ill man and a Haitian housekeeper—Colón had had a formidable past.[5] He had clearly been a big man in his youth, since he had been *alcalde* or mayor before rising to become manager of La Manicera in 1985, an industrial firm and franchise of the global food behemoth Unilever that stood out since it was so clearly a "machine in the garden" in this context.[6] This chapter explores another version of the *fukú de Colón* beyond its embodiment in Columbian seed animals, instead swirling around a man called Columbus. Yet, as we shall see, the bacá as surreptitious theft narrative in Colón's testimony may also have been a shield with which he sought to camouflage his role in the corruption and violence of the Trujillo regime.

PEANUTS AND POLITICS

La Manicera's founding and expansion charts key transitions in twentieth-century Dominican history. It was founded in 1937, in the wake of the massacre of Haitian-Dominicans, as part of the "Dominicanization of the frontier" campaign, as local capital took advantage of the land and labor opportunities freed up as thousands of people were slaughtered or emigrated. The firm later became a key foreign exchange earner during the shift toward structural adjustment policies after the Trujillo regime came to an end in 1961. But this was no ordinary peanut oil company. The plant later became the most important agroindustrial firm in the Dominican Republic, exceeded in importance only by the sugar industry, the twentieth-century pillar of the agroexport economy. It thus became a harbinger of the shift from state capitalism to neoliberalism that resulted from Ronald Reagan's 1980s Caribbean Basin Initiative, which encouraged the development of apparel assembly industries after sugar prices collapsed, and which eventually contributed to the economy's free fall in 1982 as the currency was devalued, debt arrears skyrocketed out of control, and the Dominican Republic stepped up to take the lead in a Latin American debt servicing boycott.[7] The firm also stood out because, unlike much of the sugar industry, it was locally owned.[8]

Founded by José María Bonetti Burgos and Jesús Armenteros Seisdedos, La Manicera (Sociedad Industrial Dominicana, MercaSID) eventually became part of the Dutch franchise Unilever in 1971; today Unilever is one of the largest multinational corporations in the world, expanding from oil, margarine, and soap products for domestic use into palm oil, flower, and citrus exports and personal care products. It is presently the local distributor for major brands such as Kellogg's, Hershey's, General Mills, Kimberly-Clark, and Häagen-Dazs. It was the first industrial refinery of its kind in the Dominican Republic, rendering oil from coconut, palm, and peanuts.[9] In the local theater of Bánica, La Manicera stood out dramatically since it was the sole industrial firm in a region dominated by extensive ranching and small-scale subsistence agriculture. On the Haitian side of the central frontier, in Belladère and Thomassique, there were a few scattered ox-driven sugar mills, but there was nothing comparable on the Dominican side, where access to forested mountain slopes had long enabled local herders to raise livestock with little investment of labor time, a pattern that enabled considerable autonomy from the cash nexus. Rumored to have been built in remote Bánica to avoid

US restrictions on toxic fertilizer and pesticide use, La Manicera was also distinctive because it hired largely women to clean the harvested peanuts; it had 36 female workers and 9 men, with another 5 men employed to drive the tractors during the harvest.[10] There may also have been interest in camouflaging the use of fertilizers and pesticides as well as solvents with harsh environmental effects, such as petroleum-derived hexame and caustic soda, which are used in oil extraction, by in effect hiding the plant in the central frontier. The peanuts were intercropped with *gandules* (pigeon peas) and corn, and the refined oil was exported to the United States.

The closure of the plant had significant local impact in part due to the fact that it loaned seed on credit in a context in which funding from other sources, such as the state-run Banco Agrícola, is almost impossible to obtain for smallholders. The plant had processed a new crop every three months, and La Manicera sold farm implements and oxen at cost, which meant a steady stream of support for small producers. However, the terms of its loans rendered repayment difficult, since unlike government loans, which are disbursed in cash, private company loans were disbursed in product, and the price was set on the day the smallholder received the loan, which means that the loan was obtained when the price was high and the smallholder might have to repay it when the price was low. It also meant that the loan recipients had to sell all their product to the company, and they had to do so months after they had used up the loan, which created a strong incentive to underrepresent crop yields.[11]

Importantly, La Manicera was one of the first in a honeycomb of companies founded through the predatory state capitalism that was a signature feature of the Trujillo regime. As historian Frank Moya Pons explains, high global prices for primary agricultural products after the Korean War provided ready capital for a new industrial elite to embark on a project of import substitution industrialization personally controlled by Trujillo, who gave out favors and protection to those who were willing to play according to his rules.[12] Like Trujillo himself, La Manicera founder José María Bonetti Burgos had risen from a humble background to become extraordinarily wealthy through ties to the dictator and access to the system of regional monopolies, perks given in exchange for loyalty to the regime. Early on, Bonetti had become a key member of Trujillo's inner circle due to his "strong personality" and lack of gross character flaws.[13] La Manicera was the first firm that Trujillo utilized to camouflage his family's takeover of the economy through proxies, rendering Bonetti a screen for the dictator's predations. Thus the firm belonged to Bonetti and Armenteros in name only; in fact, Héctor Trujillo, the dictator's brother, and his two sons were the true owners, replacing foreign investors after a fire in 1940. All capital inputs benefited from the same protections that the regime afforded other Trujillo investment properties and were fully exempt from taxes.[14] Unlike other Trujillista cronies, Bonetti lacked political ambition, which is surely why Trujillo trusted him, since as historian Robert Crassweller put it, "he was all business"; shrewdly, Bonetti thrived through generous profit-sharing with Trujillo. Among other ventures, he partnered with Trujillo's brother Negro in a shoe company, the cartons of which he used to transport cash siphoned off from the army and the office of the presidency.[15] Under the Trujillato, political domination and capital accumulation were inextricably braided together; however, only those within the "court society" of the regime were allowed to generate wealth, and while politics could be extremely lucrative, access to state monopolies was brutally policed.[16]

Oral historians frequently remove narratives from their social and linguistic context in order to analyze them as textual evidence. The case of Colón's tale of theft run amok indicates that this approach can be very misleading. Thus his story is also an object lesson in how hearsay can provide the context without which a narrative can be seriously misunderstood. Gossip can establish what sociologist Erving Goffman has called the "frame" for the speech act, providing the ground for the focal event.[17] As historian Luise White has observed, hearsay can reveal layers of collective experience unseen via public discourse.[18] Colón's bacá infestation story reveals how hearsay can also provide a means of interpreting the silences in oral testimony.[19] More than that, it can provide an important cross-check that can elucidate when and how informants deceive, thus enabling us to interrogate what historian Gyan Prakash might call the aporetic condition of deceit.[20] In this case, Colón's obsession with worker pillaging may have been a phantasmic screen memory concealing a history of his participation in a system of extortion and betrayal that he was trying, however unsuccessfully, to forget; thus this may have been a "motivated cover-up," obscured to me at first because of my ignorance of the implicit local knowledge of his role in the Trujillo regime's bureaucracy.[21] Alternatively, it may have been an attempt to exculpate himself by naming the open secret of rampant pillaging and corruption at the firm, though he implicated workers rather than company executives. It is possible Colón may have felt himself victimized, since he failed to reap the benefits.

On their own, these stories of demonic theft at La Manicera might be taken as tales of resistance to an industrial form of work alien to a region only partially dependent upon market exchange. They could thus be interpreted as expressions of alienation from the industrial labor culture of the firm—as popular resistance narratives of worker revenge or the "infrapolitics of subordinate groups."[22] Indeed, this is what I assumed until much later, when a conversation with some of his neighbors turned to the subject of Colón and his misdeeds. I eventually discovered that Colón's tales of worker theft were actually a mask for the fact that the theft was carried out not by the workers but rather by the firm owners and perhaps even Colón himself, as we shall see.[23] This case calls upon oral historians to develop a more layered understanding of discourse, as the monolithic concept of "testimony" that represents only the public transcript can have a flattening effect.[24] It is also a call to draw upon rumor as a means to excavate implicit social knowledge that otherwise remains concealed to the oral historian.[25]

In popular memory, the Trujillo period is recalled as a time when, in strong contrast to today, petty corruption was held effectively in check; when, it is said, one could leave a *chelito* (coin) on a park bench overnight and in the morning it would still be there.[26] Some scholars have contrasted this regime to that of Haitian strongman François Duvalier, where kleptocracy was institutionalized at every level of the social pyramid, on the presumption that under Trujillo the rules of the game allowed only the dictator, his family, and a few select cronies to engage in rampant pillaging of the economy via state monopolies and kickbacks. In this view, generalized corruption was not the norm, which enabled the Trujillato to succeed as a developmentalist regime, thus avoiding the failed-state category.[27] There is ample evidence, however, that this was patently not the case. The "Public Forum" column ("Foro Público") of *El Caribe* newspaper from 1948 to 1961—which printed more than thirty thousand letters in all—offers a treasure trove of evidence that local-level administration was riddled with everyday practices of graft and corruption.

As I have discussed elsewhere, the largest percentage of "Public Forum" letters were written by citizens accusing the civil service of inefficiency, corruption, or improper conduct.[28] Indeed, the column served as a populist escape valve for grievances against the regime, some of which were responded to, actually effecting change. In "Public Forum" letters, civil servants were accused of being ineffective, unprepared, inebriated at work, or just plain foolish; for example, the governor of San Pedro "must have come straight from an insane asylum"; the president of the Altamira *ayuntamiento* (city council) was described as useless and absolutely "comatose"; and the military of Samaná was said to have paid someone off so as to enable loud drunken parties until 2:30 a.m., against curfew regulations.[29] Another example was the *gran macuteo* (grand profiteering operation) of military service teacher Morel Pantaleón, who was accused of extracting not one but several requisite informal taxes from his charges, including a monthly fee of 50 centavos purportedly for his students' food when they were supposed to be provided with rations free of charge; a tax of 50 centavos each for the use of commissary-provided wooden rifles; and finally, on top of that, 50 centavos each for their course completion certificate.[30] Another example of bureaucratic malfeasance was the case of Lucho Nuñez Soriano of Santiago, who made off with fees collected for ID card renewals, licenses, patents, and taxes; about this, someone asked facetiously, "Is this an office of bureaucrats or gangsters?"[31] The use of the state for private ends—what political scientists call prebendalism— was rife under the Trujillato, as in the case of Domingo de la Cruz in Villa Mella, who openly used the municipality's truck to cart pipes and wood to his farm, and sold state supplies off to the highest bidder.[32] From the perspective of the regime, this kind of denunciatory harassment achieved the desired effect of terrorizing the civil service and keeping it in check, but it also provided a public archive of regime graft at all levels of government.

Accusations of impropriety and dishonor represented but a small fraction of the many thousands of denunciations publicly brandished in the press. Indeed, the overwhelming majority document the various and sundry tactics civil servants deployed to use their position to extract revenue from their underlings. Corruption was rampant within the civil service; however, given the monopolistic hold the state had on the economy, it is not surprising that this frequently involved collusion between the private sector and the public sector. This was the case for a group of over a hundred peasant proprietors whose land was appropriated by a cabal of landowners with the support of the mayor and governor in the frontier town of Santiago Rodríguez, notwithstanding the fact that they had held usufruct for over fifty years.[33] Published denunciations in *El Caribe* indicate that the official practice of siphoning off a 10 percent "tax" for the Dominican Party, which went straight into Trujillo's personal bank account, seems to have trickled down the bureaucratic chain, becoming a perceived entitlement among lower-level functionaries as well, especially within firms under the control of regime insiders. For example, one worker complained that La Manicera was paying workers not in cash but rather in *vales* (scrip), which had to be redeemed at the company store; to make matters worse, the clerks were skimming off an additional 10 percent above and beyond that from worker salaries. Additionally, the manager, Manuel Bobadilla, also stood accused of helping himself to an additional 15 percent of profit when weighing product.[34] Given the fact that the company drew employees from as far afield as the town of El Seibo, located some two hundred miles away in the northeastern corner of the country, by all accounts workers were deeply dismayed by the raw deal they got at La Manicera.

HAUNTING TALES

How might these bacá tales be characterized in terms of genre? Luise White defines genre in oral testimony as a "special kind of story that, while drawing on other kinds of stories and everyday experiences in each retelling, retains a specific set of plot and details. It is the pattern of the tale, not the circumstances of the telling, that makes a story recognizable as belonging to a genre."[35] Certainly these worker theft stories contrast in terms of narrative plotline, but they are also very different in voice and emotional tenor than the "I fought the bacá" tales discussed in chapter 6.

If bacá encounter testimonies are exhilarating heroic tales, the surreptitious bacá thievery narratives are part of a larger corpus of haunting stories that hinge upon a domestic invasion by these phantasmal abhorrent creatures; specifically, they are stories of a familiar place rendered ghastly by being overrun by infernal creatures. They are eerie and frightening. Since the transgressive beast is not conquered, there is no moral closure; their lingering threat conjures a deep unease approaching "spiritual doom," since these creatures appear small and impish but their invisibility renders them invincible. They invoke the mood of "the darker side of faith"—the notion that evil is ever-present and is constantly lurking in the recesses of our everyday spaces.[36] These haunting narratives have a different spatial dimension as well. Since the monster appears in the form of a swarm, there is not a singular contest with the Other; the enemy is invisible yet omnipresent. Indeed, one of the distinctive features of these tales is that the bacá invades the workplace or the home, familiar spaces that one frequents daily and knows intimately. Their presence renders these familiar spaces strange and even what Sigmund Freud would term uncanny.[37] The bacá presence is registered as a sensation that is tangible—even visceral—and is most often heard or felt. As Yael Navaro-Yashin says, "The banishing of the abject might be an ideological, performative, or rhetorical move." But what if the evil cannot be removed?[38] Indeed, the subfuscous tone of anxious dread in these accounts stems from the fact that there is no means of actually banishing this form of evil. These stories are also about the "familiar becoming strange" in another sense as well, since they take everyday domestic items associated with the home, such as a dog or an egg, and emplot them as supernatural agents, this transposition effecting a sense of "intense dread."[39]

THEFT AND THE VIOLATION OF SOCIAL EXCHANGE

Theft is a common topic of conversation in everyday conversation in Bánica today. Older ranchers such as José María Rivera of Hato Viejo, Guayabal, complain that you can hardly sustain a herd today given the pervasiveness of livestock theft, a narrative with an implicit contrast to the orderly police state of the Trujillo period. Abel Alcántara, who raises fighting cocks, had his prized rooster stolen, much to his dismay; at a whopping thirteen pounds, it had become so large that his neighbors called it a *pollo chivo* (goat chicken).

But the conversation that emerged about Colón outside Román Alcántara's house in 2014 invoked the trope of theft in a different register, one that served to recast the meaning of Colón's story altogether.[40] Colón was accused of violating the most basic rules of reciprocity. This was not a violation of the concept of moral economy, since it did not concern the right to subsistence; it referred to the social ties and obligations forged through the swaps of goods and favors that are a constitutive part of social life in this context. As anthropologist Parker Shipton has said, social life is forged through fiduciary culture—through the bonds of trust that undergird exchanges forged through debt and credit.[41]

The conversation about Colón emerged in a very specific backstage "microgeography"—Román Alcántara's patio, which was adjacent to Colón's house (fig. 5.2). But Román's abode was far humbler, a small house with a thatched roof and an outdoor kitchen.[42] The conversation

5.2 Román Alcántara (*right*) with his wife, Beba. Bánica, Dominican Republic, 2008. Photo by the author.

commenced with the question of what accounted for Colón's miserable condition—old, blind, and alone—which had been the norm for decades. Apparently he became *tuerta*, or blind in one eye, in the 1980s, so his eyesight was already failing when La Manicera folded in 1990. When Román said, "No one wants a life like that; death is preferable," I initially wasn't sure if he was referring to Colón's blindness or his isolation, but it soon became clear that his social seclusion was the issue.[43] In Dominican culture, solitude is by definition involuntary and intolerable. I soon came to realize that his isolation was not the cause of his misery, however; rather, it was seen as symptomatic of a far broader breach of the social contract. Colón was not the victim I had assumed him to be; in the community's view, he was doing penance for past wicked deeds.

As Román, a retired elementary school teacher, proceeded to catalog Colón's multiple breaches of social protocol, I noticed that all the typical vectors of social exchange were reversed for Colón. First, he never took care of his children, which is why they did not take care of him and why he cannot visit them in the capital and elsewhere, where they reside. Then there was the Haitian caretaker, who purported to be taking care of him; while she appeared to be feeding him, it was alleged that she was actually pilfering food for herself. Then the conversation shifted to Colón's past. Abel said it was alleged that during the Trujillo regime Colón had been a torturer, removing the fingernails of enemies of the regime. Román challenged this view, however, saying that Colón himself didn't do it, but he forced others to do the dirty work. A surreptitious shill, according to Román, Colón served as a spy for the regime; he would report to state authorities those who were unfaithful to the Trujillista cause. In this context, denunciation could land one in grave political danger, and it could result in the loss of one's job, social honor, or worse.[44] In a form of political and economic collusion characteristic of the crony capitalism of the Trujillato, Colón's exalted managerial position at La Manicera was, in this view, a reward for his political work denouncing regime enemies to the Dominican Party, the official party of the state. As Román put it, "This guy is paying for all of it, until he pays for what he did."[45] Of course, rumors that Colón had participated in the surveillance and torture apparatus of the regime are not surprising given the fact of his position as *jefe* (administrator) at La Manicera, which was known to have been actually Trujillo's firm. In a comment that highlighted the multiple ways in which Colón had violated the rules of social exchange, Víctor, who was also part of the conversation, recounted that once he had been present at a wake when a guy approached Colón and exclaimed, "Do you know the damage you did to men who owed you nothing?" Víctor went on, "He is paying for this."[46]

This peripheral hearsay cast the meaning of theft in Colón's testimony, then, in a dramatically different light. To be fair, the fog of secrecy camouflaging the regime's rampant predation and corruption has left its imprint in a widespread "hermeneutics of suspicion" and the presumption that state power was driven by clandestine back-channel rationales.[47] Given the assumption that power during the Trujillo regime operated according to hidden logics and was by definition inscrutable, one has reason to be skeptical of the veracity of these allegations against Colón; he may have been presumed to be part of the Trujillista surveillance and torture apparatus merely because of his position at La Manicera, for example. But as anthropologist Michael Jackson reminds us, "One does not have to believe in the truth claims of the system for it to work in a practical and psychological sense."[48] In providing a frame or context for the problem of theft at La Manicera, this hearsay does serve to cast his testimony in a very different light. Jackson has said of the difference between stories and explanations that certain kinds of emotional truths are conveyed via secondary narratives that elude the public first-person register, a fact that may help explain the contrast in "structure of feeling" between the two discursive regimes, since the hearsay about Colón unleashed a torrent of anger from his neighbors.[49] Gossip thus provided the semantic context without which the true moral of the story to this particular audience could not be discerned.

Returning to Colón's story about clandestine thievery at La Manicera, how should we interpret it? Theft was not an "inadvertent detail," since it was the core motif of his testimony.[50] Perhaps these hauntings represent not traces of labor power, as Karl Marx would have it, but rather memories of rapacious theft from Colón's superiors that he witnessed and wanted to speak out about but could not utter at the time. In this context, perhaps Colón's tale of covert theft run amok was actually a call for atonement, a plaintive request that someone clean up a system of institutionalized avarice once and for all—a system that was born under Trujillo but which grew and morphed under the rule of his right-hand man, Joaquín Balaguer. Balaguer was responsible for expanding the culture of petty corruption and transforming the generalized system of terror of the Trujillo regime.[51] Balaguer, Trujillo's key collaborator, held many positions during the regime, most nefariously serving as minister of foreign relations when the 1937 massacre took place, which obliged him to rationalize it to the outraged international community. Yet Balaguer went on to serve as president for decades (1960–62, 1966–78, and 1986–96), most notoriously during the dark period remembered as "the Twelve Years" (1966–78), when paramilitary groups were given free rein to attack civil resistance groups and poor dark-skinned urban youth in particular.[52] Yet these years are also known as the period of "the Dominican Miracle" due to exceptional growth rates (9 percent), said to be achieved through export-oriented foreign investment in tourism and manufacturing but actually fueled by exceptionally high international sugar prices—a boom period when ample profits enabled plenty of dividends to be repurposed for kickbacks and extortion. Like Colón, Balaguer masked the problem of corruption through constantly haranguing about the problem in his speeches. He even went so far as justifying intentionally underpaying the police, for example, on the grounds that they were able to take bribes from civilians for minor, everyday things such as moving violations and parking infractions; similarly, because civil servants levied informal "taxes" on obtaining motor vehicle licenses and passports, these illicit bribes were effectively a legitimate portion of their salary, commensurable to server tips in a restaurant.[53] These flows of stealth money to state functionaries also confirm how in Latin America political and economic transgressions can be seamlessly fused.[54]

The analysis developed here has hinged on La Manicera's relationship to the Trujillo regime, which provided the local context for the company's history, but another layer to the story is Unilever's dark past of labor exploitation and its own history of subterfuge. As historian Timothy Burke has noted, the challenge of studying the history of commodities is that many of their meanings are concealed in everyday life.[55] The precursor of Unilever got its start as English soap producer Lever and Co. in the 1880s and began collaborating with two Dutch margarine companies, Van den Burgh and Jurgens, in 1908 as industrial techniques were developed to turn fats into solids.[56] The global demand for lubricants for heavy industrial machinery such as steam engines and locomotive axles exploded at the turn of the century, and Lever and Co. established sources of supply for palm oil.[57] The firm later expanded into foodstuffs to feed the French military and profited from glycerin sales, which surged during World War I since glycerin was an ingredient used in gunpowder.[58] Founder William Lever developed a system of "dictatorial benevolence" that benefited European labor, called "prosperity sharing," in which soap factory workers lived in a planned community called Port Sunlight, near Liverpool.[59] Soap came to be seen as a measure of "white civilization" and progress for Europe, which gives new resonance to the famous 1940s ad campaign by Unilever (the company name since 1929) for the laundry detergent Persil, based on the slogan "Persil Washes Whiter," a brand identity that for some came to represent "absolute loving kindness."[60]

Yet the growth of Lever and Co. came at a brutal cost to the Nigerian and Congolese workers producing the raw palm oil it required.[61] Through the Belgian King Leopold II, William Lever acquired leases totaling 1.8 million acres for palm oil plantations, which drew upon the same brutal tactics used during the rubber boom to secure labor for this highly dangerous and underpaid work. Palm oil plantations liberally deployed the infamous *chicotte*, a hippopotamus-hide whip, as well as rape and maiming, to terrorize workers into staying on the job, conditions that were declared "abominable" by observers.[62] Protests eventually erupted on palm oil plantations in the Congo and Nigeria in 1929, in which police killed fifty women and injured many more. Lever also profited handsomely during World War I by providing soap and margarine to British troops at a time when the price of palm oil exploded due to the blockade.

A distinctive feature of Unilever's exponential growth as a company was the fact that it relied heavily on advertising—thus the "brand's sparkle."[63] Advertising is a form of dissimulation, since by "shoveling smoke" it "features messages that its creators and its audience know to be false."[64] From developing the first soap branding through placing colorful label designs on soap wrappings and boxes and spending lavishly on promotion, one might say that Unilever gave birth to modern advertising in Europe.[65] And margarine, one of its signature products, was destined for its own kind of "Pepsi generation" through offering a "range of functional and emotional choices" for its products.[66] A glance through trade journals from the 1950s reveals the constant presence of Unilever promotional films presented alongside talks in British regional townships such as Derby and Manchester on "Dairy Cookery," "Christmas Fare," and "Advertising and the Housewife."[67] And Ernest Dichter, who invented consumer research techniques such as focus groups in the 1950s, brought a Freudian approach to ads that helped ease consumer reticence, particularly among women, over products such as margarine, powdered milk, and frozen food, thus assisting, for example, in the doubling of British consumption of frozen meat pies, fish sticks, and sausage rolls in the 1970s and 1980s at a time when Unilever was seeking to expand one of its product "pillars," frozen foods.[68] In his motivational research for Palmolive dish soap Dichter argued that Unilever should focus on "emotional soap" over "reality soap," since dishwashing was a "symbol of female drudgery" for housewives.[69] Through establishing institutes in Switzerland and Germany, Dichter exported his marketing techniques to Europe.[70]

Returning to the subject of Colón and his tales of predatory demons: We might consider Colón's testimony a kind of analogous reasoning told in the third person, which, while remaining short of naming the beast, called attention to it, even if it did so within a poetics of indirection common to both gossip and Spanish elocution (which favors the indirect subject).[71] Then there is the issue of Colón's progressive blindness. While the community perceived it as a curse resulting from his past sins, one could also view it alternatively as a kind of hysteria, an intense phantasm haunting him and causing him distress—a specter of the violence of a system that perhaps in his view rendered him a victim.[72] We cannot know the whole truth about Colón's story, after all. While the historiography of the Trujillato has wanted to parse people into heroes and victims, the on-the-ground experience of individuals was often far more contradictory, ambivalent, and fraught than this dichotomy would allow. As anthropologist Ann Laura Stoler has noted, often the "bottom men" are scapegoated for crimes merely because they are more vulnerable than those at the top. Certainly while Colón was a big man in Bánica, he was part of a power pyramid that extended all the way to the grandmaster Trujillo himself.[73] An alternative reading of the bacás stalking La Manicera, however, is that they may have been Haitian baka avatars sent to clandestinely collect the property Haitian Dominicans left behind when they fled the 1937 massacre. This reading aligns with other popular taboos about touching the remains—the houses, crops, and farm animals—left behind by those who were slaughtered or fled that heinous event, since La Manicera was founded in the wake of the slaughter and in the border region where it took place.[74] And, of course, Colón had to live with the popular opprobrium of his nickname: the name of Columbus is a curse in the Dominican Republic, bearing the *fukú* of the Italian navigator who brought death and disease to the island. Herein lies a popular theory of memory in which events of the past leave tangible traces in the present. As Theodor Adorno and Max Horkheimer have said, "Men work their despair out on the dead"—and, in the case of Colón and his spirit demons, on the living too.[75]

CHAPTER SIX

BIG MEN & TALL TAILS

Yes, strange things occur because they always do. If you want a story, I will give you one. One night I was coming from La Cañita. It was 11 p.m. when I left the place. I knew where I was going, and when I arrived at the entrance, which was covered [with brush], out comes a horse—an anxious horse that suddenly stopped in front of me and boxed me in, and I said to myself, "My friend, are you going to let me pass?" Now, with good reason, I turned back. Then I don't know what the horse did, but it went somewhere, and when I arrived at Don Maro, there was the horse waiting for me. Now this was for real. I said, "I'm not coming back here!" I grabbed some stones and threw them at it, and I returned to La Cañita, and there it was again. My friend, this was not easy and I had to be alert. At that time, I had a girlfriend there; her name was Juanita. And when I arrived at her place, she said to me, "What happened?" I said, "A horse appeared to me." And she said, "But no—those are my horses. Those horses are troublesome [*mañoso*]."[1] And I said, "Those things are not toys." She had a huge fist and she said "Go to sleep here!"; I said, "No, I'm leaving because something is going on." And then she says, "No, go to sleep." And I say, "No, I'm not going to sleep!" So I left and when I returned, a boy who had an ox had died. They said, "You won't find anyone going to La Cañita," but I had to return there. I have to return, and I knew that I'm going to have to see that horse again. I got on my mule. I said, "I'm going with you; I'm not going alone."

So I left. I got on my mule and I started out. And when I arrived it was the hour of the drunks. In the alley at Servida and Punto Lírico two men were coming. And there was the horse again! So I pulled back my mule. I said to myself, "They are going to kill me." It said to me, "Who are you?" I said, "I am someone." It was then 6 a.m. I said to myself, last night I had a brush with a horse that was going to eat me. Around 1 a.m. Nothing happened, though. But that is what happened to me.

This chapter considers what José presents here—"dramatic action" stories that rural Dominican men recount about their encounters with demonic bacá spirits in Bánica and its surrounding rural areas.[2] These are devil pact narratives that reveal the occluded logic of sacrifice behind mysterious financial gains. They trace the backstage transactions of value until the violent climax when someone dies and an animal appears (as in the story above, in which a boy dies and a horse appears), which links the two events together through spirit transmutation.[3] They are narratives of encounter with an "epistemological danger"—something inchoate and uninterpretable—what linguist William Labov calls "danger of death" narratives.[4] On the one hand, these are stories of epic encounters with supernatural beasts, stories of men facing their deepest fears and risking their lives to fend off these preternatural adversaries. Yet they are also tales of men revealing feelings of vulnerability and indecision, attributes not allowed expression within the script of hegemonic masculinity, since in other contexts they could render one a loser (*fracasado*).[5] Anthropologist Johannes Fabian, who has called for an "ethnography of speaking," would identify these storytelling events as cultural performances that enact deep cultural codes.[6] But what work do these stories do? Why do Dominican men need the bacá? And what implicit codes govern their layers of meaning?[7] This chapter seeks to define this genre of narrative and considers in particular how mobility in these testimonial accounts relates to the social construction of masculinity in frontier rural communities. We will also examine the history of the horse on Hispaniola, which plays a central role in José's account.

These narratives are conveyed as eyewitness testimonies and thus are recounted as personal experience within the genre of realism. Yet they are also cued as *cuentos*, a device that brackets them as stories, and they are told in a breathless, dramatic tone and in an animated fashion so as to relive the experience and vividly engage the listener.[8] These are not at all codified verses that are honed and polished through frequent repetition.[9] Anthropologist Ann Laura Stoler has written about how vernacular speech forms such as rumor are layered, and this is certainly the case here. As she says, "Discrepant stories provide ethnographic entry into the confused space in which people lived, to the fragmented knowledge on which they relied."[10] These stories unfold processually in an ambulatory way, replete with twists and turns and detours. The accounts unfold in halting, uncertain terms in episodic fashion as the narrator gropes through the incidents; and as he speaks, the narrator often stands up and enacts his encounter. Thus these accounts conform to Richard Bauman's concept of "performed stories" that dramatically recount an event and vicariously reexperience it.[11] As historical sources, these stories convey many small "rhetorical truths," but their multivalence resists a singular bottom-line interpretation.

Scholars of slavery have sought to uncover "vernacular conceptions of freedom" at a time when "freedom rang hollow" in the post-emancipation period.[12] Bacá stories highlight mobility as a core value for men, in part a legacy of the extensive ranching and hunting economies through which many slaves found freedom and in which many Dominican freedmen participated after emancipation. As anthropologist Brian Larkin has proposed, infrastructures can structure subjects, creating "forms of desire and fantasy that can take on fetish-like aspects," creating a "kind of mentality and way of being in the world" through creating a "politics of as if."[13] Through establishing a "metaphoric predicate," this genre of bacá narratives establishes a correspondence between the narrator and a long-standing Dominican freedmen's vehicle of mobility, the horse—which also served as a central frame for male personhood in the Afro-Atlantic world, where one defining feature of slavery was the fact that it immobilized subjects. Through this encounter—the recounting of which also highlights his freedom of movement—José becomes a subject through his encounter with this iconic creature of empire that once empowered the conquistadores and enabled the conquest of the Indigenous population. In Santo Domingo, one of the few locations in the Caribbean to have a predominantly free population as early as the seventeenth century, the horse conveyed a thrilling and highly prized sense of freedom, mastery, and empowerment.[14] Anthropologist James Fernández notes that "there are always some people who feel more strongly their painful position in social space," and this is absolutely the case for José, who is a day laborer and thus is dependent in his everyday life, a posture that feminizes him.[15] Narratives such as the one presented at the start of this chapter help craft a reputation for José as a mobile agent who can fend for himself, stand up to bossy women, and claim his *dignidad* (dignity), but they also enable him to reveal fear and indecision, characteristics at odds with his self-presentation as a man of *respeto* (respect).[16]

OF HORSES AND MEN

José's narrative establishes certain telling contrastive analogies, most notably between the seen and the unseen, and between the demonic horse and the narrator's trusty mule.[17] Europeans brought to the Americas a host of pack animals, which were useful tools for colonial expansion, and seed animals for provisioning early settlers.[18] The horse and cow arrived first in Santo Domingo with Christopher Columbus in 1493; from there they were sent to Cuba, Mexico, and Venezuela. Horses were bred for export to Puerto Rico and Florida, eventually enabling Francisco Pizarro's conquest of Peru in 1531; Iberian purebred equines continued to be imported from Cuba to Jamaica even when creole horses were bred locally.[19] Even if this trade was illicit, in 1567 there was a constant stream of vessels transporting horses from Puerto Plata to Florida.[20] The abundance of feral cattle and horses enabled the early ranchers to have herds as large as twenty thousand animals; during this era of excess, aged animals or those without beautiful markings would be culled.[21] A traveler to the San Juan Valley exclaimed that the abundance of cattle and the skills of the riders was "one of the world's wonders." He said that the herd was so large that when the riders went in to collect the cattle for the roundup, the ground shuddered like an earthquake.[22] These beasts became the basis of a feral hunting economy that by the eighteenth century came to be called the *edad del cuerno*, or the era of horns.[23]

The cattle ranchers who emerged in the eighteenth century proudly rode horses to neighboring Saint-Domingue, where they sold their cattle. Their wills indicate that those with herds of fifty cattle and eighty pigs could be counted upon to have a horse or two, *una silla jineta* (saddle), and accoutrements such as a machete, a knife, a *lanza de monte* (a mounted lance for felling feral cattle), and the corresponding clothing among their prized possessions. One rancher in Bayaguana, a major cattle-ranching area in the northeast, had twenty cattle and one horse.[24] Only the largest ranchers, with herds of eight hundred or more cattle, had several horses.[25] Being seen on a horse was so important in nineteenth-century Brazil that some people would mount a horse to go open a gate a few yards from their house.[26]

Swapped for slaves, contraband mules started to pour into Saint-Domingue from Venezuela and Curaçao, which together exported some eight thousand mules in 1793. The animals were used to power sugar mills as the colony ramped up its sugar production in the eighteenth century. The Dominican northern region called the Cibao also provided mules to plantations on the western portion of the island.[27] As historian Linda Rupert duly notes, muleteers became "an iconic image of smuggling."[28] Contraband trade in mules, cattle, and horses became the central pillar of Santo Domingo's economy by the mid-eighteenth century as Saint-Domingue became a major sugar producer; the French colony, a net importer, had 63,000 horses and mules and 93,000 cattle in 1754. Burros and mules continued to be the central mode of interior transport before the advent of road-building in the twentieth century. With transport infrastructure in the Caribbean oriented toward getting sugar out of the plantation, roads and later railroads were built to move cane. Even after those were built, mules were still needed to haul food and firewood to market, and not just in the interior; everywhere, donkeys carried casks of potable water to households for sale.[29] Even in the capital city of Santo Domingo, goods flowed into the city via the Ozama River, where the "very patient work heroes"—the burro drivers known as *burriqueros*—collected kindling, produce, and poultry in their rough-hewn carts and brought them to markets across the city.[30] Indeed, even after aqueducts were built, water carriers using burros were beloved figures, if said to be rustic and foul-mouthed liars—in *costumbrista* writer Ramón Jiménez's colorful vocabulary, "embustero, pícaro, pendenciero y malhablado" (liar, mischievous, quarrelsome, and foul-mouthed) individuals who slept in the weeds and gambled away their minor profits.[31] When the French commissioner was fleeing Toussaint Louverture's revolutionary army, he deployed a mule train to carry his property into the interior.[32]

Historian John Crowley has noted how eighteenth-century visual imagery of Cuban sugar plantations erased the slave so as to stress "hypertechnical images" of evaporative vats and roller mills, but it also excised animal power. In an inversion of the European pastoral paradigm, terminology like the "Jamaica Train" for sugar refining cast the mills as pure machinery with no reference to the live "horse power" that sustained them.[33] Yet oxen and mules were key factors of production for agriculture, and they were efficient, as the volume of sugar produced by mule-driven sugar mills was competitive with, if not superior to, that produced by water-powered mills. Guided by slaves, animal labor drove the plantation. In indigo production, the cog-wheel levers were also kept in motion by mules.[34] In the era before nitrogen fertilizer, mule dung and cattle urine were absolutely necessary for healthy soil; they protected it from depletion by sugar monoculture. And while cattle may have been edited out of eighteenth-century lithography of the sugar plantation, on the ground they were ubiquitous. As eighteenth-century British pro-slavery politician and historian Bryan Edwards noted, "I believe, indeed, there are a great many overseers who give their land no aid of any kind, other than that of shifting the cattle from one pen to another, on the spot intended for planting."[35] As previously noted, animal inputs such as "bullock's blood" and "fine animal charcoal" (bone char), along with bird excrement, have long been central ingredients used in sugar manufacturing.[36] The preponderance of mules and burros among the Dominican laboring classes was apparent in eighteenth-century wills; for example, Cristóbal Diaz de Paredes upon his death left eleven burros and mules and sixty pigs.[37]

Animals such as horses, oxen, and burros that worked in tandem with humans, becoming extensions of the body, were particularly beloved, and were not eaten.[38] But the horse is the charismatic prestige animal par excellence, the animal seen as most proximate to humans. The fact that the horse stood apart is evident in several ways. For one, there is a long tradition of horse panegyric in Latin America. Bernardo de Balbuena penned a poem in 1622 that cast Mexico's greatness in terms of the quality of its horses, and Luis José Peguero, writing in 1763 in Baní, penned poetically that an equine's color was indicative of its personality—gray indicated a jumper, just as piebalds were mellow.[39] Horses have long played central roles in the important rituals of the *campo* (countryside), marriages and baptisms.[40] In rural *coplas* (four line poems or songs) and sayings, frequently a man's steed and his woman are pitted against one another, and often the horse wins. For example, a woman might forget to brush one's teeth, but a man never fails to groom his horse. It was also said that one of the key weaknesses of Dominican men is that they love to talk about the temperament and antics of their horses in "hyperbolic *tertulias*" (social gatherings).[41] A strong sense of commensality is apparent in the treatment of companion animals such as the family mule, which long provided rural transportation in the interior.[42] Fed, stroked, spoken to, their feet checked and trimmed, they were individuated through names, as seen in the novel *Over* (1939) by Ramón Marrero Aristy.[43]

In Juan Bosch's classic 1936 novel about nineteenth-century *caudillismo* (strongman rule), La Mañosa ("Tricky"), who gives the book its title, is the beloved family mule, leader of a train for a rural merchant who sells beans, corn, and tobacco in the interior; the animal's resilience, courage, pluck, and personality render her a beloved symbol of creole identity. In Bosch's words: "As dark as half burnt wood, her gaze was intelligent and loving, her footing fine and sure, her hooves small, round, black and tough. Everything about her was colorful and pleasing."[44] Blackness in this context was embraced: Black oxen might be nicknamed "Negrito," a diminutive that conveys affection. Blackness also featured in rustic food products such as molasses and unprocessed sugar; as the saying goes, "The blackest brown sugar [*raspadura*] is the best for coffee."[45] As Bosch's narrator says, "My mule? For all the money in the world I would not give her away, and not because of her performance, but rather because I care for her as if she was a person."[46] Her owner's greatest gesture of trust was loaning this very special animal to his compadre General Fello Canario when his horse was injured in the middle of a military campaign.[47] While this treatment is imbued with sentimental nostalgia, in part due to Bosch's socialist politics, farm animals held far more than mere utilitarian value. But there may be another reason beyond that the mule has been embraced as a symbol of creole mestizo identity. The word *mulatto*, derived from the Portuguese *mula*, meaning "mule," is a part of a strong interface in vocabularies of mixture between humans and animals that emerged in the eighteenth century. The Castas paintings produced in Mexico for a Spanish audience, for example, illustrate the racial types *coyote*, which was a cross between a "mestindio and a castiza" (thus a mixture of Indian, Iberian, and mestizo); mulatto, which was the offspring of a Spanish man and a Negro woman; and *lobo* or wolf, which emerged from a Negro and an Indian.[48]

An anonymous copla went as follows:

Voy a ensillá mi caballo
Porque burro no e' montura.

I'm going to saddle up my horse
Because a donkey is not a mount.[49]

As a key symbol of Iberian nobility and equestrian showmanship, the horse was long a central component of royal display in Spain, and its association with nobility is evident in the New World context.[50] Horses were important prestige animals, requisite to staging performances of power, and they provided the appropriate frame for nineteenth-century caudillos, for whom riding skills were an important part of their political charisma at a time when the heroic masculinity of the nation-building soldier reigned supreme.[51] Caribbean historian Hilary Beckles argues that "the iconography of the black male warrior as liberator and protector was enshrined within the discourse of nation building."[52] For example, it was said of Dominican statesman Ramón Cáceres, "Ese si era jinete" (Now *he* was an equestrian). Stories of Ulises Heureaux's assassination include not only his travails but those of his mount; it was said that he was shot on his horse, falling to the ground, but succeeded in getting back on and riding off for an honorable exit.[53] Famed Dominican general Máximo Gómez, who helped secure Cuban independence from Spain, was said to have been "the last American rider"; as a means of denunciation, his detractors claimed that he and his troops were barefoot and horseless.[54] The importance of the steed as a font of masculine pride is a theme in the classic sugar novel *Cañas y bueyes* (Sugar cane and oxen) (1936) by Francisco E. Moscoso Puello, in which the local magistrate (*alcalde pedáneo*) Alipio does pirouettes on his steed Biscochito ("Little Cake") to show off and, in particular, impress the ladies; in Dominican popular parlance this form of exhibitionism is called being a *comparona*.[55] Though his horse apparently was his sole asset, he loaned it to pretty girls, perhaps hoping for recompense. In the words of Moscoso Puello, "That horse was the envy of the town. It was a beast among beasts."[56] While the horse helped the Haitian revolutionary chieftains win against the armies of France, England, and Spain, it also enabled the wholesale devastation of the Indigenous population, so it is a sign of authority as well as subjugation. The horse was more than a mere prop for male authority; it helped constitute it.

This helps explain why Haitian military commanders such as Toussaint Louverture and Jean-Jacques Dessalines are most frequently imaged on horseback, and why Rafael Trujillo was frequently photographed in equestrian attire (figs. 6.1 and 6.2). For example, when freedman Juan Aponte was jailed for sedition in Cuba in 1812 for treasonous drawings, these included sketches of Haitian revolutionaries atop their steeds.[57] In the quintessential political form that emerged in the nineteenth

6.1 Portrait of François Dominic Toussaint Louverture (1743–1803), in uniform, mounted on his horse. French school, ca. 1800. Sotheby's Lot 198 PF2139. Art Digital Studio © Sotheby's.

century, the caudillo is defined as the man on horseback, and the horse was the pedestal that gave the caudillo social distance from the plebe and thus accorded him respeto (respect); the horse conferred social honor to the rider, providing "ceremonial distance" or deference.[58] This was especially important for mixed-race *hombres de mando* (men in command) like Trujillo, who otherwise did not have the trappings of class respectability, which is why Trujillo announced his candidacy on horseback, and why his motto to his followers was "*Seguiré a caballo*" (I will follow on horseback).[59] Indeed, during the Cuban war of independence, whether one fought on horseback or on foot was a marker of race and status, since former slaves rarely had horses during the early phases of the insurgency, acquiring them either in battle or as they rose in military rank.[60]

The fact that animal breeding became an alibi for racial improvement helps us understand why in the 1950s the mixed-race Rafael Trujillo inaugurated a system of *ferias ganaderas* (livestock fairs), an animal genealogical registry, and a national studbook, all intended to improve bovine breeding—and to showcase the racial purity of the nation at the

6.2 Rafael Trujillo, around the time of his presidential candidacy, with his horse, Caonabo, 1930. Courtesy of Centro León, Santiago, Dominican Republic.

very least through its animal surrogates. These measures served other purposes as well, such as displaying his affinities with strongmen from other cattle-ranching nations such as Anastasio Somoza of Nicaragua, while also associating Trujillo with the fecundity and breeding prowess of his professional studs, earning him labels such as *primer ganadero dominicano* (first Dominican cattleman). Trujillo's farm Hacienda Fundación won awards for animals of "most distinguished race" and "pure English blood," labels that cast Trujillo as an aristocrat by association.[61] The premier theater of horse-riding skills was of course "the sport of kings": polo, a game originally created to train mounted military in Iran and which was popularized throughout the British Empire via tea planters and colonial officers. Trujillo officialized the sport by forming the Ciudad Trujillo polo team, which competed against the United States and Mexico, enabling a masculine display of power and control over

6.3 St. George, also known as the vodou/vodú deity Ogou, on his steed. Chromolithograph, undated.

others and, of course, associating the regime with famed jetsetter Porfirio Rubirosa, the philanderer and polo player extraordinaire, to whom the term *playboy* was often applied and who was known for showing up at the Bagatelle polo club in Paris in his blue Ferrari.[62]

As Ann Norton Greene has noted, the horse is an elite animal, and its "physical power . . . reinforced other kinds of power—aristocratic, military, political, sexual, religious."[63] The horse's authority extends to its role in vanquishing supernatural enemies. A common chromolithograph of St. George (often associated with the deity Ogou) showcases him sitting on top of a white steed, poised and ready to fight dragons and other satanic avatars (fig. 6.3). This motif of a horse facilitating metaphysical warfare is also present in Haitian sequin artist Myrlande Constant's epochal tapestry of the 2010 Haitian earthquake, in which a mounted equine figure fights off a series of *malfecteurs* (evildoers) unleashed by the catastrophe.[64]

In England and New England, nineteenth-century breeding practices rendered animal bloodlines important status markers, and there was an avid market in horse loans, but this was not the case in the Dominican countryside, where relations of clientage and ties of social reciprocity enabled individuals of stature to secure rides when needed. This was the case in *La Mañosa* when caudillo Fello Macario needed a mount and cashed in his social debts to borrow one from a trusted ally. Indeed, the importance of relations of trust being traceable through swapping horses can be seen in a passage from Manuel del Cabral's epic poem *Compadre Mon* (1940) about riding "with a guitar and on your horse."[65] As historian Emilio Rodriguez Demorizi put it, "The biggest respect [*deferencia*] one could pay a friend was loaning him one's horse."[66] Yet the status hierarchy was clearly apparent when the recipient of the request to borrow a horse had to reveal with embarrassment, "But all I have is a mule."[67]

GENDERED HISTORIES

Twentieth-century Dominican development has marginalized the cattle regions that once reigned supreme. The Dominican economy entered into a period of steep decline with the onset of neoliberalism as traditional export prices collapsed in the 1980s. As sugar exports decreased steeply, a debt crisis emerged at that time, as the Dominican Republic was forced into austerity measures by the IMF.[68] The crisis that ensued when food subsidies were withdrawn inspired food riots that spread to South America, bringing down the presidency of Jorge Blanco (1982–86). The 1980s experiment in export free trade zones encouraged by Ronald Reagan's Caribbean Basin Initiative brought jobs initially, but these soon evaporated as firms fled to first to Mexico and later to China, and the informal sector became an expanding safety net for the poor. Joaquín Balaguer (president 1960–62, 1966–78, and 1986–1996) aggressively promoted tourism, and by the 1990s it had become a central driver for the economy.[69] This sector is now driving growth rates that lead Latin America and the Caribbean as a whole, although little if any of these profits trickle down to rural areas.[70] High-end tourism such as all-inclusive resorts create few jobs outside of low-paid work in hotel services. Moreover, sugar plantations as well as all-inclusive resorts are enclaves without backward or forward economic linkages and do not enhance the agrarian sector.[71] IMF requirements for lowering tariff barriers have also contributed to overall food dependency.

These trends have been compounded by a highly urban development orientation that has basically left the Dominican countryside to fend for itself. Historians of Latin American politics have long focused on rhetoric to interpret political subjectivities and logics of citizenship.[72] But we also need to study infrastructure, since technological systems convey ontologies that also constitute subjects through conveying a sense of inclusion within modernity.[73] For example, as part of a master plan to alleviate urban traffic, the government of Leonel Fernández (2004–12) spent $700 million to build an underground metro to meet transport needs in the capital city, Santo Domingo.[74] Like the nineteenth-century train, the metro conveyed a fantasy of mobility that *capitaleño* (capital) elites found captivating, as it created a simulacra of cosmopolitan life in places like New York.[75] Importantly, Fernández was the first Dominican president to have grown up in the United States. Yet simultaneously in Bánica, public infrastructure was entirely neglected, as the *síndico* (mayor) left the irrigation system broken and languishing for decades.[76] Rafael Hipólito Mejía won the presidency in 2000 on the grounds that he would refocus state attention on underserved rural communities, even though he actually had a history of undermining them, since as minister of agriculture he was the one who executed the devastating pig slaughter in 1979, discussed in chapter 4 . In point of fact, government spending on rural areas has decreased steeply since 1995, and the share of agriculture in the GDP has declined by half, from 12 percent to 6 percent.[77]

A mood of rural despondency is reflected in the rise in popularity of *música del amargue* (bitter music), which expresses the shame of poverty and the longing for status items that might attract a girlfriend. The genre called bachata had long been a sign of rurality, but as it became urbanized, especially through the meteoric rise of the New York–based band Aventura, amargue's melodramatic expressivity came to speak for the emotional toll of poverty experienced by those left behind by emigration.[78] This music's backward-looking view challenges the national narrative of progress. Singer Luis Miguel, whose song "Se acabó lo bonito" (The beauty is over) was a blockbuster hit during the early 2010s when I was visiting Bánica, is characteristic of this genre, in which men chronicle the pain and humiliation of poverty within a gloomy emotional timbre. "Sangre de guano," for example, offers a visceral critique of urban elitism and its duplicity through the story of a girl who passes up the narrator for a guy with a car; the protagonist has only a motorcycle (a central mode of transport in rural townships), and her father ridicules him because he is broke.[79] Amargue has become the music of the informal proletariat, favored by those with street occupations such as day laborers, police, blacksmiths, dockworkers, and market vendors.

This pattern of development has helped give rise to a significant gender imbalance. Inflation and the decline of the peso as a result of economic restructuring forced more women into the labor force in the 1980s.[80] The *zonas francas* (export free trade zones) created jobs in sewing, and job creation within hotel chains has been primarily in cleaning services, both of which are perceived as "women's work." Women's labor has been prioritized in nontraditional agroexports, such as off-season vegetables and flowers, as these have expanded, and women are often paid less.[81] Women have also dominated migration to the United States in a context in which it has become a significant marker of respectability and middle-class status on the island.[82] While the central frontier has less outmigration than larger cities, several families in Bánica have relatives in the United States, and they are principally women. The pattern of female outmigration has been reinforced by the fact that upward of fifty thousand Dominicans incarcerated in the United States have been deported back to the island since the early 1990s, and 93 percent of them are male.[83] Women's participation in the labor force actually doubled in the 1980s, as men's declined, and women also rely on their children for income.[84]

As women acquired an income, becoming heads of households, they had more leverage to stand up to their partners. Ethnomusicologist Deborah Pacini Hernandez charted a trend in popular music in the 1980s, in particular within bachata lyrics, in which women were cast as the problematic Other—for example, as prevaricating betrayers who reduced their menfolk to *pariguayos* (bumpkins, fools) as they took over the role of family breadwinner.[85] To make matters worse, the Dominican *campo* continues to have high rates of unemployment and underemployment, partly due to patrilineal inheritance, since the eldest son typically inherits the farm, leaving the other siblings adrift; furthermore, the ubiquity of Haitian labor lowers wages within the border agricultural sector and serves to stigmatize male day labor.[86] The gender gap applies to education as well. Most Dominican boys do not reach the fifth grade, and girls do far better in school than boys throughout elementary and high school.[87]

José's story of man versus horse also forces us to contend with the important relationship Dominican men have long held with their equine mounts, which in the post-emancipation period enabled what historian

Aisha Finch has called "the luxury of mobility" while also providing a crucial frame of authority for Dominican masculinity.[88] The importance of the horse to social status has deep Iberian roots and was reinforced during the Haitian Revolution, when the horse as a prestige animal was claimed by freedmen of color. This importance can also be seen linguistically, in the fact that the term for "gentleman" (*caballero*) derives from the term for "horse" (*caballo*). Consequently, the fact that the demon in José's story appears in equine form is significant. The horse, of course, was brought by Columbus and early Spanish settlers and has long served as a crucial tool of colonization and subjugation within slavery.[89]

TRICKSTER TALES?

While some scholars allege that it is the pleasure of audience voyeurism that explains the popular fascination of tales of evil and keeps them alive through frequent retelling, in this case it may be just as much the way these cuentos (oral narratives) fashion the protagonist into an epic hero through his ability to withstand extraordinary dangers.[90] Of course, the epic is part of the Western canon, and a key feature of these stories is that they are tales of men traveling alone who encounter obstacles and overcome them. This type of identity quest is part of the modernist canon, as men set out on voyages on which they are faced with great challenges, and they return home having proven their manhood and honor. Narrators in epic tales are often cast as social avengers, and epic narratives in oral form are certainly told of popular heroic outlaws such as faith healer Díos Olivorio Mateo, who in the early twentieth century evaded the law and has come to represent the local community of the Dominican southwest and its values.[91]

But there are also clearly ways in which these tales diverge from the epic canon. The epic form is characterized by clear moral binaries and by progression over time as the narrator grows from his voyage.[92] Yet if the European canon of epic narratives is often characterized by linear movement from periphery to center, travel in these oral Dominican tales, by contrast, has "non-linear complexities," as the passage of the protagonist in the bush is blocked by a terrifying beast and he has to valiantly evade the obstacle by changing course, doubling back, and constantly innovating his itinerary.[93] Moreover, these stories are not conveyed as narrative histories but rather as successions of anecdotes without a clear moral coda.[94] These tales of encounter also feature front-and-center frightening altercations with infernal beasts, with superhuman deeds in virtual battle, but the protagonist is not a hero but an underdog with daring "rascality."[95] Indeed, he deploys evasive tactics such as lying, hiding, and cheating to escape, rendering these stories similar to traditional trickster tales, which are exceedingly popular in former slave societies, albeit in this case conveyed as eyewitness testimonies.[96] These stories showcase the "indomitable individualism" of the narrator, his wits, his cunning, and his pride.[97] "A mulatto Don Quijote," the narrator is a "boldly imaginative" and visionary knight errant, a man who in vain tries to carve out a righteous life within a fallen and corrupt world.[98] These battles provide a proscenium for garnering respect, and so they may be construed as "social identity projects" through which the protagonist acquires respeto—a key frame for male personhood and a sense of worth often unavailable to poor rural men through their labor—through his valor in facing down hazards. This is what José is referring to when he says that he "became someone"; what he means is that he has been granted his "moral worth as a social person."[99]

Folklorist Lewis Hyde treats the larger arc of trickster tales in the Western tradition, first canonized by the Greeks. But bacá stories have a very particular history, since they are told by narrators within a context of a history of slavery. As such, they should be located within the larger corpus of African American trickster tales, which also revel in overcoming challenges. In the Caribbean, they are traditionally told in the third person, as mythic tales in which the folk hero is camouflaged in animal guise, and are told with the intention of entertainment.[100] They are celebrations of everyday rogues and heroes—underclass men who escape everyday dangers on their own without the help of others, using only their wits and cunning.[101] This "veiled discourse of dignity and self-assertion"—thus social honor—offers symbolic resistance to forms of everyday domination, in particular, historical slavery; they are satisfying because of the ways in which they challenge the public transcript of deference requisite within the corridors of power. As literary critic Henry Louis Gates reminds us, "The black tradition is double voiced."[102] These cuentos also form part of a tradition of indirection within subaltern speech characteristic of former slaves, who were often presumed to be on the other side of the law, as well as being part of a long history of dissimulation due to the centrality of illicit contraband in the borderlands; these features frame aspects of the stories as purposeful forms of "veiled communication."[103] The nocturnal journey setting is important because it is a reminder of the subversive nature of this content: Nighttime, travel, and solitude contrast with the degrading everyday world of work under those with superior status, and during the period of slavery, nighttime was one of the few times when slaves could convene without supervision.[104] Highlighting these men as clever individuals surely holds a special thrill in the post-emancipation period, since slavery removed all markers of individuation, including proper names.[105]

It should not surprise that similar narratives have long been passed down. Consider Alexandre Dumas's *Les Trois Mousquetaires* (*The Three Musketeers*, 1844) and other tales. Dumas was the grandson of an enslaved woman and a renegade nobleman who fought in the French cavalry during the Haitian Revolution; Dumas's father rose to command a free legion during the French Revolution. Those real-life stories provide ample fodder for Dumas's popular novels of men on horseback.[106] For example, Cuban independence leader Antonio Maceo was long steeped in Dumas's novels as well as biographies of Toussaint Louverture, the Haitian revolutionary chieftain on horseback.[107]

Caribbean folk heroes engaged in epic travels can pass years in the monte or bush, a space of danger and transformation where the spirits reside, and which confers special wisdom. Former Cuban slave Esteban Montejo vanished into the monte for seven years; Dominican faith healer Olivorio Mateo returned as a prophet after seven days underwater.[108] But in other ways bacá tales would more likely be characterized as *petites histoires* (little histories), since the journeys they recount are not transcendental but everyday scenarios—returning from the farm, visiting a girlfriend, or collecting pay from an employer.[109] They are about travel on everyday roads and mountain paths, not "the forest primeval"; these are secular not otherworldly journeys.[110] One key feature is the way these narratives locate the protagonist squarely within the public domain of the street, which is important since the street is the premier proscenium of manhood in Latin America.[111]

José's story ultimately, however, fails to conform to a key feature of the epic genre—the story of a hero who works in the service of the nation. As an underdog and an outsider, the narrator of bacá tales demonstrates several motifs common to the picaresque genre (the *pícaro*), such as the first-person voice, the underclass social setting, horizontal travel, and episodic plot development.[112] A social orphan, the narrator is adrift and stands apart from society. He is forced to become a rascal due to his struggle for existence in a hostile world. A "coward with a cause," José in this account is the bold individual who stands up to a powerful demon, though he fails to slay it.[113] There are also elements of the pícaro in the mobile and sexually available woman who dresses him down; indeed, her inappropriately domineering behavior defies the social script for the honorable female.[114] This characteristically Spanish genre likely had an influence on maritime adventure tales such as that of Alexandre Exquemelin, who traveled to Tortuga as a French *engagé* and recounted his experiences alongside Henry Morgan and other pirates.[115]

TRAVELER'S TALES

> Everybody knows, we gonna walk, we gonna walk, walk, walk, walk down freedom street.
>
> **KEN BOOTHE** | "Freedom Street"

Walter Benjamin has charted how popular narratives represent the experience of labor. This makes sense if these bacá narratives are centrally about freedom defined as mobility, since the border has long been a central corridor of both the cattle trade and the military, both of which are itinerant professions.[116] The peripatetic lifestyle of hateros is well described in Víctor Garrido's aptly titled memoir, *En la ruta de mi vida, 1886–1966* (In the route of my life, 1886–1966; 1970); Garrido's father spent months on the road driving his cattle to Haiti for sale. The military has left its mark on this region as well. The province and neighboring town of Elías Piña were named for a colonel of the Dominican army during the 1844 independence war against Haiti who died trying to retake Bánica from Haitian forces; Bánica's sister township in Haiti, across the Artibonite River, is named for "proud and vain" Georges Biassou, the Haitian commander and monarchist who sided with the Spanish during the revolutionary war.[117] Bánica's relationship to the sites of many important battles of the independence wars, such as the adjacent town, Las Matas de Farfán, helps explain why Rafael Damirón termed it part of the "deep south"—a place where men would take to the interior with a Remington and a steed. Bánica served as a transit point for revolutionary soldiers, including the "heroic mulattos" Buenaventura Báez and Ulises Heureaux, even though it is not geographically part of the southern corridor.[118]

While the story of cattle theft had long been a popular narrative in the border region, the eighteenth-century cattle boom created a new figure, the *metedor* or *corredor*, who, flaunting prohibitions, moved large numbers of cattle across the border to take advantage of the fact that the price for cattle in Saint-Domingue could be double or triple that in Santo Domingo. These corredores or runners acted with impunity in the central frontier corridor from Azua to Hinche. Their tactic was to declare a nonexistent theft, pay off the border guards, and drive cattle to Saint-Domingue for sale in Guarico (then the name for Cap-Haïtien).[119] These stockmen were the tígueres of their day, exemplifying a rags-to-riches trajectory enabled by their skills as smooth talkers and by their mastery of the arts of duplicity. Many used their earnings to purchase their freedom if they weren't free already. Quintessential go-betweens, these were "men of words" whose central skill was their narrative abilities, which made them persuasive and eloquent speakers.[120] The chicanery of these highly mobile border crossers was enabled by their multilingualism, as well as their ability to spin a yarn that convinced authorities that they were not who they seemed to be; one would imagine that they likely also relished boasting about their successes after the fact.[121] Through their skills at verbal performance they resemble another eighteenth-century figure of cosmopolitan mobility, the sailor, whose stories "highlighted fighting, drinking, sex, virility, and masculinity" and were later canonized as voyage narratives.[122] Many stockmen gained fame as arrogant braggadocios and womanizers. In colonial Saint-Domingue, they were also frequently said to be thieves, "lazy, argumentative and bold-faced liars."[123] Historian Antonio Gutiérrez Escudero has argued that the genre of the picaresque was popularized in the Dominican Republic through the eighteenth-century cattle trade when it became the lifeline of the national economy and as the metedores came to rule the island. Contraband became dominant, and when authorities tried to stop the trade, the metedores rose up in rebellion.[124] Thus cattle contraband became a key infrastructure for the picaresque genre and its characteristic dissimulation; indeed, Gutiérrez Escudero goes so far as to claim that the illicit cattle trade rendered the figure of the pícaro a national culture hero.[125]

Since the metedores became local culture heroes at a time when slavery was the norm, outsiders found them an affront. Indeed, travelers developed a robust critical commentary on the "natural economy" of these frugal and independent "masterless men" who, because they were not involved in agriculture, appeared to spend their days lying around and not working, and as a result were met with contempt.[126] In an era in which labor coercion was the norm, these autonomous freedmen, hunters, and ranchers, who "spent their days astride an old mule, visiting farms and drinking coffee, in picturesque attitude somewhere between potentates and beggars," seemed like an affront and a portent of doom.[127] As one contemporary observer exclaimed of Santo Domingo, "It is a nation without industry, of men who fail to accumulate, of great torpidness. . . . If these slave owners, indolent and incapable of making any effort, don't make use of their slaves—carelessly lying around in their hammocks and strumming their guitars—both the will and the muscles of their slaves will be lost, victims of their lethargy."[128] Equally alarmed at the absence of agriculture in the interior, Dominican authorities instead blamed it on the "excessive" number of rural freedmen who had access to ample state lands and a feral animal commons; this produced "blacks without discipline or subjection" and "loafers," and their existence prompted anti-vagrancy legislation.[129] In fact, Martinique jurist Moreau de Saint-Méry explicitly racialized this discourse when he complained that owners were unable to treat their slaves with the superiority that was required in part because the owners were themselves mestizos.[130]

In a former slave plantation society, the sheer mobility of the men in bacá narratives denotes that they are freedmen, not slaves; indeed, in the nineteenth century status accrued to those exemplary slaves whose professions entailed mobility, such as cart drivers, coachmen, muleteers, or soldiers—male occupations of distinction that have long been lionized in popular song.[131] As slaves moved off the plantation and into urban areas, the Cuban songs called *pregones* lovingly celebrated the itinerant food vendors who sold snack foods such as agua de coco (coconut water), peanuts, mamey, pineapple, vegetables, and herbs such as *romerio* and *altamisa* for cooking, cosmetic, and aphrodisiac uses. Songs about fruit vendors were also a stock theme in turn-of-the-century Dominican music such as the *boleros* by Grupo Dominicano titled "Los mangos de Baní" (The mangos from Baní) and "El platanero" (The plantain vendor).[132] Indeed, vegetables made their mark even in the names of musical genres such as cebolla (onion).[133] Cebolla songs chart the emergence of urban freedmen's occupations in the working-class barrios of nineteenth-century Havana, occupations that required a pressed shirt; thus *leña* (firewood) was needed not only for cooking fuel but also to fire up the iron. These songs include nicknames such as "El Doctor" for a vendor; such nicknames marked status as freedmen sought to claim respectability they had long been denied.[134] Cebolla songs imitate vendors' calls as they walked down the street, at times engaging in saucy flirtation, using the fruits for sale as props with the housewives and domestics who purchased from them.[135]

Our narrator at the beginning of this chapter, José, casts himself as a trickster, which is an underclass hero popular throughout the African diaspora. As "lords of in-between" and quintessential boundary crossers, tricksters are frequently on the run. Bacá narratives are invariably emplotted on roads; they are journeys in which the protagonist faces dangerous adversaries that test him, but he invariably lands on his feet. These dangers are especially frightening because they are confronted in darkness, rendering it difficult to make out exactly who or what the adversary is; thus the narrative presents an aura of confusion.[136] Indeed, the opacity in these narratives is itself a marker of underdog experience, since these protagonists are clearly not "masters of all they surveyed."[137] It has been argued that part of the trickster's role is to create boundaries or reveal obscured categorical distinctions, thus foregrounding the ability to create order in the fog. As writer Lewis Hyde states, the trickster is the "mythic embodiment of ambiguity and ambivalence, doubleness and duplicity, contradiction and paradox."[138]

Henry Louis Gates has argued that the trickster genre originated in West Africa. For example, the beloved Yoruba god of chance, Eshu, figures prominently as a reminder of the determinant role of luck in everyday life, which has become almost metaphysical in its importance.[139] Yet the meaning of travel takes on a particular valence in the African diaspora, where enslaved peoples were for centuries defined by immobility, shackled and tied to the plantation. Movement was a privilege earned or stolen, not given, and mobility was one of the perks lavished upon loyal slaves, who might become muleteers, overseers, or livestock drivers. The freedman was a go-between within colonial society who was cast as dangerous in large part due to his physical and social mobility. In a context in which most African-descended people were bound to the plantation, freedpeople with the privilege of movement, such as female domestics (charged with fetching water and going to market) and free urban male artisans (including carpenters, masons, tailors, livestock handlers, and blacksmiths) were often accused of sedition and assumed to be the masterminds of slave revolts, and sometimes they were: Toussaint Louverture, a coachman, became a national hero.[140] They posed a double threat to the plantocracy because many freedmen were skilled with arms due to their high preponderance in the military or *maréchaussée* (military police).[141]

Cuban *son* was a musical genre that developed in the eastern region around Santiago de Cuba, the site of early freedman culture. Son obsessively chronicles mobility as a form of status signaling. For example, the song "Tu veras" (You'll see) ponders where the protagonist will go when his girlfriend arrives: "When my girlfriend comes, I will go to Viejo, I will give her my hat; if I go to Havana, I will bring my girlfriend, I will pack my bag."[142] Another example is Antonio Machín's "A Baracoa me voy" (I'm going to Baracoa), which celebrates hitting the road and heading to Baracoa, even if there is no paved road. Dominican merengue also frequently references mobility through the use of verbs such as *going, arriving*, and *fleeing*; in that genre, conditions of stasis are often vilified.[143] Indeed, the ability to travel unfettered was itself a marker of privilege, signaling that the protagonist was clearly a freedman—in this context, quite an achievement. Along these lines, these popular bacá encounter narratives must be seen as first and foremost modes of braggadocio, as they signal status via freedom of movement, courage, and at times one's prodigious sexual liaisons.[144]

Bacá stories have elements shared with stories about the popular figure of the tíguere, a deeply Dominican character that is a local variant of the trickster, a "good rogue" who subversively rises to become powerful.[145] Unlike St. Miguel, however, the narrator does not defeat his supernatural opponent; instead, he just narrowly escapes it via the age-old dexterity of the disempowered, what Brazilian anthropologist Roberto DaMatta calls the "clever dodge."[146] The tíguere is a survivor who emerges well from any situation, his audacity and courage reflecting the experience and values of the underclasses.[147] The tíguere is a social climber who uses verbal dexterity and "hyperfluency" as a means of social ascent.[148] Unlike the social avenger, he does not seek to destroy his opponent; rather, he aims to shrewdly outmaneuver it.[149] With the protagonist narrowly escaping the claws of the demonic monster, these stories reverse the arrows of the relationship, as the underdog is transformed into a figure of power; they also underscore the uniqueness of the protagonist's individual survival skills, championing street smarts over sheer physical might. The tíguere is thus by definition an individual who succeeds in elevating himself above his peers in a context of informality.[150]

A quintessentially urban "man of the crowd," the tíguere requires the anonymity of the city, but we catch a glimpse of the rural origins of this figure within stories about encounters with the bacá.[151]

Bacá narratives showcase the cunning of the protagonist as well as the pleasure of taking on an opponent in a ritual contest—an important detail, since facing off with an adversary highlights the protagonist's activity (as opposed to passivity) and competition, rivalry, as well as seduction are the masculine troika par excellence.[152] But bacá stories are not the only everyday fora of this kind. Popular Caribbean male pastimes such as reciting the poetry form called décimas (long an everyday art form showcased at the local *colmado* or corner grocery), cockfighting, and playing dominoes also entail facing off with a rival (dominoes also showcases one's command of rule-breaking through *trucos* or tricks).[153] This is also the case for ritual events. In the Máscaras masquerade of Elías Piña, men in teams dress up in makeshift costumes and whip the opposing group in territorial contests. Haitian and Dominican *rará* or *gagá* bands process on Good Friday and engage in ritual stand-offs with other teams.[154] There are also individualist displays of popular male swagger, such as the Gede-inspired *vagabon* or the West Indian rude boy. All these narratives should be seen as speech acts that conform to a broader idiom of Afro-Atlantic masculine displays of male courage and skill.[155] As folklorist Richard Bauman has argued, these verbal displays should be seen as cultural performances that demonstrate the manly valor of the protagonist as he skillfully resists confrontation with a supernatural foe, thus rendering him a "man of worth" and earning him the admiration and respect of the public; in Bauman's words, they are intended to conjure "conspicuous honor for the camera."[156] The need to glorify manhood by being "theatrically heroic" was quite apparent in José's telling of his tale, since as he told the story he stood up and pantomimed his frantic escape from the demonic horse; this was in stark contrast to his body language when he described his family background and work history at the commencement of his life narrative, which was far more subdued and contained.[157] One way men earn their manhood is through altercations with bacá; another is via dogfighting, where, as Evans, Gauthier, and Forsyth have put it, "Gaming, in this context, functions to distribute honor and status among males who have little access to alternative routes for legitimate successes which might allow them to measure up as 'real men.'" Through their bacá foil, plebeian men thus can perform a "masculine ideal" that would be unattainable otherwise.[158]

In addition to their reflection of popular underclass values, these stories can be read as a form of working-class autobiography. Bacá stories are popular across classes, told by day laborers, teachers, and *alcaldes*; however, they are resolutely male stories. Women are familiar with the bacá but do not have violent encounters with them. When women possess them, the bacá are protective. Luisa, a healer in Bánica of Haitian descent, told me that she fashions bacá for clients, and women in Santo Domingo have recounted to me that they kept bacá as power objects to shield them from evil and bad luck.[159] Bacá practices thus reveal a key cultural contrast for gender construction in Latin America. If women secure bacá to shelter themselves (and by extension their children, as part of collective selves), men deploy them to combat rivals and stand out as individuals and thus hone their reputation among their peers.[160] Conflict is foundational to male relationships, and when rupture occurs, it makes itself known through *chismorreo* (gossip, which women help spread, of course). Indeed, if women are loath to engage with bacá directly, they participate in the circulation of bacá narratives either by helping identify them or by spreading the news.[161]

SORCERY AND GENDER

Why the striking gender difference in how women and men model bacá? Relations between humans and their divinities are a projection of social relations.[162] Anthropologist Robert Hertz might argue that it has to do with the cultural tendency toward binaries; thus women are associated with the right hand of the sacred (angelic spirits and rule-making), and men with the left hand (the demonic and rule-breaking), just as the realm of the dead is often imaged as the inverse of society.[163] I would assert, however, that the split within bacá practice in this case has more to do with the patterns of gender in this particular township. Since Bánica is home to the Cofradía of San Francisco, which has long been organized by women and which gives them a direct link to the Catholic Church, women are loath to publicly repeat bacá stories, which the church casts as demonic. Worse still, in a culture of conjuring, merely uttering a bacá's name could summon it.[164] Additionally, middle-class women in Bánica frequently work as nurses and pharmacists, jobs that locate them within the sanctioned domain of medical knowledge, and this may encourage them to keep silent about this phenomenon, which is said to cause illness.

Yet women certainly participate in the shaping and sharing of these narratives in private. For example, one critical issue is identifying the beast as a spirit demon rather than a garden-variety animal, and when men arrive home and are still processing their experiences, women may identify the beast as a bacá.[165]

Yet even if women traffic in bacá stories in the concealed spaces of the kitchen and the bedroom while these narratives are still private gossip and not yet public rumor, these narratives travel along male circuits and sites of discourse. Men recount these stories while butchering meat at market or while relaxing with friends with a beer after work or on Sunday. Religious studies scholar David Frankfurter has called attention to the chains of transmission of "unverified news" in storytelling about the demonic. In recounting these tales, men cast themselves as "heroic, solitary warriors against evil"; their discernment of forces invisible to the majority and their ability to escape those accrues to them a "preternatural power."[166] This expertise locates them almost on a par with the "experts in evil," the Dominican curanderos or Haitian bòkò, who are able to diagnose the invisible forces behind an illness or a string of misfortunes, and accords them access to a significant form of social power.[167]

Brazilian anthropologist Roberto DaMatta has described how the figure of the rogue hero is often established in relation to a foil in a paradigm he describes as triangulation.[168] Even as these narratives centrally concern the ferocity of the supernatural predator and how the protagonist narrowly escapes its clutches through his habilidad or wiles, in the process these stories show off other masculine attributes; for example, the seductive appeal of the protagonist, and hence his sexual potency, is demonstrated by the presence of girlfriends in the tales. (In urban contexts this aspect of tigueraje would be cast as the pursuit of multiple sexual conquests, but in rural settings these extramarital relationships tend to be serial and hence more orderly.)[169] An indication that the girlfriend is a prop to demonstrate the tíguere's sexual agency is indicated by the fact that she is left nameless in the story and thus is not accorded social personhood.[170] In a pattern identified by anthropologist Brendan Thornton, these narratives of supernatural tíguere transgression also enable men who otherwise seek to characterize themselves as hardworking hombres de trabajo (men of work) to have a "residual identity" as tíguere hustlers—hombre hombres—which enables them simultaneously to be respectable and to have a tough male reputation.[171] Through engaging in spirit predation and violent encounters with the ambient dead, they can thus be granted respect among their male peers for their capacity for violence while maintaining the façade of respectability that they need as fathers and heads of household.[172]

A central foil in these narratives, of course, is the monster itself, which establishes the competitive rival that is a key prop of masculinity. As anthropologist Christian Krohn-Hansen has observed, one piece of evidence that courage in the face of an opponent is a key aspect of manhood in the Hispanophone world is the fact that the word *guapo* means both "valiant" and "handsome," indicating that bellicose men are especially attractive.[173] And through their behavior, the ambient dead are themselves imaged as masculine foes par excellence. This is uncannily similar to what anthropologist Todd Ochoa has seen in his work on Palo Monte in Cuba. In this space of interaction with the spirit world, the best *nfumbe* (spirit entities) should be forceful, as he puts it, "overbearing in its dominance, and rebellious in its submission. . . . built, vitalized, and engaged in a struggle for command."[174] Indeed, in Palo Monte the verb for dealing with the *prenda* (spirit cauldron) is *arrear*, the term used to refer to driving mules or cattle, and is an action that requires "aggressive posturing."[175] Anthropologist Stephan Palmié has noted how working the prenda within Palo Monte draws upon the imagery of "force and coercion" from slavery, in which the *nganga* (spirit urn) must be actually beaten to compel it to work.[176] It could also be argued that slavery helped shape an exaggeratedly forceful genre of Black masculinity evident in these practices as well. A potent reminder is that in the West Indies, the very word *spirit* long meant "to kidnap," a practice associated with enslavement.[177] The constant threat from malevolent invisible foes requires a male warrior who can keep these forces at bay.[178] Sociologist Mimi Sheller said that "oppositional militarism" underpinned Haitian politics in the post-emancipation period; one might say this was the case for male everyday relations with the spirit world in the Caribbean as well.[179]

Interestingly, the figure of the tíguere became generalized as a quintessentially Dominican social type in the 1950s during the regime of despot Rafael Trujillo, as political repression became suffocatingly harsh toward the twilight of his thirty-year rule. This period has been described as asphyxiating, as people felt completely trapped by a regime that was now striking previously protected targets such as women and priests.[180] In this context, the tíguere enacted a form of symbolic rebellion that was similar to what British sociologist Dick Hebdige has described for the youth subcultures of postwar Britain, where standing out as an underclass youthful male put someone at risk of clashing with the police. As Hebdige aptly describes it, "Subculture forms up in the space between surveillance and the evasion of surveillance, it translates the fact of being under scrutiny into the pleasure of being watched. It is a hiding in the light."[181]

But developing a reputation as a risk-taker also requires that stories about one's achievements become part of the community rumor mill, which is where the bacá narratives come in handy.[182] The stories' characteristic logic of "binary moralism"—and hence their melodramatic tone—evinces their origins within oral culture and also probably assists them in accruing the necessary symbolic capital so that they are more likely to be retold and thus burnish the reputation of the protagonist.[183] As historian of rumor Luise White has put it, the veracity of these narratives is based not on their truth value but rather on their eloquence, which renders them engaging enough to be retold.[184] The atmosphere of harrowing danger and forceful drama in known quotidian settings likely makes these stories especially compelling and encourages their circulation. As we have seen, stories about successful engagements with ferocious spirit demons in which the protagonist prevails over his supernatural foe also surely burnish the protagonist's masculine aura. As Todd Ochoa describes men's relationships with their power objects in Cuba, which serve as both a foil for and a reflection of the men who keep them: "Prendas and [their] keepers alike revel in the stories of a prenda's stubbornness, rebelliousness, and ruthless despotism."[185] Strong men are as only as robust as their ngangas, it seems. The prevalence of these stories, and their utility in assuaging a wounded masculinity (which is always a nagging threat if you are poor, since other masculine trappings such as fatherhood and a steady job are at best precarious), may also encourage the logic of personalization, in which the stories of others are retold as if the storyteller was the protagonist even if he was not; this would make these akin to exemplary narratives, which articulate a "higher kind of truth to which its hero is the witness."[186]

One aspect of masculinity is being physically imposing, and one could argue that certain forms of spirit predation enhance one's manliness by extending one's body into space.[187] Heroic masculinity frequently involves crafting a larger-than-life persona—for example, through practices available to Haitian sorcerers such as having an invisible battalion of zonbi ready to fight at one's disposal, being able to send a zonbi across the globe, or being able to turn into a massive snake or canine.[188] But within the domain of everyday life, on Hispaniola it has long been the steed that increases one's stature. This may be why the Haitian Creole term for the human host for a deity is *chwal* (horse), a reminder that the horse has long provided a foundational root metaphor; anthropologist Maya Deren notes the popular Haitian saying that "great gods cannot ride little horses."[189] The importance of the horse as a key prop for masculine prowess is a legacy of slavery, which, as historian Hilary Beckles reminds us, entailed "the military defeat and subsequent violent subordination of black males by white men" and thus "the conquest and control of the black male body"; this set men up to assert themselves in the postemancipation period.[190]

BACÁ ENCOUNTERS AS LIFE NARRATIVES

El que nada tiene, nada vale.
He who has nothing is worth nothing.
JOSÉ ALCÁNTARA

Much of the scholarly work on oral history has focused on individuals with histories of protest and struggle that became important emblems of identity and served to refocus their life narratives after key events that transformed them from workers into militants.[191] Labor history was understandably a dominant concern of oral historians who came of age in the 1960s and wished to document labor struggles for which the archival record was biased or absent.[192] And the *testimonio* genre elevated the voices of those with a firmly articulated subaltern political identity in an effort to document political oppression and popular violence.[193] But given the absence of formal labor organization in these frontier Dominican communities outside of relations of kinship and patronage and the prevalence of informal labor, there is no heroic dividend to be derived from one's identity as a worker in this context. Patron-client relations expressed through relations of *compadrazgo* and *apadrinamiento* (godparenthood) do not produce the kind of contestatory political identities that forge mythic types and moral stories found among labor militants; by sharp contrast, they tend to forge ties of vertical identification with and loyalty to social superiors.[194] Notwithstanding national growth rates, today most Bánica residents are subsistence farmers with greatly diminished herds. The cash-starved countryside depends on supplementary income from overseas remittances, a larger percentage of which accrues to female-headed households.[195]

In José's extended oral narrative, he casts the world of work as a place where he lacks agency, where he was a victim of circumstance subject to the whims of family and bosses. This stands in sharp contrast to the backwoods proscenium, where he was a master and commander of his destiny, making his own decisions about where to go and defying his girlfriend's threatening fist.[196] The problem with identifying with one's work is quite apparent at the start of his life narrative, in which José noted that because of his grandfather's—his primary caretaker's—departure, he had to take responsibility for his siblings at age thirteen, which meant that his schooling concluded in the seventh grade; this is a common story within the context of the Caribbean matrifocal family, where men pair up with girlfriends and thus establish multiple households with competing familial obligations.[197] As José explained, even if someone is lucky enough to have a conuco or subsistence plot, products such as yucca, corn, and plantains bring only pocket change at market, since everyone grows them. So he had to travel all over town looking for day jobs unloading trucks or mopping, and as he described it, *luchando* (struggling).[198] The prevalence of unpaid family labor in the countryside contributes to low wages, which, as noted earlier, is compounded in the border region by the abundance of Haitian day labor.[199] The split between José's self and person, his private and public identities, is apparent as well in the fact that he spent less than 14 percent of the interview talking about his work; the overwhelming majority of the interview showcased his bacá encounters. His discussion of his work life lacks specific detail and is interspersed with verbal shields to cover up unpleasantries he would prefer not to talk about. These verbal shields take the form of statements such as "He who has nothing is nothing," "Life is not easy," and "It's not easy to obtain 100 pesos" (about $2); sociologist Erving Goffman would describe such statements as "linguistic covers."[200]

A compounding factor in the reluctance of Dominican men to identify with their work is the denigration of manual labor in postemancipation societies, as well as the erosion of work in the Dominican Republic, where many among the working poor today are forced to rely on the informal sector, popularly termed *chiripeo*.[201] While in urban areas family *microempresas* (microenterprises) such as an arepa stand can provide basic subsistence, this is considerably more difficult in the countryside, where the market is far smaller because people lack discretionary income.[202] In the past, ample access to state lands and collective lands called *terrenos comuneros* knitted clans together through cross-cousin marriage and made for ample land, but land access became very tight during the Trujillo regime due to population growth and the monopolistic policies of the regime, reaching crisis-level proportions in the early 1960s, at which point the traditionally conservative Catholic Church began to speak out in favor of land redistribution.[203] Indeed, President Juan Bosch's support for land reform made him the object of a CIA-backed coup that ousted him from power after just seven months in office. Today 77 percent of all Dominican farms are less than five hectares.[204]

José prefers to pull a veil over his work because engaging in rural day labor for others is considered shameful for men, especially in the context of the Haitian-Dominican border, where many agricultural tasks today are regularly performed by Haitian citizens and Dominicans who are ethnic Haitians; for most of the twentieth century these groups were employed as hyper-exploited *braceros* in the cane fields of the Dominican Republic, a deeply reviled task associated with slavery. Ironically, those with property exude pride in their ability to "improve the land, ripen the tobacco and fatten the pig," notwithstanding the fact that they almost invariably have hired male workers to cultivate the land and do not do so with their own hands.[205] The sense of duty to give back, in which one takes pride in one's land but does not work it, is apparent in rural landowner Ceferina Chaves's comment: "To the poor, one must leave something, so they can have a *divi divi* [a local fruit] of my land, they can have it," a kind of creole version of "Let them eat cake."[206] This attitude is common throughout the post-emancipation Caribbean, where one legacy of slavery has been the notion that working for others is "fundamentally alienating," compounded by the fact that in rendering a worker dependent, it is feminizing.[207]

This is a key reason that hustler figures like the tíguere and the Haitian vagabon, who "work without sweating," are such popular antiheroes today.[208] As art historian Katherine Smith has put it, "The vagabon social type is common throughout the Afro-Atlantic in part because under the system of slavery, idleness was theft. Like the lie that reveals artifice, this act of theft undermined the tenets of slavery through the assertion of willfulness."[209] If under slavery freedom of movement was a privilege enabling access to higher-status work, such as cattle herding, and skilled work such as masonry, tobacco cultivation, dock work, and itinerant sales, after emancipation mobility was curtailed as permits became necessary to move people and animals in the interior, the US occupation instituted corvée labor as a form of punishment, and the Trujillo regime implemented vagrancy laws with the aim of expanding agriculture. In his extended narrative, José evinces a strong sense of victimization as he casts his constant movement to obtain odd jobs as part of his deep fatigue; as he states, "I had to walk a lot and work a lot."[210]

In this context, then, bacá narratives in which poor men reenact encounters with supernatural foes on remote country roads appear to fit within a larger repertoire of transatlantic masculine performances in which plebeian men "flaunt their exclusion" in various ways.[211] Carolyn Cooper has described the bawdy, sexually aggressive speech style of dancehall music, just as Katherine Smith has charted the popular embrace of Gede, the god of sex and death; both offer forms of embodied resistance for disenfranchised young men in Jamaica and Port-au-Prince, Haiti, who may not have regular work but through the lwa (deity) Bawon Samdi can marshal zonbi power to make things happen if needed.[212] But if talk about work highlights one's lack of male agency, by contrast bacá stories showcase it, as the protagonist shrewdly deliberates a course of action, standing up against actors obstructing his way, including bossy girlfriends, violent drunks, and "extraordinary beings" of various types.[213] The problem of one's actual social identity is masked, it seems, by the virtual social identity forged through encounters with bacá, just as the stigma of manual labor and poverty in everyday life is camouflaged through tales of heroism and bravery in the domain of the spirit world.[214]

CONCLUSION

> This race in which the beast was the hunter and the man the hunted
> left a profound impression on my father's mind.
> **TOM REISS** | *The Black Count*

Personal narratives have been said to convey foundational structures that are occluded in polished stories that have been retold many times.[215] Yet what work do the bacá-encounter narratives do, and what kinds of "involuntary memory" do they engage? These narratives might be classed alongside the genre of slave narratives, joining canonical voices of exemplary escapees such as former slaves Esteban Montejo and Olaudah Equiano, except that bacá narratives do not have the structure of progression that those do.[216] Bacá stories are aimless and ambulatory, presenting an "opaque and blind mobility."[217] As forms of memory, they are ephemeral, appearing in flashes, yet their "shock experience" may also provoke trauma.

Given the centrality of mobility in these accounts, they are certainly freedman's tales, but they also invoke a distinct sensation of fugitivity—a sense of being watched and hunted by an invisible force, of an ever-present danger lurking around every corner, one that is hard to discern but is clearly there. In this sense, they reflect the *longue durée* history of the island, one in which Dominican men had the privilege of early freedom compared to their neighbors, but that freedom was constantly at risk, since well into the late nineteenth century freedmen could be abducted into slavery in neighboring Cuba and Puerto Rico. Because of this risk, Dominican men, who have a long history of being skilled hunters, are rendered potential victims of predation.[218] In this sense, bacá stories bear an uncanny resemblance to the specter of slave-catching in postcolonial Sierra Leone, where "marauding spirits" skulk about in the darkness waiting to seize people on country roads.[219] Freud might say that the case of José's horse sighting was similar to the case of a patient who suffered trauma and whose dreams recapitulate the catastrophic incident, but what José experienced was perhaps more akin to a recurring nightmare.[220]

I have argued that as "performative utterances," these narratives are centrally masculine performances of mastery, and thus rituals of rebellion against the deferential script of ceremonial etiquette required of poor men in rural contexts. They enable men like José to, in his own words, "become someone," to claim personhood and forge a masculine identity usually unavailable to the marginalized.[221] Yet these narratives also enable men to reveal weakness, fear, and vulnerability, when doing so in other contexts would cast a shadow on their virility. If metaphor is a transaction across contexts, these popular narratives may be said to be what literary theorist Saidiya Hartman has termed "critical fabulations," which both remasculinize plebeian men, who lack social honor due to their dependence and precarity, and enable them to demonstrate feelings disavowed within hegemonic masculinity, such as fear and uncertainty.[222] Walter Benjamin has noted how the mimetic gift is produced through sensory contact, as well as how it has been expressed in practices of the occult.[223] So we might consider the conjuring of the horse as a form of sympathetic magic that renders the horse a mimetic figuration for José, becoming his alter ego and in a way his spirit double. Much as the nickname Caballo ("Horse") confers a kind of studly strength upon the recipient, the horse apparition revisits a "secretly familiar" visceral bond between equines and humans on Hispaniola that celebrates the freedman's mobility. As Michael Taussig has said of the mimetic facility, "Once the mimetic has sprung into being, a terrifically ambiguous power is established; there is born the power to represent the world, yet that same power is a power to falsify, mask, and pose."[224] These storytelling events enable José to strike a pose as a man of action; he can be, as David Leverenz has put it, "the master of everything not quite seen, dark, and below the belt," but without the tone of elegiac nostalgia or sadism evoked by the US myth of the heroic frontiersman and its myth of "regeneration through violence."[225]

Bacá stories have a blasphemous character since they violate the code of deference—and hence respectability—that governs Dominican everyday life. That is why they are told in private settings among close, trusted friends, especially in a context in which the economy is still controlled by a handful of founding ranching clans who reclaimed this area for stock raising after the Haitian Revolution. But I want to stress that plebeian Dominican men need the bacá just as much as Haitians do; the monster provides a crucial identity prop for poor Haitians and Dominicans on both sides of the border to achieve respect in a context that affords few other means for doing so. Just as the Haitian wizard Ernst Nelson acquires power and esteem through his skills at crafting zonbi that enable him to solve his neighbors' most urgent problems, José's successful evasion of the bacá renders him a successful tíguere fighting off a supernatural foe, thus becoming a man of action as he defies his domineering girlfriend and takes back the road from the spirit demon.[226] In fighting off the bacá, he acquires agency in a way that is not otherwise easily possible in his everyday life, and in doing so he is able to shed the label of "idleness" (holgazanería) that has long haunted Dominican freedmen and subsistence peasants, who due to their access to a feral animal commons could resist wage labor until very late in the game.[227] Per historian Walter Johnson's critique of agency, however, this is not about "preserving his humanity"; rather, as I have argued, it is about crafting a hegemonic masculine profile. This is clearly not a liberal model of selfhood, since José had no choice in the matter, but he rose to the occasion and lived to tell the tale.[228] And he's been telling it ever since.

CHAPTER SEVEN

BECOMING ANIMAL

FOOD, SEX, & THE ANIMAL GROTESQUE

Carnival traditions in the Atlantic world engage in playful parody of fig-ures of authority and stock characters from everyday life. But popular Dominican masquerade traditions avoid elite satire, which is a common feature of Caribbean Carnival, and instead center animals. From the Lechón (pig), with its horns and long snout, to the ebony-clad Cocorí-camo, which brandishes a horse or ox skull, mane, and large teeth, and Roba la Gallina (the chicken thief), whose frame is dwarfed by enormous breasts and buttocks, the invasive species brought by Columbus have been repurposed into playful transvestites and fearsome monsters. But animals also figure importantly in other forms of popular performance. In the 1960s the political opposition imaged freedom in the form of a "liberty ham," and when artist Chiqui Mendoza wanted to portray the campy burlesque *merengue típico* singer Fefita, he portrayed her dancing with free-range goats.[1]

But how do we account for the veritable obsession with the animal within Carnival and beyond in the Dominican Republic? I argue that this fascination with fauna is the result of an intersubjectivity forged by a long history of hunting and ranching, which were essentially forms of predation as well.[2] No wonder bakas have eyes that glow red like animals hunted in the dead of night. But it should also be seen as one of the afterlives of slavery, since "underground" storytelling through animal trickster tales and double voicing is a common feature of Black Atlantic vernacular speech.[3] Animals are an important media due to the relationship between animals and slaves on the plantation where they shared a sense of "fraught proximity" as the enslaved black person and the nonhuman animal were positioned as twin captives in mutual subjugation.[4] As a result, literary critic Joshua Bennett has argued that slaves looked to animals as the promise of life beyond confinement through wildness and flight as the animal became a vehicle for reclaiming one's humanity. If anti-Black racism sought to animalize Black folk, nonhuman animals offered an alternative model of personhood based on empathy and care; this might explain how former slaves seem to have found a model of "becoming human" through becoming animal.[5] Wild boar and cattle also serve as embodied memories of life before state subjugation, when free access to feral pigs, cattle, and goats in the open range monte sustained first runaway slaves and later the free peasantry outside of slavery and plantation labor. This vision is both nostalgic and utopian, since it seeks to conjure the period before plantation agriculture felled the forest, when free-range herds still dominated the interior.

This study has linked baka/bacá spirit demons to the historical process of colonialism and the Columbian exchange, proposing that they should be seen as phantasms of the trauma of conquest. These popular revenant sightings convey experiences of trauma that were masked by "forgetting and dissociation" due to horror as the Amerindian population collapsed; they represent the aporia of "unclaimed experience."[6] Yet in this reworking of past trauma through haunting, Haitians and Dominicans are not alone, of course. Within Palo Mayombe, Cubans also revisit the ravages of slavery through their ritual restaging of colonial slave hunts in what anthropologist Kenneth Routon has described as a "ritual poetics of history." As Routon puts it, "Palo . . . does not so much as memorialize as mimic the social predations and power arrangements associated with the institution of slavery."[7] The excessive mortality of slavery gave rise to practices in which participants work with the dead as a form of visceral empowerment.[8] In Haiti, slavery is remembered and reenacted through ritual work; one might say that slave descendants today enslave spirits as supernatural assistants.[9] The use of canine imagery and horsehair in divination practices and the use of bull horns in Carnival masks also work through the power of mimesis.[10] The Lansè-Kòd of Haitian Carnival draw upon the iconography of power within slavery to craft their fearsome profile, their skin darkened with crude oil, cracking their hemp whips that turn people into animals, just as their secret society counterparts are rumored to do.[11] We have seen how the animals brought by Columbus were perceived as predatory vermin, yet also how these invasive species have been repurposed today as power objects, with bone shards and bull horns harnessed to do ritual work today (figs. 7.1 and 7.2).[12] As Fernando Ortiz has said, "horns have a sacred-magical character. Their sounds keep malevolent spirits away," and sealed with a mirror they are used by Mayomberos for divination and to charge themselves with magical force.[13] But this popular culture of mimesis—of seeking to harness the power of the original through imitation—extends beyond the domain of sorcery and idioms of ritual power and the culture of trauma.[14]

Cuban literary critic Jorge Mañach theorized *choteo*, the Caribbean culture of ribald joking and banter—the popular humor mill that turns despair into laughter—as a form of resilience derived from a history of foreign intervention.[15] I want to suggest that the baka should be located within a popular culture of resistance manifest in cultural performances of symbolic freedom and carnivalesque license rooted in a history of slavery.[16] Haitians and Dominicans fashion themselves as animals within a range of ludic genres, from nicknaming to Carnival costumes, that recreate elements of what historian Gabriel de Avilez Rocha has called "*cimarrón* (runaway slave) ecologies."[17] Haitians and Dominicans may be located on opposite sides of the baka's depredations, but both groups need it as an identity prop that enables men to become popular heroes through playing to win in "rituals of aggression" that burnish their male reputations through bombast and swagger.[18]

Mourning and the elegiac are not the only genres available in the afterlives of slavery; performative practices that embrace and celebrate marronage can also be seen as countermemories of captivity and Black death, "critical fabulations" that refigure the past through conjuring a space of playful exuberance.[19] In this sense, while bacá phantoms do exhibit "repetition compulsion," the Freudian model of mourning does not allow for totems that spark identification and that may well represent a survival strategy.[20] A case in point is the preeminent Dominican Carnival figure Lechón Joyero, which is covered with tiny mirrored embellishments, has spiked horns, and sports the characteristic whip; it is the centerpiece of Carnival in the city of Santiago de los Caballeros. The use of mirrors conforms to Central African Kikongo forms of spiritual protection, which ward off evil through "astonishment," representing "fugitive

7.1 Artist Ronald Edmond's vodou power objects with horns and baby faces, beaded banners called *dwapo*, and sequin-encrusted bottles. When these objects have been prepared, they can be used for sorcery. Marché de Fer, Port-au-Prince, Haiti, 2011. Photo by the author.

7.2 A Haitian altar with a horn with vèvè sacred designs for Ti Karang, on the Day of the Dead. Port-au-Prince, Haiti, 2011. Photo by the author.

specters from a graveyard realm."[21] As art historian Krista Thompson reminds us, due to the anonymity and lack of personhood of blackness under slavery—a fact exemplified by the nineteenth-century bandit termed "El Negro Incognito" (The Incognito Black), who emerged in the wake of the Haitian Revolution—there is a visual politics of bling in the Caribbean.[22] In this light, the Lechón's insistence on being seen through pervasive shine should be seen as a kind of "infrapolitics," a camouflaged form of resistance to anonymity.[23] This chapter considers how the runaway slave and the free-range hunting ecology of feral swine and cattle that long sustained marronage are commemorated through "embodied memories" in popular culture and everyday life.[24]

This study thus far has stressed the way the baka has served to divide the island through forming part of a racial assemblage that casts those of darker hue as the masters of the "dark arts." But as we have seen, it also conjures a shared history that harkens back to the sixteenth-century buccaneering economy, which brought together Amerindian and African runaways with European debt servants in a hunting system on the margins of colonialism. As one of the Lansè-Kòd troupe members, Adescar Sanil, has said, "Carnival is a great way to understand history, especially in our country, Haiti."[25]

MAROON PEASANTRY

The runaway slave has become an iconic figure of martial resistance in the Caribbean. This is due to the violent war of attrition that the Jamaican and Surinamese maroons were subjected to; in the case of Jamaica, it involved importing vicious Cuban dogs of war. For decades maroon communities were forced to defend themselves, becoming "communities at war, fighting for their very existence."[26] The maroon was later redeemed in the twentieth century, becoming an iconic sign of Black resistance, especially in nations with large former slave populations, such as Brazil and Haiti.[27] Due to its predominantly mestizo national identity, however, the Dominican Republic as a nation has not embraced the cimarrón in this way. Yet the fact that sugar only became dominant in the Dominican Republic in the twentieth century, and even then was confined to the southern coast, coupled with low population density and the refuge provided by three major mountain chains, gave rise to a pervasive history of marronage. Indeed, the very term *maroon* was born in the Spanish colony of Santo Domingo. The first African in the New World "escaped to the Indians" after arriving with Governor Ovando in Santo Domingo in 1503. They had traveled to Hispaniola to contend with a rebellion of Indigenous and Spanish miners that had halted production, an affront to which the authorities responded by killing the miners' wives and burning the miners alive.[28] And the Taíno cacique Enriquillo fled to the hills after his wife and mule were stolen from him; there he maintained an insurgent community of indigenes and Africans at large for a decade and a half, and after his surrender the community kept going for another fourteen years.[29] As noted by a French sailor in 1620, the first buccaneer communities of Hispaniola also incorporated African maroons. The sailor came upon a *nègre* and a *marron* by a roasting device they called a *boucan*, and were soon joined by French crew deserters.[30] In an effort to curtail maritime contraband activity, authorities forced the northern coastal populations of Hispaniola to resettle in 1605, yet this move actually enhanced opportunities for escape, since it created a large no-man's-land. Indeed, one might say that the first African slave revolt in the Americas, which took place on Hispaniola in 1521, commenced three centuries of marronage, as the later emergence of intensive sugar plantation agriculture in Saint-Domingue encouraged a slow but steady exodus of runaway slaves and freedmen taking refuge across the border, and in particular across the mountain chain between Neiba and San Juan de la Maguana and the central frontier, which continued through the nineteenth century in response to repressive labor forms and taxation.[31] As historian Anne Eller has shown, maritime maroons also sought refuge from Cuba and Puerto Rico, for slavery raged in those places through the late nineteenth century, while slavery was abolished across Hispaniola in 1822. This may explain the shared figures of Cuban and Dominican Carnival such as Cocorícamo and the large-bowed horns of several masks including the Lechón (fig. 7.3).[32]

If the maroon has not been embraced in Santo Domingo in the same way as it has elsewhere, this is the result of the politics of national identity within a twentieth-century state project of national whitening.[33] But it also has to do with the fact that the maroon, in this case, was not an embattled martial minority. Rather, it seamlessly blended into the colonial-era peasantry, which until the US occupation was characterized by a lack of private property in land and a generalized culture of free-range hunting.[34] This very different history of marronage in colonial Santo Domingo is readily observed in the case of Maniel, a community of maroons

7.3 The Dominican Cocorícamo masquerade in procession. Photo by Mariano Hernández for Rubén Durán, dir., *Cimarrón Spirit: Afro-Dominican Maroon Culture*, (2015). Courtesy of Mariano Hernández.

that lasted over a century in the mountains of Bahoruco, a region that long served as a safe haven for runaway slaves.[35] Spanish authorities sought to reduce this community through various military incursions, but the maroons succeeded in evading them by escaping into the dense forest, by setting traps that maimed their adversaries, and by establishing alliances with the monteros.[36] The bellicose view of the maroon was promulgated by eighteenth-century chronicler M. L. E. Moreau de Saint-Méry, a supporter of slavery who was traumatized by the slave uprising in Saint-Domingue; he portrayed the community as "terrible brigands," and his discussion of the problem of runaway slaves conformed to the Gothic narrative of the Haitian Revolution, in which slave insurgents were cast as predatory savages.[37] The reality of Maniel, however, was very different.

While the governor of Santo Domingo declared his intent on numerous occasions to dislodge the cimarrones of Maniel, he was unable to do so in part because the community appears to have become embedded within the cattle-ranching San Juan Valley through patron-client relations.[38] Early on in the campaign, troops were able to capture seven members of the fugitive community, which at its peak had more than one thousand people, but the maroons (which included one man from Bánica) on several occasions proposed settlement in exchange for peace, only to later evade authorities. The maroon settlements of Maniel and Naranjo expanded dramatically during the Haitian revolutionary insurgency; at one point the Haitian military commander Vincent Ogé even took refuge there. But these "fierce separatists" sustained themselves for decades through forging alliances with local hateros and monteros who served as key intermediaries between them and the state, and they were involved in extensive relations of debt with locals, who clearly relied upon their hunting skills for meat and meat products.[39] Travelers to Saint-Domingue during the Haitian Revolution casually reference the fact that they bought meat and pork tallow from the hunters. The maroon settlement also traded wood with the coastal community of Petit Trou, which was a major contraband depot. Unable to defeat them militarily, Spanish authorities tried to beseech them into settling in a township, offering them land, food for a year, and the right to bear arms and tools (even though Indigenous and African slaves had long been barred from carrying guns); these tactics eventually resulted in their establishment of a town.[40] Maniel and Naranjo were the largest maroon communities, but the eastern part of the Spanish region was long a draw for runaway slaves from Saint-Domingue, a pattern that continued into the nineteenth century as Haitian state efforts to promote export agriculture fueled a trickle of migrants across the border, especially in the central frontier, where entire townships such as Restauración and Guayajayuco were founded by migrants of Haitian origin.[41] The blending of maroon practices into the peasantry is also suggested by François-Richard de Tussac, a botanist, who noted in 1792 the preference for escaped slaves to build their huts deep in the forest.[42]

The pervasiveness of marronage over time, its eventual dispersion, and its embeddedness within the Dominican free peasantry distributed its cultural features throughout society.[43] Hunting is the common denominator that conveys the memory of the cimarrón from the caves and mountains where they took refuge to other sites, such as the military, which relied on hunting skills because soldiers were not allocated provisions, and to the interior communities of freedmen, who relied on hunting as a supplemental protein and income source. Practices convey memories as well as senses and emotional dispositions.[44] From the fact that maroon staple foods such as *víveres* (starchy tubers and roots such as ñame, batata, yautía, and yuca) and pork are such beloved feast foods—which Johnhenry González refers to as part of the "agriculture of escape" since the root crops were grown wild and hidden from authorities—to the cultural proclivity for hunting, the signs of marronage are ubiquitous, though without the race marking characteristic of places where maroons were an embattled minority.[45]

Notwithstanding the official narrative of "Indo-Hispanic identity," many spectral traces of marronage remain.[46] They can be found in place names in the Dominican countryside, such as Angola, a rural parish of Las Matas de Farfán, as well as Congo, La Cimarrona, and El Maniel; some place names honor slave rebels such as Sebastian Lemba, who led a slave revolt in San Juan in 1532.[47] The Morne á Mantegue (Lard Mountain) commemorates the preeminent maroon foods, the feral pig and *mangú*, a dish of mashed plantain.[48] Teeth filing, which formed part of Central African Kikongo male initiation ceremonies and which became popular as part of fierce male self-presentation among Cuban freedmen and especially virile dockworkers, was also prevalent in rural areas of the Dominican Republic into the twentieth century.[49] Another reference to marronage is the word *mambí*, which became a term of esteem for the nineteenth-century Cuban independence war fighters. But the word is derived from the Kikongo word *mbi* and was actually first used on Hispaniola to refer to runaway slaves.[50] Spanish troops deployed during the 1865 Dominican War for Independence brought the term to Cuba, where it came to refer to anyone who defied Spanish authority. The social memory of the runaway slave is also conjured in the feared phantasm the *biembién* (come come), which appears like a runaway slave in the forests around Bahoruco—the site of Enriquillo's revolt—armed with sharp teeth and nails, and which when you approach it attacks like a wild animal.[51] These specters live deep in the wooded hills, and in Haiti they are said to be spirits of the dead, since they lack the ability to speak.[52] And the Bizango secret society of Haiti originated as a maroon organization named for the Bissagos Islands of Guinea-Bissau, which had its own history of marronage, since it was an important site of slave extraction.[53]

Anthropologist Stephan Palmié might describe these signs of fugitivity as ambivalent "moral artifacts," since they conjure respect as well as a certain measure of fear because they represent illegitimate forms of power. But they are also active hauntings, specters of subjugated knowledge that refuse to retreat and that represent a kind of "incomplete capture."[54] It might also be argued that the iconography found in caves where Indigenous slaves and later maroons took refuge reference aspects of cimarrón subterfuge, since the cave walls were frequently decorated with creatures such as bats and owls, which were seen as nocturnal manifestations of souls of the dead by the Taíno; also, of course, cimarrones were forced to move around at night. Many caves, such as the sacred cave of San Francisco in Bánica, continue to be important sites of pilgrimage today.[55]

Help her, Anaisa
They sent a bacá to the poor woman
And at night she turns into an animal
I know it's a spell in animal form
With red eyes, she meows
She also turns into a horse
The spirit of the dead appears neighing.

CUCO VALOY, "Anaisa"[56]

A CARNIVAL OF ANIMALS

French historian Le Roy Ladurie has described Carnival as a "total social fact" that contains economic, religious, magical, and morphological elements.[57] One might say that the centrality of the pig and the bull within Haitian and Dominican Carnival renders those animals national totems, since the central figures are the Dominican Lechón (suckling pig), the Haitian Lansè-Kòd (a figure that turns people into cattle), and the Dominican Cocorícamo and Los Toros, which are fearsome bovines. One indication of the embeddedness of the bull in Dominican popular culture is the fact that cofradia members are sometimes called *toreros* (bullfighters), and a particular genre of sacred song is called *tonadas de toros* (bull tunes), perhaps resulting from the fact that some cofradias historically submitted a tithe to the Catholic Church in the form of cattle.[58] Indeed, Moreau de Saint-Méry elided the distinction between Dominicans and their cattle when he derided the Spanish colony of Santo Domingo as completely degenerate since its people, horses, and cattle were all "shocking mixtures" since they failed to practice selective breeding. He went on to advise the French to recolonize it for its own good so that both the humans and the nonhuman fauna could benefit from "scrupulous attending to the improvement of the race."[59] Linguistic evidence also suggests these animals' associations with the bacá, since the term bacá resonates with *vaca* (cow), and the pigs that came to Hispaniola were called *baquiras*.[60]

As the last of the charismatic megafauna, the bull has long served as an icon of "power, force and leadership" and is the forefather of Caribbean masquerade.[61] Folklorist Robert Nicholls has noted that aggressive horned animal characters in Caribbean Carnival bear a resemblance to the figures in the masquerades of West African peoples such as the Bijugos of the Bissagos Islands, who sport life-size replicas of bull heads during initiation ceremonies and for whom cattle are an important symbol of power and wealth.[62] Horned masks may reference Christian iconography of the devil as a goat as well as the slave trade, since slaves were often ransomed or purchased with cattle.[63] Slavery brought skilled African herders to the Americas, which likely nourished masquerade costumes such as Mocko Jumbie of St. Thomas, which features a horse on stilts and includes a horse skull and cow horns that are often painted red to heighten their ferocious appearance.[64] The Jamaican Horsehead sports a mule skull with a threatening open mouth brandishing large teeth and resembles a Bamana masquerade figure that eats constantly and demands gifts of food as a sign of authority.[65] These masquerade characters carry whips to clear the path for the procession and infuse the ceremony with energy, although the Lechón also inspires laughter, since he is hypersexualized with sausages or bananas swinging from his *morcilla* or rope sausage belt.[66] Whips are also used in certain festival traditions as aural metaphors of force and are intended to appropriate this emblem of power from slavery to create "sonic territorialization" as groups assume control of particular domains; the sound of the whip also conveys transgression.[67] These performances of raw power resonate with Bakongo power figures (minkisi), which may be covered with metal nails.[68] In the Americas, the bull has become a popular means to convey the antisocial "insubordinate outsider," which "embodies masculine values of strength, jocularity, sexual potency, and aggressive retaliation."[69]

In contrast to scholars who emphasize Carnival's rule-breaking aspect, art historian Samuel Kinser has said that Carnival entails an "exemplary . . . enlargement of the everyday."[70] National Carnival has long been controlled by the state, and in Cuba *comparsa* groups would process to and salute authorities, who paid their respects by giving them gifts and would shut things down when fighting ensued.[71] But there are also popular masquerades that occur around Christmas and Easter and that are organized in a more grassroots fashion by communities themselves, rather than being policed by authorities; they are called "maroon carnivals" in the Dominican Republic.[72] The most well-studied is the Dia de Reyes of Cuba on January 6, when the Afro-Cuban cabildos in the nineteenth century processed in costume as *diablitos* (little devils), wearing masks adorned with palm fronds and horns.[73] Another is the Cocorícamo, which wears a cow skull as a mask, a mane of horsehair and palm fronds, and pants covered by a skirt (fig. 7.4).[74] Of all these Carnival figures, Cuban folklorist Fernando Ortiz claimed that Cocorícamo generates the most compelling *maná*—a rush of supernatural force or energy.[75] Cocorícamo derives from the Kikongo word *koko*, which means "spirit"; this may account for how Cocorícamo conjures a visceral kind of identification of both "actualization and anxiety."[76] The word *Cocorícamo* has been absorbed into Cuban vernacular speech as a term for something extravagant, monstrous, terrible, inexplicably mysterious, "extraordinary, ineffable or superhuman," which may implicitly convey popular fear of and reverence for the maroon.[77] Scholars have linked these horned costumes to Africa, yet in the Dominican context, horns may reference marronage, since rebelling slaves at times wore skins and affixed horns to their clothing to render themselves more fearsome alongside their knives and guns.[78] Jamaican maroons carried obeah charms of goat horns, affixed the jawbone of a defeated European to their horns, and wore his teeth as protective talismans around their ankles and wrists.[79] The Afro-Cuban Diablito masquerade processed during an annual celebration called the Fiesta de los Ñames (yam feast).[80] The malevolent baka is also associated with marronage through the maroon festivals of Easter, since recipes to make a baka frequently start with planting an egg in the ground on Viernes Santo (Holy Friday) and since slaves were said to be able to hide from authorities through shape-shifting.[81]

These maroon carnivals have adopted outsider mascots as a means of acquiring respect through illegitimate forms of power as a form of rebellion against the norms of respectability that have long excluded them.[82] Like Batman, the devil became a popular emblem of street masculinity for freedmen.[83] In Panama, Congo Carnival traditions celebrate cimarrón resistance through staging mock battles between good and evil as the figure Devil Mayor leaps across rooftops and he and his minions battle evil enslavers; in Haiti, an effigy of Judas is burned.[84] A polysemic symbol, the whip is an assertion of power, a symbol of resistance to slavery, and a remembrance of slave suffering, and is prominent in popular Carnival

7.4 Cuban Cocorícamo Carnival figure with ox mask with horns. From Fernando Ortiz, *Los bailes y el teatro de los negros en el folklore de Cuba* (Havana: Editorial Letras Cubanas, 1981).

7.5 Los Toros of Monte Cristi, Dominican Republic. Photo by Rubén Durán, Carnival in the Dominican Republic, 2009–10. Courtesy of Artstor.

traditions.[85] In Bánica, men impersonate the devil with grotesque masks that combine animal elements, blackface, wigs, and other detritus; they wear long gowns and furiously whip each other, as also happens in the Toros masquerade of Monte Cristi (fig. 7.5).[86] In Haiti, the Lansè-Kòd camouflage their faces and wear horns to look menacing, and they carry sisal cords as a reminder that slavery is over (fig. 7.6).[87] And in Trinidad, the Devil Band includes staged dance combats.[88] As ethnographer Renée Craft puts it, Congo practitioners have reappropriated the Christian devil and repurposed it as parody as they celebrate self-determination and freedom as a form of "counteraesthetics."[89] Representations of the devil in Latin America often combine a beastly referent with humor to celebrate underdog revenge.[90] And in the Dominican Republic, the devil has become the transcendent character of carnival.[91]

These horned Carnival figures are representations of the Christian devil, but outside of their ability to engage in clandestine telepathic transport and their shape-shifting skills, they bear little resemblance to the terrifying and all-powerful figure of Satan that drove Europe to witch hunts. The Iberian early modern devil was already flawed when it arrived

7.6 Twa Lansè-Kòd (The Three Rope Throwers). Jacmel, Haiti, 1996. Photo by Leah Gordon.

in the Americas. The Dominican Carnival character Diablo Cojuelo represents the Moors who were defeated by St. James, the patron saint of Spain, in an eleventh-century battle and eventually became demons who chased infidels back to church in seventeenth-century Spain. But Diablo Cojuelo was also the title of a seventeenth-century Spanish picaresque novel that featured a rogue antihero from the underclass, thus embodying the slyness of the trickster, "who lives on his wits just short of delinquency," defends himself with "guile and wits," and fails to evolve into a moral person.[92]

The "King of Carnival," Diablo Cojuelo, is said to have a limp due to his fall from heaven, so he is wounded and thus not at all the very powerful being portrayed during the Spanish Inquisition. Perhaps this is why it is often named in a minor key, as in the Afro-Cuban cabildo masquerade

7.7 *Libète: Viv Dyab* (Freedom: Djab Lives), mural in Port-au-Prince, with Haitian ougan who works with Legba, 2007. Photo by Frank Polyak.

Diablito, when little devils process on January 6.[93] As ethnomusicologist Sydney Hutchinson has noted, the fact that he is injured both humanizes him and accords him swagger, while burnishing his mischievous reputation. The devil's lameness also associates him with Legba (who is represented as San Antonio in Dominican vodú), the god of the crossroads, who carries a cane and opens the way (fig. 7.7); the Lechones similarly clear the path for their procession, establishing a perimeter around them through the crack of their whips, as do Yoruba Egungun masqueraders.[94] The offbeat syncopation in merengue típico—the aural version of a limp—is also implicitly associated with blackness, since it is said to come from the Haitian *carabiné*, a couple dance that emerged in the nineteenth century.[95] In keeping with other antiheroes, these minor devils are characterized by acts of "festive laughter," including sexual excess and ritual profanation (the latter includes the celebration of bandits and deserters like a wounded general who fled the Dominican revolutionary war effort to dance instead, and other cowards and deserters).[96] Lewdness also serves as a language of aggression among the Gede spirits of Haiti, who publicly curse people's genitalia on the Day of the Dead, just as Lechón's banana publicizes his sexual prowess.[97]

This "oppositional style," which celebrates rogues and tricksters, has carried over into secular domains of popular culture as well. The 1970s Panamanian rock artist Everardo Sandoya was ascribed the nickname "The Devil."[98] Timba brava, a popular dance music in Cuba, was born in Black working-class neighborhoods and conveys an "untamed 'maroon' identity" through its vulgar lyrics, bold horn instrumentation, and characteristic "percussive attack." Timba brava conveys a maroon aesthetic through male *guaperia* (courage, handsomeness) by flaunting associations between Black people, eroticism, and aggression, a style of strident virility prohibited during slavery.[99] The surge in popularity of Haitian *vagabondaj* (vagabondage) through embracing the raucous and saucy spirits of the dead is a celebration of the oppositional values, as Katherine Smith colorfully puts it, of "vivacity and decrepitude."[100] The vagabon's popularity among former slave populations should not surprise, since as a hustler, he "works without sweating"; he thus embodies "slackness," which is a revolt against middle-class respectability and forms part of the broader corpus of "African-Atlantic transgressive masculinities" such as the Dominican tíguere and the West Indian rude boy, whose key tactic is flirtation and who use the dance floor as their proscenium.[101] The tíguere has become the central figure of Dominican underclass *hombria* (manhood), and it connotes illicit paths to upward mobility, from hustling to sleeping with American tourists.[102] This popular culture of transgression helps explain why drug kingpins have become objects of national fascination; one of these is José Figueroa, "the Pablo Escobar of the Caribbean," who at one point controlled 90 percent of the cocaine passing into the United States and who was long the fugitive most wanted by Puerto Rican and Dominican authorities.[103] As noted in chapter 2, Figueroa escaped from jail and took refuge in the Dominican Republic, and he evaded authorities for a decade through multiple plastic surgeries, payoffs, and subventions of free reggaetón concerts.[104] As Smith has said, "The vagabon and his cohort are revered as antiheroes because they flaunt their exclusion."[105]

As we have seen, feral pigs and cattle long formed the core of an important hunting commons that united free Blacks, plebeian Europeans, and runaway slaves, with the animals becoming "entangled objects" that wove together poor folk across the island. Areas of *crianza libre* (free grazing lands) were often located on the periphery of extensive cattle

7.8 A member of a Dominican Cocorícamo masquerade troup wearing a horse mask. Photo by Mariano Hernández for Rubén Durán, dir., *Cimarrón Spirit: Afro-Dominican Maroon Culture* (2015).

ranches, and hunters would do occasional work for ranchers, such as chasing roaming cattle, when they needed cash; over time a type of sharecropping system arose in which stockmen granted access to hunting on their hatos.[106] Yet the pig and the bull as national totems have strongly contrastive histories as well, since the expansion of the cattle trade to Saint-Domingue, which peaked in the late eighteenth century, reduced the hunting commons. But most importantly, the family pig was a prestige food that was eaten only on special occasions, whereas cattle hides and meat were export commodities; thus the pig, as gift, contrasts with the cow, as commodity. Indeed, the pig was an "inalienable possession" that nourished and provided cash for the family; as a commodity, cattle had an enigmatic "mystical" air of "magic and necromancy," because they were alienated from the labor relations that produced them.[107] The pig is also an important symbol of the divine in Haiti, where it is the prized food for Èzili Dantò, the goddess who embodies femininity and Black rage.[108] Karl Marx wrote that commodities assume a "fantastic form" that conceals the social relations of their production. Yet the Lansè-Kòd, who turn people into cattle, actually reveal the enigmatic secret on which slavery depended.

In a gesture akin to sympathetic magic, Haitian and Dominican men seek to adopt animal characteristics within a range of ludic genres, from Carnival characters to nicknaming practices, that celebrate a free-range cimarrón ethos. This helps explain the exorbitant profusion of animal nicknames. Consider contemporary Puerto Rican recording artist Bad

Bunny; the 1970s *merenguero* Johnny Ventura, who became known as "El Caballo Major" (Big Horse); and even Fidel Castro, who was called "El Caballo." Other popular emblems of male praise are *gallo* (cock) and *león* (lion); these can be doubled up, as in tíguere león. Dominican nicknames are heraldic attributions of masculine respect and tend to veer toward charismatic predators such as the gorilla, dog, shark, and lion. The notorious tíguere (tiger) has become the most important emblem of street masculinity and popular antihero since the 1950s, but "Mule," "Goat," "Burro," and "Old Horse" (*penco*) are common monikers as well. As forms of rebellion against everyday plebeian status, nicknaming practices can be seen as verbal charms, not unlike Amerindian masking practices in which the "warrior's prowess was manifested and articulated through identification with fearsome predators."[109] The quest to "animalize" oneself in this way is an everyday rite of reversal, since Carnival costumes such as Horsehead, Cowhead, and Lechón are centrally manifestations of the animal world that exuberantly celebrate their feral nature through taking over the streets in competitive displays of masculine rivalry (fig. 7.8).[110] If there is any doubt that animal nicknaming represents a male desire to embrace one's inner transgressive spirit, the desire is confirmed by the fact that its opposite is *manso*, which means "timid" and "docile" and can refer to a castrated bull or horse.[111] At times animal nicknames even adopt a jocular tone as forms of "playful profanation," as in "Perrón" (Large Dog).[112] This form of speech play is an important component of *relajarse* (horseplay), typically among men and often accompanied by plenty of alcohol and laughter—a kind of banter that ultimately produces solidarity or *confianza* (trust) among men, drawing upon idioms of deference but in such a way as to invoke an imagined brotherhood of studs.[113]

MONTE ADENTRO (INTO THE DEEP BUSH)

Soy un lobo domesticado
I am a tamed wolf
FRANKIE RUIZ | "Soy un lobo domesticado"

The spirit of the carnivalesque bleeds into popular culture in the Caribbean, especially as it relates to male verbal arts. Folklorist Roger Abrahams set the stage for the discussion of everyday verbal performances of this kind with a description of "speech mas," a feature of Trinidadian

Carnival, in which a captain is elected on the basis of his wit.[114] But his discussion then moves on to quotidian male performance genres such as rhyming and talking bad—what anthropologist Antonio Lauria calls "rituals of profanation"—which occur on street corners and in rum shops and include erotic verbal play as well as banter and gossip.[115] As seen among hip-hop artists, a key component of this male ludic culture are nicknames that serve as "symbolic individuators" and confer a "mock heroic identity on their bearers."[116] They can be expressions of affect and respect or profanation, such as *beisbolero* (baseball player) Ronnie Belliard, who was called "Teletubby," or strongman Fulgencio Batista, who was nicknamed "El Hombre" (The Man) by his followers and "El Negro" (The Black) by the elite who loathed him.[117] And then there is Ernst Nelson, whose name evokes both the historic British admiral as well as a popular spiced rum, Admiral Nelson.

Caribbean nicknames can be extravagant, such as one given to a Jamaican boy who was named after all eleven cricket players of a London team after they scored an important victory.[118] And they can also express braggadocio, such as the case of a 1920s murderer from Villa Mella, a community descended from freed slaves, who was given the moniker "El Bacá" because he was said to have hexed his victim before killing him.[119] They can also be very funny, such as Fermin Mercedes, a candidate running for alderman (*regidor*), whose nickname was "Chupa Rabo" (ass kisser).[120] Cuban writer Jorge Mañach has theorized the way *choteo* or male banter converts everything into "mockery, sarcasm and ridicule," taking nothing seriously, as a form of "metaphysical rebellion," a habit of disrespect for authority resulting from a long history of foreign intervention.[121]

But another reason for the popularity of heraldic nicknaming is certainly slavery, since slaves were often given their owner's name or were refused surnames since "the unnaming and renaming of new arrivants from Africa was, for their masters, an integral part of the act of taking possession."[122] And without acknowledged fathers, slaves lacked the double-barreled last name that is a marker of personhood in the Iberian world: *sin otro apellido* (without a second surname) or its short form, "s.o.a.," became a stigma of illegitimacy and thus a "hidden marker" of race that carried on beyond emancipation.[123] So when a serial killer took control of the Dominican countryside during the Haitian Revolution, no wonder he was called "El Negro Incognito" (The Invisible Black), lacking a name or any form of social personhood.[124] Nicknaming is also a way of taking control of one's public identity, something that has particular salience for former slaves. Naming has been said to be a form of "deep play," but as a "veiled discourse of identity and self-assertion," it can also be a form of "infrapolitics."[125]

The Egungun masquerade of the Yoruba honors the ancestors through personifying them, just as maroon carnival heretically casts the cimarrón as the primordial Dominican forefather. In doing so, it contradicts the ethnonationalism of the Dominican state, which has reigned supreme since the 1920s US occupation and which defines Dominicans as "constitutionally white."[126] Through the language of grotesque realism and the liberating principle of laughter, it creates a "countermemory" by forging a filial connection to a maroon past, and it does so through casting identity via the preeminent maroon food, pork.[127] If the cattle trade served to define a contrast between the two sides of the island, the free-range creole pig did the obverse. It formed part of the household, since it ate table scraps, and was a symbol of commensality, since it is the prestigious feast food served on important holidays and at patron saint festivals; thus it is also a sacred food. If eating blurs the boundary between food and the eater, it should be no surprise that the pig is the star of Carnival, since it casts Dominican men as having unfettered mobility, like the feral creole pigs and the "ham of liberty" of Dominican political caricature. Though it is considered "unclean" in parts of Europe, the pig has been localized in the Caribbean as a highly valued prestige food with near-mythic reverence, one that conveys the magic of the gift, in contrast to other meats, such as beef, which became commodities.[128] Feasts are ritual activities of commensality with condensed meanings, and the pig is the most important sacrificial food for the gods at major events; in Bánica, women from the cofradia of San Francisco come together as a collectivity to prepare massive vats of food for the faithful.[129]

The veritable obsession within popular culture with the pig and the cow appears in the national dishes which are served at Easter and Noche Buena and in the porcine and bovine referents that, as we have seen, are key elements of Carnival costumes. Haiti's national dish, the beloved *soup joumou*, is made from a combination of meats and starches such as maize, plantain, and root vegetables and bears more than a family resemblance to the Dominican *sancocho*—"the country's most cherished dish"—which also showcases a variety of meats alongside yucca, malanga, yam, and pumpkin.[130] But one key point of distinction is the meat selection, since sancocho should have pork and soup joumou should include beef.

The Iberian link to the pig is also enshrined in Cuba, where sancocho is actually a term for pig feed. The other significant difference between these two stews is the national narrative within which they are embedded: Soup joumou is said to have nourished the maroons who fought the Haitian Revolution, whereas sancocho is the *comida criolla* (creole food) par excellence, akin to the storied *ajiaco* (mixed meat) soup of Cuba, which Fernando Ortiz defined as the epitome of transculturation and race mixture.[131] Nor is food the only lingering trace of a cimarrón past; according to Arcadio Díaz Quiñones, so is the Hispanic Caribbean ethos of *bregar* (struggle), which is a kind of resilient stoicism in the face of precarity and suffering born of life on the run.[132] Dominican men's identification with the free-range creole pig is a sign of their subaltern everyday culture of resistance to being tied down or governed by others, which is a key feature of Caribbean manhood.[133] Men dressing as animals is not exactly shape-shifting, of course. However, by traversing the divide between human and animal, it is a celebration of metamorphosis and hybridity—an often unacknowledged feature of the island given the fact that for centuries slaves flowed eastward onto Dominican terrain.

> I had a pig in the kitchen and I lost it
> In the living room, the kitchen, the patio
> Where are you my little pig?
> I had it saved for the party
> Now I wonder where it may be
> Where is the little foot of my piglet?
> Where is the head of my piglet?
> They stole it, they ate it
> I love to care for my pig
> Oh to eat fried pork!
> Give me a piece of that *fritura* (fried meat), Mommy!
> My pig!
> **PEDRITO CALVO**, "El cochino" (The pig)[134]

THE PIG WITH THE GOLDEN ASS

An example of Mikhail Bakhtin's festive laughter of carnival, "ambivalent in its triumph and desire, gaiety and degradation"—and one might add, in its exuberant embrace of transgressive bodily acts such as ravenous devouring and fornication—is the figure of the sow, which is cast as a surrogate woman in drinking tales such as an elaborate cuento I heard in which the Christmas pig became an object of sexual desire. In this story, a man went to pick up a *lechón* (piglet) for Christmas dinner, selecting one with a golden ass (*nalgitas doraditas*). But en route home, he started contemplating its derriere to the point where he could no longer contain himself, and he pulled over to the side of the road, removed the animal from the trunk, and consummated his desire with the *marranita* (piglet) on the side of the road.[135] To be sure, the story was told to an audience of mostly men, was lubricated by plenty of alcohol, and was intended to be hilarious, so this was quite clearly a *relajo* or a *vacilón*—"an exchange of sardonic commentary, off-color jokes, and inventive twists of the vernacular tongue."[136] The story was doubly hilarious due to the novel twist on the sex-in-the-barnyard genre, since here sex occurred with the centerpiece of the Christmas meal, thus offering a conjoining of food and sex genres of the grotesque.[137] In exploring the meanings of tales of sex with animals, I am following historian Reinaldo Román's edict that scholars should not "dismiss the vulgar" out of hand; even sardonic joking commentary of this sort reveals something of the hidden codes of culture that frequently remain occluded in everyday life.[138]

Talk about animal sex must be contextualized within the broader domain of verbal euphemism in the Caribbean, through which talk about sex is often camouflaged through talk about food.[139] Fruit is often used as an erotic trope to disguise sexual desire, with mangos, for example, serving as synecdoches for ripe young girls, as in the song "El Mango" by Charanga Forever in which a woman is chastised for having lost the bloom of youth, thus for no longer being a mango, due to her wrinkles.[140] In many popular songs, fruit is a metaphor for sexual conquest, as well as a frequent form of surreptitious speech about sexual hunger and how men can get carried away by their lusty appetite. And for a man to note this in public actually augments his reputation, since in the words of Peter Wilson, "men are esteemed for their virility, and are granted a freedom which they are expected to exploit."[141] If tropical fruit, juicy and flavorful, is most often chosen as a vehicle for conveying male lust, animals—which are just one step removed from the dinner table in the rural Caribbean, where meat products are frequently purchased live at market—can do some of this work as well. Animal tropes can be references to domination and possession, which are key elements of sexual desire, as when the narrator proclaims he wants to make a woman "his." Romantic liaisons can be referenced as well through the barnyard language of possession, such as being *amarrado,* a term also used to refer to tying up a patio pig or dog.[142] The verb for "to pick," as in "to pick a fruit"—*coger*—is a common slang for a "casual" sex act, its meaning deriving from the popular legitimacy of free access to public produce in the colonial period due to the separation of usufruct claims in Iberian law which parsed cultivation, grazing, and picking rights. A minor reference to the word *coger* is all it takes to allude to sex.[143] To further add to the interface of food and sex, of course, the names of patio animals are frequently used as terms of endearment, such as *pollita,* "chick," for beloved subordinates such as women and children.

Anthropologist Roger Lancaster has argued that in Latin America machismo is a means of structuring power relations between and among men, one in which manhood is contingent upon performing the active role in sexual intercourse. Men gain status by winning sexual contests in which women are the media but not the audience. Value is accorded to those who take the active part in sexual transactions, the object of which is to become an hombre hombre and thus avoid shame.[144] Lancaster's argument, which places the stress within this political economy of male status on playing the active role, downplays the object of desire and lessens the distinction of whether the sex object is male or female. This helps explain why the object of sexual lust can readily be a beast. Of course, Caribbean manhood is dependent upon associations with nature; it is assumed that male desire is natural and cannot be effectively bridled, that—like the feral horses that dominated the interior plains in the seventeenth and eighteenth centuries—men can only rein in their sexual energies to a degree. For this reason, power games and competition are a defining feature of manhood.[145] Wilson claims that the Iberian Caribbean offers the most explicit system of these values, since there "*machismo* is both an absolute and relative measure of a man's worth."[146]

Let us return now to the theme of eating as a metaphor of commensality as well as community malfeasance. As Johannes Fabian has noted, eating is an act of power, and eating alone (*comer solo*) is a strong label of popular opprobrium in the Dominican Republic; meat-eating is also an idiom of male dominance.[147] Indeed, one of the reasons the bacá (and its owner) is so wicked is because it eats alone and selfishly gains at other's expense; if you do not feed it, it will eat you or yours. The fact that eating is so important in this context may be a result of the hunting ethos, within which "relations modulated by that between predator and prey ... makes the act of ingestion a logical operator," as well as the fact that familiarization of animals centrally involves feeding them.[148] As Norton has said, "The essence of making kin is feeding."[149] Catholic Carnival, of course, is followed by a period of abstinence, when meat-eating is prohibited, as followers share the experience of sacrifice that defines Easter (that is where Carnival gets its name: *carne vale*, "farewell to the flesh"). In Haiti, eating is a root metaphor, connoting "abundance, friendship, sex and above all, power"; nourishing the gods is critically important because that is how they obtain the sustenance and strength they need to protect their devotees.[150] Death is expressed as being "eaten," a term that when taken up by cultural outsiders has led to moral panics.[151] Yet witchcraft is often defined by a "poetics of predation" involving taboo forms of flesh consumption.[152] In Sierra Leone, witches are said to roast kebabs of human meat, which anthropologist Rosalind Shaw has argued is a memory of the slave trade, which positioned Europeans as diabolical consumers of African bodies.[153] Due to beliefs about shape-shifting, in Haiti there is widespread popular suspicion about meat due to fears that it could actually be human flesh, so if it foams white—the color of death—when cooked, it must be discarded.[154]

As the anthropologist Clifford Geertz has said, forms of animal masquerade such as Carnival, animal nicknaming practices, and comestible comedy are forms of "deep play" that reveal more than they conceal.[155] I have argued here that animal histories can help explain the central role played by nonhuman fauna within popular cultural forms such as Carnival and storytelling idioms on Hispaniola, where—unlike in Europe and among Dominican elites, werewolves and the "zone of indistinction between beast and man" became the basis for sovereign violence—the figure of the animal is embraced within popular culture since it represents "unfettered possibility and promise."[156] These mimetic representations of furtive animal specters are thus forms of remembrance that have kept alive the possibility of a "fugitive elsewhere" through slavery and beyond.[157] And through consuming their respective national dishes, which feature beef and pork, Haitians and Dominicans in a way eat each other. Thus foodways reveal a more entangled story of national identity on the island, one alluded to in Carmen Boullosa's novel about buccaneering, *They're Cows, We're Pigs.*[158]

The charisma of the baka should be seen as an example of the perennial "allure of evil." Yet it is also a stark reminder that the word *apocalypse* derives from the word for "revelation."[159] An emblem of horror that represents the spirit of capitalism in the Americas, the baka has several layers of meaning. But demonstrating why pigs, cattle, horses, and dogs have become so culturally important as figures of mourning as well as popular puissance requires tracing their material histories as well as their emotional significance.[160] As we have seen, the baka channels histories of trauma and fear, yet as a "veiled assertion of a clandestine countermemory" of marronage and unsanctioned forms of power, it has also become a source of empowerment and delight for Haitian and Dominican men alike, who need this cultural object as an identity prop that keeps alive the promise of freedom. Shape-shifting has long been a technique of escape, enabling popular rebels such as Haitian fugitives Clément Barbot and Benoît Batraville and Dominican outlaws such as El Negro Incognito to elude authorities.[161] Another memory of marronage is the fact that *makandal*, the name of a maroon leader, became the generic term for protective amulets and poisons in eighteenth-century Saint-Domingue.[162] As Bakhtin reminds us, "The most intense and productive life of culture takes place on the boundaries." This is a reminder that we need to listen to these "unauthorized performances" on the Haitian-Dominican frontier a lot more carefully.[163]

NOTES

PREFACE. FROM THE MOUTH OF THE GOAT

1   *Boca del chivo* (goat's mouth) in Dominican Spanish means "gossip." The baka forms part of a "squad" (to quote Herskovits) of spirit demons that includes the *lougawou, galipote, zonbi, djab,* and other supernatural entities. These have received considerably more treatment in Haitian ethnography than in the ethnography of the Dominican Republic but are usually only mentioned in passing. An exception on Haiti is Thylefors, "Poverty and Sorcery," chaps. 6 and 7. See also Hurbon, *Voodoo,* 60; Hurbon, *Le barbare imaginaire*; Sheller, *Consuming the Caribbean,* chap. 5; Rigaud, *Secrets of Voodoo,* 84; Herskovits, *Life in a Haitian Valley,* 239–43, 336, 340, 352; Métraux, *Voodoo in Haiti,* 288–89; Deren, *Divine Horsemen,* 113, 136, 285; Brown, *Mama Lola,* 143; Ackermann and Gauthier, "The Ways and Nature of the Zombi"; Bourguignon, "The Persistence of Folk Belief"; Charlier, *Zombies*; Davis, *Passage of Darkness*; Simpson, "Loup Garou and Loa Tales"; Simpson, "Magical Practices"; Lauro, *The Transatlantic Zombie.* A very similar phenomenon in the Anglophone Caribbean is the duppy or the jumbie, which is mentioned in Hurston, *Tell My Horse,* 43; Fernández Olmos and Paravisini-Gebert, eds., *Creole Religions of the Caribbean*; and Wong, *Jumbie Tales.* For Dominican treatments of the bacá, see Ubiñas Renville, *Historias y leyendas,* 129–39; Ubiñas Renville, *Mitos, creencias y leyendas,* 25–28, 40, 193, 292, 352–55; Labourt, *Sana, sana,* 183–86; Inoa, *Diccionario de dominicanismos,* 29; Krohn-Hansen, "Magic, Money and Alterity," 136; Brendbekken, "Beyond Vodou," 37; Deive, *Vodú y magia*; Roorda, Derby, and González, *Dominican Republic Reader,* 413; Pérez y Pérez, *Algunas,* 13; and García-Cartagena, *Bacá.* The demonic creature of Puerto Rico, the *chupacabra,* which killed animals (which the baka can do as well), is treated in Román, *Governing Spirits*; and Derby, "Imperial Secrets." Davis, *La otra ciencia,* discusses forms of protection from errant spirits in chap. 5; see also Rigaud, *Secrets of Voodoo,* 85, for a discussion of *ougans* (vodou priests) sending and removing spirits. Richman, *Migration and Vodou,* has a chapter on Haitian spirit work that forms

part of the dreaded *petwo* or *pwen* vodou practice; sorcery is also treated in the epilogue. Esteban Deive discusses Dominican witchcraft in *Vodú y magia*, chap. 9. As with *bacá* and *baka*, I use *vodú* for Dominican instances of this religious complex and *vodou* for Haitian ones, although when I quote authors who used alternative spellings I have left those as is.

2 Derby, "Haitians, Magic, and Money." For more on the 1937 massacre, see Derby and Turits, *Terreurs de frontière*; Turits, "A World Destroyed"; Cadeau, *More Than a Massacre*; Paulino, *Dividing Hispaniola*; Bosch Carcuro, *Masacre de 1937*; Myers and Paulino, *The Border of Lights Reader*.

3 Derby, *The Dictator's Seduction*, chap. 6.

4 Derby and Werner, "The Devil Wears Dockers." In this case the bacá appeared in the form of a small black man, as it often does. Herskovits mentions that the dead can be imaged as dwarves in *Life in a Haitian Valley*, 249.

5 See Pires, Strange, and Mello's excellent article "The *Bakru* Speaks." West Indians formed part of the labor force for the Dominican sugar industry in the early twentieth century, and Dominican faith healer Olivorio Mateo's assistant was West Indian.

6 Taussig treats public secrecy in *Defacement*, 5. Perhaps due to a long history of authoritarian rule under the Trujillo and Balaguer regimes and periodic campaigns against vodú, many Dominicans prefer to keep their relationship to the spirit world private, as in the merengue song "La cruz de palo bonito," which contains encoded references to vodú elements such as the palo de cruz (plant of the cross), which offers protection from powerful spirit demons such as bacás and zonbi. The song also indirectly references a practitioner's devotion to St. Antonio (who, as a *lwa*, is known as Legba). See "'La Cruz de Palo Bonito' por Miriam Cruz." Thanks to Raúl Fernández for this reference. For more on similar Caribbean errant spirits, see Crosson, *Experiments with Power*; Paton, *The Cultural Politics of Obeah*; Paton and Forde, eds, *Obeah and Other Powers*; and Ochoa, *Society of the Dead*. A key difference between obeah and vodú/vodou, however, is that in the West Indian nations of Trinidad, Jamaica, and the Bahamas obeah remains illegal today.

7 *Campesino* is the Spanish term for "small cultivator," although some border livestock producers consider it disrespectful. See Bautista, *Si me permiten hablar* (that text spells *bacá* as *vaca*, but the accent and pronunciation indicate that it refers to a spirit demon and not a bovine).

8 Lachatañeré, *¡¡Oh mío Yemaya!!*, a collection of Orisha foundational narratives from Cuba, for example, contains no shape-shifting. How-

ever, within the foundational narrative of the Abakúa secret society in Cuba, a fish is converted into Sikán; see Brown, *The Light Inside*, 46.

9   I discuss this in "Trujillo, the Goat." For example, in popular speech *chivo* has a variety of meanings: It can refer to something that is phenomenal, someone who is nervous, or someone who cannot be trusted. And *chivirica* means "coquettish." Many more of these popular sayings can be found at https://www.tiktok.com/@felixbaezr/video /7358835990401944878 (accessed August 24, 2024). Herskovits mentions Haitian sayings about goats in *Life in a Haitian Valley*, 265.

10   Thus conforming to the Arawak distinction (identified by Santos-Granero) between long-domesticated plants, which are classed as sublime, and the more recently domesticated ones, which are classed as grotesque. See Santos-Granero, "The Virtuous Manioc and the Horny Barbasco." I discuss a similar cultural splitting among Dominicans between gringo and creole chickens in Derby, "Gringo Chickens with Worms."

11   Ricoeur, "Memory—History—Forgetting," 475.

12   Sugar cane was grown during the colonial period, but the Dominican economy was not dominated by sugar, it never had a sugar boom as did Saint-Domingue and Cuba, and sugar remained regionally specific. See González Llana, "Isla de Santo Domingo." On sugar and Cuban deforestation, see Funes Monzote, *From Rainforest to Cane Field*.

13   DeLoughrey and Handley, *Postcolonial Ecologies*, 9. As revenants, they are thus specters of history; see Musharbash and Presterudstuen, "Introduction," 10; Johnson, *Spirited Things*.

14   Anne Eller uses the term "center-island" in *We Dream Together*. For more on the history of Haitian-Dominican relations, see Fumagalli, *On the Edge*; Eller, *We Dream Together*; Nessler, *An Islandwide Struggle*; Walker, "Strains of Unity"; Ulrickson, "'*Esclavos que fueron*'"; Turits and Derby, "Haitian-Dominican History."

15   Alicia Sangro Blasco, personal communication; Beckman, "What's Left of Macondo?" This genre commenced in the Caribbean, however, with Cuban writer Alejo Carpentier's *The Kingdom of This World*, which included runaway slave Makandal's shape-shifting.

16   Hirsch and Spitzer, "Testimonial Objects," 358. For more on Indigenous slavery, see Stone, "War and Rescate."

17   For more on the massacre, see Turits and Derby, "Haitian-Dominican History"; Derby and Turits, *Terreurs de frontière*; Paulino, *Dividing Hispaniola*; Cadeau, *More Than a Massacre*; Hintzen, *De la masacre*; García-Peña, *Borders of Dominicanidad*. Haitians are linked to the "bitter money" derived from cane cutting, which is associated with slavery; see Shipton, *Bitter Money*, and Derby, "Haitians in the Dominican Republic."

18   Quoting Derek Walcott. See Stoler, "Introduction."

19　　　　Diamond, *Collapse*; Wucker, *Why the Cocks Fight*.

20　　　　As monsters typically do; see Cohen, "Monster Culture (Seven Theses)." Krohn-Hansen has argued that bacá narratives forge a divide between Haitians and Dominicans on the island ("Magic, Money and Alterity").

21　　　　Tsing, "Unruly Edges," 144. For works that offer an entangled view of the island, see Matibag, *Haitian-Dominican Counterpoint*; Eller, *We Dream Together*; Nessler, *An Islandwide Struggle*; Fumagalli, *On the Edge*; Mayes and Jayaram, *Transnational Hispaniola*; and Maríñez, *Spirals in the Caribbean*.

22　　　　Smith, "Dialoging with the Urban Dead." Smith and I observed Dominican *curanderos* (popular healers) receiving the spirits through a Barbancourt pour in visits in 2015 with ten healers in Elías Piña. Dominican vodú is treated in Davis, *La otra ciencia*; Andújar Persinal, *Identidad cultural*; and Ripley, *Imágenes de posesión*. Haitian vodou is treated in Deren, *Divine Horsemen*; Métraux, *Voodoo in Haiti*; Richman, *Migration and Vodou*; Brown, *Mama Lola*; and Ramsey, *The Spirits and the Law*. It should be noted that the spirits are called the 21 *divisiones* or *les mistères* or *los misterios* by many practitioners, however, and not vodou/vodú.

23　　　　Meyer, "Religion and Materiality"; Smith, "Dialoging with the Urban Dead"; Gómez, *The Experiential Caribbean*.

24　　　　Although when the highway was built from Thomassique, Haiti, to Hato Viejo, Dominican Republic, motorcycles started appearing more and more. Foul smells can also indicate foul play; I was told that a sign that a Dominican zonbi maker in Elías Piña was up to no good was the horrific odor of his shrine. For more on sensing the spirit world, see Gómez, *The Experiential Caribbean*.

25　　　　Eller, *We Dream Together*.

26　　　　Hinche (Hincha) was located within Dominican terrain through the eighteenth century. Another set of cattle networks linked the elite of Santiago de los Caballeros with Dajabón and Cap-Haitiën, but it is very difficult to cross the Dominican frontier from Pedro Santana to Dajabón, so these were distinct routes. For more on these northern links, see Cassá, "Rebelión de los capitanes." For more on Bánica's colonial past, see Hernández González, *La colonización de la frontera*, 133–45; Mora Oviedo, *Bánica*.

27　　　　For more on Ramírez, see Lundahl and Lundius, *Peasants and Religion*.

28　　　　These beliefs are not uncommon. Caudillos (rural strongmen) Buenaventura Báez and Pablo Mamá were also said to have such protection, as did a rebel leader who called himself Romaine-la-Prophetésse during the Haitian Revolution (Eller, *We Dream Together*, 42; Eller, "Raining Blood," 435; Vanhee, "Central African Popular Christianity,"

259; and Rey, *The Priest and the Prophetess*). There has been extensive intermarriage between these clans, as can be seen in the list of names in Mora Oviedo, *Bánica*, 192–99. This anecdote also is a reminder that the border has long served as a refuge for outlaws from both sides of the island; Baud, "Una frontera—refugio"; Baud, "Una frontera para cruzar," 5–28.

29 Dominican general Valentín Alcántara defected to the Haitian army in the nineteenth century. This view also associates Haitian vodou with the ability to magically generate cash; see Derby, "Haitians, Magic, and Money"; Filan, *Vodou Money Magic*.

30 "The Roots of *La Sentencia*: An Interview with Rachel Nolan"; Wooding, "Haitian Immigrants and Their Descendants." Another border-crossing phenomenon is that the Haiti-based series of clinics Partners in Health has a Dominican partner organization, Socios en Salud, that provides primary health care to Dominicans and Haitians in Elías Piña; see Garry, "Crossing Rivers." For more on cultural mixing on the border, see Derby, "Doña Pico's Story."

31 Altman, "Revolt of Enriquillo."

32 Yingling, "Maroons of Santo Domingo," 27.

33 Clastres, *Society Against the State*; Baud, "Una frontera—refugio"; Baud, "Una frontera para cruzar." The Haitian opposition that ousted Jean-Bertrand Aristide also took refuge in the border area, and crossing the border has long served as a means to escape political authorities, as was the case for Don León Ventura, co-founder of the Palma Sola Liborista community, which sprang up upon Trujillo's death, and the Union Patriotique, a Haitian Dominican organization, formed against the US occupation of Haiti but organized across the border (Martínez, *Palma Sola*; Lundius, *The Great Power of God*; Lundahl and Lundius, *Peasants and Religion*). Today this rather unpoliced area may be a site of drug and human trafficking as well in ways that complicate the link between licit and illicit activity, since some local officials appear to be involved in contemporary illicit trade. See Schendel and Abraham, *Illicit Flows*, 7; Baud and Van Schendel, "Toward a Comparative History of Borderlands"; Baud, "State-Building and Borderlands."

34 For more on the closure of the border due to cholera, see Andrews, "Sinks for the Press."

35 Block, "Healing Waters of the Caribbean."

36 Lundius, *The Great Power of God*; Lundahl and Lundius, *Peasants and Religion*; Bettelheim and Derby, "Olivorio Altars and *Espiritismo*." For more on the crackdown on popular *curanderismo* during the US occupation, see García-Peña, *Borders of Dominicanidad*.

37 Lundius, *The Great Power of God*, 103–12; Lundahl and Lundius, *Peasants and Religion*. There is an image of Bánica's thermal baths in

Moreau de Saint-Méry, "Vue de l'entrée." Martha Ellen Davis describes this region as part of a "mystical geography"; see her prize-winning book, *La otra ciencia*; her edited volume, *La ruta hacia Liborio*; and her documentary, *The Dominican Southwest*. See also Bettelheim and Derby, "Olivorio Altars and *Espiritismo*," and Giovanni Saviño's documentaries about the religious practices of the region: *Misterios, La comarca fija de Liborio*, and *The Culture of Palo*. This region also has *indio* ancestral spirits who live under the water; see Pešoutová, *Indigenous Ancestors*.

38   Pešoutová, *Indigenous Ancestors*, 242–47.

39   Krohn-Hansen, "Magic, Money and Alterity," 134.

40   Sharpe, *In the Wake*. Historian Joseph Miller has noted how "evidence of the past survives, yet it is often indirect, muffled and mixed in complex ways with information from the present"; he also describes anecdotes as an important oral genre in Miller, "Introduction."

41   The course was called "After the Earthquake: Popular Memory as History in Haiti" and was funded by a LASA/Ford Special Project Grant, took place in 2011, and was co-taught with Watson Denis, Teresa Barnett, and Andrew Apter.

42   *Pájaro* literally means "bird," but in this context it is a figure of evil and forms part of a range of avian-related euphemisms for death, such as the owl, which is said to be an *ave de mala suerte*, an omen of bad luck or even death. It is not just the bacá that is frightening to some, however. Fear of the spirit world drives many into evangelical Protestantism and Adventism since Catholicism may be seen as coterminous with vodú/vodou; see McAlister, "From Slave Revolt"; Thornton, *Negotiating Respect*. Thus conversion can serve as a defense against sorcery as well as a license to practice it. It can also be seen as a more powerful form of protection; see Richman, "The Vodou State"; Richman, "A More Powerful Sorcerer."

43   James, *Doña María's Story*, 173.

44   Benjamin, "The Storyteller," 100. On island memories of trauma, see Suárez, *Tears of Hispaniola*.

45   Ricoeur, "Memory—History—Forgetting," 475.

46   Crosby, *The Columbian Exchange*.

47   Ricoeur, "Memory—History—Forgetting," 478. A massive lighthouse, the Faro a Colón, was built by Joaquín Balaguer in 1992 for the five-hundredth anniversary of Columbus's arrival, and Dominican authorities claim that the country houses his remains. See Krohn-Hansen, "A Tomb for Columbus in Santo Domingo."

48   Blanco and Peeren, "Introduction," 11–12; Caruth, "Unclaimed Experience." Jeffrey Alexander has theorized cultural trauma as when "members of a collectivity feel they have been subjected to a horrendous

event that leaves indelible marks upon their group consciousness" ("Toward a Cultural Theory of Trauma," 307).

49   Whitehead, *Of Cannibals and Kings*, 54.

INTRODUCTION. SPIRITS, HISTORY, AND POWER

Epigraph: Boukman Eksperyans, *Libète (Pran Pou Pran Li!)*, Island Records, 1995.

Passages of this introduction were previously published in "Island of the Dead," BBC *History Revealed Magazine*, April 2022.

1   For more on Nelson, see Smith, "Dialoging with the Urban Dead." For more on Haitian secret societies, see Laguerre, *Voodoo and Politics in Haiti*; Davis, *Passage of Darkness*. Secte Rouge and Cochon Gris secret society members are reported to turn into cattle and pigs and then return to human form in Hurston, *Tell My Horse*, 216.

2   This comment reflects the braggadocio I discuss in chapter 7, but in actual fact baka shape-shifting is not random, as Perez y Perez, *Algunas de las creencias y supersticiones*, 13, and others contend. The Haitian term for shape-shifting is *dedoubleman*.

3   Eating is also the idiom for soul removal through witchcraft among the Bakongo; see MacGaffey, *Religion and Society*, 143, 145, 147; Bockie, *Death and the Invisible Powers*.

4   Here is the interview in Creole:

> EN: Moun sosyete Bizango o Sanpwèl kap tounen nan ason, tankou yon kalbas, tankou yon lamp ou yon kart—yo kap tounen sa ki li vle nan tè. Yo kap tounen kochon, yo kap tounen chen. Yo kap tounen bèf ou kochon ou kabrit. Si se kochon, nan sosyete Bizango, ou pa kap manje-li. Yo kap tounen chen. Depi ou fè pati sosyete Bizango ou Sanpwèl, li pèdi anpil bagay, lè ou enskri nan sosyete, lè ou antre nan sa. Si ou gen yon pitit, nan sosyete a, sosyete kap pran piti ou. Sanpwèl manje vyann. Si se moun ki te tounen animal, yo kap manje li. Si ou manje vyann la, fòk ou peye pou li. Ler ou antre nan sosyete sa, yon moun fòk antre ou. Gason ak fanm kap mache nan sosyete sa paske se sosyete Sanpwèl ki rele van. Nan Sanpwèl fanm kap antre. Lè yo fè ceremoni, yo gen yon boutèy espesyal, yon boutèy maji a. Yo gen yon boutèy espesyal—se nam Sanpwèl sa a ki te kontwole sa. Boutèy yo kap tounen nimpò ki animal. Yo kap tounen nan ti chen, ti chat, nan kochon. Tout ce posib. Yo kap ale nimpò ki plas. Nan sosyete Sanpwèl, yo kap ale a Pot-au-Prince o Jérémie ak Sanpwèl. Yo kap ale a Jérémie. Nan yon nuit, sosyete Sanpwèl kap vizite tout Ayiti.

LD: Eske ou kap manje moun nan fòm animal?

EN: Non, paske se nan fòm animal sèlman nan nuit. Si se yon kochon lougawou, se yon malfaitè. Moun Sanpwèl ak moun Bizango se moun malfaitè. Lougawou kap tounen animal e lap tounen kay. Li tounen chat o gwo kochon ou li ka tounen nan gwo bèf. Si ou vann sa nan mache, lap mò. Bèf sa, lè ou manje sa, lap tiye li.

5   Haitians call these practices *maji*. I use the term *sorcery* here with some trepidation since during the colonial period such allegations fueled anti-Black racism and could land African-descended subjects in jail, since *sortilèges* (spells) were outlawed and there were periodic crackdowns against African-derived religions during the US occupation and the Trujillo regime. See García-Peña, *Borders of Dominicanidad*; Ramsey, *The Spirits and the Law*; Paton and Forde, *Obeah and Other Powers*; Paton, *Cultural Politics of Obeah*. However, scholars of popular religion in Brazil, Cuba, and Amazonia, where sorcery is not illegal today, use the term; see Parés and Sansi-Roca, *Sorcery in the Black Atlantic*; Taussig, "History as Sorcery"; Richman, *Migration and Vodou*; Whitehead and Wright, *In Darkness and Secrecy*.

6   By "commodity familiar" I mean spectral manifestations of capitalism—a variant of Marx's commodity fetishism.

7   Smith, "Dialoging with the Urban Dead," 67. This is what Karen Richman has termed the "interpersonal theory of disease" ("Mortuary Rites," 154). On bottles used for wanga or spells, see McAlister, "A Sorcerer's Bottle," 305–22. On illness sent via sorcery, see Farmer, "Sending Sickness," 6–27; Farmer, *AIDS and Accusation*. This function corresponds to the justice logic of assault sorcery; see Crosson, *Experiments with Power*; Charlier, *Zombies*; Davis, *Passage of Darkness*. Elizabeth McAlister treats secret societies and their spiritual work with zonbi in *Rara!*, chap. 3. For Cuban secret societies, see Miller, *Voice of the Leopard*; Brown, *The Light Inside*. I use the Haitian spelling zonbi when referring to its meanings on the island of Hispaniola, and the spelling *zombie* when referring to the Hollywood representations.

8   Skulls and bones are "spirit-embodying" objects; see Thompson, *Flash of the Spirit*, 118.

9   As Crosson has put it in *Experiments with Power*. See also Whitehead and Finnström, *Virtual War and Magical Death*, 20.

10   Dayan, *Haiti, History, and the Gods*, 37; McAlister, "Slaves, Cannibals, and Infected Hyper-Whites," 457.

11   McAlister, *Rara!*, chap. 3; Forde, "Introduction," 2; Lauro, *The Transatlantic Zombie*, 17–18; Hartman, *Lose Your Mother*, 85, 97; Sharpe, *In the Wake*; Patterson, *Slavery and Social Death*.

12   Loichot, *Water Graves*, 12–13; Dayan, *Haiti, History, and the Gods*, 254. Forde calls these "bad deaths" in "Introduction," 5; see also Brown, *The Reaper's Garden*, 248, on "duppies." Richman stresses the importance of mortuary rites in Haiti in "Mortuary Rites," 142.

13   Brendbekken, "Beyond Vodou," 36. The quote from Georges René was taken from a conversation at a ceremony on November 1, 2010—the first Day of the Dead after the 2010 Haitian earthquake. This was a very charged event, of course, since three hundred thousand people had perished as a result of the earthquake.

14   Forde, "Introduction," 4; Routon, "Conjuring the Past," 641; Palmié, *Wizards and Scientists*, 159–200.

15   Brendbekken, "Beyond Vodou," 35.

16   I heard these stories when I arrived in Santo Domingo two weeks after the Haitian earthquake, which occurred in January 2010. The lougawou is gendered female and is typically a woman who turns into a turkey; this accords with the fact that most traveling Haitian vendors are women. For more on these—which are called *brujas* in the Dominican Republic—see Anatol, *The Things That Fly in the Night*; Simpson, "Loup Garou and Loa Tales"; Simpson, "Haitian Magic," 97. The *loup-garou* is also part of French folklore; see Milin, *Les chiens de Dieu*; Smith, *Monsters of the Gévaudan*.

17   Richman, "Mortuary Rites," 147; Kahn, "Smugglers, Migrants, and Demons"; McAlister, *Rara!*, chap. 3; Santos-Granero, "Introduction." In Haiti, pwen has been called a form of sympathetic magic; see Richman, *Migration and Vodou*, 16. Intriguingly, there is an ethnic group in Central Africa called the Baka who are rumored to have shape-shifting abilities; see Köhler, "Half-Man, Half-Elephant."

18   Whitehead and Wright, *In Darkness and Secrecy*, 2–3. Beck, *To Windward of the Land*, discusses the *bolum, baku, bok*, or bakru, xxxi; however, in the West Indies, due to the long history of criminal prosecution of obeah, these forms of magic are seen by some as the work of the devil (Beck, *To Windward of the Land*, 218–19; Paton, *The Cultural Politics of Obeah*; Savage, "Slave Poison/Slave Medicine," as well as other essays in Paton and Forde, *Obeah and Other Powers*; Ramsey, *The Spirits and the Law*; Smith, "Genealogies of Gede"; Wong, *Jumbie Tales*). See Crossons, "What Obeah Does Do" on moral ambivalence toward obeah in Trinidad.

19   Van Berkel, *The Voyages of Adriaan van Berkel to Guiana*. Guyana was a Dutch colony for a time and Amerindians often served as guides there. Thanks to Vikram Tamboli for this citation.

20   I am grateful to an anonymous reader for these etymological insights. For more on sorcery as a form of resistance to slavery, see Garrigus, *A Secret Among the Blacks*; Garrigus, "Like an Epidemic." *Becara* was the

term for "white man" in colonial Jamaica (Thicknesse, *Memoirs and Anecdotes*, 77).

21   On the zombie, see Ackermann and Gauthier, "The Ways and Nature of the Zombi"; Davis, *Passage of Darkness*; Charlier, *Zombies*; Lauro, *The Transatlantic Zombie*; McAlister, "Slaves, Cannibals, and Infected Hyper-Whites"; McAlister, *Rara!*; Sheller, *Consuming the Caribbean*; Derby, "Zemis and Zombies." It is important to note that Black Atlantic religious practices are constantly innovating in relation to new technologies, a point stressed by Sánchez in "Channel-Surfing."

22   Davis, "Afro-Dominican Religious Brotherhoods," 60; Forde and Hume, *Passages and Afterworlds*; Gómez, *The Experiential Caribbean*; Bennett, *Vibrant Matter*. On the US version of the zombie, see Lauro, *The Transatlantic Zombie*.

23   Oliver, *Caciques and Cemí Idols*, 50; Viveiros de Castro, "Cosmological Deixis"; Viveiros de Castro, *From the Enemy's Point of View*; García Garagarza, "The Year the People Turned into Cattle"; Musgrave-Portilla, "The Nahualli"; Sousa, *The Woman Who Turned Into a Jaguar*; Derby, "Zemis and Zombies."

24   Erikson, "Myth and Material Culture," 107; McAlister, *Rara!*, 104. The bottle as spirit container is also referenced in baccoo narratives in Guyana, since the baccoo pelts its adversaries with bottles and bricks; see "Buxton Baccoos Keep Up Attacks on Family." Thanks to Vikram Tamboli for this reference.

25   MacGaffey, "Complexity, Astonishment and Power"; MacGaffey, "The Personhood of Ritual Objects"; Gonzalez, *Maroon Nation*; Roberts, "'Perfect' Lions"; Pratten, *The Man-Leopard Murders*.

26   Viveiros de Castro, "Cosmological Deixis," 470–71; MacGaffey, *Kongo Political Culture*.

27   Crespo Vargas, "Inquisición y artes mágicas," 350; Lewis, *Hall of Mirrors*; Hagler, "Exhuming the Nahualli"; Sousa, *The Woman Who Turned Into a Jaguar*; Norton, *The Tame and the Wild*, chap. 2.

28   Bynum, *Metamorphosis and Identity*, 30.

29   An example of what Farmer has called "sending sickness." The visceral power of jealousy is discussed in Brown, *Mama Lola*; Taussig, *Shamanism, Colonialism, and the Wild Man*.

30   McAlister, *Rara!*, chap. 3.

31   Davis, *Passage of Darkness*, 112–14.

32   On genre, see White, "'They Could Make Their Victims Dull,'" 1383.

33   Simpkins, Johnson, and Brice, "The Makandal Text Network." For more on vodou as resistance during the colonial period, see Pluchon, *Vaudou, sorciers, empoisonneurs*.

34   In Haitian Creole this is called an *angajman*; see Herskovits, *Life in a Haitian Valley*, 242; Krohn-Hansen, "Magic, Money and Alterity." For

another example of devil pacts as explanations for wealth, see Tutino, "From Involution to Revolution in Mexico," 813. For more on devil pact narratives, see Crain, "Poetics and Politics"; Edelman, "Landlords and the Devil"; de la Torre, "The Well That Wept Blood"; Gordillo, "The Breath of the Devils"; Gordillo, *Landscapes of Devils*. Profit made from sugar, which in particular is associated with slavery, is what Parker Shipton describes as "bitter money" in *Bitter Money*.

35 For discussion of stories of zombie labor working at the US-owned HASCO sugar plant in the 1910s, see Seabrook, *The Magic Island*, chap. 2; Richman, *Migration and Vodou*. In his introduction to *The Social Life of Things*, Appadurai also notes that concealment of money flows can give rise to forms of fetishism. Georg Simmel discusses the money form in his essay on secrecy, noting the "unattainable secrecy" its "facilities of dissimulation" enable; see Simmel, "The Sociology of Secrecy," 467.

36 On banana consumption in the United States, see Striffler and Moberg, *Banana Wars*. A prime example of Chiquita's promotion of banana consumption in the United States is *Chiquita Banana's Recipe Book*, which contains thirty-seven ways to incorporate bananas into sweet and savory dishes. Thanks to Elizabeth McQueen for this citation. Zonbi meat is that of a spirit which has been shapeshifted into an animal. For more on zonbi meat, see Bulamah, *Ruínas circulares*, 121–22. It is usually beef but it can be pig or horse.

37 For more on these associations between illicit powers and foreignness, see Pires, Strange, and Mello, "The *Bakru* Speaks," 14; Richman, *Migration and Vodou*, 154; Beck, "West Indian Sea Magic," 194–202, esp. 195; Derby "Imperial Idols"; Weismantel, "White Cannibals"; Weismantel, *Cholas and Pishtacos*; Santos-Granero and Barclay, "Bundles, Stampers, and Flying Gringos." On commodity aesthetics, see Palmié, "Thinking with *Ngangas*," 860.

38 Nash, *We Eat the Mines*; Ferry, *I Am Rich Potosí*; Taussig, *The Devil and Commodity Fetishism*.

39 Wachtel, *Gods and Vampires*, 83.

40 Weismantel, *Cholas and Pishtacos*, 194.

41 Thanks to an anonymous reader for this insight.

42 Personal communication, 2011. The binary moralism of Christianity is also not shared by polytheistic religious systems such as Haitian vodou and Dominican vodú. However, evangelical Protestants and some Catholics may see them as witchcraft. Chakrabarty takes up the problem of translating minority histories in "Minority Histories, Subaltern Pasts."

43 Marx and Engels, *The Marx-Engels Reader*, 324.

44 The term *superexploitation* is from Wald, "Gulf and Western's 'Slave Labor Camp'"; see also Melillo, "The First Green Revolution." This

practice also came to associate Haitians with cane cutting, a debased form of labor associated with slavery, which in turn gave rise to anti-Haitianism; Turits and Derby, "Haitian-Dominican," 43–53.

45   On HASCO, see Seabrook, *Magic Island*, cited in Ramsey, *The Spirits and the Law*; Wald, "Gulf and Western's 'Slave Labor Camp' in Dominican Republic"; Derby and Werner, "The Devil Wears Dockers." These rumors often appear during moments of global economic distress for which the reasons are not clear on the ground, such as the Depression in the 1930s and the debt crisis in the 1970s (when prices shot up overnight for basic commodities under IMF austerity policies, resulting in massive protests).

46   Wareing, "'Violently Taken Away,'" 1–22.

47   Stone, "War and Rescate"; Van Deusen, *Global Indios*.

48   Wheat, *Atlantic Africa and the Spanish Caribbean*.

49   Norton, *The Tame and the Wild*, 77. For Marx, placer mining would be considered merchant capitalism, the antecedent to industrial capitalism.

50   Altman, *Life and Society*, chap. 2.

51   Eagle notes that West Africans were placed in the gold mines of Hispaniola ("The Early Slave Trade," 142). On West African mining, see D'Avignon, *A Ritual Geology*, chap. 2. As she explains, Europeans interpreted this spirit world as the work of the devil. See also McNaughton, *The Mande Blacksmiths*, 48–50, on blacksmiths' secret powers; Herbert, *Red Gold of Africa*; Roberts, "The Place of Iron in African Cosmologies"; Rosen, *Fires of Gold*, 38; and chapter 2.

52   See Bockie, *Death and the Invisible Powers*, which explores Kongo mortuary beliefs and notes that the term *eating* is used frequently to convey spirit predation (see, for example, 46 and 51). Eating is also a motif in popular narratives of diabolism in Gordillo, "The Breath of the Devils," 40–42; Gould, *To Lead as Equals*, 29; Nash, *We Eat the Mines*, ix.

53   McNaughton, *Mande Blacksmiths*, 48–50. Roberts discusses the "'enchanted technologies' of iron smelting" in "The Place of Iron in African Cosmologies."

54   Burnard and Garrigus, *The Plantation Machine*; Richman, *Vodou and Migration*.

55   Taussig, *Devil and Commodity Fetishism*.

56   Palmié, "Thinking with *Ngangas*," 864.

57   Mintz, *Sweetness and Power*. Palo Monte in Cuba also involves a pact; see Palmié, "Thinking with *Ngangas*," 862.

58   Richman, *Migration and Vodou*, 218.

59   White, *Speaking with Vampires*, chap. 1; West and Sanders, *Transparency and Conspiracy*, 6; Derby, "Haitians, Magic, and Money."

60   Derby and Werner, "The Devil Wears Dockers."

61   Richman, *Migration and Vodou*, 154; Smith, "Dialoging with the Urban
        Dead," 78.

62   Richman, *Migration and Vodou*, 224, contrasts the terms *do* and *work* as
        moral antinomies that correspond to the right and left hands of vodou,
        gine versus maji. *Trabajo* is also a term for sorcery in Cuba.

63   Pietz, "The Spirit of Civilization," 29–30.

64   Equiano cited in Woodard, *The Delectable Negro*, 40. Descourtilz men-
        tions that slaves thought they had been captured so that Europeans
        could drink their blood (*Voyages d'un naturaliste*, 25). Turner discusses
        the history of cannibalism narratives dating from slavery in *I Heard It
        Through the Grapevine*, chap. 1. Eating is also an idiom for commodifi-
        cation and inequality in Gordillo, "The Breath of the Devils." Interest-
        ingly, while individual eating is suspect (hence the vilified *comer solo*;
        Mateo, "The 'Eat Alones,'" 373), feeding others is a social good (Rich-
        man, *Migration and Vodou*, 160; Stevens, "Manje in Haitian Culture"). I
        return to this topic in chapter 7.

65   Gomes da Cunha and van Velzen, "Through Maroon Worlds," 256. We
        also heard about a violent baka attack in Carriacou (Grenada) from
        Winston Fleury (personal communication, 2013), so this specter exists
        beyond Hispaniola.

66   Comaroff and Comaroff, "Occult Economies," 282.

67   Rumors about whether Balaguer's longevity in office could be ex-
        plained though mystical protection were fueled through his sister
        Emma, who participated in Santería. In addition, Balaguer was widely
        rumored to have little men who swept spirits away from his home with
        tiny brooms. Bacá rumors could also be registering covert repression
        (denied by the regime as well), as we shall see in chapter 5. For more
        on the Trujillo regime, see Derby, *The Dictator's Seduction*; Turits, *Foun-
        dations of Despotism*; Roorda, *The Dictator Next Door*. On Dominican
        politics, see Hartlyn, *The Struggle for Democratic Politics*.

68   While the topic is beyond the scope of this account, the United
        States, of course, has played a major role in enabling and support-
        ing these regimes starting with the military occupation of Haiti and
        the Dominican Republic by the United States (1915–34 and 1916–24,
        respectively), when the first national armies were created. Rafael
        Trujillo was an officer in the US-trained national guard, from which
        he launched the coup that landed him in office for over thirty years.
        The United States intervened to oust the democratically elected
        regime of Juan Bosch in 1965, and the Duvalier dynasty was sup-
        ported by the United States for its role in keeping communism out of
        the hemisphere. For more on these events, see Renda, *Taking Haiti*;
        Roorda, *The Dictator Next Door*; McPherson, *The Invaded*; Calder, *The*

Impact of Intervention; Gleijeses, *The Dominican Crisis*; Abbott, *Haiti*. Yoder treats Balaguer's use of "sports patronage" to curry favor with the masses through baseball in *Pitching Democracy*, 108.

69   Gregory, *The Devil Behind the Mirror*, chap. 1; Krohn-Hansen, *Jobless Growth*.

70   Krohn-Hansen, *Jobless Growth*, 18.

71   Asmann, "Drug Ring Exposes Massive Money Laundering." The extensive political graft of the PLD since its ascendency in the 1990s came to light in 2017 in the Odebrecht corruption scandal, in which Dominican politicians were exposed as having partaken in some $92 million of illicit profit; see Pineda, "Dominican Republic Arrests Officials." Thanks to Samuel Bonilla Bogaert for bringing this issue to my attention.

72   Hippert, *Not Even a Grain of Rice*; Krohn-Hansen, *Jobless Growth*.

73   For an example of state violence under Balaguer, see Del Pilar Sánchez, "Bosch forma escuela durante polémica."

74   Derby, "Haitians, Magic, and Money."

75   Comaroff and Comaroff, "Occult Economies." This accords with Dayan's assertion that there was a surge in evil spirits in Haiti in the 1990s with the rise of export subcontracting, internal migration, violence, and poverty; see Dayan, "Vodoun, or the Voice of the Gods," 29.

76   Thornton, *Negotiating Respect*, 4.

77   McAlister, "The Militarization of Prayer in America," 2; Thornton, *Negotiating Respect*, chap. 3.

78   Richman, "The Vodou State," 277; Richman, "Religion at the Epicenter."

79   "Pat Robertson Says Haiti Paying for 'Pact with the Devil'"; McAlister, "From Slave Revolt."

80   Richman, "The Vodou State," 281.

81   For example, "Haiti Rumors Woman"; "Aterrador un baca golpea hombre"; "Dicen 'Bacá' atemoriza residentes en Oviedo"; "Aparece un bacá en el paraje Limonae"; "Existen o no existen los Bacá." Davis, *The Dominican Southwest*, includes two interviews about the bacá, clearly demonstrating the fear of this phenomenon on the part of someone who I presume to be a Pentecostalist. For more on evangelical Protestantism in Haiti, see McAlister, "Possessing the Land for Jesus."

82   Jackson, *Paths Toward a Clearing*, 149; West, *Ethnographic Sorcery*, 63. The previous paradigm for understanding identification with animals, of course, was totemism; see Smith, "I Am a Parrot (Red)."

83   West, *Ethnographic Sorcery*, 57; Thylefors, "Poverty and Sorcery in Haiti."

84   Kahn, "Smugglers, Migrants, and Demons."

85   Otten, *A Lycanthropy Reader*, xiii.

86   Csordas, "Embodiment as a Paradigm," 15.

87   Bourdieu, *Outline of a Theory of Practice*, 78.

CHAPTER 1. PRETERNATURALIA: OF TALKING COWS

Epigraph: Cohen, "Monster Culture," 3–25. Thanks to María Elena García for bringing this text to my attention.

Earlier versions of this chapter were presented at the "Thinking with Animals" panel at the Dominican Studies Institute conference in 2020; at the University of California, Irvine in 2015; at the University of Florida, Gainesville; and at the University of Leiden in 2016 where it benefited from commentary by Peter Pels, among others. Some passages of this chapter were previously published in "Zemis and Zombies: Amerindian Healing Legacies on Hispaniola," in *Medicine and Healing in the Age of Slavery*, edited by Sean Morey Smith and Christopher D. E. Willoughby (Baton Rouge: Louisiana State University Press, 2021), and in "Doña Pico's Story and the Long History of the Haitian-Dominican Borderlands," *Revue d'Histoire Haïtienne*.

1   Moreno Fraginals, *El ingenio*; Mintz, *Caribbean Transformations*, Mintz, *Sweetness and Power*.

2   An important exception is Norton, *The Tame and the Wild*, 77 and chap. 3, which underscores the role of livestock in the dispossession of the indigenous population in the Americas.

3   Watts, cited in DeLoughrey, Gosson, and Handley, *Caribbean Literature*, 19; Morban Laucer, "Fauna extinguida."

4   Mychajliw, "On the Extinction (and Survival)." For more on the history of extinctions in Latin America, see Vergara, "Animals in Latin American History."

5   Liliana Dávalos and Miguel Núñez Novas cited in Weisberger, "Humans Doomed Caribbean's 'Lost World.'" Some eastern Caribbean islands have maintained more robust animal populations, but Hispaniola was the launching pad for Spanish colonialism and its violent dispossession.

6   Mychajliw, "On the Extinction (and Survival)." See also Upham, "Past and Present."

7   Benítez-Rojo, *The Repeating Island*.

8   Del Toro, "Foreword," ix.

9   What the Comaroffs and Sanders and West have called an occult cosmology; see Sanders and West, "Power Revealed and Concealed," 6. *Pájaro*, which means "bird," in this context is a generic term Dominicans use to describe the devil or any animal that might be evil,

particularly suspicious ones; see Inoa, *Diccionario de dominicanismos*, 167. As supernatural assistants, baka bear a strong resemblance to the ààlè of Nigeria, which are both agents of a particular individual and mystical power objects; see Doris, *Vigilant Things*, 71.

10 "LD" indicates my follow-up questions.

11 Freud, "The Uncanny."

12 See Freud, "The Uncanny," 219. Thus it fulfills Eliade's criteria of the sacred; Eliade cited in Csordas, "Embodiment," 20. Some Haitians say that the galipote is a Dominican phenomenon found in the border region (Elizabeth McAlister, personal communication).

13 Tortorici, "Visceral Archives of the Body." See also Holland, Ochoa, and Tompkins, "On the Visceral."

14 Herskovits, *Life in a Haitian Valley*, 246. Dunham mentions stories she heard of the eighteen-foot-high red-eyed Gran Boeuf (Great Cow), held by French general Leclerc, who invaded Haiti during the revolution (*Island Possessed*, 250). These changelings have been represented as being able to turn into insects, but this is not part of baka shape-shifting grammar today; for examples, see Cestero, *La sangre*; Carpentier, *The Kingdom of This World*. Jamaica has demonic cattle called rolling calves that have bells and red eyes; see Wong, *Jumbie Tales*. They also appear as horses, as we will see in chapter 6.

15 People may say that these spirit demons can change into anything, but the animal referent is actually very specifically the seed animals brought by Columbus. Rigaud, *Secrets of Voodoo*, 86, mentions dogs and horses as Gede *mystères*. Altman, *Life and Society*, chap. 2, charts the precarity of life on Hispaniola in the early days of conquest.

16 Crosby, *The Columbian Exchange*.

17 Anderson, *Creatures of Empire*.

18 Cohn, *Europe's Inner Demons*; Breslaw, *Witches of the Atlantic*.

19 Guha, *The Small Voice of History*; Tsing, Swanson, Gan, and Bubandt, *Arts of Living*; Nance, *The Historical Animal*; Brantz, "Introduction"; Few and Tortorici, *Centering Animals*. See also Chakrabarty, "Minority Histories, Subaltern Pasts."

20 As in the salsa chorus "Yo tengo una gallina en la casa" (I have a hen at home). Turner, "'We Are Parrots,' 'Twins Are Birds'"; Fernandez, *Beyond Metaphor*, 130. On intimacy and empathy between human and nonhuman animals, see Sanders, "Actions Speak Louder"; Shapiro, "Understanding Dogs"; Norton, "Subaltern Technologies," 30. For a call to consider indigenous meanings of ecologies, see Mancall, "Pigs for Historians."

21 Radcliffe-Brown, "On Social Structure," 36. See Blakley, *Empire of Brutality*, on animals as vehicles of slave dehumanization.

22 Bulamah, "From Marrons to Kreyòl"; Fudge, "A Left-Handed Blow"; Tejera, "Public Enemies."

23   See Williams-Forson on "performance and play" in *Building Houses*, 22; Santner, *Stranded Objects*, 9, 11.

24   Csordas, "Embodiment," 23.

25   Taussig, *Shamanism, Colonialism*, 367; Csordas, "Embodiment," 15.

26   Shaw, *Memories of the Slave Trade*.

27   Bourdieu, *The Logic of Practice*, 56; Roach, *Cities of the Dead*, 10.

28   Benjamin, "Some Motifs in Baudelaire," 114–15.

29   Tsing, Swanson, Gan, and Bubandt, *Arts of Living*, 5.

30   Holland, Ochoa, and Tompkins, "On the Visceral," 395.

31   Bentley, *Dictionary and Grammar of the Kongo Language*; Gordon, *Ghostly Matters*, xix; Trouillot, *Silencing the Past*, 14, 82. On "repressed memory," see Apter and Derby, "Introduction," xv. On the *fukú* or *fucú*, see Díaz, *Oscar Wao*, 1; Inoa, *Diccionario*, 110. This makes the baka a phantasm of what Stoler has called imperial ruination; see her *Imperial Debris*.

32   Stewart and Strathern, *Witchcraft, Sorcery, Rumors, and Gossip*, 30.

33   Stoler, "'In Cold Blood'" 154; Taussig, *Shamanism, Colonialism, and the Wild Man*, 465.

34   White, *Speaking with Vampires*, 41, 51.

35   Corbin cited in White, *Speaking with Vampires*, 81–82.

36   Dimock, *Through Other Continents*; Fuentes, *Dispossessed Lives*, 7. Freud actually uses the term *dregs*; see Freud, *Introductory Lectures*, 31.

37   The island was called La Española during the colonial period but was Anglicized as Hispaniola in the twentieth century. On indigenous demographic decline, see Wilson, *Hispaniola*.

38   Crosby, *The Columbian Exchange*, 75; Rouse, *The Criollo*, 28. Thanks to Stephen Bell for bringing the latter text to my attention.

39   Bishko, "The Peninsular Background"; contrast with Anderson, *Creatures of Empire*, and Mancall, *Nature and Culture in the Early Modern Atlantic*.

40   Bishko, "The Peninsular Background," 496.

41   Even the restrained writer Crosby describes Hispaniola as a "death camp" (*The Columbian Exchange*, 75); Norton, *The Tame and the Wild*, 77.

42   MacGaffey, "Twins, Simbi Spirits"; Deren, *Divine Horsemen*, 38; Métraux, *Voodoo in Haiti*, 152.

43   Sharpe, *In the Wake*, 13, 15.

44   Freud, *Totem and Taboo*, 14.

45   Interestingly, horses in Milot, Haiti, are called camels. Rodrigo Bulamah, personal communication.

46   Alvarez Chanca cited in Deive, *Antología de la flora y fauna*, 36.

47   Crosby, *The Columbian Exchange*, 76.

48   Fernández de Oviedo y Valdés, *Historia general*, 3:79, 2:117. Typically it was feral animals, rather than animals from one's herd, that were

slaughtered for meat. For more on the broader context of the early settler colony, see Wheat, *Atlantic Africa*.

49   Mizelle, *Pig*, 42–43.

50   Exquemelin, *The History of the Buccaneers*, 37.

51   Fernández de Oviedo y Valdés, *Historia general*, 2:42; Exquemelin, *The History of the Buccaneers*, 37.

52   Fernández de Oviedo y Valdés, *Historia general*, 3:80; Marvin, *Wolf*, 7.

53   Karnowski, "A Population of Hard to Eradicate 'Super Pigs.'"

54   Alonso de Zuazo in Deive, *Antología de la flora y fauna*, 39; Crosby, *The Columbian Exchange*, 85. For parallels to New England, where pigs provoked battles between colonists and Amerindians, see Anderson, *Creatures of Empire*.

55   As happened elsewhere, since overgrazing can weaken grasses, favoring the secondary growth of arid-zone thorny plants; see Melville, *A Plague of Sheep*, 99; Crosby, *Germs, Seeds and Animals*, 55; Exquemelin, *The Buccaneers of America*, 28.

56   Crosby, *Germs, Seeds and Animals*, 53–54.

57   García Garagaza, "The Year the People Turned Into Cattle," 32.

58   Pešoutová, *Indigenous Ancestors*, 247. The goat also invokes the Christian iconography of the horned devil, of course. I discuss this resonance in Derby, "Trujillo, the Goat." For more on the illustrated manuscript in figure 1.1, with full digital reproduction, see "Histoire Naturelle des Indes," Morgan Library and Museum, https://www.themorgan.org/collection/Histoire-Naturelle-des-Indes.

59   For more on the role of animals in Spanish colonial domination, see Norton, *The Tame and the Wild*, chap. 3.

60   Johnson, "The Introduction of the Horse," 599; Wright, *The Early History of Cuba*, 29.

61   Padron, "Los caballos de la conquista," 641; Norton, *The Tame and the Wild*, 81.

62   Pagán Perdomo, *Sir Robert H. Schomburgk*, 52. This challenges Todorov's argument in *The Conquest of America*.

63   Tortorici, "Visceral Archives of the Body," 407–37. For more on smell and slavery, see Kettler, *Smell of Slavery*; Kettler, "The Miasmic Theft of Modernity."

64   Las Casas cited in Varner and Varner, *Dogs of the Conquest*, 30–31; Fernández de Oviedo y Valdés, *Historia general*, 2:149.

65   Varner and Varner, *Dogs of the Conquest*, 13–14, 32; Norton, *The Tame and the Wild*, 85.

66   Exquemelin, *The Buccaneers of America*, 39. As *cuir de courdoue*, these were fashioned into wall tapestries and luxe interior furnishings.

67   Padron, "Los caballos de la conquista," 642. Fernández de Oviedo y Valdés was so fascinated by the silent dogs that he brought one to

Panama to see if it would bark there; he also beat and stabbed them to see if he could induce a sound. Gerbi, *Nature in the New World*, 296; Fernández de Oviedo y Valdés, *Historia general*, 3:65–69.

68 The Taíno also engaged in night hunting and skillfully collected fire-flies to light their way (Fernández de Oviedo y Valdés, *Historia general*, 3:180).

69 Crosby, *The Columbian Exchange*, 91. On how sensoria contribute to terror, see Shalhoub-Kevorkian, "The Occupation of the Senses."

70 Charlier, *Zombies*, 88, 95; Padron, "Los caballos de la conquista," 644. Walton mentions the cave of St. Anna near Santo Domingo and another in the center of the country with "many more visible marks of its being used as a species of catacomb"; see Walton, *Present State*, 353.

71 *Horse* is the term for "medium" in Haiti and in Palo Mayombe in Cuba, as is the dog within Cuban Palo Monte; Hurston, *Tell My Horse*; Cabrera, *Reglas de Congo*, 123, 216. Descourtilz describes a wanga or spirit object in the form of a snake with a dog head in *Voyages d'un naturaliste*, 3:114, 156.

72 On the early freedman majority in the Dominican Republic, see Turits, "Slavery and the Pursuit of Freedom"; Turits, *Foundations of Despotism*; Dubois and Turits, *Freedom Roots*.

73 Rupert, *Creolization and Contraband*; Guisti-Cordero, "Beyond Sugar Revolutions"; Deive, *Tangomangos*.

74 Benítez-Rojo, *The Repeating Island*; Burnard and Garrigus, *Plantation Machine*.

75 Evans-Pritchard, *The Nuer*, 48. Philippe Descola has remarked that the forms of animism and "ontological mimetism" he found in Amazonia are shared by herding pastoralists; see his *Beyond Nature and Culture*, 326–37.

76 As Anne Eller reminds us in her important article "Rumors of Slavery" and book *We Dream Together*. Abolitionist David Turnbull's papers record numerous examples of freedmen kidnapped into slavery; see his book *Travels in the West*.

77 Forde, "Introduction," *Passages and Afterworlds*.

78 Turner, *The Ritual Process*, 95.

79 The term "ambient dead" is from Ochoa, *Society of the Dead*. See Del Toro, "Foreword." Not all renditions of the baka and galipote locate them within a larger community of the undead; important exceptions are Davis, *La otra ciencia*, 133–88, and Bourguignon, "Persistence of Folk Belief," 36–46; the latter argues that cannibalism rumors or the logic of sacrifice (mange moun) is the common denominator among these malignant entities. For more on the Haitian trickster par excellence, the Gede, see Katherine Smith, "Genealogies of Gede," 85–101.

80 As in Haiti, where, Richman has argued, fears of vodou can drive
people into evangelical Protestantism; see Richman, "Religion at the
Epicenter"; McAlister, "Possessing the Land for Jesus."

81 Ávila Suero, *Barreras*, 72.

82 JuanMa S. M., personal communication, June 18, 2018. See Simmel,
"The Sociology of Secrecy," 464.

83 I have observed this gendered pattern, but it is not cast this way in
the literature. Roger Lancaster discusses agency versus passivity as
gendered binaries in *Life Is Hard,* chap. 8. On the baka versus the lougawou, see Herskovits, *Life in a Haitian Valley*, 239–43; Wilentz, *Farewell,
Fred Voodoo*. Nocturnal witches eating children appear elsewhere in the
Antilles and have deep roots in European and African folklore. David
Chariandy defines these as "female vampires" in *Soucouyant*, 135. Lewis
and Weismantel discuss implicit gendered meanings in their work on
witchcraft; see Lewis, *Hall of Mirrors*; Weismantel, *Cholas and Pishtacos*.

84 Wynter cited in Weheliye, *Habeas Viscus*, 21.

85 On Haiti in the Dominican religious imagination, see Davis, *La otra
ciencia*, 90. Lara Putnam makes the point that obeah and voodoo are
definitive racial markers in "Rites of Power," 244.

86 *Baraguabael* in Rivero Glean and Chávez Spínola, *Catauro de seres*,
84–85. Yet they also bear a strong resemblance to African spirit gods;
see Douglas, "Animals in Lele Religious Symbolism," esp. 48.

87 Sánchez, "Channel-Surfing," 388–434. The animism-totemism distinction is made by Descola in *Beyond Nature and Culture* and in Viveiros
de Castro, "Cosmological Deixis."

88 Doris, *Vigilant Things*, 16.

89 Geurts describes this as part of "vodu metaphysics" in *Culture and the
Senses*, 191–93.

90 Descola's "predatory animism" or Whitehead's "assault sorcery." A baka
can thus be planted to protect a garden, just as fishermen use clandestine charms to ensure a good catch (Beck, "West Indian Sea Magic," 197).

91 Carpentier, *The Kingdom of This World*; Weaver, *Medical Revolutionaries*, 92; Garrigus, *A Secret Among the Blacks*.

92 Krug, *Fugitive Modernities*.

93 See the Cuban *son* song "Choncholí se va pa'l monte" by Familia Valera
Miranda. Thanks to Raúl Fernández for this reference. While this song
treats lore about the wars of independence and runaway slaves, the
timing is suggestive, since this was written in 1912, just after US sugar
plantations were invading the area, which may have produced a wave
of maroon nostalgia.

94 It is also problematic because, as demonic, it implicitly locates them
within a Christian moral rubric; see Brown, *Mama Lola*, 143; Métraux,
Voodoo in Haiti, 288; Deren, *Divine Horsemen*, 285.

95   Although he was talking about dreams and parapraxes; see Freud, *Introductory Lectures*, 31.

96   Their role as vampires is a signal feature of the lougawou or *soucouyant*; see White, *Speaking with Vampires*; Scheper-Hughes, *Death Without Weeping*; Hurbon, *Voodoo*, 60; Hurston, *Tell My Horse*, 201; Herskovits, *Life in a Haitian Valley*, 246. See also Hurbon, *Le barbare imaginaire*. The figure of the Pishtaco also draws upon a devil pact tale, since Indian fat is said to be used to pay the foreign debt of Peru; see Wachtel, *Gods and Vampires*, 82–83. Accusations of human sacrifice have long been leveled at Haiti; see Forde, "Introduction," 5–6; Ramsey, *The Spirits and the Law*. In Cuba, where Haitians were brought to cut cane in the early twentieth century, Haitians were rumored to have Faustian pacts through their human-made djab spirits, which are also called baka, *démon*, or *lugán* (which may well be a rendition of lougawou); see Rivero Glean and Chávez Spínola, *Catauro de seres*, 192–93.

97   Putnam, "Rites of Power," 243–67; Weheliye, *Habeas Viscus*.

98   Whitten and Torres, *Blackness in Latin America and the Caribbean*, 12–13.

99   Peter Wade discusses the ambivalence of *mestizaje* in *Blackness and Race Mixture*, 1–4.

100   Wilentz, *Farewell, Fred Voodoo*; Massumi, "The Future Birth of the Affective Fact," 53. On Gothic Haiti, see John Savage, "Slave Poison/Slave Medicine"; Hoermann, "'A Very Hell of Horrors'"; Johnson, *The Fear of French Negroes*.

101   Cestero, *La sangre*, 56–57.

102   Edward Long quoted in Brown, *The Reaper's Garden*, 139.

103   Deirdre Cooper Owens discusses black "superbodies" in *Medical Bondage*; Jackson, *Becoming Human*, 13, notes how gender plays an important role in racialization.

104   Tomislav Z. Longinović makes this point for Serbs in Europe in *Vampire Nation*. On Gothic narratives of the Haitian revolution, see Geggus, "Atrocity, Race, and Region." Bosch, *La mañosa*, 125, mentions a protective spell acquired in Haiti that could stave off shape-shifter demons and ambient dead; even in Trinidad, obeah power objects are often called *wanga*, which is a Haitian term (Crosson, *Experiments with Power*). This extends to South America. As Whitten and Torres put it, "The imagery of black Haiti held by mainland South American whites (*mestizos*) suggests an undesirable power of blackness within *mestizaje* that is to be feared and controlled. It suggests a racialist revulsion and spiritual awe of latent and nascent power" (Whitten and Torres, *Blackness in Latin America and the Caribbean*, 1:12–13).

105   See Smith, "Lansetkòd."

106   "Racial assemblage" is from Weheliye, *Habeas Viscus*. See also Whitten and Torres, *Blackness in Latin America and the Caribbean*, 1:13.

107   Silverstein, "The Secret Life of Texts," in Silverstein and Urban, eds.,
        Natural Histories of Discourse, 81–82.

108   Burton, *A Mission to Gelele*.

109   Lewis, *Hall of Mirrors*, chap. 5.

110   Jackson, *Becoming Human*, 4. As do the Huitoto indigenous peoples of
        Colombia. See Taussig, *Shamanism, Colonialism, and the Wild Man*, 133.

111   Weismantel, *Cholas and Pishtacos*, chap. 5 (notwithstanding the fact
        that they are frequently described as black; see 182).

112   Taussig, *Defacement*.

113   Alfred Métraux, quoted in Taussig, *Shamanism, Colonialism, and the
        Wild Man*, 217. I have also heard Americans say that the dogs in Bánica
        are racist and bark at Haitians.

114   Arnold, *Monsters, Tricksters, and Sacred Cows*, 9.

115   Taussig, *Shamanism, Colonialism, and the Wild Man*, 219.

116   For example, Seabrook, *The Magic Island*. As well as during anti-
        superstition campaigns such as the nineteenth-century Bizoton affair.
        See Ramsey, *The Spirits and the Law*, chap. 3.

117   Whitten and Torres, *Blackness in Latin America and the Caribbean*, 1:12.

118   For example, Haitians are cast as a "silent invasion"(quoting Balaguer,
        La isla al revés) in Gautreaux-Piñero, "Lo de Haití."

119   Duara, "Linear History and the Nation-State," 33.

120   Except when the border is closed, as it was after the 1937 massacre
        of ethnic Haitians; see Michel Laguerre's *Voodoo and Politics in Haiti*,
        which argues that Saut D'Eau (Sodo) was created by President Elie
        Lescot in order to provide Haitians with an alternative to Dominican
        pilgrimage sites when their access was cut off after the massacre. I ob-
        served Haitian pilgrims at the Higüey pilgrimage in 1992, and Hurston
        notes Dominicans visiting Saut D'Eau (Hurston, *Tell My Horse*, 228).

121   Richman, "Possession and Attachment," 207; Johnson, *Spirited Things*.

122   Spyer, *Border Fetishisms*, 2.

123   Pietz, "The Problem of the Fetish, I."

124   This observation draws upon interviews conducted with Katherine
        Smith in Elías Piña among ten Dominican curanderos, all of whom ac-
        quired their spiritual powers in Haiti. Taussig, *Shamanism, Colonialism,
        and the Wild Man*. The prostitute anecdote is from Katherine Smith,
        "Le Monde Invisible." Palmié notes that anti-Haitianism and "vigorous
        traffic in magical powers across the Haitian-Dominican border" are
        not mutually exclusive ("Other Powers," 327–28). Martha Ellen Davis
        discusses "mystical geographies" as well as the case of the women who
        sought a Haitian "work" (trabajo) to remove seven spirits that had
        made her ill in *La otra ciencia*, 88–93, 122.

125   This is a totemic logic of identification with a predatory prestige
        animal, which Descola terms "ontological mimeticism" (*Beyond Nature*

and Culture, 325). The term *man-god* is from Román, *Governing Spirits*. Katherine Smith argues that the popularity of the ribald figure of the oversexed underworld trickster Gede brandishing his phallus arose during the US occupation of Haiti, during which time men were disarmed and many were killed by US Marines; see Smith, "Genealogies of Gede," 92. For more on the nahualli, see Hagler, "Exhuming the Nahualli."

126   Cohen, "Monster Culture (Seven Theses)," 19. This claim relates to what Lewis terms the "unsanctioned" realm of witchcraft; see her *Hall of Mirrors*.

127   See Pires, Strange, and Mello's argument about the bakru as an ethnic mediator in "The *Bakru* Speaks."

128   Labat, *The Memoirs of Père Labat*, 168, 175. He is struck by how eager the colonists are to acquire clothing and makes note that they even bought "half rotten thread," which they paid for with new Mexican coin (190).

129   Gutiérrez Escudero, "El hato ganadero," 380; Ulrickson, "'*Esclavos que fueron*.'"

130   Gutiérrez Escudero, "El hato ganadero," 387.

131   Derby, "Haitians, Magic, and Money." Indeed the Latin term *naturalia* refers to goods or kind as opposed to money or the sex organs.

132   Arawak origin myths often include snakes as guardians, however.

133   Rupert, *Creolization and Contraband*, 170.

134   For more on maroons on Hispaniola, see Rocha, "Maroons in the Montes."

135   Morgan, "Slaves and Livestock," 47. He notes that names were also shared between slaves and livestock, and racial meanings bled across varieties of "stock," as it was said that black cattle thrived better in the West Indies than cattle of other colors.

136   For livestock labor and leatherwork in Saint-Domingue, see Garrigus, *Before Haiti*, 78–80. For more on animal labor in Latin America, see Neufeld, "Animal Perspectives."

137   Rupert, *Creolization and Contraband*, 173; Garrigus, "'Like an Epidemic'"; Blakley, "'To Get a Cargo of Flesh, Bone, and Blood.'" Govindrajan discusses human-animal relatedness in *Animal Intimacies*, 4.

138   Lambert, "Master-Horse-Slave," 618–41.

139   Sanders, "Actions Speak Louder," 45–52.

140   For more on animal care in Saint-Domingue, see Weaver, *Medical Revolutionaries*, chap. 5.

141   Mandelblatt, "Pen-Keeping"; Shepherd, *Livestock, Sugar and Slavery*; Silié, *Economía, esclavitud y población*.

142   Edwards, *The History, Civil and Commercial, of the British Colonies*, 3:161; Mintz and Hall, *The Origins of the Jamaican Internal Marketing System*,

19; Trouillot, "Culture on the Edges"; Dubois and Turits, *Freedom Roots*, 91; DeLoughrey, "Yam, Roots, and Rot"; Wynter, "Novel and History."

143   Scott, "Reclaiming Gregoria's Mule," 181–216.

144   For more on animal labor, see Jocelyne Porcher, "Animal Work," 302–18.

145   Franklin, *The Present State of Hayti (Santo Domingo)*; Walker, "Strains of Unity," 41.

146   Scott, "Reclaiming Gregoria's Mule," 193.

147   Anderson, *Mahogany*.

148   Rodríguez Demorizi, *Enciclopedia dominicana del caballo*, 325–26. Thanks to Hélène Cardona for this translation.

149   Rodríguez Demorizi, *Enciclopedia dominicana del caballo*, 85.

150   Orchestra Aragón recorded this classic in the 1940s, but it was likely an earlier composition.

151   Evans-Pritchard, *The Nuer*, 88; Douglas, "Animals in Lele Religious Symbolism."

152   Norton, *The Tame and the Wild*, 115. On mimesis via hunting, see also Viveiros de Castro, "Cosmological Deixis," 472; Whitehead, "Conclusion: Loving, Being, Killing Animals."

153   Candea, "'I Fell in Love.'" For more on companion species, see Haraway, *The Companion Species Manifesto*; Haraway, *When Species Meet*.

154   Eduardo Kohn argues that among the Runa it creates an "ontological blurring"; see his "How Dogs Dream," 7.

155   I heard about these practices in interviews with cattle ranchers; prayers are noted in the list of cures in Ávila Suero, *Barreras*, 94–109. As Baldemiro, a curandero, put it about his special powers (*poderes especiales*): "As a person who God gave a divine light, [as] someone whose hand can be divine. Because I was born and raised on the mountain and when I came down I had these special powers" ("Como una persona a quien Dios le dirigió una luz divina, [como] alguien cuya mano puede ser divina. Porque yo era de la montaña, criado en la montaña y cuando bajé aquí, al lugar, fue haciendo esa obra"; cited in Ávila Suero, *Barreras*, 161). Here he stresses his strong link to the monte, but in the longer interview he also stresses his faith and the saints who direct him in his preparation of baths, teas, and medicinal botellas or decoctions (157). Certain adjectives are also shared between animals and people, such as *travieso* (mischievous). Thanks to Pablo Gómez for calling this to my attention.

156   Frazier's "Law of Contact," paraphrased in Taussig, *Mimesis and Alterity*, 21.

157   Ávila Suero, *Barreras*, 107.

158   Ávila Suero, *Barreras*, 59, notes the curative properties of goat milk. The burro milk incident was recounted to me by Martín Alcántara in

June 2016. His grandfather, who had spent three days "under water" (a popular idiom for how powers of divination and mediumship are acquired), was thrown in jail in Azua, but when he proved his healing skills, he was released by the *guardia* (police). Another case of someone brought back from the dead by a healer is recounted in Ávila Suero, *Barreras*, 91. Sometimes popular healers are called *médico-curanderos* to accord them more respectability given a long history of curandero persecution (Ávila Suero, *Barreras*, 92).

159   Norton terms this "intersubjectivity" in *The Tame and the Wild*, 35.

160   Rodríguez Demorizi, *Enciclopedia dominicana del caballo*, 87; Price, "Fishing Rites," 17.

161   Kohn, "How Dogs Dream"; Kohn, *How Forests Think*.

162   Garrido, *En la ruta de mi vida*, 12. Thanks to Pablo Gómez for translation assistance.

163   Beckwith, *Black Roadways*, 85–86.

164   Bosch, *La mañosa*, 32; "The Letter of Emancipation," in Cabrera, *Afro-Cuban Tales*, 159–62. Thanks to Judith Bettelheim for suggesting this reference to me. The Cuban song "Cuidadito" also references a talking bird (Raúl Fernández, personal communication).

165   Descartes, "From the Letters," 61.

166   Mullin, "Mirrors and Windows," 201–24.

167   Haraway, *Primate Visions*; Ritvo, *The Animal Estate*.

168   Willerslev, *Soul Hunters*, 27.

169   Willerslev, *Soul Hunters*, 83. Thanks to David Sutton for bringing this book to my attention. See also Pedersen, *Not Quite Shamans*; Kohn, *How Forests Think*.

170   Whitehead, "Conclusion: Loving, Being, Killing Animals," 336.

171   Serpell, *In the Company of Animals*, 5.

172   Prestol Castillo, *You Can Cross the Massacre on Foot*; Mora Oviedo, *Bánica*, 178–79.

173   Shanklin, "Sustenance and Symbol," 375–403.

174   As in the title of Averill's book: *A Day for the Hunter, A Day for the Prey*. On the cultural significance of the creole pig in Haiti, see Gordon and Parisio, *A Pig's Tale*.

175   Judith Carney, personal communication, from her reading of Moreau de Saint-Méry, *Description . . . de la partie française*.

CHAPTER 2. THE MYSTERIOUS MURDER OF JAVIER

This essay was presented at the Sugar Conference at the John Carter Brown Library in 2013; at the Department of History, Northwestern University in 2014; at the Department of History, New York University in 2014; at the panel "Transnational Hispaniola" at the annual meeting of the Latin American Studies Association in 2014; and at the conference "Animals, Agency, and Slaving" at UCLA in 2020. It benefited greatly from commentary at these venues, especially from Chip Carey, Karen Richman, Zeb Tortorici, and Tracey Dewart. Special thanks to Judith Bettelheim for her generosity in guiding me through the literature on Caribbean festival arts.

1   Actually refounded, since Bánica was the site of an indigenous *cacicazgo* and was founded in 1504, but many left Elías Piña as the sugar economy dried up due to the Haitian Revolutionary War (1791–1804) and the period of postrevolutionary military incursions from Haiti into the Dominican border, which are detailed in Nessler, *An Islandwide Struggle*. For more on Bánica's history see Mora Oviedo, *Bánica*.

2   News reports wrote of it as a death and not a suicide (perhaps due to the stigma of suicide), even though his wife and son were present at the time and so there was certainly no confusion; see Ney Suero, "Hallan muerto a encargado junta distrital." On sorcery or what is called "sent sickness" in Haiti, see Farmer, "Bad Blood, Spoiled Milk"; Richman, *Migration and Vodou*, 207. As Neil Whitehead reminds us, there is a "cultural plurality of notions of death" (*Dark Shamans*, 40)

3   Taussig, *Shamanism, Colonialism, and the Wild Man*, 394–95. On the baka and jealousy, see Brown, *Mama Lola*, chap. 5.

4   Guisti-Cordero, "Beyond Sugar Revolutions"; Guisti-Cordero, "Sugar and Livestock"; Hernández González, *El sur dominicano*. Rubén Silié has written extensively on the *hato* economy of Santo Domingo; see his essay "The Hato and the Conuco" and his book *Economía, esclavitud y población*.

5   Ulrickson, "'*Esclavos que fueron*'"; Bragadir, "Contested Topographies"; Bragadir, "Shifting Territories," 23–43.

6   Manuel de Azlor quoted in Rodríguez Demorizi, *Viajeros de Francia*, 28.

7   Ginzburg, "Clues," 96–125.

8   Freud, *Jokes*.

9   Seigworth and Gregg, "An Inventory of Shimmers," 1–28; Koselleck, "Terror and Dream," esp. 221.

10   Since they are revenants that suck blood. For the definition of a vampire, see Dundes, *The Vampire*; Whitehead, *Dark Shamans*.

11   White, *Speaking with Vampires*, 50.

12   Seigworth and Gregg, "Introduction," 13. On popular fears of reenslavement on Hispaniola in the nineteenth century, see Eller, "Rumors of Slavery"; Eller, *We Dream Together*; Nessler, *An Islandwide Struggle*.

13   Karl Marx cited in Taussig, *The Devil and Commodity Fetishism*. Hernández González notes that cattle and horses were swapped for

slaves in *La colonización de la frontera*, 151, as does Ulrickson in "'Esclavos que fueron.'" Silié, *Economía, esclavitud y población*, has a chapter on
specie shortage and its impact on the cattle economy.

14   Livingston and Puar, "Introduction," 10. On animism within contexts
        of hunting and pastoralism, see Viveiros de Castro, *From the Enemy's
        Point of View*; Viveiros de Castro, "Cosmological Deixis," 469–88;
        Whitehead, "Conclusion: Loving, Being, Killing Animals"; Descola,
        Beyond Nature and Culture. Beliefs involving shape-shifting are com-
        mon among pastoralists; see Pedersen, *Not Quite Shamans*; Willerslev,
        Soul Hunters; Ingold, "On Reindeer and Men"; Ingold, *The Perception
        of the Environment*. Pels discusses the relationship between animism
        and fetishism in "The Spirit of Matter." Reinaldo Funes Monzote has
        stressed that this early form of Caribbean extensive cattle culture was
        actually hunting since the animals were feral; see Funes Monzote,
        "Cultura ganadera."

15   Río Moreno, *Guerreros y ganaderos I: Caballos y équidos españoles*;
        Río Moreno, *Ganadería, plantaciones y comercio*; Norton, "Subaltern
        Technologies."

16   Palmer, "Land Use and Landscape Change." Grasslands and scrub are
        delimited in the frontier by two large forested mountain chains.

17   López y Sebastián and Río Moreno, "La ganadería vacuna," 37.

18   Alvarez Chanca cited in Deive, *Antología de la flora y fauna*, 37. The
        buccaneers were also avid meat-eaters, as evidenced by a duel that
        erupted over marrow bones; Exquemelin, *The Buccaneers of America*,
        101. For more on elite hunting in Spain, see Norton, *The Tame and the
        Wild*, chap. 1.

19   Fernández de Oviedo y Valdés, *Historia general*, 2:68.

20   Las Casas cited in Frank Moya Pons, *Después de Colón*, 108; Earle,
        The Body of the Conquistador, 44. The Burgos Laws required that the
        indigenes be given a primarily plant-based diet (Moya Pons, *Después
        de Colón*, 88). Interestingly, slaves were given some beef to eat, likely
        since they were valuable commodities (de Echoagoian, cited in Carney
        and Rosomoff, *In the Shadow of Slavery*, 108). On gender and meat
        consumption, see Adams, *Sexual Politics of Meat*.

21   Gerbi, *Nature in the New World*, 279.

22   Las Casas quoted in Moya Pons, *Después de Colón*, 15.

23   Moya Pons, *Después de Colón*, 128–29.

24   Wilk, "The Extractive Economy," 301.

25   Long, *History of Jamaica*, 240; Benítez-Rojo, *The Repeating Island*, 51.

26   Paravisini-Gebert, "'Extinct Through Human Causes.'"

27   Pestana, "Hispaniola," *English Conquest of Jamaica*, 74, 77; contrast with
        Melville, *A Plague of Sheep*.

28   Exquemelin, *The Buccaneers of America*; Curtis, "Masterless People."

29   Benítez-Rojo, *The Repeating Island*, 51; Gutiérrez Escudero, "El hato ganadero," 357.

30   Gutiérrez Escudero, "Contrabando en el Caribe," 73; Gutiérrez Escudero, "El hato ganadero," 380.

31   Jarvis, *In the Eye of All Trade*, 249–52. On the turtle commons of the eastern Caribbean, see Crawford, *The Last Turtlemen of the Caribbean.*

32   González relates this to the creation of *tierras realengas* and later *terrenos comuneros* that allowed usufruct access for hunting; see González, "Monterías y campesinos monteros," 521–29; González, "Hunting and the Free Peasantry"; González, *De esclavos a campesinos*; Rocha, "Maroons in the Montes," 15–35. These collective rights were complex, though, since montería (hunting) rights to wild animals were also recognized and there were *sitios comuneros* dedicated to montería where pigs could be left to forage (González, "Monterías y campesinos monteros," 534).

33   Labat, *The Memoirs of Père Labat*, 175; Exquemelin, *The Buccaneers of America*, 33.

34   Rodríguez Demorizi, *Lengua y folklore*, 308.

35   Exquemelin, *The Buccaneers of America*; Lescallier, "Nociones sobre los principales lugares."

36   González, "Monterías y campesinos monteros," 516–17.

37   González, "Monterías y campesinos monteros," 518–19.

38   Pestana, *The English Conquest of Jamaica*, 84; Exquemelin, *The Buccaneers of America*, 37.

39   Horse: Goodson to Thurloe, 24 January 1655/6, 453. Boiled hides: Ysassi, "Two Spanish Documents (30 April 1656)," Ysassi to brother (31). Proclamation, 26 July 1656. Some evidence suggests that men ate horse even when provisions were comparatively available. See Doyley, Journal, 6v. Prisoners (whom he also worried would spy): Brayne to John Thurloe, 10 January 1656/7, *SPT*, V:778. Fear: Doyley to [Committee on America], September? 1657, f. 144. All from Pestana, *The English Conquest of Jamaica*. Thanks to Carla Pestana for these citations.

40   Labat, *The Memoirs of Père Labat*, 176.

41   González, "Monterías y campesinos monteros," 514.

42   *Catalogue d'objets d'art . . . , meubles, belle tenture en cuir de Cordoue.*

43   Dubois, *Avengers of the New World*, 21.

44   Dubois, *Avengers of the New World*, 19.

45   The system of *pesas* is described in Gutiérrez Escudero, "El hato ganadero," 371; Sánchez Valverde, *Idea del valor.*

46   Hernández González, *El sur dominicano (1680–1795)*, 1:253.

47   Gutiérrez Escudero, "El hato ganadero," 366–67.

48   Gutiérrez Escudero, "El hato ganadero," 354; Bragadir, "Contested Topographies."

49   After Santiago, which had been primarily a site of agriculture and export crops such as tobacco until the cattle boom. See Gutiérrez Escudero, "El hato ganadero," 353, 363, 369; Mora Oviedo, *Bánica*. For more on the history of the border, see Hernández González, *La colonización de la frontera*; Hernández González, *El sur dominicano (1680–1795)*, 2 vols. Until the eighteenth century, Hinche was the most important town in the central frontier (Hernández González, *La colonización de la frontera*, 159).

50   Gutiérrez Escudero, "El hato ganadero," 364. The narrative of cattle theft thus has a long history of use as a cover for other crimes: the 1937 massacre of ethnic Haitians by the Trujillo regime was claimed falsely by authorities to be a rejoinder to border cattle rustling.

51   Gutiérrez Escudero, "El hato ganadero," 354, 358. Cattle were an important source of upward mobility in Saint-Domingue as well and contributed to the social honor of being mounted on a horse. For more on the terrenos comuneros, which were also found in Cuba, see Turits, *Foundations of Despotism*.

52   Gutiérrez Escudero, "El hato ganadero," 374; Moreau de Saint-Méry, *Description . . . de la partie française*, 223, reveals that there were few ranches near the Artibonite sugar zone. Saint Rose, for example, had 3 sugar plantations, 329 coffee plantations, 3 indigo farms, and 2 cattle ranches; see also p. 134 for the north.

53   Gutiérrez Escudero, "El hato ganadero," 380–81. Indian slaves were also traded for livestock; see Stone, "War and Rescate," 51.

54   Lescallier, "Itinerario desde Santo Domingo," 58.

55   Garrido, *En la ruta*, 12. These hatos were often organized as collective property and shares were used for access to montería; see Hernández González, *La colonización de la frontera*, 157; Hernández González, *El sur dominicano (1680–1795)*, 1:136–37.

56   Lescallier, "Nociones sobre los principales lugares," 9, 27.

57   Lescallier, "Nociones sobre los principales lugares," 27.

58   Lescallier, "Nociones sobre los principales lugares," 27; Albert, "Reseña topográfica," 79.

59   Moreau de Saint-Méry, *Description . . . de la partie espagnole*.

60   Exquemelin, *The Buccaneers of America*, 41, 21.

61   Labat, *Nouveau voyages*, 175–77.

62   Similar to other pastoral cultures, where dairy forms an important protein source; Gutiérrez Escudero, "El hato ganadero," 346. Hernández González notes that the diet was principally composed of plantain, sweet potato (batata), milk, and dried meat, but their principal protein source was dairy; they ate meat infrequently (*La colonización de la frontera*, 158–59).

63   Silié, *Economía, esclavitud y población*, 39.

64   Sánchez Valverde, *Idea del valor*, 186–88. This passage is reproduced in
      both Silié, *Economía, esclavitud y población*; and Moreau de Saint-Méry,
      Description . . . de la partie espagnole.

65   Sánchez Valverde, *Idea del valor*, 189.

66   Bernardo y Estrada, *Manual de agrimensura cubana*, n. 254, cited in
      Sánchez Valverde, *Idea del valor*, 195. For more on the montero, see
      Raymundo González's many works on the subject, including *De escla-
      vos a campesinos.*

67   Sánchez Valverde, *Idea del valor*, 192. Valverde felt that only through
      massive slave imports would Santo Domingo improve its lot; see
      Nessler, *An Islandwide Struggle*, 118.

68   Sánchez Valverde, *Idea del valor*, 192.

69   Long, *The History of Jamaica*, 2:85–87.

70   Hernández González, *El sur dominicano*, 1:254–55.

71   Hernández González, *El sur dominicano*, 1:254.

72   Sánchez Valverde, "The Idea of Value," 88–90.

73   Labat, *Voyages aux isles de l'Amérique*, 218.

74   Slaves and cattle appear alongside one another in parish ledgers, for
      example, in Long, *The History of Jamaica*, 2:191.

75   Silié, *Economía, esclavitud y población*, 106.

76   As with all farm animals such as pigs or mules; see Scott, "Reclaiming
      Gregoria's Mule."

77   Thornton, *Africa and Africans*, 135.

78   Sluyter, *Black Ranching Frontiers*, 12.

79   Sluyter, *Black Ranching Frontiers*, 8.

80   Almada, *Brief Treatise*, 11–12.

81   Mitchell, *Blood Sport*, 30.

82   Mitchell, *Blood Sport*, 47–50.

83   Mitchell, *Blood Sport*, 86–88.

84   Mitchell, *Blood Sport*, 89.

85   Coleman, *Vicious*, 11.

86   The term is a Spanish translation from Ernest Hemingway; see Mitch-
      ell, *Blood Sport*, 89–90.

87   Hernández González, *El sur dominicano (1680–1795)*, vol. 2, 108.

88   Jiménez, *Al amor del bohío*, 387–88; Bosch, *La manōsa*.

89   Ubiñas Renville, *Historias y leyendas*, 50.

90   See the novel by Ramón Marrero Aristy, *Over*. On the forma-
      tion of human-companion animal intersubjectivity established
      through interaction and the significance of naming, which endows
      the animal with "virtual personhood," see Sanders, "Actions Speak
      Louder."

91   Louis, *When Night Falls*, 37–40; see also Des Prés, *Children of Yayoute*.
      This is similar to the Dominican prohibition against eating your own

herd; they should remain objects of exchange, and meat was to be hunted from feral animals (Gutiérrez Escudero, "El hato ganadero," 346).

92   Puckett, *Folk Beliefs*, 324.

93   Deive, *La mala vida*, 29.

94   Anne Eller, personal communication.

95   Rigaud, *Secrets of Voodoo*, 157–59.

96   Thompson, "From the Isle Beneath the Sea," 113.

97   Seabrook, *The Magic Island*, 50.

98   Puckett, *Folk Beliefs*, 196. On slave attacks on cattle, see Blakley, "'To Get a Cargo of Flesh, Bone, and Blood,'" 85–111.

99   Puckett, *Folk Beliefs*, 118. I observed this at the *peristil* (vodou temple) Narivéh in Haiti in 2018 with Georges René, Jean-Daniel Lafontant, and Josefine Wallace.

100   For more on the petwo/rada distinction, see Deren, *Divine Horsemen*, 61–62. This is redolent of what Katherine Smith terms the Bizango aesthetic; see Smith, "Lansetkòd," 80. On the incorporation of foreign signs into vodou, see Derby, "Imperial Idols."

101   Bennett, *Being Property Once Myself*, 3.

102   Velten, *Cow*, 31.

103   Gran Toro and Toro Lisa are sometimes called Criminel and form part of the petwo line of dangerous spirits; see James, Millet, and Alarcón, *El vodú en Cuba*, 230. Toro is the head of the petwo line of spirits and is allied with the Bizango secret society (Georges René, personal communication).

104   Beck, *To Windward of the Land*, xxxv; Seabrook, *The Magic Island*, 50.

105   Cited in Cosentino, *Sacred Arts of Haitian Vodou*, 36. Interestingly, both the Cowhead and Horsehead masks of Jamaica have three legs; see Nunley and Bettelheim, *Caribbean Festival Arts*, 54. Celtic influence came from northern Spain.

106   Thompson, "From the Isle Beneath the Sea," 104–6; Ridore, "Yahweh," 135. For more on horns in West Indian Carnival figures such as the Horsehead and within Jonkonnu masquerade, which are adorned with mule skulls and tusks of boars and oxen and which may date from the Spanish era in Jamaica (although Bettelheim and Nunley link this to masking traditions in Mali, where pastoralism is also prevalent, and British masquerades that include a horse skull), see Nunley and Bettelheim, *Caribbean Festival Arts*, 4; Nicholls, *The Jumbies' Playing Ground*, which traces the use of horns to Guinea Bissau, where cattle were a symbol of "wealth and power" (149–50).

107   The Cocorícamo masquerade is also found in Cuba. The word *Cocorícamo* is derived from the Kikongo and Yoruba words *koko* and *eri oko*; see Ortiz, *Nuevo catauro*, 147. For more on horned masks, see Nunley

and Bettelheim, *Caribbean Festival Arts*, 47; Kinser, *Carnival, American Style*, 207.

108   Kinser, *Carnival, American Style*, 211; Agamben, *Homo Sacer*, 105.

109   Leach, "Anthropological Aspects of Language," 158.

110   Kinser, *Carnival, American Style*, 210; Hutchinson, "'A Limp with Rhythm,'" 98.

111   See Lomax, *Alan Lomax in Haiti*, for evidence of bull sacrifice in Haiti in the 1930s. The need in Haiti for a steer for sacrifice is mentioned in Richman, *Migration and Vodou*, 254, and Deren, *Divine Horsemen*, 199, but I am not aware of cattle being used in sacrifice in the Dominican Republic.

112   Evans-Pritchard, "The Sacrificial Role of Cattle," 191. He suggests that this is effected through the laying on of hands, which is significant because faith healers in the Dominican countryside heal both people and animals through the laying on of hands (interview, Martín Alcántara, 2017). A large pig is the sacrificial animal of choice for the feast of San Francisco in Bánica, for example, and a black pig is the food of choice for Èzili Dantò, the quintessential mother figure in Haiti; see Gordon and Parisio, *A Pig's Tale*.

113   Simmel, "The Stranger," 402–8; Leach, "Anthropological Aspects," 156.

114   Online Etymological Dictionary, s.v. "cattle," https://www.etymonline .com/search?q=cattle.

115   As in tales of demonic cows in Colombia, Nicaragua, Mexico, and Jamaica—all sites of extensive cattle ranching. See Edelman, "Landlords and the Devil"; Gould, *To Lead as Equals*; García Garagarza, "The Year the People Turned Into Cattle." Martha Beckwith noted that "talking cows are an omen of death" in Jamaica in her *Black Roadways*, 85.

116   Marx and Engels, *The Marx-Engels Reader*, 321; Douglas, *Natural Symbols*.

117   Lévi-Strauss, *The Raw and the Cooked*, 35–37.

118   Nunley and Bettelheim, *Caribbean Festival Arts*, 37. The word *lechón* means piglet, but the Lechón mask actually looks like a combination of a duck and a bull (*Second Face: Museum of Cultural Masks*, https://www .maskmuseum.org/mask/lechon-1/)—although, to be fair, the creole pig (now very rare after the 1979 mass slaughter), which was feral, had a longer snout than contemporary pigs as well as tusks. The Fundación Museo del Carnaval Dominicana in Santo Domingo confirms that the mask Lechón has the face of a pig ("Lechones de Santiago" display).

119   As Girard states, "The *monstrous double* is also to be found wherever we encounter an 'I' and an 'Other' caught up in a constant interchange of differences" (Girard, *Violence and the Sacred*, 164).

120   Lizardo, "Tres aspectos." In Los Toros of Monte Cristi Carnival, they whip each other in pairs, as they do in the Semana Santa (Holy Week)

tradition of *las máscaras* in Bánica and elsewhere in the province of Elías Piña. Thanks to Brendan Thornton for the Monte Cristi data. As Bettelheim notes, however, the use of swinging bladders to scare children was common in European carnival traditions as well. Rara occurs during Holy Week in Haiti, and fighting occurs within rara when bands meet up; see McAlister, *Rara!*, 155–56. Dominican *cimarrón* carnivals in the border areas of Elías Piña and San Juan de la Maguana are treated in Durán, *Cimarrón Spirit*.

121   Smith, "Lansetkòd," 80.

122   This incident inspired Trouillot's novel *The Infamous Rosalie*. Thanks to Sophie Mariñez for this suggestion.

123   This is also the case with las máscaras of Bánica. Evans-Pritchard interprets the fact that the Nuer take their names from their cattle as evidence of their deep identification with them; see Evans-Pritchard, "The Sacrificial Role of Cattle," 183.

124   Ulrickson, "'Esclavos que fueron.'"

125   Evans-Pritchard, "Customs and Beliefs Relating to Twins," 236; Turner, *The Ritual Process*, 47.

126   Evans-Pritchard, *The Nuer*, 18–19; Evans-Pritchard, "The Sacrificial Role of Cattle," 82. The belief in species "transmigration" is a feature of both Amerindian and West African cultures; see Smith, "I Am a Parrot (Red)"; Bockie, *Death and the Invisible Powers*.

127   Kinser, *Carnival, American Style*, xv.

128   DaMatta, *Carnivals, Rogues, and Heroes*, 47. See Weheliye's discussion of how humanity is disciplined "into full humans, not-quite-humans, and non-humans" in *Habeas Viscus*, 3.

129   Hutchinson, "The Cattle of Money," 311; Comaroff and Comaroff, "Goodly Beasts, Beastly Goods."

130   Palmié, "Thinking with *Ngangas*," 854.

131   Parry and Bloch, *Money and the Morality of Exchange*, 1.

132   I must say that this story is pure popular conjecture. I have no evidence to back this rumor up.

133   Solidarité Fwontaliye, "A Stand Against Statelessness"; *Tráfico de seres humanos y migraciones*.

134   For more on the Odebrecht scandal, see Gallas, "Brazil's Odebrecht Corruption"; Fieser, "A Graft Machine's Collapse"; Conde, "R. Dominicana. Haitiano, fobia y poder." The PLD stranglehold was broken in 2020 when the Modern Revolutionary Party candidate Luis Abinader won the election. During Leonel Fernández's first term, $100 million in government funds mysteriously disappeared (United Nations High Commissioner for Refugees, "Freedom in the World 2008—Dominican Republic"). For more on Dominican politics, see Krohn-Hansen, *Political Authoritarianism*; Hartlyn, *The Struggle for Democratic Politics*.

Contraband has a deep history in the Dominican Republic, however; see Ponce Vázquez, *Islanders and Empire*.

135 Drug shipments increased 800 percent between 2011 and 2013 under the presidencies of Leonel Fernández and Danilo Medina. See Austin and Held, "The Dominican Republic"; Narconon, "Cocaine and Other Drugs"; Jacobs, "Major Drug Trafficker"; Associated Press, "Two Ex-MLB Players Accused." Money laundering was run through nightclubs staffed with women trafficked from Colombia and Venezuela and former baseball players.

136 Baxter, "Law Enforcement."

137 "José Figueroa Acosta Arrested."

138 Reyes, "Narco se convierte en leyenda."

139 "DNCD apresa sindico de Bánica por 'sospechoso,'" *San Juan de la Maguana en la Red*, accesssed July 19, 2012, SanJuanDR.com.

140 Sanders and West, "Power Revealed and Concealed," 6. Morten Axel Pedersen uses the concept of isomorphism in his *Not Quite Shamans*, 79 and 213.

141 Shaw, *Memories of the Slave Trade*, 15.

142 Shaw, *Memories of the Slave Trade*, 15.

143 Landers, *Atlantic Creoles*, chap. 2; Ferrer, "Haiti, Free Soil, and Antislavery"; Ferrer, *Freedom's Mirror*, 168; Nessler, *An Islandwide Struggle*, 35.

144 Shaw, *Memories of the Slave Trade*, 258, 243; Geschiere, *The Modernity of Witchcraft*; Bayart, *The State in Africa*.

145 Apter and Derby, "Introduction," xxiv.

146 Fricker, *Epistemic Injustice*, 89, 6; Sanders and West, "Power Revealed and Concealed," 12; Derby, "Beyond Fugitive Speech"; Scott, *Domination and the Arts of Resistance*.

147 Anderson, *Creatures of Empire*; Forde, "The Moral Economy of Spiritual Work."

148 Blachette, Zoega, and Fontenelle, *A Manual of the Art of Making and Refining Sugar*, 89.

149 Hoermann, "'A Very Hell of Horrors.'"

150 Routon, "Conjuring the Past," 643.

151 Bataille and Stoekl, *Visions of Excess*.

152 Marx, "The Fetishism of Commodities and the Secret Thereof."

153 Shaw, *Memories of the Slave Trade*, 5.

CHAPTER 3. THE INSCRUTABLE JAILBREAK OF CLÉMENT BARBOT

Epigraph: Quoted in Routon, *Hidden Powers of State*, 64.

Earlier versions of this essay were presented at the panel "*Cuidado con el perro que muere callado*: Canines as Agents of Violence and

Resistance on Hispaniola," Latin American Studies Association Meetings, San Francisco, 2012; "B/Ordering Violence: Boundaries, Indigeneity, and Gender in the Americas, Caribbean Borderlands Near and Far," University of Washington, Seattle, 2012; "Animal Crossings: Man and Beast at the Margins of Culture," American Anthropological Association Meetings, 2012; at The Miller Center for Historical Studies, University of Maryland, 2013; and at "Witches at Stake: Legacies of a Cultural Icon," Department of German and Romance Languages and Literatures, graduate student conference, at Johns Hopkins University, 2019.

1   This story is also recounted in Joseph, *For Whom the Dogs Spy*, 59.

2   This story was told to me by Toni Monnin. See Heinl and Heinl, *Written in Blood*, 636; Abbott, *Haiti*, 110–12.

3   These rumors are related to the fact that Duvalier incorporated vodou priests into the paramilitary forces as a means of terror; see Laguerre, *Voodoo and Politics in Haiti*; Laguerre, *Military and Society in Haiti*; Rotberg, "Vodun and the Politics of Haiti."

4   Kettler, *The Smell of Slavery*; Johnson, "'You Should Give Them Blacks to Eat'"; Yingling and Parry, "The Canine Terror."

5   Ahmed, *The Cultural Politics of Emotion*, 11. For a call to consider the material as well as symbolic traces of animals, see Weismantel and Pearson, "Does 'the Animal' Exist?" For an effort to bring sound and taste into ethnography, see Stoller, *The Taste of Ethnographic Things*.

6   Comaroff and Comaroff cited in Shaw, *Memories of the Slave Trade*, 226. Johnson draws upon visual representations of "canine warfare" in colonial engravings and literature to explore its cultural impact; as she states, "Common in occurrence yet uncommonly extreme in their viciousness, such tactics have left their mark on collective memory." See Johnson, *The Fear of French Negroes*, 46.

7   Turner, "Commentary: Ethno-Ethnohistory," 237.

8   Dayan, *The Law Is a White Dog*, loc. 75.

9   Norton, *The Tame and the Wild*, 83–86.

10   Yingling and Parry, "The Canine Terror"; and Parry and Yingling, "Slave Hounds and Abolition."

11   See Gordon, *Ghostly Matters*, xvi, on haunting as unresolved social violence; Cohen, "Monster Culture (Seven Theses)," 19; and Chamoiseau, *Slave Old Man*, on the mastiff as a "monster." See also Dixa Ramírez, *Colonial Phantoms*, on another kind of ghosting.

12   Courlander, "The Cat, the Dog and Death." See also Chéry, *Le chien comme métaphore en Haïti*. Thanks to Leah Gordon for this reference.

13   Bell, "Twenty Dollars," 111.

14   Large, "Rosanna," 167.

15   Thanks to Alison Bruey for the following 1944 poem about the *cadejos*: Carlos Luis Saenz, "El Cadejos," in Zeledón C., *Leyendas ticas de la tierra*, 14–15.

> Las cadenas del cadejos,
> ay, ay, ay, las cadenas,
> las cadenas del cadejos
> son largos como mi pena.
> Son largas como mi pena!
> La noche se hace mas negra;
> se apagaron las estrellas;
> en la tumba de mi madre
> crece una cruz de tinieblas.
> La noche se hace mas negra!
> No me maldigan los hombres
> ni vengan tras de mi huella;
> dejenme con mi alma sola
> y con mis largas cadenas.
> Y con mis largas cadenas!

See also Puckett, *Folk Beliefs*.

16   Dogs also served as psychopomps for the Greeks; see McHugh, *Dog*, 40–42; Laman cited in Ochoa, *Society of the Dead*, 275n9.

17   Thanks to Rebecca Dirksen for suggesting this connection, and Katherine Smith for the anecdote from her research among the Sanpwèl; see also McAlister, *Rara!*, 88.

18   Rigaud, *Secrets of Voodoo*, mentions the protective use of baka, while McAlister describes this as part of the hot side of vodou practice. The term *assault sorcery* is from Neil Whitehead's work; see Whitehead and Wright, *In Darkness and Secrecy*.

19   Whitehead and Wright, *In Darkness and Secrecy*, 3.

20   Chochotte, "Making Peasants *Chèf* "; Laguerre, *The Military and Society*.

21   Scott, *Domination and the Arts of Resistance*, 199.

22   Garrigus, *A Secret Among the Blacks*; Gaillard, *La guérilla de Batraville*.

23   Derby, *Dictator's Seduction*, chap. 6. As, it was said, did Venezuelan strongman Rómulo Betancourt; see Vidal and Whitehead, "Dark Shamans and the Shamanic State," 58. This rumor may have had something to do with the fact that Trujillo had Haitian provenance through his maternal line.

24   Whitehead and Finnström, *Virtual War and Magical Death*, 19, 21.

25   Milin, *Les chiens de Dieu*.

26   Linebaugh, *The London Hanged*; Paul, *The Poverty of Disaster*. For a more historicist rendering of the origins of French loup-garou lore, see Smith, *Monsters of the Gévaudan*.

27   Pratten, *The Man-Leopard Murders*; Roberts, "'Perfect' Lions, 'Perfect' Leaders"; Van Bockhaven, "Leopard-Men of the Congo"; Whitehead, *Dark Shamans.*

28   Milin, *Les chiens de Dieu*, 21; Evans, Gauthier, and Forsyth, "Dogfighting." On Abakúa, see Brown, *The Light Inside*; Miller, *Voice of the Leopard*; Cabrera, *La sociedad secreta Abakúa.*

29   Lewis, *Hall of Mirrors*, 103–5; Sousa, *The Woman Who Turned Into a Jaguar*. A strong element of misogyny courses through these tales, likely when told by men, since it is more often that male shape-shifting is cast as a skill associated with chivalry, whereas when women do it the intent is to engage in heinous acts of social violation such as infanticide, a version that has become canonized in Caribbean stories of the *soucouyant* or lougawou. See Milin, *Les chiens de Dieu*, 93; Chariandy, *Soucouyant*; Jäger, "Is Little Red Riding Hood Wearing a Liberty Cap?"

30   Douglas, *Natural Symbols.*

31   On the use of dogs in Dominican hunting practices, see Davis, "La Montería." See also Ingold, *The Appropriation of Nature*; Roberts, "'Perfect' Lions, 'Perfect' Leaders."

32   Whitehead, *Dark Shamans*, 49.

33   White, "The Forms of Wildness."

34   Stoller, *Embodying Colonial Memories*, 6, 130.

35   Beier, "The Yoruba Attitude Toward Dogs"; Beier, "Dog Magic of Yoruba Hunters." Animal skulls are also a regular feature of Yoruba shrines.

36   Gottlieb, *The Afterlife Is Where We Come From.*

37   Gottlieb, "Dog: Ally or Traitor?," 480. Thanks to Andrew Apter for this citation.

38   McAlister, "A Sorcerer's Bottle," 305–22.

39   MacGaffey, *Art and Healing of the Bakongo*, 4; MacGaffey, "Ethnography and the Closing of the Frontier," 267.

40   Thompson, *Flash of the Spirit*, 121. Thanks to Judith Bettelheim for suggesting this cite.

41   Taussig, *Mimesis and Alterity*, 150.

42   Alexander and Smith, *The Cambridge Companion to Durkheim*, 275.

43   Freud, "The Uncanny."

44   Thoby-Marcelin, *The Beast of the Haitian Hills*, 83.

45   Thoby-Marcelin, *The Beast of the Haitian Hills*, 99; Thompson, "From the Isle Beneath the Sea," 111.

46   Interestingly, however, in Haiti galipotes are seen as uniquely Dominican (Elizabeth McAlister, personal communication).

47   González, "Monterías y campesinos monteros"; Davis, "La Montería." Lipe Collado told me that he went hunting for feral goats in the 1950s.

48   Gosse, *A Naturalist's Sojourn in Jamaica*, 388.

49   Rainsford, *An Historical Account*, 424.

50   Hogan, *History of the Irish Wolfdog*, 6–7, 104. In fact, their global popularity among nobles culled them nearly to extinction until the breed was revived by Irish nationalists eager to demonstrate their superiority to the English mastiff in the late nineteenth century.

51   For the history of dog breeding, see Ritvo, *The Animal Estate*.

52   Fernández de Zafra, "El terror de los esclavos."

53   Johnson, "'You Should Give Them Blacks to Eat'"; Yingling and Parry, "The Canine Terror."

54   Norton, *The Tame and the Wild*, 85.

55   Casas, *A Short Account*, 16.

56   Varner and Varner, *Dogs of the Conquest*, 6.

57   Varner and Varner, *Dogs of the Conquest*, 7, 13.

58   Johnson, "'You Should Give Them Blacks to Eat,'" 68.

59   Dallas cited in Barcia Paz, *Seeds of Insurrection*, 60.

60   Gosse, *A Naturalist's Sojourn*, 389.

61   Sloane, *A Voyage to the Islands*, 1:xvi–xvii.

62   "Hog-Raising in Cuba."

63   Dallas, *The History of the Maroons*, 57.

64   Dallas, *The History of the Maroons*, 101.

65   Dallas, *The History of the Maroons*, 108.

66   Dallas, *The History of the Maroons*, 67.

67   Dallas, *The History of the Maroons*, 127, 119.

68   Edwards and the Governor and Assembly of Jamaica, *The Proceedings*.

69   Dallas, *The History of the Maroons*, 287.

70   Dallas, *The History of the Maroons*, 169.

71   Ardouin and Madiou cited in Johnson, *The Fear of French Negroes*, 26. While Quentin Tarantino has been criticized for the excessive violence of his film *Django Unchained*, such violence was actually not uncommon in Atlantic slave societies, as we have seen here.

72   Rainsford, *An Historical Account* (1805), 423–29.

73   Rainsford, *An Historical Account* (1805), 426–27; Ferrer, *Freedom's Mirror*, 184.

74   Rainsford, *An Historical Account* (1805), 426.

75   I am drawing upon the methodology of White, *Speaking with Vampires*, 6–8.

76   Among others, Balaguer, *La isla al revés*; Peña Batlle, *Orígenes del estado haitiano*.

77   Interestingly, Joaquín Balaguer casts Haitians also as uncontrollable animals—however, as rabbits—in his anti-Haitian tract *La isla al revés*, due to his Malthusian interest in highlighting their irrepressible fecundity.

78	Derby and Turits, *Terreurs de frontière*; Turits, "A World Destroyed"; Paulino, *Dividing Hispaniola*; Cadeau, *More Than a Massacre*.
79	Rainsford, *An Historical Account* (1805), 339.
80	Barcia Paz, *Seeds of Insurrection*, 58–59.
81	Gascón, "The Military of Santo Domingo," 432.
82	Dallas, *History of the Maroons*, cited in Barcia Paz, *Seeds of Insurrection*, 58, 60–61.
83	Fouchard, *The Haitian Maroons*. Another contrastive aspect of dog practices on the island is the relative neglect of dogs in Haiti compared with Dominican public dogs, which are cared for.
84	Goffman, *Relations in Public*, chap. 3; Goffman, *The Presentation of Self in Everyday Life*.
85	Somers, "The Narrative Constitution of Identity."
86	Varner and Varner, *Dogs of the Conquest*, 23.
87	Whitehead, "The Taste of Death," 232.
88	Rainsford, *An Historical Account* (1805), 429; Trouillot, *Silencing the Past*.
89	Palmié, *Wizards and Scientists*, 11–12.
90	Taussig, "History as Sorcery," 95.
91	Richman, *Migration and Vodou*, 164; Deren, *Divine Horsemen*, 62, 69.
92	Marisa J. Fuentes speaks of "body memory" in *Dispossessed Lives*, 16.
93	As a captured spirit sent to do work at a distance. See Whitehead and Wright, *In Darkness and Secrecy*, 1–21; Deren, *Divine Horsemen*, app. B.
94	Descourtilz, *Voyages d'un naturaliste*, 3:114.
95	Routon, "Conjuring the Past," 633, 643; Cabrera, *Reglas de Congo*, 216n16; Ochoa, *Society of the Dead*, 120.
96	Special thanks to Katherine Smith for this datum and photo.
97	Palmié, *Wizards and Scientists*, 175; Hertz, *Death and the Right Hand*.
98	Depestre, *Hadriana in All My Dreams*, 129, 137.
99	Ochoa, *Society of the Dead*, 226; Rigaud, *Vè-vè*, 562. Thanks to Katherine Smith for drawing this source to my attention.
100	Mobley, "The Mystery of the 'Mondongue' Midwife in Saint Domingue."
101	Herskovits, *Life in a Haitian Valley*, 248.
102	Marvin, "Wolves in Sheep's (and Others') Clothing," 67.
103	Freeland, "Natural Evil in the Horror Film," 67.

CHAPTER 4. CREOLE PIGS AS MEMENTO MORI

Earlier drafts of this chapter were presented at "Pig Out: Hogs and Humans in Global and Historical Context," Agrarian Studies Program, Yale University, in 2015; the conference on "Trees Take Us to the Gods:

Vodou and the Environment," sponsored by Kosamba: A Scholarly Association for the Study of Haitian Vodou, in 2015; and the panel "Debating the Patterns of Migration, Economics and History of Hispaniola" at the annual meeting of the Caribbean Studies Association, in 2016. Passages of the chapter were previously published in "Male Heroism, Demonic Pigs, and Memories of Violence in the Haitian-Dominican Borderlands," UCLA *Center for the Study of Women Update*, May 10, 2010.

1   According to Barbara Fuchs's criteria; see Fuchs, *Knowing Fictions*, 113; Fuchs, "Suspended Judgments," 449. Thanks to Sarah Stein for bringing this work to my attention. Hegel is equally a pícaro. After a stint at the computer center, he joined the army only to later become a self-taught artist and move to Santo Domingo, where his work has been acclaimed. Strikingly handsome, he left behind several children in Bánica.

2   An excerpt from this account can be found on my YouTube channel: "Creole Pigs," YouTube, posted by Robin Derby, October 12, 2015, https://www.youtube.com/watch?v=F8JKHRF0z50&t=42s. His neighbor was female, which also indicates how women can be implicated indirectly in chains of rumor transmission about bacá specters.

3   After the 1979 slaughter the creole pig was declared extinct; however, it appears that some did survive in the interior. See Matos Espinosa, "Caza de venados." Thanks to Pauline Kulstad for bringing this article to my attention.

4   Walton, *Present State of the Spanish Colonies*, 1:284. M. E. Descourtilz called it a brown pig and said it was hunted in Santo Domingo when palm kernels were ripe, as the pigs adored them (*Voyages d'un naturaliste*, 2:171–72). Thanks to Elizabeth Landers for this citation.

5   The program, which was called the African Swine Fever Flu Eradication Project and Plan to Develop Pig Raising, involved the governments of the United States, Canada, and Mexico, the United Nations Food and Agriculture Organization (FAO), the International Development Bank, and the University of Georgia and was coordinated by the Institute for International Cooperation, a subgroup of the Organization of American States. Dominicans call swine fever *cacedó*.

6   Geary, *Phantoms of Remembrance*; Moreau de Saint-Méry, *Description . . . de la partie française*, 262. Santo Domingo mahogany became a prized export for high-end furniture through the 1920s Arts and Crafts movement; see Anderson, *Mahogany*.

7   Hartman, *Lose Your Mother*, 6.

8   Bulamah, "Pode um porco falar?" Sidney Mintz pioneered the study of Caribbean provision grounds; see Mintz, "Slavery and the Rise of Peasantries."

9	As in the Andes; see Archetti, *Guinea-Pigs*.
10	Bennett, *Being Property Once Myself*, 3.
11	Clarke, *Pig Tails 'n' Breadfruit*, 127–28.
12	This locates Hispaniola within a broader culture of global pig ritual systems; see Gordon and Parisio, *A Pig's Tale*; Rappaport, *Pigs for the Ancestors*; Strathern, *The Gender of the Gift*; and Alvarez Blásquez, *O libro do porco*, 24–27, which has a section on why pork is sacred in Galicia, Spain, mentioning that a pig's tooth, for example, can protect against evil eye.
13	For a rich consideration of the cultural significance of the pig within Christianity, see Fabre-Vassas, *The Singular Beast*.
14	Norton, "The Chicken or the *Iegue*"; Norton, *The Tame and the Wild*; Archetti, *Guinea-Pigs*. See also Fausto, "Feasting on People"; Descola, *In the Society of Nature*; Viveiros de Castro, "Cosmological Deixis"; Kohn, *How Forests Think*. Marcel Mauss terms these phenomena systems of total prestation; see Mauss, *The Gift*.
15	Connolly and Fuentes, "Introduction," 111. Thanks to Anne Eller for bringing this special issue to my attention.
16	Connolly and Fuentes, "Introduction," 115; Mauss, *The Gift*, 54.
17	Doris, *Vigilant Things*, 58; Derby, "Zemis and Zombies."
18	Schefer and Cordier, *Recueil de voyages*, 88, 92–93, 99.
19	Street, "Feral Animals in Hispaniola," 400–401.
20	Scott, *The Art of Not Being Governed*.
21	Funes Monzote, *From Rainforest to Cane Field*; Moreno Fraginals, *El ingenio*.
22	Durland, "The Forests of the Dominican Republic," 206.
23	Moscoso Puello, "From Paris to Santo Domingo," 200.
24	On the ceremony at Bois Caiman, see Dubois, *Avengers of the New World*, 99–100. Yet gray or red pigs can be diabolic, and can indicate sickness: see Herskovits, *Life in a Haitian Valley*, 242; Courlander, *The Drum and the Hoe*, 96.
25	Parrinder, "Activities of African Witches"; Dulin, "Vulnerable Minds."
26	Beckwith, *Black Roadways*.
27	Norton, "The Chicken or the *Iegue*" includes an anecdote from Oviedo of a Taíno man who hunted with a group of familiarized pigs. An important exception is the Cochons Sans Poils, a feared secret society; see Herskovits, *Life in a Haitian Valley*, 243. The goat has also been indigenized, as can be seen in the beloved Haitian childhood game *osselets*, played with goat knuckles. I discuss the significance of the goat in Derby, "Trujillo, the Goat."
28	Gordon, *Ghostly Matters*, 19.
29	Ferme describes this as the "underneath" in Ferme, *The Underneath of Things*.

30   Stoler, *Along the Archival Grain*, 19–23, drawing upon Certeau, *Heterologies*, 150–55.

31   For an example of how these bacá narratives have been folklorized, see Ubiñas Renville, *Mitos, creencias y leyendas dominicanas*, 129–37. I am drawing upon Kathleen Stewart's *Ordinary Affects*, 52.

32   Comaroff and Comaroff, "Goodly Beasts, Beastly Goods"; Hutchinson, "The Cattle of Money"; Evans-Pritchard, *The Nuer*.

33   The pig is the favored sacrifice for a petwo rite, which is associated with sorcery; see Richman, *Migration and Vodou*. In 1994 Andrew Apter and I met a *curandera* in Regla just outside Havana, Cuba, who kept an enormous hog in her bathtub, one solution to the food crisis of the Special Period.

34   Beckwith, *Black Roadways*, 61. I am not sure, however, that the creole pig was always the sacrificial animal par excellence, since a nineteenth-century traveler to Arcahaie noted the sacrifice of a white cock and goat (although the purported cannibalism allegations here indicate this source is not to be considered trustworthy); St. John, *Hayti*, 201. Pigs do not appear frequently as sacrificial animals in the vodou literature. The cornmeal porridge served at ritual feasts is called *mayi moulin* in Haiti and *chenchen* in the Dominican Republic, but a *plato seco* (dry plate or ritual snack, including sesame, peanuts, and candy) also includes corn in the form of popcorn. Rigoberta Menchú in her memoir also notes that she took care of the family pig as a child; see Menchú, *I, Rigoberta Menchú*.

35   This is the Cuban version from José Ortega (personal communication). Patín Maceo recounts a slightly different one in *Dominicanismos*, 161.

36   Phillips, "The Pig in Medieval Iconography."

37   For example, Beinart, Middleton, and Pooley, *Wild Things*; Aderinto, *Animality and Colonial Subjecthood in Africa*. Exceptions include Few and Tortorici, *Centering Animals*.

38   Kohn, "How Dogs Dream," 7.

39   Norton, "The Chicken or the *Iegue*," 34; Norton, *The Tame and the Wild*. Interestingly, Cuban hunting manuals classify livestock into three categories, not two; see "La caza es arte y sabiduria de guerrear et de vencer" in Cuba, *Ley de caza*. Thanks to Reinaldo Funes Monzote for this citation.

40   Van Dooren and Rose, "Lively Ethnography."

41   Although Sluyter argues that the use of the lance on horseback is Fulani; see Sluyter, *Black Ranching Frontiers*.

42   Street, "Feral Animals in Hispaniola," 404.

43   Ligon, *True and Exact History*.

44   Although Mintz leaves out swine and poultry from his model; see Mintz, "Slavery and the Rise of Peasantries."

45   Scott, *Slave Emancipation in Cuba*; Scott, "Reclaiming Gregoria's Mule."

46   Ligon, *True and Exact History*, 7, 34, 37; Beckwith, *Black Roadways*.

47   Weiner, *Inalienable Possessions*, x.

48   Parsons, "The Acorn-Hog Economy," 215, 227; Sarg, "Comment on élève et on tue le cochon en Alsace Bossue."

49   Hémardinquer, "The Family Pig of the Ancien Régime," 50–72; Parsons, "The Acorn-Hog Economy," 230.

50   See Silié, *Economía, esclavitud y población*.

51   Tejera, "Public Enemies: The Revolutionary and the Pig." For more on the official discourse of indolence, see Ramírez-D'Oleo, "Insolence, Indolence."

52   Walton, *Present State of the Spanish Colonies*, 372.

53   Scott, *The Art of Not Being Governed*.

54   Scott, *The Art of Not Being Governed*, 203; Sartorius, "Transitory Trust"; Eller, "To Cap-Haïten, with My Family."

55   Malcolmson and Mastoris, *The English Pig*, chap. 7.

56   Smith, *Kinship and Community in Carriacou*; Beck, *To Windward of the Land*, xxxiv, 219.

57   Beck, *To Windward of the Land*; Musgrave-Portilla, "The Nahualli or Transforming Wizard," 10–11.

58   Beckwith, *Black Roadways*, 202.

59   Moreau de Saint-Méry on the snake cult of Saint-Domingue: *Description . . . de la partie française*; Beck, *To Windward of the Land*, xxxii.

60   Walton, *Present State of the Spanish Colonies*, 1:19.

61   Vega and Michel, *Asuntos dominicanos*, 15.

62   Walton, *Present State of the Spanish Colonies*, 1:33. See González, *De esclavos a campesinos*.

63   Rodríguez Demorizi, *Lengua y folklore*, 308. Pedro Francisco Bonó's novel *El montero* inaccurately portrays the Dominican hunter as part of a landed peasantry, however.

64   The montero is the equivalent of the figure of the Puerto Rican *jíbaro* and was late to be embraced by Dominican elites (Scarano, "The *Jíbaro* Masquerade"). For an early twentieth-century Dominican view of the jíbaro as a poor peasant displaced by sugar companies and forced into nomadism, who "cannot be educated and must be left to wallow in his ignorance, anemia, and poverty," see Pérez, *Geografía y sociedad*, 259.

65   Lane, *Pillaging the Empire*, 120.

66   Gascón, "The Military of Santo Domingo," 433.

67   Bonó, "In the Army Camp at Bermejo."

68   "La caza es arte y sabiduria de guerrear et de vencer," in Cuba, *Ley de caza*.

69   Salvajes (wild), amansados o domesticados (tamed), mansos o domésticos (tame).

70	Norton, *The Tame and the Wild.*
71	"Shooting and Hunting in Florida," 2–3.
72	*Charleston Courier*, November 18, 1857.
73	Bennett, *Being Property Once Myself*, 4–5.
74	Long, *The History of Jamaica*, 22. He also reports that "they were not married but herded together very much like cattle, living in communal quarters."
75	Whitehead, "Conclusion: Loving, Being, Killing Animals," 334.
76	The concept of spirit guardian is from Pedersen, *Not Quite Shamans.*
77	Much like the *wurumbu* as described by Fardon, *Between God, the Dead and the Wild*, 35–37.
78	Puckett, *Folk Beliefs*, 314, 505.
79	Ochoa, *Society of the Dead*, 154. For dog parts used among the Bakongo in spells, see MacGaffey, *Art and Healing*, 28, 55.
80	Park, Burgess, and McKenzie, *The City*, 137.
81	Arzeno Rodríguez, *Enrique Blanco*, 32.
82	Norton, "The Chicken or the *Iegue*," 39.
83	For a critique of animal studies for not taking into account "racializing assemblages and thus the nonpersonhood of human subjects," see Alexander Weheliye, *Habeas Viscus*. Thanks to Robin Kelley for this suggestion.
84	Associación de Academias de la Lengua Española, *Diccionario de americanismos*, s.v. "cochón," accessed March 7, 2025, https://www.asale.org/damer/coch%C3%B3n.
85	Neel Ahuja cited in Whitehead, "Conclusion: Loving, Being, Killing Animals," 331. An exception is Ko, *Racism as Zoological Witchcraft*.
86	Rémy, "The Animal Issue in Xenotransplantation."
87	This is suggested by estimates compiled by the University of Minnesota on the potential damage to the US pork industry reaching $5 billion; see Ebert, "Porkbarrelling Pigs in Haiti." On the vulnerability of the US pork industry, see "Timeline: The History of Smithfield Foods." Vertical integration and precision genetic engineering—what the company calls the "birth to bacon approach"—ended up making Smithfield Foods the world's largest hog producer and pork processor; see Barboza, "Goliath of the Hog World."
88	The literature on this event only treats Haiti, yet the same measures were taken on both sides of the island.
89	Sánchez Botija, "Peste porcina Africana," 991–1029.
90	Diederich, "Swine Fever Ironies,"104. The pig slaughter in Haiti has received critical attention, but not that of the Dominican Republic. See Bulamah, "Pode um porco falar?" Sophie Moore mistakenly claims that Dominican pigs were not killed; see her "Chronic Carriers," 94.

91 Cruz Duran, "Análisis de las consecuencias económico-sociales."

92 Farmer, "Swine Aid"; Bulamah, "Pode um porco falar?"

93 Hernandez, *Bachata*, 154.

94 For more on this debt crisis and the bread riots, which spread all the way to Venezuela, see Derby, "Haitians in the Dominican Republic."

95 I don't have evidence of protest for Haiti, but surely there was; however, under the Duvalier regime it would have been very risky to challenge a military action.

96 They said, "We are poor people and in this humble section we live more by livestock raising than anything else" (somos gentes pobres y que en este humilde seccion, se vive mas de la crianza que de otra cosa). Letter to President Antonio Guzmán Fernández and Hipólito Mejía, Secretary of State for Agriculture, from a group of 105 petitioners from Sección El Guayabal, Distrito Municipal de Postrer Río, Provincia Independencia, March 22, 1979; papers of Héctor Incháustegui Cabral, Secretario de Estado sin Cartera, Ministerio de Industria y Commerce (hereafter MIC), Archivo General de la Nación, Dominican Republic (hereafter AGN).

97 Deive, *Antología de la flora y fauna*, 333.

98 Arthur and Dash, *Libète*, 105.

99 Cited in Ortner, "Is Female to Male," 13.

100 Lawrence, "Menstrual Politics," 117–37. In the Dominican countryside, menstruating women should stay away from cultivated fields.

101 Knight, *Waiting for Wolves in Japan*, 50, 78.

102 Deren, *Divine Horsemen*, 138–41; Gordon and Parisio, *A Pig's Tale*.

103 Telegram to President Antonio Guzmán Fernández from Cornelio Florian Recio, Sección de Boca de Cachón, Jimaní, on behalf of 32 petitioners who lost 85 animals in the slaughter, Tamayo, January 21, 1979; papers of Héctor Incháustegui Cabral, Secretario de Estado sin Cartera, MIC, AGN.

104 Weiner, *Inalienable Possessions*, quoting Mauss, *The Gift*, 50.

105 Smith, *The Matrifocal Family*.

106 To President Antonio Guzmán Fernández, from Miguelina Matos Ledesma, María Fortuna Matos Ledesma, and 23 other petitioners, Tamayo, January 31, 1979; papers of Héctor Incháustegui Cabral, Secretario de Estado sin Cartera, MIC, AGN.

107 Interview by the author, Bánica, July 2010.

108 Telegram to Pedro Bello Heredia, secretary of state for agriculture, "Reclamación de pago de cerdos," from the governor, quoting various claimants, Jimaní, July 20, 1979, MIC, AGN.

109 Telegram to President Antonio Guzmán Fernández, "Informe sobre sacrificio de cerdos," from Héctor Incháustegui Cabral, secretario de estado sin cartera, on behalf of Leovigildo Florian, Luciano Pérez, and

Saturnino Cuevas, who lost 85 pigs, Jimaní, April 19, 1979; papers of Héctor Incháustegui Cabral, Secretario de Estado sin Cartera, MIC, AGN.

110 Letter to President Antonio Guzmán Fernández, from Baron Monterom and 23 other petitioners, Tamayo, January 23, 1979, papers of Héctor Incháustegui Cabral, Secretario de Estado sin Cartera, MIC, AGN; interview by the author, Bánica, July 2010.

111 Receipts for the campaign against porcine fever diffusion, radio announcements, from the Fondo Especial para el Desarrollo Agropecuario: $300 RD, February 12, 1979; $240 and $375 RD, April 23, 1979; MIC, AGN.

112 Telegram to Hipólito Mejía, secretary of state for agriculture, "Informe sobre sacrificio de cerdos," from Héctor Incháustegui Cabral, secretario de estado sin cartera, on behalf of Leovigildo Florian, Luciano Pérez, and Saturnino Cuevas, Jimaní, April 19, 1979, MIC, AGN.

113 Quoted in telegram to Hipólito Mejía, secretary of state for agriculture, "Informe sobre el sacrificio de cerdos," from Héctor Incháustegui Cabral, secretario de estado sin cartera, on behalf of Leovigildo Florian, Luciano Pérez, and Saturnino Cuevas, sección Boca de Cachón, Jimaní, April 19, 1979, MIC, AGN.

114 Most pig farmers had fewer than 10, about a third had 25–30, and a handful had 70–80 hogs (estimate from a sample of lists of "personas que del este del municipio que perdieron sus cerdos para controlar la peste porcina para recompensarle en parte sus perdidas sufridas, A su pres. Antonio Guzmán, del Gobernador Civil Provincia Independencia, Jimaní," January 11, 1979, MIC, AGN). A survey from Independencia, Jimaní, revealed that most people had only 2 pigs; letter to Presidente Antonio Guzmán Fernández from Pedro Dello Heredia, Gobernador Civil, Jimaní, January 22, 1979, MIC, AGN.

115 To Ing. Agron. Rafael Martínez Richiez, sub-secretario administrativo, Secretaría de Estado de Agricultura, from Orlando Sánchez Díaz, secretario ejecutivo fiebre porcina Africana, "Asunto: Solicitud para Cotización," March 13, 1979, MA, AGN.

116 Köhler, "Half-Man, Half-Elephant."

117 Joiris, "Hunting Rituals"; Köhler, "Half-Man, Half-Elephant," 69.

118 MacGaffey, "Complexity, Astonishment and Power," 193; Thompson, *The Four Moments of the Sun*, 27.

119 Mubitana, "Wiko Masquerades."

120 Douglas, *Purity and Danger*; Taussig, "What Color Is the Sacred?"; Taussig, *Defacement*, 52.

121 Beauvoir-Dominique, "Underground Realms of Being."

122 Fausto, "Feasting on People," 510.

123 Girard, *Violence and the Sacred*, 1–3. Brett Mizelle develops another explanation for the ambivalence of the pig in secular contexts in his *Pig*, 180.

124   Interview, July, 2009, Bánica.
125   Radcliffe-Brown, "On Joking Relationships," esp. 199–200.
126   Tejeda Ortíz, *El carnaval dominicano*, 207.
127   Smith, *Kinship and Community in Carriacou*, 133. For more on the djablesse, see Gugolati, "La Djablesse."
128   Fabre-Vassas, *The Singular Beast*, 302.
129   One of my informants alleged that the jabalí bacá emerged during the swine fever crisis, which commenced in 1979.
130   Arthur and Dash, *Libète*, 228.
131   Ebert, "Porkbarrelling Pigs in Haiti."
132   Haiti was self-sufficient in rice until the early 1980s. See Sundaram and Chowdhury, "Agricultural Trade Liberalization"; Famine Early Warning System Network, "Central American and Caribbean."
133   Ewing-Chow, "Five Overlooked Facts." For more on structural adjustment, see Klein, *The Shock Doctrine*; for its impact on the Caribbean, see McAfee, *Storm Signals*.
134   According to my informants, replacement pigs were not made available to border farmers. US pigs are given ractopamine to make them grow faster, which can actually make them violent. See Bottemiller, "Codex Adopts Ractopamine Limits"; Roberts, *Food Law in the United States*.
135   Varner and Varner, *Dogs of the Conquest*; Johnson, *The Fear of French Negroes*.
136   White, *Speaking with Vampires*, 85.
137   Appadurai, *The Social Life of Things*, 12.
138   Weismantel, *Food, Gender, and Poverty*, 169.
139   Connerton, *The Spirit of Mourning*, 17.
140   Gordon, *Ghostly Matters*, xvi, 63; Santner, *Stranded Objects*, 147.
141   Lydia Cabrera notes that Cubans do not use the term *bosque* (forest) but rather *el monte*, which means "mountain" or the "wilds" (Cabrera, *El monte*, 67), or *manigua*, "swamp."
142   For more on early slavery and its demise in the Dominican Republic, see Turits, "Slavery and the Pursuit of Freedom."
143   Pané, "Antiquities of the Indians," cited in Whitehead, *Of Cannibals and Kings*, 85n5. As one of Cabrera's informants put it, "Las medicinas están vivas en el monte" (The medicines are alive in the forest), since every plant has a supernatural force (Cabrera, *El monte*, 18).
144   Cabrera, *El monte*, 83, 109.
145   Deren, *Divine Horsemen*, 98–100; Cabrera, *El monte*, 109.
146   Palmié, *Wizards and Scientists*, 184.
147   Rocha, "Maroons in the Montes," 20; Palmié, *Wizards and Scientists*, 186.
148   A logic explored in Knight, *Waiting for Wolves in Japan*, 73.
149   Hurston, *Tell My Horse*, 39.

150   Anecdote from Jean-Claude Delbeau in Dayan, *Haiti, History, and the Gods*, 264–65, in a discussion of the skin removal theme in baka narratives. Luise White posits vampires to be signs of colonial extraction in *Speaking with Vampires*, 5; I discuss the creole-gringo contrast within poultry in Derby, "Gringo Chicken with Worms."

151   Métraux describes the careful attention to detail in a sacrifice in *Voodoo in Haiti*, 168–69. As he states, "Nothing that is concerned with sacrifice, either closely or remotely, is exempt from ritual."

152   Fausto articulates these as opposed logics in "Feasting on People."

153   Bourguignon, "The Persistence of Folk Belief."

154   See Girard, *Violence and the Sacred*, 250–51. Vincent Brown describes how duppy spirits can be either malevolent or benign in *The Reaper's Garden*, 224.

155   Simpson, "Magical Practices in Northern Haiti."

156   Hurston, *Tell My Horse*, 201, 207–9.

157   In Japan there are also shape-shifting wild boars that disguise themselves as human; Knight, *Waiting for Wolves in Japan*, 48.

158   Deren, *Divine Horsemen*, 143–44; Gordon and Parisio, *A Pig's Tale*.

CHAPTER 5. SPECTERS OF COLUMBUS

Epigraph: Derrida, *Specters of Marx*, 121.

This chapter was presented in 2015 at two panels: "Mapping Routes Through the Haitian-Dominican Borderlands," at the annual meeting of the Latin American Studies Association, and "Whispers in the Archive: Rumor and Gossip as Primary Sources," at the American Historical Association, where it benefited from comments by Lynn Hunt and others.

1   Colón was Abel Alcántara's *padrino* or godfather and thus compadre of his father, Martín Alcántara. Juan Alcántara is a more distant relative.

2   See Derrida, *The Animal That Therefore I Am*. Contrast Derrida's perspective on the gaze with Berger, "Why Look at Animals?" This oral version of the baka as a clandestine swarm of thieving spirit demons requires the use of *gad*, a protective device to keep malign spirits away.

3   Others translate *pendejo* as "dumbass," "asshole," or "wanker."

4   Chakrabarty, "Minority Histories."

5   Chakrabarty, "Minority Histories," 101, 110.

6   I am quoting Leo Marx's classic *The Machine in the Garden* here, but this also resonates with Sidney Mintz's claim in his book *Sweetness and Power* about how the industrial plantation merged the field and the factory. Another parallel example of a curse becoming affixed to

a commercial establishment is the hardware store Ferreteria Read, which was owned by Trujillo's brother-in-law; riots and looting occurred there in 1961 after Trujillo's assassination, and Antonio de la Maza, who had killed Trujillo, was shot to death there along with Juan Tomás Diaz. The store was originally owned by a man who was murdered by a man with the nickname "Bacá"—likely due to rumors that had surged about a bacá at the establishment. Thanks to Pauline Kulstad for providing me with this information. I also consulted "SIM asesinan a Antonio de la Maza y a Juan Tomás Diaz" at Perfil224.com, a now defunct website, accessed April 23, 2022.

7   Werner, *Global Displacements*, 34–36.

8   Moya Pons, *Empresarios en conflicto*, 299. During his time in office, Rafael Trujillo bought up many sugar holdings, in particular those of Canadian firms. In fact, Central La Romana was the only sugar company not bought out by Trujillo; it was owned by the Gulf and Western Corporation until 1984.

9   Moya Pons, *Empresarios en conflicto*, 38.

10   Martín Alcántara, father of Abel, personal communication, October 10, 2015. It also employed child labor, which may have been an additional reason to seek to keep the plant as invisible as possible.

11   Pauline Kulstad, personal communication. Bánica's peanut farmers form part of a border peanut producer community that extends north through Restauración, Loma de Cabrera, and Dajabón. Controlled by the Sociedad Industrial Dominicana (SID), these producers tried intermittently to organize a union around 1979—efforts that were met with fierce repression from authorities. See Martínez, "La victoria del cimarrón." These efforts to tie labor to the estate through loans bear comparison to debt peonage; see McCreery, "Debt Peonage."

12   Moya Pons, *Empresarios en conflicto*, 42.

13   Crassweller, *Trujillo*.

14   Moya Pons, *Empresarios en conflicto*, 37–39.

15   Crassweller, *Trujillo*, 170, 267. The Bonetti family continues to engage in acts of populist generosity reminiscent of Trujillo's pattern of pervasive corruption combined with dramatic acts of populist largesse—seen, for example, in the 2012 inauguration of a cockfighting stadium in Santo Domingo named for Alberto Bonetti Burgos; see "Gallos: Tony García presiderá coliseo Bonetti Burgos."

16   This strategy worked for José María Bonetti Burgos, since his relative José Miguel Bonetti became president of the Industrial Association of the Dominican Republic. Moya Pons, *Empresarios en conflicto*, 228.

17   Goffman's "frame analysis" is cited in Duranti and Goodwin, *Rethinking Context*, 9.

18   White, *Speaking with Vampires*, 36; Derby, "Beyond Fugitive Speech."

19 Passerini, *Fascism in Popular Memory*.

20 Prakash cited in James, *Doña María's Story*, 231.

21 Taylor, "To Follow a Rule," 41.

22 Scott, *Domination and the Arts of Resistance*; Passerini, *Fascism in Popular Memory*; Taussig, *The Devil and Commodity Fetishism*.

23 For accusations that Bonetti was siphoning money from the peanut processing plant, see "Directivos de fábrica de aceite de maní continúan manejos propios del Trujillato: Trataran salvar privilegios con ofertas del dinero," *Union Cívica*, January 6, 1962; and "Harina, cemento y maní," *Union Cívica*, March 6, 1962.

24 This is taken up in Daniel James's *Doña María's Story*, in which different levels of narration are discussed (134).

25 Taylor, "To Follow a Rule," 50.

26 As Martín Alcántara told me, in describing the orderly past versus the rampant crime of today, "Then there was life, today it's hard" ("Habia vida, hoy es duro").

27 Richard Lee Turits describes the Trujillo regime as developmentalist with limited everyday corruption; see his important book *Foundations of Despotism*.

28 Derby, *The Dictator's Seduction*, chap. 4.

29 See Felipe Ozuna, "Edificación cangreja"; Santiago Rodríguez, "Conducta bochornosa"; and Osvaldo Acosta, "Jugadora impune"; all in *El Caribe*, December 25, 1958. See also Leoncio Gan (name cut off), "Anomalias en Altamira," *El Caribe*, March 21, 1958.

30 Raymundo Canales, "Mantiene macuteo," *El Caribe*, March 21, 1958.

31 Justo Franco, "Un tipo diligente," *El Caribe*, March 23, 1958. It is possible, however, that Justo Franco—"Just Frank"—was a plant for the regime who was tasked with creating denunciations.

32 Gaspar Ortiz, "Tiene macuteo"; Gustavo Canales, "Manejos raros"; both in *El Caribe*, April 5, 1958. The term *prebendalism* is from Joseph, *Democracy and Prebendal Politics in Nigeria*.

33 Pascual Gómez, "Quitan tierras," *El Caribe*, April 5, 1958.

34 Raúl In (last name cut off), "Se quejan de injusticia," *El Caribe*, April 22, 1958. I wish to thank José Antinoe Fiallo for these denunciations, which he shared with me from his collection.

35 White, *Speaking with Vampires*, 6.

36 Del Toro, "Foreword," vii, ix.

37 Freud, "The Uncanny."

38 Navaro-Yashin, *The Make-Believe Space*, 151.

39 Freeland, "Natural Evil in the Horror Film."

40 Román is Martín Alcántara's first cousin.

41 This is similar to the reciprocity negation in Canessa's argument about the Pishtaco in *Intimate Indigeneities*, 182. On moral economy, see

Scott, *Moral Economy of the Peasant*; Thompson, "The Moral Economy of the English Crowd." See also Shipton, *The Nature of Entrustment*, xi.

42 Ogborn, *The Freedom of Speech*, 20.

43 In Spanish, "Una vida así, no la quiere nadie—la muerte es mejor."

44 See Mario Vargas Llosa's *The Feast of the Goat* for a gruesome but not inaccurate story of denunciation and its multiple social effects during the Trujillo regime.

45 This is drawn from a conversation in July 2013 at which Erik Peña and I were both present, but I have worked from Erik's recording of the event. Many thanks to Erik for sharing this material with me.

46 In Spanish, "¡Ud. sabe el daño que él hizo a hombres que no deben nada! Por eso esta pagando con esta."

47 West and Sanders, *Transparency and Conspiracy*, 12.

48 Jackson, *Paths Toward a Clearing*, 66.

49 The concept of "structure of feeling" is from Williams, *The Country and the City*, 58.

50 Ginzburg, "Clues."

51 See State Sugar Council, "Dominican, Cut the Cane!"

52 Hartlyn, *The Struggle for Democratic Politics*; CIA Special Report, "The Twelve Years"; Martínez, "Why Not, Dr. Balaguer?"; Díaz, "The Ghosts of Gloria Lara." This period provides a crepuscular backdrop for Alcántara Almánzar's short stories in *Where the Dream Ends*.

53 Balaguer continued with his predecessor Trujillo's emphasis on large public works projects that camouflaged equally large kickbacks. In fact, Saudi Garcia reports that in the 1970s the mining industry was reporting such exceptionally large mysterious net losses that they became a concern to authorities; see Garcia, "Environmental Maroonage." For more on Balaguer's discourse of corruption, see Liberato, *Joaquín Balaguer, Memory, and Diaspora*, 119.

54 Edelman, "Landlords and the Devil."

55 Burke, *Lifebuoy Men*, 9.

56 See "1900–1950—Joining Forces, Unilever Comes to Life," accessed April 29, 2025, https://www.unilever.com/our-company/our-history-and-archives/1900-1950.

57 Robins, *Oil Palm*, loc. 2131.

58 Zuckerman, *Planet Palm*, 73.

59 Wilson, *The History of Unilever*, 146–47.

60 Jones, *Renewing Unilever*, 132.

61 Burke, *Lifebuoy Men*, 1. Promotional materials for palm oil exclaimed, "Profits 100%"; see Billows and Beckwith, *Palm Oil and Kernels*.

62 Zuckerman, *Planet Palm*, 77–78. Lever himself was lionized in the official Unilever history as an "enlightened capitalist," as opposed to the "palm oil ruffians," yet he once had the feet cut off a Congolese chief's

daughter to obtain her brass anklets. Wilson, *The History of Unilever*, 1:142; Zuckerman, *Planet Palm*, 70.

63   Jones, *Renewing Unilever*, 150.

64   Schudson, *Advertising*, 11. See Mazzarella, *Shoveling Smoke*.

65   Sunlight was the first soap with packaging and a copyright; previously soap was sold in "anonymous bars." Reader, *Unilever: A Short History*, 11.

66   Jones, *Renewing Unilever*, 122, 125.

67   Unilever film showings are listed at least fourteen times in the pages of the *Magazine of the Women's Gas Council* just from 1958 to 1962; see, for example, that magazine's issue from January 1958, in the online resource *Food and Drink in History*.

68   Jones, *Renewing Unilever*, 97; Moira A. Hillson, "Frozen Foods in the UK," *Food Market Journal*, 25 (1984), in *Food and Drink in History*; Unilever Technical Staff, "What Is Margarine? An Account of Public Service," 1936, in *Food and Drink in History*. Unilever came to hold 70 percent of the UK mushy pea market by 1983; see "Canned Foods in the UK," September 1984, in *Food and Drink in History*. Unilever also acquired Chesebrough-Ponds in 1986 and expanded into personal care items as well as specialized chemicals. Dichter founded the Institute for Motivational Research in New York and grew it into a multimillion-dollar global business, and he singlehandedly conducted market research studies for many Unilever products in the 1950s; see *Food and Drink in History*. Vitamins were added to margarine and powdered milk to ensure that they had "high nutritive quality" and to combat consumer prejudice such as rumors that margarine was made from "stinking inedible whale oil"; see "What Is Margarine?" and Abbott, "False Advertising: An Expose of the Propaganda Against Margarine and the Margarine Industry," *Institute of Margarine Manufacturers Bulletin*, no. 12 (March 1928), both in *Food and Drink in History*.

69   Dichter, "Summary of a Psychological Research Study on the Sales and Advertising Problems of Palmolive Soap," March 1952, in *Food and Drink in History*. Indeed, most of Unilever's advertising was oriented toward "the average housewife. In the UK, we called her mum"; Jones, *Renewing Unilever*, 116.

70   For more on Dichter, see "Retail Therapy," in *Food and Drink in History*.

71   Michael Jackson discusses analogy in *Paths Toward a Clearing*, 172; Pamela Stewart and Andrew Strathern stress the "interpretive ambiguity" intrinsic to rumor in *Witchcraft, Sorcery, Rumors, and Gossip*, 30.

72   This is the Marxist concept of haunting from Horkheimer and Adorno, "On the Theory of Ghosts." See also Gordon, *Ghostly Matters*, 20.

73 Gordon, *Ghostly Matters*, 24. Colón's situation is like the case of Valk sketched by Stoler in *Along the Archival Grain*, 233.

74 See Derby, "Haitians, Magic, and Money," 522.

75 Adorno and Horkheimer, "On the Theory of Ghosts." As in Derrida's formulation, these spirit demons hover between the living and the dead; see Sprinker, *Ghostly Demarcations*, 137.

CHAPTER 6. BIG MEN AND TALL TAILS

Earlier versions of this chapter were presented at the panel "Ecology and Ethnohistory: Problems and Approaches," at the annual meeting of the American Society for Ethnohistory, and at the conference "Writing Nature," at the French Department, UCLA, both in 2018.

1 The term *mañoso* likely derives from the Creole term *manié*. The Dominican term connotes "ability, dexterity and bad habits and usually is applied to animals, both beasts of burden and pets"; Martha Ellen Davis, personal communication, 2018. It appears frequently in its Creole form, *mañie*, in Prestol Castillo, *Pablo Mamá* (translated as *You Can Cross the Massacre on Foot*).

2 Interview with José, who is one of Martín Alcántara's field hands, April 2, 2012. See also Labov, "The Transformation of Experience."

3 The fact that devil pact genre is a deep narrative structure on the island can be seen in Danticat, *Claire of the Sea Light*, in which every birth is accompanied by a death; see also Weismantel, *Cholas and Pishtacos*, 194.

4 Johnstone, *Stories, Community, and Place*, 35; Labov, "The Transformation of Experience."

5 Moya, "Power Games and Totalitarian Masculinity," 126. Thanks to Randol Contreras for this insight.

6 Fabian, *Power and Performance*, 7.

7 Finnegan, *The Oral and Beyond*, 2.

8 Goffman, *Frame Analysis*, 435; Labov, "The Transformation of Experience." On testimony, see Paik, *Rightlessness*, 15.

9 As in the story of the *puerquita con las nalgitas doraditas* (the pig with the golden ass), discussed in chapter 7.

10 Stoler, *Along the Archival Grain*, 185.

11 Bauman, *Story, Performance, and Event*, 77; Goffman, *Forms of Talk*.

12 Rebecca Scott's pathbreaking book *Slave Emancipation in Cuba* and her subsequent works commenced a conversation that has continued with Lightfoot's *Troubling Freedom*; Fuentes's, *Dispossessed Lives*; and Nessler's *An Islandwide Struggle*. Quotes are from Nessler, *An Islandwide*

Struggle, 5, and Lightfoot, *Troubling Freedom*, 9. Bulamah has described how lack of mobility in Haiti—colloquially termed *lòk*—is a popular expression for misery within rural communities; see his "*Lòk*: Pandemics and (Im)mobility."

13   Larkin, "The Politics and Poetics of Infrastructure," 329, 331.

14   Dubois and Turits, *Freedom Roots*. Bulamah discusses mobility and its constraints in "*Lòk*."

15   James Fernández, "The Mission of Metaphor," esp. 58. He underscores that these sign images also convey affectivity (31).

16   Wilson, "Reputation and Respectability"; Lauria, "'Respeto,' 'Relajo.'"

17   Structuralists such as Mary Douglas and Alan Dundes use contrastive oppositions as an analytical tool; see Douglas, "Deciphering a Meal," 260, and Dundes, "Structuralism and Folklore." Horses also appear as demonic vehicles in US spirit visions; see Hyatt, *Hoodoo—Conjuration—Witchcraft—Rootwork*, 29. For a Haitian lougawou as a white horse, see Simpson, "Loup Garou and Loa Tales," 223.

18   Ligon, *True and Exact History*, 22. On donkeys and settler colonialism in southern Africa, see Jacobs, "The Great Bophuthatswana Donkey Massacre."

19   Márquez, "Los primeros caballos que pisaron América"; Rodríguez Demorizi, *Enciclopedia dominicana del caballo*, 8; Lambert, "Master-Horse-Slave," 623. On the equine history of Spain, see Renton, *Feral Empire*. Thanks to Vetilio Alfau Durán, who referred me to the *Enciclopedia dominicana del caballo*, which is a rich compendia of equine history and lore.

20   Rodríguez Demorizi, *Enciclopedia dominicana del caballo*, 8.

21   Rodríguez Demorizi, *Enciclopedia dominicana del caballo*, 91.

22   Rodríguez Demorizi, *Enciclopedia dominicana del caballo*, 9.

23   Rodríguez Demorizi, *Enciclopedia dominicana del caballo*, 325.

24   Hernández González, *El sur dominicano*, 1:57.

25   Hernández González, *El sur dominicano*, 1:61.

26   Chasteen, *Heroes on Horseback*, 32.

27   Rupert, *Creolization and Contraband*, 170–71. Yet these might have been primarily for export, since few mules apparently were used on the island; Rodríguez Demorizi, *Enciclopedia dominicana del caballo*, 8. Andrew Walker, "Strains of Unity," 39.

28   Rupert, *Creolization and Contraband*, 170. The privilege of their mobility also made them key organizational figures in the independence wars.

29   Hazard, *Santo Domingo*, 186. Hazard noted that "the familiar donkey, while in every part of the world an object of ridicule and amusement," was ubiquitous in Santo Domingo (202).

30   Alemar, *Escritos de Luís E. Alemar*, 135.

31 Jiménez, *Al amor del bohío*, 65.

32 Hazard, *Santo Domingo*, 130.

33 Crowley, "Sugar Machines," 403–36; Marx, *The Machine in the Garden*; Moreno Fraginals, *El ingenio*, 160–62.

34 Edwards, *The History, Civil and Commercial*, 332. He is actually describing indigo production on Hispaniola (330); he discusses sugar mills on 263.

35 Edwards, *The History, Civil and Commercial*, 255.

36 Five to six pounds of bones and two pounds of dried blood per hundred gallons of sugar; see Evans, *The Sugar-Planter's Manual*, 126, 199. It is interesting to note that while animal and human labor power are rendered invisible, the language of corporality is used in the sugar-making process, such as *defecación* and *leche* (defecation and milk) (Moreno Fraginals, *El ingenio*, 131, 141).

37 Hernández González, *El sur dominicano*, 1:57.

38 Keri Brandt uses the concept of "kinesthetic empathy" to describe embodied communication between horses and humans; see Brandt, "A Language of Their Own," 316.

39 Rodríguez Demorizi, *Enciclopedia dominicana del caballo*, 90.

40 Examples include R. Emilio Jiménez, *Al amor del bohío*, 1, 8.

41 Rodríguez Demorizi, *Enciclopedia dominicana del caballo*, 261.

42 See Porcher, "Animal Work," 302–18. Codependence between oxen and men is a theme in Manuel del Cabral's *Compadre Mon* (1940): "Hasta los bueyes de los ojos llanos / tras el boyero que regresa triste / con la palabra hombre entre las manos" (Even the dull-eyed oxen, after the herdsman who returns sad with the word *man* in his hands), 36. Thanks to Lizabeth Paravisini-Gebert for suggesting this text to me.

43 Marrero Aristy, *Over*.

44 In Spanish, "Era oscura como la madera a medio quemar; tenía la mirada inteligente y cariñosa; las patas finas y seguras; las pezuñas menudas, redondas, negras y duras. Todo en ella era vistoso y simpatico." Bosch, *La mañosa*, 39.

45 Of course, white sugar was exported, which left only brown sugar or honey available for coffee sweetening (Martín Alcántara, personal communication, June 2016). When Marcy Norton and I interviewed another of Martín's farm hands in June 2016, the oxen were named Negrito, Media Luna, Chino, and Chinito Piloto. Ethnic monikers are common terms of endearment for both people and animals in the Caribbean, and these translate roughly into "My Dear," "Honey," or "Baby."

46 In Spanish, "Mi mula? Por todos los cuartos del mundo no la doy. Y no es solo porque me desempeñe, sino porque le tengo cariño, como si fuera persona." Bosch, *La mañosa*, 38. It is worth noting here that the

term *mañosa* is used for people as well as animals, especially little boys; see Prestol Castillo, *You Can Cross the Massacre on Foot.*

47 This text images the caudillo as an honorable nationalist, yet military officers were often imperious and abusive; see Gascón, "The Military of Santo Domingo." Popular songs about the abuses of generals are cited in Damirón, *De nuestro sur remoto.*

48 Twiss, *Travels Through Portugal and Spain,* cited in Deans-Smith, "Creating the Colonial Subject," 191.

49 Garrido de Boggs, *Reseña histórica del folklore,* 122.

50 See Renton, *Feral Empire.*

51 Peluffo, "Heroic Masculinities and the War of the Pacific."

52 Beckles, "Black Masculinity," 240.

53 Rodríguez Demorizi, *Enciclopedia dominicana del caballo,* 261. Even important works on caudillismo fail to even include the word *horse* in their index; see Brunk and Fallaw, *Heroes and Hero Cults in Latin America*; Fuente, *Children of Facundo*; Salvatore, *Wandering Paysanos.*

54 Rodríguez Demorizi, *Enciclopedia dominicana del caballo,* 271; see also the tale of Cuban soldier *mambí* abjection from the independence war cited in Ferrer, *Insurgent Cuba,* 114.

55 Peter Wilson discusses another form of status competition—"putting down"—in *Crab Antics,* 119; see also Vargas, *De la casa a la calle,* 95.

56 In Spanish, "Ese caballo era la envidia del lugar. Era bestia entre las bestias." Moscoso Puello, *Cañas y bueyes,* cited in Rodríguez Demorizi, *Enciclopedia dominicana del caballo,* 264–66.

57 Palmié, *Wizards and Scientists,* chap. 1.

58 Goffman and Lauria stress deference as accorded through ceremonial idioms; see Goffman, "The Nature of Deference and Demeanor," 63, 65, 77; and Lauria, "'Respeto,' 'Relajo.'"

59 Rodríguez Demorizi, *Enciclopedia dominicana del caballo,* 339–40.

60 Ferrer, *Insurgent Cuba,* 48.

61 Rodríguez Demorizi, *Enciclopedia dominicana del caballo,* 159–64, 273. An important chapter in the history of Dominican stock breeding occurred during the US occupation period. The first horse racing stadium—the Hipódromo—was built in 1917 and the winners were turned into studs (Rodríguez Demorizi, *Enciclopedia dominicana del caballo,* 183–85).

62 Rodríguez Demorizi, *Enciclopedia dominicana del caballo,* 279; Moya, "Power Games and Totalitarian Masculinity" (2004); Foges, "Porfirio Rubirosa."

63 Greene, *Horses at Work,* 5, cited in Lambert, "Master-Horse-Slave," 621.

64 Smith and Philogene, *Myrlande Constant.*

65 Cabral, *Compadre Mon,* 66.

66 Rodríguez Demorizi, *Enciclopedia dominicana del caballo,* 260.

67   Bosch, *La mañosa*, 117–18. On British cattle breeding, see Ritvo, *The Animal Estate*; Kences, "The Horses and Horse Trades." A classic work on relations of trust and reciprocity is Eisenstadt and Roniger, *Patrons, Clients and Friends*. Clientage relations were especially important in the nineteenth-century Dominican interior due to the low level of monetization and state formation. Social debts were a key form of political capital, as seen in this turn of phrase expressing the vast political power of General Wenceslao Ramírez in the early twentieth century: "That he was friends of all the principal men of the country and all the governments wanted his friendship and his services" (Garrido, *Espigas históricas*, 267).

68   Gregory, *The Devil Behind the Mirror*, 30.

69   Gregory, *The Devil Behind the Mirror*, 24.

70   World Bank, "The World Bank in Dominican Republic"; "The Strange Economic Miracle."

71   LeGrand, "Living in Macondo."

72   See, for example, works on Peronism by Laclau, *On Populist Reason*; James, *Resistance and Integration*; and Karush and Chamosa, *The New Cultural History of Peronism*.

73   Larkin, "The Politics and Poetics of Infrastructure," esp. 333.

74   "El metro lleva costo."

75   Baud, *Historia de un sueño*. The metro was also a colossal font for PLD kickbacks, as has long been the case with public works in the Dominican Republic; see *"La corrupción sin castigo": Casos denunciados*, 107. Thanks to Pauline Kulstad González for bringing this to my attention. The Odebrecht scandal also involved large public works that camouflaged bribes to officials, see Pineda, "Dominican Republic Arrests Officials."

76   And in a region that forms part of the extended periphery of the rice-producing zone of San Juan de la Maguana, which thus requires irrigation.

77   De Ferranti et al., *Beyond the City*, 135. Data is drawn from the FAO and the World Bank; see Stefanelli, *Country Fact Sheet*; Werner, "Placing the State," 9. There has recently been very strong growth in organically grown crops such as cacao and bananas, but this has been regionally specific, occurring in Azua and Barahona in the south and Valverde and Montecristi in the north; see Raynolds, "The Organic Agro-Export Boom." The lack of an effective *síndico* (mayor) to advocate for Bánica until the last elections has been a key hindrance.

78   Dent correlates the rise in popularity of *música sertaneja* in Brazil with neoliberalism; see Dent, *River of Tears*, 8.

79   I have been inspired by work on Peronist melodrama here. See Karush and Chamosa, *The New Cultural History of Peronism*, 1–20; James, *Resistance and Integration*. But the critique of elites charted by Karush

and Chamosa and by James is not, of course, from the perspective of rural sectors. Thomson in "Indexing and Interpreting Emotion" notes how difficult it is to chart emotions within life narratives, which is why I have found that reading popular songs against life narratives can be a useful technique of comparison. Pacini Hernandez discusses música del amargue in *Bachata*, 168; see also Incháustegui, *El disco*, 26.

80 Marple, "Machismo, Femicide, and Sex Tourism."

81 See Raynolds, "Harnessing Women's Work"; Barndt, "On the Move for Food."

82 Massey, Fischer, and Capoferro, "International Migration and Gender"; this article explains the female predominance in Dominican migration terms of a "matrifocal system." See also Guarnizo, "Los Dominicanyorks."

83 Northern Manhattan Coalition for Immigrant Rights, "Deportado, Dominicano, y Humano;" Brotherton, "Dominican Republic: The Deportees."

84 This deepened the pattern of matrifocality that is a feature of former slave societies; see Smith, *Kinship and Class in the West Indies*. For more on children providing income to their mothers, see Wolseth, *Life on the Malecón*.

85 Safa, "Female-Headed Households"; Pacini Hernandez, *Bachata*, chap. 5. These forms of verbal aggression have taken a disturbing turn toward physical violence recently, as the country now has the third-highest rate of femicide in Latin America; see Marple, "Machismo, Femicide, and Sex Tourism."

86 Werner, *Global Displacements*.

87 Wasch, "Children Left Behind," 107. Thanks to Andrew Mitchell for this citation.

88 Finch, *Rethinking Slave Rebellion in Cuba*, 54.

89 Lambert, "Master-Horse-Slave."

90 Frankfurter, *Evil Incarnate*, 80. Labov and Waletzky confirm that the greater the sense of danger, the more effective the narrative ("Narrative Analysis," 30).

91 Eric Hobsbawm on social banditry in *Primitive Rebels*. On Olivorismo, see Davis, *La ruta hacia Liborio*; Davis, *The Dominican Southwest*; Lundius, *The Great Power of God*; and Lundahl and Lundius, *Peasants and Religion*.

92 James, *Doña María's Story*, 162–63.

93 Fernando Coronil in Ortiz, *Cuban Counterpoint*, xlii.

94 James, *Doña María's Story*, 171.

95 Abrams, *A Glossary of Literary Terms*, 76. Thanks to Elizabeth De-Loughrey for this citation. Ortiz uses the term *rascality* in his description of tobacco in *Cuban Counterpoint*, 18.

96   Marshall, *Anansi's Journey*, 91; the author traces this genre to the Akan peoples of Ghana.

97   This contrasts with epic tales; see James, *Doña María's Story*, 162.

98   All portrayed as the prototypically Cuban characteristics of tobacco in Ortiz, *Cuban Counterpoint*, 16, 22, 24. "Mulatto Don Quijote" is from Prestol Castillo, *You Can Cross the Massacre on Foot*.

99   See James, *Doña María's Story*, 163; James, *Resistance and Integration*; Lauria, "'Respeto,' 'Relajo,'" 64

100   Abrahams, *Afro-American Folktales*; Goss and Barnes, eds., *Talk That Talk*.

101   Abrahams, *Afro-American Folktales*, 6.

102   Gates, *The Signifying Monkey*, xxv; Scott, *Domination and the Arts of Resistance*, 137.

103   Padilla discusses cuentos as a means of self-fashioning for tourists in *Caribbean Pleasure Industry*, 130.

104   The concept of framing device is from Goffman, *Frame Analysis*, chap. 13. On nocturnal movement within Cuban slavery, see Finch, *Rethinking Slave Rebellion*, 66.

105   Zeuske, "Hidden Markers, Open Secrets."

106   Reiss, *The Black Count*. Thanks to Judith Bettelheim for bringing this text to my attention.

107   Ferrer, *Insurgent Cuba*, 58. Anthropologist Roberto DaMatta argues that the story of the Count of Monte Cristo is the paradigmatic rogue in Brazil; see DaMatta, *Carnivals, Rogues, and Heroes*, 206.

108   Cabrera, *El monte*, cited in González Echevarría, "Biografía de un cimarrón," 119; Lundius, *The Great Power of God*. Enrique Blanco, a renegade solider during the Trujillo period, also conforms to this motif; see Arzeno Rodríguez, *Enrique Blanco*. On the whiteness of the epic literary form, see Farrell, "Walcott's *Omeros*." Spending time underwater with the *indio* spirits is often said to be how clairvoyants receive their special powers in this region, the number seven being a marker of numinosity.

109   *Petite histoire* is from González Echevarría, "Biografía de un cimarrón," 116. A bacá narrative about a worker getting paid and having his salary usurped by a bacá appears in Davis, *The Dominican Southwest*.

110   Schama, *Landscape and Memory*, 15.

111   DaMatta, *Carnivals, Rogues, and Heroes*; Moya, "Power Games and Totalitarian Masculinity" (2002), 114.

112   Dunn, "Spanish Picaresque Fiction."

113   Guillén, "Toward a Definition of the Picaresque," 107.

114   Kuffner, *Fictions of Containment*.

115   Exquemelin, *The Buccaneers of America*.

116   Benjamin, *The Storyteller*.

117   Vega B., "Elías Piña"; Landers, *Atlantic Creoles in the Age of Revolutions*, 83.

118   Damirón, *De nuestro sur remoto*, 4, 25. Compare this to the version stressing violence in Pestol Castillo's *Pablo Mamá* (viii), albeit with the moral binarism characteristic of melodrama and a deeply dark view of rural life in which life is cheap and even the mosquitoes kill.

119   Gutiérrez Escudero, "El hato ganadero," 363–64. Gutiérrez Escudero links the metedor to the picaresque on the basis of his actions, but my argument is more about his skills in spinning yarns about his travels.

120   Abrahams, *The Man-of-Words in the West Indies*.

121   Moreau de Saint-Méry, *Description topographique . . . de la partie française*, 1:651–53, cited in Geggus, *The Haitian Revolution*, 20.

122   Rediker, *Outlaws of the Atlantic*, 19, 22.

123   Geggus, *The Haitian Revolution*, 22.

124   In the Rebellion of the Captains; see Gutiérrez Escudero, "El hato ganadero," 374; Cassá, "Rebelión de los capitanes."

125   Frank Moya Pons also claims that contraband, largely by montero hunters and stockmen, was a kind of "free cimarronaje" and became a Dominican "cultural phenomenon"; see Moya Pons, *La otra historia dominicana*, 96; and Gutiérrez Escudero, "El hato ganadero." For other forms of creole self-fashioning, see Scarano, "The *Jíbaro* Masquerade."

126   The term "masterless men" is from Scott, *The Common Wind*; see also Baretta and Markoff, "Civilization and Barbarism," 596.

127   Prestol Castillo, *You Can Cross the Massacre on Foot*, 17.

128   Rodríguez Demorizi, *Viajeros de Francia*, 117.

129   Sánchez Valverde, cited in Moya Pons, *La otra historia dominicana*, 130; Hernández González, *El sur dominicano*, 2:138–39; Sánchez Valverde, *Idea del valor*, 284–85. Compare this portrayal to José María Pichardo's description of a cash cropping farmer of tobacco and cacao, of whom "organization, seriousness, pulchritude, intelligence, make powerful business, and from there are born great successes" (Pichardo, *Tierra adentro*, 26). See Ramírez-D'Oleo, "Insolence, Indolence."

130   Moreau de Saint-Méry, *Descripción de la parte espanõla*, cited in Moya Pons, *La otra historia dominicana*, 131.

131   Ada Ferrer mentions mobility as one of the draws of joining the military in *Insurgent Cuba*, 33.

132   Grupo Dominicano, "Los Mangos de Baní," 1929, in "A History of Dominican Music in the United States"; Incháustegui, *El disco*, 14.

133   Incháustegui, *El disco*, 27.

134   In "El yerbero," the *yerbero mayor* declares himself *el doctor*.

135   El carbonero complains about the cost of firewood in Barrio Obrero. Examples abound, including "El botellero," "El carbonero," "Frutas del Caney," "Coco seco," "Rica pulpa," "Se va el dulcerito," "Pirulí," "El

yerbero," "Hojas para baño," and "Cao cao maní picao." Thanks to Raúl Fernández for these suggestions.

136   Labov and Waletzky, "Narrative Analysis," 29.

137   Burnett, *Masters of All They Surveyed*; Malamud, "Zoo Spectatorship," 219. Édouard Glissant has argued in favor of opacity as a mode of resistance; see his "For Opacity."

138   Hyde, *Trickster Makes This World*, 7. Thanks to Julie Franks for bringing this text to my attention.

139   Gates, *The Signifying Monkey*, xxiii.

140   Palmié, *Wizards and Scientists*, chap. 1.

141   Sartorius, *Ever Faithful*. Peguero notes that the Dominican military became larger than most Latin American nations as slaves sought freedom; see her *The Militarization of Culture*.

142   In Spanish, "Cuando venga mi prieta, me voy para Viejo, que le doy mi sombrero; si me voy para la Havana, me llevo a mi prieta, preparar la maleta." Trio Matamoros, *35 canciones desde Cuba con amor*. Thanks to Raúl Fernández for this suggestion.

143   As seems fitting, since musicians had to travel to work. Mobility emerges when the theme veers away from romance; see Austerlitz, *Merengue*, 1, 18, 21, 28, 35, 46–47. Themes of mobility such as coming and going also pop up in riddles and poetry such as *coplas*; see Jiménez, *Al amor del bohío*, 37–38; Garrido de Boggs, *Reseña histórica*, 75, in which a girl is exhorted to collect the calf and take it to the paddock. See further Garrido de Boggs, *Reseña histórica* 86–89, 97–102, 136; page 136 includes the verse "Con la Cruz vinimos, con la Cruz nos vamos, llegó, llegó, llegó, llegando" (We came with the cross, we leave with the cross, arrived, arrived, arrived, arriving), which accords with the fact that this would be sung by a cofradia member who often travels on pilgrimage.

144   Palmié, *Wizards and Scientists*, chap. 1. These liaisons are often enabled by mobility, as evidenced in lore about drivers, for example.

145   DaMatta, *Carnivals, Rogues, and Heroes*, 219.

146   DaMatta, *Carnivals, Rogues, and Heroes*, 235.

147   Collado, *El tíguere dominicano*; Krohn-Hansen, "Masculinity and the Political."

148   Bauman, "Performance," 100.

149   DaMatta, *Carnivals, Rogues, and Heroes*, 236.

150   On how these stories champion the protagonist as a survivor, see Collado, *El tíguere dominicano*, 26; DaMatta, *Carnivals, Rogues, and Heroes*, 209. See also Gates, *The Signifying Monkey*, 59.

151   Benjamin, "The Paris of the Second Empire."

152   Wilson, "Reputation and Respectability"; Fuller, "The Social Constitution of Gender," 137.

153   Vargas, "Everyday Life in a Poor Barrio," 452.

154   On playing dominos, see Vargas, *De la casa a la calle*, 102, but while she discusses the pervasiveness of trickery within dominoes, she does not consider the masculine pleasures of rivalry, which is an important idiom of Dominican masculinity. For rará, see McAlister, *Rará!*. A great demonstration of masculine rivalry is "Johnny Ventura con Anthony Rios."

155   Smith, "Atis Rezistans."

156   Bauman, "Verbal Art as Performance"; "Performance and Honor in 13th-Century Iceland," esp. 143. While Bauman was criticized for a lack of attention to female gender self-styling, much of his work concerns masculinity.

157   Bauman, "Performance and Honor in 13th-Century Iceland," 142.

158   Evans, Gauthier, and Forsyth, "Dogfighting," 217.

159   I did not encounter women in Bánica with protective bakas, but I did on a previous research visit in 1990, when I interviewed poor women who received housing from the Trujillo regime in the neighborhoods of Ensanche Luperón and María Auxiliadora in the northern portion of the city near Rio Ozama; see Derby, *The Dictator's Seduction*, chap. 6. This gendering is not universal. In Haiti, bakas are often imaged as diminutive protective spirits, and in the eastern Caribbean the baku is more like a Haitian djab, which brings you what you want via a contractual relationship; see Beck, *To Windward of the Land*, 224. Thanks to Bill Gannett for providing this reference. For more on the Haitian djab, see Jeffrey Kahn, "Smugglers, Migrants, and Demons."

160   Wilson, "Reputation and Respectability."

161   Vargas, *De la casa a la calle*, 136.

162   Barber, "How Man Makes God in West Africa."

163   Hertz, *Death and the Right Hand*. The opposed terms *angelic* and *demonic*, which are Christian categories, of course, is from Fanger, *Conjuring Spirits*, vii.

164   For this reason I was chastised by Doña Pico Mora, who led the San Francisco cofradía in 2010, for saying *diablo* as a curse. There is also an evangelical Protestant community in Bánica, but I did not speak with them, since they operated within another set of social networks.

165   For evidence of this, see "Creole Pigs," YouTube, posted by Robin Derby, October 12, 2015, https://www.youtube.com/watch?v=F8JKHRFoz50.

166   Frankfurter, *Evil Incarnate*, 32.

167   Frankfurter, *Evil Incarnate*, chap. 3. These figures have long been persecuted by authorities; however, in popular circles they are seen as useful problem-solvers when nothing else works. Dominicans cannot make them, but they can undo these spells. See the interview with Irio

Rodríguez in Roorda, Derby, and González, *Dominican Republic Reader*, 411–14.

168 DaMatta, *Carnivals, Rogues, and Heroes*, 208.

169 Thornton, *Negotiating Respect*, 176; Ramírez, *What It Means to Be a Man*, chap. 3.

170 See José's story at the beginning of this chapter. See also Contreras, *The Stickup Kids*, and Gregory, *The Devil Behind the Mirror*, 153. Of course, her namelessness might also have been a product of the fact that I was an outsider and I did not know her.

171 As Brendan Thornton has argued for evangelical converts in his book *Negotiating Respect*, 175.

172 Here I am drawing upon Ochoa, who calls similarly agentive *muertos* in Cuba "ambient dead." He does not consider masculinity in his account, yet this gender argument may well also work for his Cuban Palo material; see his *Society of the Dead*. On violence and respect, in addition to Thornton, *Negotiating Respect*, see Contreras, *The Stickup Kids*; and Bourgois, *In Search of Respect*.

173 Krohn-Hansen, "Masculinity and the Political," 112.

174 Ochoa, *Society of the Dead*, 188–89.

175 Ochoa, *Society of the Dead*, 190.

176 The term is from the Kikongo word for sorcerer or healer (Ochoa, *Society of the Dead*, Introduction).

177 As Hilary Beckles has argued (although in "Black Masculinity in Caribbean Slavery" he links it to post-emancipation violence in Jamaica, not to symbolic violence, as I am doing here). See also Palmié, *Wizards and Scientists*, 174–75. On the verb *to spirit*, see John Donoghue, "Indentured Servitude," 893–902. Thanks to Carla Pestana for clarifying the use of this term.

178 Beckles argues that "the iconography of the black male warrior as liberator and protector was enshrined within the discourse of nation building" (Beckles, "Black Masculinity in Caribbean Slavery," 240).

179 Sheller, "Sword-Bearing Citizens."

180 I have in mind the famous case of the Mirabal assassinations; for more on this, see Roorda, "The Murder of the Mirabal Sisters"; and Collado, *El tíguere dominicano*, 34.

181 Hebdige, *Hiding in the Light*, 35.

182 Wilson's "Reputation and Respectability." I discuss the tíguere in Derby, *The Dictator's Seduction*, chap. 5, with an emphasis on its other features such as sexuality and upward mobility.

183 Karush, "Populism, Melodrama, and the Market," 25.

184 White, *Speaking with Vampires*, 31.

185 Ochoa, *Society of the Dead*, 109.

186   Patai, "Whose Truth?" 270; Portelli, *The Death of Luigi Trastulli*, 23.

187   This idea was suggested to me by Roberto Strongman's comments at the conference "New Approaches to Black Atlantic Religion," UC Humanities Faculty Working Group, October 27, 2018, UCLA. For what he terms the "multiplicity of self," see his "Transcorporeality in Vodou."

188   The snake reference is from Beck, *To Windward of the Land*, 226.

189   Frontispiece, Deren, *Divine Horsemen*.

190   Beckles, "Black Masculinity," 228–29.

191   Portelli, *The Death of Luigi Trastulli*; Castillo Bueno, *Reyíta*; James, *Doña María's Story*.

192   Perks and Thomson, *The Oral History Reader*.

193   Echenique, "Documenting Realities of Oppression."

194   Moya Pons, *La otra historia dominicana*, 127; James, *Doña María's Story*, chap. 2. Emília da Costa argues this for the post-emancipation period in Brazil in her *The Brazilian Empire*. I have in mind clientelism within the domain of labor relations here; however, Dominican politics are also deeply clientelistic. See Werner, "Placing the State in the Contemporary Food Regime."

195   Kimhi, "International Remittances."

196   Contreras makes the point in *The Stickup Kids* that Dominican men feel that work for others is a violation of their masculine agency. Contrast this to Aisha Finch's slave testimonies from the 1840s Cuban revolt *la escalera*, in which slaves detailed their tasks as workers in great detail; see Finch, *Rethinking Slave Rebellion in Cuba*.

197   Smith, *The Matrifocal Family*.

198   These are the odd jobs he mentioned. The fact that Haitians today monopolize agricultural day labor in the borderlands contributes to its stigmatization, or perhaps he would have preferred a modern "white" job, which he did not have, of course.

199   Del Rosario and Morrobel, *Ocupación y pobreza rural*, 136. Thanks to Marion Traub-Werner for recommending this study.

200   "La vida no es tan fácil," "No es fácil aquí de conseguir 100 pesos"; Goffman, *Strategic Interaction*, 14.

201   A case in point would be a friend who was a lecturer in French at the Catholic University in Santo Domingo but whose family income was actually provided by a *fritura* or fried-meat stand in his barrio (neighborhood), a fact that took years of building *confianza* or trust for him to reveal. See Krohn-Hansen, *Jobless Growth*; Vargas, *De la casa a la calle*, 31. The denigration of labor seems to be a characteristic of post-emancipation societies, since by contrast poor Peruvian men take pride in their work; see Fuller, "The Social Constitution of Gender Identity."

202   A case in point is someone who is responsible for his family's ranch but has only occasional work as a tailor, which is his only income

stream. For more on this, see Derby and Werner, "The Devil Wears Dockers."

203   Roorda, Derby, and González, *Dominican Republic Reader*, 395–97; Turits, *Foundations of Despotism*.

204   Werner, "Placing the State," 9. This essay discusses land reform under the Balaguer regime.

205   Roorda, Derby, and González, *The Dominican Republic Reader*, 180–83.

206   Roorda, Derby, and González, *The Dominican Republic Reader*, 181–82. I have edited the language slightly here.

207   Cooper, "Erotic Maroonage," 80.

208   This apt definition emerged in a focus group I conducted on tigueraje in Bánica in 2015.

209   Smith, "Atis Rezistans," 133.

210   "Yo he caminado mucho, he hecho mucho trabajo." This comment also contrasts mounted mobility with walking, which is tiring and stigmatized.

211   Smith, "Atis Rezistans," 132.

212   Cooper, "Erotic Maroonage"; Smith, "Atis Rezistans."

213   Asma, *On Monsters*, 3. I use the term *agency* with all the caveats considered in Walter Johnson's insightful essay "On Agency."

214   Goffman, *Stigma*, 2.

215   Labov and Waletzky, "Narrative Analysis."

216   Barnet, *Biography of a Runaway Slave*; Gates, "Introduction."

217   Certeau, *The Practice of Everyday Life*, 93.

218   Eller, "Rumors of Slavery," 662; Nessler, *An Islandwide Struggle*.

219   Shaw, *Memories of the Slave Trade*, 56, 131.

220   Freud cited in Benjamin, "Some Motifs in Baudelaire," 115.

221   Austin, "Performative Utterances"; Goffman, "The Nature of Deference and Demeanor." Goffman discusses "ceremonial profanations" or defamation of social superiors as a technique of obtaining "the ceremonial grounds of selfhood" among those for whom "the only ceremonial statements that are possible for him are improper ones" (93), but he does not discuss the crafting of self through alternative domains.

222   I am grateful to Randol Contreras for suggesting this reading of these stories to me. On hegemonic masculinity in the Dominican Republic, see Moya, "Power Games and Totalitarian Masculinity" (2002), who draws on R. W. Connell's work in *Masculinities*; see also Contreras, *The Stickup Kids*.

223   Benjamin, "On the Mimetic Faculty"; Taussig, *Mimesis and Alterity*.

224   The term "secretly familiar" is from Freud, cited in Taussig, *Mimesis and Alterity*, 38, 42–43, 125.

225   Slotkin cited in Leverenz, "The Last Real Man in America," 759, 753.

226   The street, of course, being the core proscenium of manhood in Latin America. While there is a long literature on the casa/calle divide, for a compact summary as it relates to Dominican masculinity, see Moya, "Power Games and Totalitarian Masculinity" (2002).

227   Balaguer, *La isla al revés*, 52; Mir, *Cuando amaban las tierra comuneras*, 181. Thanks to Lisa Paravisini for suggesting the latter text to me.

228   Johnson, "On Agency." In the context of poverty, these stories are trophies, a strong contrast to scientific explorer travel narratives; see Terrall, "Heroic Narratives."

CHAPTER 7. BECOMING ANIMAL: FOOD, SEX, AND THE ANIMAL GROTESQUE

A portion of this chapter was presented at the panel *"El hombre, la hembra, y el hambre*: Food and Sex in Cuban Culture," at the conference "Cuba: An Island in a Changing World," University of California, Riverside, 2010, where it benefited from commentary and suggestions from Raúl Fernández. Passages of this chapter were previously published in "Trujillo, the Goat: Of Beasts, Men, and Politics in the Dominican Republic," in *Centering Animals in Latin American History*, edited by Martha Few and Zeb Tortorici (Durham, NC: Duke University Press, 2013).

1   *Unión Cívica*, June 4, 1961; Gates, *Signifying Monkey*, xxi; Hutchinson, *Tigers*, 92.

2   For more on predation on Hispaniola as a mode of interaction see Norton, *The Tame and the Wild*.

3   Gates, "Introduction"; Goss and Barnes, *Talk That Talk*, 17.

4   Bennett, *Being Property Once Myself*, 2–3. See also Ko, *Racism as Zoological Witchcraft*, 106.

5   Jackson, *Becoming Human*.

6   Cvetkovitch, *Archive of Feelings*, 1–14.

7   Routon, "Conjuring the Past," 635–36.

8   Brown, *The Reaper's Garden*; Ochoa, *Society of the Dead*, 7.

9   McAlister, *Rara!*, 109. Correspondingly, Yoruba initiates are called "slaves of the river."

10   Hurston, *Tell My Horse*, 30; Taussig, *Mimesis and Alterity*; Routon, "Conjuring the Past."

11   Edmond Paul calls this the "Bizango aesthetic" in "Pa Wowo (The Dance Steps of Wowo)," 80.

12   Routon, "Conjuring the Past," 640. Antelope horn shavings are used to cure poisoning; personal communication, Lorsk Jean Charles, Racine Wellness House, Brooklyn, New York.

13   In Spanish, "los cuernos tuvieron carácter sagrado-mágico. Con sus
       sonidos, ahuyentaran los malos espiritus." *Instrumentos de la música
       Afrocubana*, vol. 5, 325–26. Specifically they use the horn of a goat, a bull
       or a deer.

14   Taussig, *Mimesis and Alterity*, xiii.

15   Mañach, *Indagación del choteo*.

16   Roach, *Cities of the Dead*, 10.

17   Presentation at Atlantic History Speaker Series, UCLA, November 11,
       2020.

18   Rohlehr, "I Lawa," 341.

19   Hartman, "The Dead Book Revisited." On how discourses of bereave-
       ment can also be a source of joy, see Santner, *Stranded Objects*, 11. This
       culture of meeting death with humor is also a feature of Mexico; see
       Lomnitz-Adler, *Death and the Idea of Mexico*.

20   Santner, *Stranded Objects*, 147.

21   Thompson, *Flash of the Spirit*, 145; MacGaffey et al., *Astonishment and
       Power*.

22   Thompson, *Shine*. On El Negro Incognito, see González, *De esclavos a
       campesinos*, 156–60.

23   Scott, *Domination and the Arts of Resistance*, 19.

24   Shaw, *Memories of the Slave Trade*.

25   Gordon and Hutton-Mills, *Kanaval*.

26   Price, *Maroon Societies*, 16; see also Deive, *Los guerrilleros negros*. The
       martial view of the maroon is also due to the fact that much of the
       scholarship on maroons have focused on Jamaica and Surinam, which
       involved protracted and violent military insurgencies, as was also the
       case for Dominica. See Honychurch, *In the Forests of Freedom*.

27   Fouchard, *The Haitian Maroons*; Krug, *Fugitive Modernities*.

28   Price, *Maroon Societies*, 1; Curtis, "Masterless People," 156–57.

29   Altman, "The Revolt of Enriquillo," 587–614; Stone, "America's First
       Slave Revolt."

30   Curtis, "Masterless People," 153.

31   Gonzalez, *Maroon Nation*; Baud, "Una frontera para cruzar." Bernardo
       Vega and Carlos Esteban Deive, who did extensive archaeological
       work on maroons, has established four zones of early maroon activity,
       two of which are in the center part of the island. See Vega and Deive,
       "Topónimos dominicanos."

32   Eller, "Rumors of Slavery."

33   This commenced under the Trujillo regime with the 1937 massacre
       of Haitian-Dominicans, continued through the Balaguer regime, and
       culminated with the 2013 ruling under Leonel Fernández that sought
       to denationalize all those born after 1929. See "A Stand Against State-
       lessness." See also Baud, "Constitutionally White"; Turits and Derby,

"Haitian-Dominican History"; Hintzen, *De la masacre*; García-Peña, *Borders of Dominicanidad.*

34 Turits, *Foundations of Despotism*, chap. 1. La Rosa Corzo also challenges the martial runaway slave narrative by emphasizing that runaway slaves in eastern Cuba were actually more likely to disperse than confront authorities; see his *Runaway Slave Settlements*, 19.

35 Altman, "The Revolt of Enriquillo."

36 Moreau de Saint-Méry, "The Border Maroons of Saint-Domingue."

37 Hoermann, "'A Very Hell of Horrors,'" 185. For more on Moreau de Saint-Méry, see Johnson, *Encyclopédie Noire*.

38 Costa has revealed the importance of patron-client relations for freedmen in Brazil as well; see Costa, *The Brazilian Empire*.

39 Quote from Yingling, "Maroons of Santo Domingo," 45; Deive, *Los cimarrones del Maniel de Neiba*, 17, 26, 30, 44, 67. See also Bragadir, "Contested Topographies"; Bragadir, "Shifting Territories."

40 Deive, *Los cimarrones del Maniel de Neiba*, 60.

41 Lundahl, *The Haitian Economy*; Brendbekken, *Hablando con la mata.*

42 Tussac, *Flore des Antilles*, 1:25. Thanks to Elizabeth Landers for this citation.

43 Deive, *Vodú y magia en Santo Domingo.*

44 Apter and Derby, *Activating the Past*, xiii–xxxiii; Csordas, "Embodiment as a Paradigm," 11; Norton, "Subaltern Technologies"; and what Norton terms intersubjectivity in *The Tame and the Wild.*

45 Holt, "Marking," 1–20. Called *víveres* or *viandas* in Spanish, some are tubers and some are roots. They are a beloved and defining feature of Antillean cuisine and are equally associated with el monte in Cuba, where in the nineteenth century they were said to actually blacken one's complexion; see Dawdy, "La 'Comida Mambisa,'" 53; Gonzalez, *Maroon Nation*, chap. 6. Sixteenth-century chronicler Oviedo notes the African preference for yams; see Carney and Rosomoff, *In the Shadow of Slavery*, 91. Hurston describes a maroon hunt for feral pork in *Tell My Horse*, chap. 3.

46 Mayes, *The Mulatto Republic*, 23.

47 There are ninety-one place names with African referents, six to Congo and five to Maniel. See Vega and Deive, "Topónimos dominicanos."

48 Street, "Feral Animals," 402; Valerio Holguín, "Oda al Mangú."

49 Morban Laucer, "Características de los dientes"; José Victoriano Betancourt cited in Ortiz, *Los negros curros*, 36. For more on the transference of Central African culture to the Americas (which Jan Vansina describes as the foundational "cultural background" among African Americans), see Heywood, *Central Africans*, xi; Landers, "The Central African Presence"; MacGaffey, "Twins, Simbi Spirits"; Vanhee, "Central

African Popular Christianity"; Rey, "Kongolese Catholic Influences";
Heywood and Thornton, *Central Africans, Atlantic Creoles*.

50   *Mbi* means "the evil one, a bad person"; see Bentley, *Dictionary and Grammar of the Kongo Language*, 869; Ortiz, *Los instrumentos de la música*, vol. 3, 445–46. Thanks to Raúl Fernández for this reference.

51   Inoa, *Diccionario de dominicanismos*, 37. Eller reports that there were sightings and even captures of these creatures during the 1860s insurrection (Eller, *We Dream Together*, 43).

52   Paulino and Castro, *Diccionario de cultura*, 59. This lexical reduplication is likely a sign that its name is derived from a West African term (Andrew Apter, personal communication).

53   Moreau de Saint-Méry, *Description . . . de la partie française*, 28; Gonzalez, *Maroon Nation*, loc. 746.

54   Palmié, *Wizards and Scientists*, 75–76; Gordon, *Ghostly Matters*, xviii; Csordas, "Embodiment as a Paradigm," 15.

55   Bogaert, "Descripción de tipos cerámicos." On bat imagery, see Garcia Arévalo, "El murciélago en la mitología"; Garcia Arévalo, "The Bat and the Owl"; Veloz Maggiolo, Renato, and Luna Calderón, "Investigaciones arqueológicas en Cueva Collantes."

56   The song, recorded in 1990 by Cuco Valoy con La Nueva Tribu, is a plea to Anaisa, the Vudú goddess of love and happiness, and it is executed in exaggerated parodic form.

> Ayúdala, Anaisa Pye
> No llore Señora, abrácese a los seres
> Ayúdala, Anaisa Pye
> Ayúdala, Anaisa Pye
> A una pobre señora le echaron un Bacá,
> que le sale de noche convertido en animal.
> Ayúdala, Anaisa Pye
> Se que es un guanguá con figura de gato,
> De ojos colorao [colorados], le sale maullando.
> miau
> Tambien le sale en forma de caballo,
> El espíritu del muerto le sale relinchando.
> brrr Niii
> Echado el guanguá, ese espíritu loco,
> Sera que le interesa el amor de su esposo?
> Ayúdala, Anaisa Pye
> La pobre señora ha pedido a Anaisa,
> Que la libren del muerto que le han echado encima.
> Ay, el Barón del Cementerio!
> Ayúdala, Anaisa Pye.

57   Le Roy Ladurie, "Carnivals in History"; Mauss, *The Gift*, 76–77. I
          am punning here on the musical piece of the same name by Camille
          Saint-Saëns.

58   This practice was originally Iberian and dates back to the seventeenth
          century. Today the Bayaguana Cofradia, which is a male sodality,
          still collects cattle and turns it over to the church; see Davis, "Afro-
          Dominican Religious Brotherhoods," 89–91, 103.

59   Moreau de Saint-Méry, *Description . . . de la partie espagnole*, 3.

60   Fernández de Oviedo y Valdés, *Historia general y natural de las Indias*,
          4:97. Although the stress is not the same in the two words *baká* and
          vaca, an important distinction.

61   Rice, *The Power of the Bull*, 251.

62   Nicholls, *The Jumbies' Playing Ground*, 149–50. Bettelheim discusses
          the Horsehead and Cowhead characters in her article "Jonkonnu and
          Other Christmas Masquerades," 54–55.

63   Baum cited in Nicholls, *The Jumbies' Playing Ground*, 149.

64   Although Bettelheim notes that these characters emerged in the twen-
          tieth century and were whitened over time (Nunley and Bettelheim,
          Caribbean Festival Arts, 48). See Nicholls, *The Jumbies' Playing Ground*,
          57–58; Sluyter, *Black Ranching Frontiers*. The horns of the Dominican
          Lechón are also often painted red, and its mask today often has the
          colors of the Dominican national flag.

65   Nunley and Bettelheim, *Caribbean Festival Arts*, 55. They also note
          the British origins of these equine costumes, as does Nicholls in *The
          Jumbies' Playing Ground*. An important difference between this Malian
          masquerade and Caribbean Carnival, however, is that the latter is
          secular.

66   Hutchinson, "'A Limp with Rhythm'"; McAlister, *Rara!*, 89.

67   Goodman, "Elegant Instruments of Imperial Influence"; Smith, *A
          Sensory History Manifesto*, 45.

68   MacGaffey, "The Personhood of Ritual Objects," 47.

69   Nicholls, *The Jumbies' Playing Ground*, 46. This author also notes how
          predatory beasts have long figured in pagan rituals in Europe.

70   Kinser, *Carnival, American Style*, xvii.

71   Orovio, *El carnaval habanero*.

72   See the excellent documentary *Cimarrón Spirit*, directed by Rubén
          Durán; Tejeda Ortíz, *El carnaval dominicano*, 509. As in Ukraine, Easter
          is a time when spirits return to visit the living; see Kramer and Var-
          enikova, "At Ukraines' Gravesites."

73   Ortiz, *Los bailes y el teatro de los negros*, 446, 468–69.

74   In the Dominican Republic it was almost always a cow, but in Cuba it
          could be an ox (Tejeda Ortíz, *El carnaval dominicano*, 514).

75   Durkheim cited in Mazzarella, *The Mana of Mass Society*, 4.

76   Mazzarella, *The Mana of Mass Society*, 5. In Cuba it is spelled
        Kokorícamo.

77   Ortiz, *Los bailes y el teatro de los negros*, 477.

78   Soto David and Pérez Terrero, "Un hallazgo arqueológico"; Matos de la
        Rosa, *San Juan de la Maguana*, 244.

79   Thicknesse, *Memoirs and Anecdotes*, 73, cited in Ebanks, "The Maroons
        of Jamaica," 94.

80   Ortiz, *Los bailes y el teatro de los negros*, 441.

81   Roorda, Derby, and Gonzalez, *Dominican Republic Reader*, 413; Ubiñas
        Renville, *Pedro Bululú*, 119. Interestingly, creole chicken is one Colum-
        bian exchange creature that has been indigenized; see Derby, "Gringo
        Chicken with Worms."

82   Rohlehr, "The Calypsonian as Artist," 93. The adoption of the devil as
        a mascot has its origins in the colonial period and the diabolization of
        Indigenous and African religion; see Lewis, *Hall of Mirrors*. For more
        on Dominican masculinity, see Horn, *Masculinity After Trujillo*.

83   Ito, "In 'Star Trek Beyond,'" *New York Times*, September 27, 2016.
        Another example is the French term *malfaiteur*, "wrongdoer," which
        in the Haitian Creole form, *malfektè*, was levied against indigenes
        and Africans in the colonial period and has become a boasting label
        for powerful sorcerers such as Ernst Nelson, whom we met in the
        introduction. See Descourtilz, *Flore pittoresque et médicale*, 7:95; Smith,
        "Dialoging with the Urban Dead," 68. The appropriation of the devil
        as a countercultural symbol first started during slavery. For example,
        Makandal's slave hut was called a devil's hut (*caze à diable*); Garrigus,
        A Secret Among the Blacks, 91.

84   McAlister, *Rara!*, chap. 5. The significance of Judas in this context is
        complicated and is well explained by McAlister, "The Jew in the Hai-
        tian Imagination."

85   Hutchinson, "A Limp with Rhythm," 100.

86   Thanks to Brendan Thornton for the Toros reference. I discuss the
        Máscaras masquerade in Derby, "Trujillo, the Goat."

87   Gordon et al., *Kanaval*, 27.

88   Abrahams, *The Man-of-Words*, xvii. Ritual combats are also a part
        of Haitian rara; McAlister, *Rara!*, 152. See also Craft, *When the Devil
        Knocks*, 4; Blier, *African Vodun*, 27.

89   Octavio Paz quoted in Limón, "Carne, Carnales, and the Carni-
        valesque," 127.

90   Octavio Paz quoted in Limón, "Carne, Carnales, and the Carni-
        valesque," 127.

91   "The Diablos Cojelo," Embajada de la República Dominicana ante el
        reino de Bélgica, accessed March 10, 2025, https://bel.mirex.gob.do/wp
        -content/uploads/2023/07/Diablo-Cojuelo-ENG.pdf.

92   Guillén, "Toward a Definition of the Picaresque," 76; Dobal, "Los lechones."

93   Hutchinson, "A Limp with Rhythm," 94; Alcántára Almánzar, *Where the Dream Ends*, 26.

94   Drewal and Drewal, "More Powerful Than Each Other."

95   This is Hutchinson's argument in her fine article "A Limp with Rhythm," 97; Hutchinson, "Entangled Rhythms," 141.

96   Bakhtin, *Rabelais and His World*, 12; Limón, "Carne, Carnales, and the Carnivalesque," 138; Hutchinson, "A Limp with Rhythm," 91; Jansen, "Los sonidos del merengue," 146.

97   On vulgarity in rara, see McAlister, *Rara!*, chap. 2. Verbal obscenity is, of course, also a feature of African American verbal arts; see Abrahams, "Playing the Dozens."

98   Bourgois, *In Search of Respect*, 8. He was a member of the psychedelic rock movement and had a vision of the devil during an acid trip. Julian Apter, personal communication.

99   Beckles, "Black Masculinity in Caribbean Society"; Vaughan, "*Timba Brava*"; Bradford and Fernández, "Cuba's Second Golden Age of Popular Music."

100   Smith, "Atis Rezistans"; Dirksen, *After the Dance*, 22–24.

101   Smith, "Atis Rezistans," 132; Dirksen, *After the Dance*, 42–46; Cooper, "Erotic Maroonage." This moniker has had deep roots ever since Descourtilz called Toussaint Louverture a *tigre* (Descourtilz, *Voyages d'un naturaliste*, 1:20).

102   On the Sanky Panky, who trolls the beaches hunting for female tourists, see Moya, "Power Games and Totalitarian Masculinity" (2002), 129; Brennan, *What's Love Got to Do with It*, as well as the runaway comedic hit film *Sanky Panky*, dir. Pintor (Coral Films, 2007). For more on Dominican masculinity, see Krohn-Hansen, "Masculinity and the Political"; Horn, *Masculinity After Trujillo*.

103   Moya, "Power Games and Totalitarian Masculinity" (2002), 117.

104   Fieser, "The Caribbean Drug Kingpin."

105   Smith, "Atis Rezistans," 132.

106   González, "Hunting and the Free Peasantry."

107   Marx and Engels, *The Marx-Engels Reader*, 324.

108   Gordon and Parisio, *A Pig's Tale*. Beyond the sacrifice at Bois Caiman, evidence that the pig is sacred in Haiti is that its bristles became protective talismans during the insurgency; see Dalmas, *Histoire de la Révolution de Saint-Domingue*, 118. Bois Caiman was claimed by evangelicals to have been a "blood pact with Satan"; see McAlister, "From Slave Revolt to a Blood Pact," 187. There is also a pig masquerade within Haitian Carnival; see Gordon et al., *Kanaval*, 103.

109   Norton, "Going to the Birds"; Norton, *The Tame and the Wild*, 122–23.
       Kivland, *Street Sovereigns*, draws on work by Karen McCarthy Brown
       to discuss the word *wanga* (charm) in chap. 4. For more on the tíguere,
       see "Quirogas Garcia 'El tíguere Dominicano.'"

110   Babcock, "Introduction," *The Reversible World*, 13–38. Horsehead is a
       prominent figure in Trinidadian Carnival; see Bettelheim, "Jonkonnu
       and Other Christmas Masquerades," 40. On the role of competition
       in Carnival, see DaMatta, *Carnival, Rogues, and Heroes*, 112; McAlister,
       Rara! On animalization, see Viveiros de Castro, *From the Enemy's Point
       of View*, 302.

111   Hutchinson, *Tigers of a Different Stripe*, 34. Trinidadian men also have
       a preference for exogenous animal nicknames, such as "Village Ram,"
       "Donkey," "Mule," and "Ram Goat" (Rohlehr, "I Lawa," 341, 343).

112   Goffman, *Interaction Ritual*, 87.

113   Bakhtin, cited in Limón, "Carne, Carnales, and the Carnivalesque."

114   Abrahams, *The Man-of-Words*, xvi.

115   Lauria, "'Respeto,' 'Relajo,'" 54.

116   Burton, "Names and Naming," 49.

117   Interestingly, even the terminology for nicknames generally is more
       elaborate in Spanish than in English, since *apodo, mote,* and *sobrenom-
       bre* all mean roughly "nickname" but have slightly different meanings.

118   Burton, "Names and Naming," 36.

119   As mentioned in Inoa, *Diccionario de dominicanismos*, 29; see the
       Boletín Judicial from 1928 to 1932. Thanks to Pauline Kulstad for this
       data. Mora Oviedo, *Bánica*, 195, also mentions *bacá* as a nickname; it
       is common in Haiti for particularly forceful individuals (Johnhenry
       Gonzalez, personal communication).

120   Since *rabo* can also refer to the penis, this could also mean "cock-
       sucker." The nicknames are cited in Pérez, "El pueblo de los apodos";
       David, "Los apodos más famosos"; Pimentel Paulino, "Motes, apodos y
       sobrenombres"; "Los extraños apodos de aspirantes políticos." Thanks
       to Pauline Kulstad for these references.

121   Glover, "Todo a Relajo"; Mañach, *Indagación del choteo*.

122   Burton, "Names and Naming," 41.

123   Zeuske, "Hidden Markers, Open Secrets."

124   Goffman, *Interaction Ritual*, 5–46. He was responsible for 29 deaths
       and 27 injuries (González, *De esclavos a campesinos*, 143).

125   Burton, "Names and Naming"; Scott, *Domination and the Arts of
       Resistance*, 183.

126   Baud, "Constitutionally White"; García-Peña, *Borders of Dominicani-
       dad*, 7.

127   Stoller, *Embodying Colonial Memories*, 30; Haraway cited in Mol, *Eating
       in Theory*, 125.

128   Miller, "Coca-Cola"; Gordon et al., *A Pig's Tale.*

129   Dietler and Hayden, *Feasts*, 1–20.

130   "Soup Joumou"; Gonzalez, "Sancocho."

131   Ajiaco is thus a symbol of Cuba's blended identity. Ortiz claimed it dated from the sixteenth century and thus was Taíno in origin from *aji*, the Indigenous term for "hot pepper"; yet the same soup is equally a symbol of national identity in Colombia and Peru. Ortiz cited in Garth, *Food and Identity in the Caribbean.* Similarly, callaloo is seen as a metaphor for the racial diversity of Trinidad and Tobago; see Bettelheim, Nunley, and Bridges, "Caribbean Festival Arts: An Introduction," 31.

132   Díaz Quiñones, "De cómo y cuándo bregar."

133   Scott, *The Art of Not Being Governed.*

134   From the album *Cuba Hits Envidia*, Vol. 1 (2008). The full song is:

> Yo tenía una cochina y se me perdió
> En la sala, la cocina, el batey
> ¿Dónde estás mi cochina tú?
> La tenía guardada para la fiesta
> Ahora me pregunto dónde estará
> ¿Dónde está la patica de mi cochina?
> ¿Dónde está la cabeza de mi cochina?
> Se la robaron, se la comieron
> A mi me gusta criar mi cochina
> ¡A comer fritura!
> ¡Dame un pedacito de fritura, mamita!
> ¡Mi cochina!

135   This story emerged during a focus group on *tígueraje* in Santo Domingo that occurred during a beer-drinking session among close friends, organized for me by Julio César Santana in August 2008. The narrator said that I had earned the appellation *tíguere culebra* (tiger snake) because I thought the story was hilarious. Here is the story in its entirety:

> On the 23rd of December, the father says come and get the little pig so that we can kill it on the 24th for Christmas Eve dinner. He goes to look for one, and he is taken to a pen where there are many little piglets. What happens next? I don't know if you realize that this is the truth? He is saying this—not me! [guffaws of laughter] He sees all the baby piglets. But the one that catches his eye is the pig with the golden ass [this phrase becomes the rhyming chorus: la puerquita con las nalgitas doraditas]. I am embarrassed to continue. The guy sees the pig with the golden ass within the group, and he says to the man, how much does it cost so I can take it home to my father? He says he would

like the one with the golden ass. And so he takes the piglet and leaves. But then what happens? He takes it and puts it in the trunk of the car—and this is true—the guy drives through Bayaguana and onward onto the Mella highway in Santo Domingo. But he could not forget the piglet with the golden ass. And in thinking about the pig, he gets aroused. Hardly anyone understands this but I am telling you exactly what I was told. He says that he stopped the car in the middle of the freeway and says, "I have to see that pig's ass." And he opens the trunk and the first thing he does is he sees the pig with the golden ass. And from there he does the original sin with it. But he felt sorry when they killed it (my wife is going to kill me) and he could not eat it during the dinner because it was *that* pig. I want to know if in the developed world there are people who would do this with a pig. Only in this country. Here adolescent boys have sex with chickens.

In Spanish:

El 23 de diciembre, papá dice ve y busca el marranito para que lo matemos el 24 para la cena. Él va y lo llevan a una cerca donde hay muchos puercos chiquitos. ¿Qué es lo que sucede? Julio, no sé si se entienda eso, que es verdad. Él ve todas las puerquitas. Pero lo que llama su atención es la puerquita con las nalgitas doraditas. ¡Lo está contando él no yo! [guffaws of laughter] A mí me da verguenza para continuar. El hombre ve una puerquita que tiene las nalgitas doraditas entre el grupo. Y él dice al señor, ¿cuánto quiere para que se la lleve a su papá? Y él dice que él prefiere la puerquita que tiene las nalgitas doraditas. Y coge su puerquita y se la lleva. ¿Pero que sucede? Se la lleve y la mete en el baúl—eso es verdad—y el tipo va manejando para Bayaguana y para abajo y para el transcurso de la carretera Mella. Pero él "no se me podía olvidar de las nalgitas de la puerquita." Y en pensar en la puerquita, el pene iba creciendo—el bimbim [Dominican term for "penis"]. Casi nadie entendío ese asunto. Pero estoy contando lo que dicen, señores. Él dice que él se paró y en el medio de la carretera y dice, "Yo tengo que ver las nalgitas de la puerquita." Y él abrió el bonete del baúl y lo primero que él vio es la puerquita con las nalgitas doraditas. Y ahí se hizo el pecado original. Pero él tuvo la pena cuando se mató la puerquita (ahí mi mujer me va a matar) y él no podía comérsela durante la cena porque era *esa* puerquita. Yo quiero saber si en el mundo desarrollado hay hombres que hacen eso con una puerquita. Solamente en este país. Los niños adolescentes hacen el sexo con las gallinas.

136   Román, *Governing Spirits*, 198; Thornton, *Negotiating Respect*, 202. Dirksen discusses Haitian *betiz*, which is "vulgar humor," in *After the Dance*, chap. 4. There was also delight as well as embarrassment at my presence at the telling of this tale, and after its recounting, the narrator

joked that this behavior was a sign of Dominican underdevelopment but that relating this tale to me as an American—given the fact that the Dominican Republic has experienced two US interventions—also made the telling of the tale a "filthy rite" intended to tweak my sense of decorum though the "satiric humor of the oppressed"; see Stephen Greenblatt, "Filthy Rites." I also once heard a tale of a Cuban boy's sexual encounter with a turkey—which led me to ponder the significance of fornication with the premier US feasting food, one that could stand in for the elegant eagle, the US national totem (Adrian López Dénis, personal communication).

137   Indeed, a regional history has a whole chapter on a "picturesque" *hijo del pueblo* (townsman) who was discovered in the carnal act with a *burra* by the owner of the beast, who had him arrested, much to his annoyance. His defense to the judge was that as a single man, he had to attend to his sexual needs, after all, and that this was preferable to raping a minor (Mora Oviedo, *Bánica*, 178–79).

138   Román, *Governing Spirits*, 196; Freud, *The Joke*. The story was cued as a testimonial narrative that the narrator had heard from the teller in the first person ("this is the truth"; "he is saying this—not me!"), but this is belied by the rhyming poetic structure of the story, which delights in repeating the chorus five times. As oral historian Ruth Finnegan has noted, poetry is a specialized verbal art form, and the repeating chorus is a telltale sign that this story has been frequently retold and thus that it is clearly an oft-repeated tale, not a testimony. See Finnegan, *The Oral and Beyond*.

139   Ohnuki-Tierney discusses how commensality can be "symbolically equated with sexual union" in *Rice as Self*, 118.

140   From *Cuba Hits Envidia—Vol. 1*.

141   Wilson, "Reputation and Respectability"; Wilson, *Crab Antics*.

142   "Ay esa mujer!" *The Rough Guide to Bachata and Merengue*.

143   As in the lyrics to the song "Cógelo ahi" by Antony Santos: "Ay, cogelo allí, allí, allí, allí; no joda tanto, cogelo allí . . . a buen gusto, cogelo allí," with the staccato percussion filling in the blanks. *The Rough Guide to Bachata and Merengue*.

144   Lancaster, *Life Is Hard*.

145   Ramírez, *What It Means to Be a Man*, 58.

146   Wilson, "Reputation and Respectability," 73.

147   Fabian, *Power and Performance*; Adams, *The Sexual Politics of Meat*, 12.

148   Strathern, "Eating (and Feeding)," 3.

149   Norton, *The Tame and the Wild*, 7, chap. 7; Norton, "The Chicken or the *Iegue*."

150   Pérez, *Religion in the Kitchen*.

151   Rodrigo Bulamah, personal communication, July 20, 2020. Eating is also an idiom for soul-stealing witchcraft among the Bakongo; see

MacGaffey, *Religion and Society in Central Africa*, 147; Bockie, *Death and the Invisible Powers*. On Haiti, see Bourguignon, "The Persistence of Folk Belief," 39. On moral panics related to cannibalism allegations in Haiti, see Herskovits, *Life in a Haitian Valley*, 246; Ramsey, *Spirits and the Law*, 83–84. See also Hurbon, "The Bizoton Affair," on a scandal that occurred during the 1864 anti-superstition campaign. A group of women were sentenced to death for cannibalism on the fantastical allegation that a water spirit had taken a child, which was killed and cooked with beans and yams in a soup pot as a sacrifice for a vodou rite; see Ramsey, *Spirits and the Law,* 83–86. Raymundo González discusses the *comegente* affair, in which a serial killer was given the nickname "People Eater"; see González, "El comegente"; Maríñez, *Spirals in the Caribbean*, chap. 1.

152   Comaroff and Comaroff, cited in Shaw, *Memories of the Slave Trade*, 262.

153   Shaw, *Memories of the Slave Trade*, 202.

154   Rodrigo Bulamah, personal communication, July 20, 2020.

155   Geertz, "Deep Play," 82.

156   Agamben, *Homo Sacer*, 107; Bennett, *Being Property Once Myself*, 3; Shaw, *Memories of the Slave Trade*, 267.

157   Hartman, *Lose Your Mother*, 97.

158   On food consumption as fashioning distinctions between self and other, see hooks, "Eating the Other"; Tompkins, *Racial Indigestion*; and Ohnuki-Tierney, "We Eat Each Other's Food to Nourish Our Body."

159   Contreras, *The Stickup Kids*; Hess, "The End Is Near."

160   Pearson and Weismantel, "Does 'the Animal' Exist?," 23.

161   Batraville was one of the Haitian cacos who fought the US occupation; see Gaillard, *La guérilla de Batraville*, 62, for more on him and allegations that he was protected by pwen. On the negro incógnito, see González, *De esclavos a campesinos*, 152; Ramírez-D'Oleo, "Insolence, Indolence."

162   Weaver, *Medical Revolutionaries*, 92; Garrigus, *A Secret Among the Blacks*.

163   Bakhtin cited in Roach, *Cities of the Dead*, 63.

BIBLIOGRAPHY

Abbott, Elizabeth. *Haiti: The Duvaliers and Their Legacy*. New York: Touchstone, 1991.

Abrahams, Roger D. *Afro-American Folktales: Stories from Black Traditions in the New World*. New York: Pantheon, 1985.

Abrahams, Roger D. *The Man-of-Words in the West Indies: Performance and the Emergence of Creole Culture*. Baltimore: Johns Hopkins University Press, 1983.

Abrahams, Roger D. "Playing the Dozens." *Journal of American Folklore* 75, no. 297 (1962): 209–20.

Abrams, M. H. *A Glossary of Literary Terms*. Boston: Wadsworth Cengage Learning, 2012.

Ackermann, Hans-W., and Jeanine Gauthier. "The Ways and Nature of the Zombi." *Journal of American Folklore* 104, no. 414 (1991): 466–94.

Adams, Carol J. *The Sexual Politics of Meat: A Feminist-Vegetarian Critical Theory*. New York: Bloomsbury Academic, 2015.

Aderinto, Saheed. *Animality and Colonial Subjecthood in Africa: The Human and Nonhuman Creatures of Nigeria*. Athens: Ohio University Press, 2022.

Agamben, Giorgio. *Homo Sacer: Sovereign Power and Bare Life*. Translated by Daniel Heller-Roazen. Stanford, CA: Stanford University Press, 1998.

Ahmed, Sara. *The Cultural Politics of Emotion*. New York: Routledge, 2015.

Albert [other name unknown]. "Reseña topográfica de la parte de Santo Domingo habitada por españoles." In *Viajeros de Francia en Santo Domingo*, edited by Emilio Rodríguez Demorizi, 77–87. Santo Domingo: Editora del Caribe, 1979.

Alcántara Almánzar, José. *Where the Dream Ends*. Translated by Lizabeth Paravisini-Gebert. Pompano Beach, FL: Caribbean Studies Press, 2018.

Alemar, Luís. *Escritos de Luís E. Alemar*. Compiled by Constancio J. Cassá. Santo Domingo: Búho, 2009.

Alexander, Jeffrey. "Toward a Cultural Theory of Trauma." In *The Collective Memory Reader*, edited by Jeffrey K. Olick, Vered Vinitzky-Seroussi, and Daniel Levy, 306–10. New York: Oxford University Press, 2011.

Alexander, Jeffrey, and Philip Smith. *The Cambridge Companion to Durkheim*. Cambridge: Cambridge University Press, 2005.

Almada, André Álvares d'. *Brief Treatise on the Rivers of Guinea*. Liverpool: Department of History, University of Liverpool, 1984.

Altman, Ida. *Life and Society in the Early Spanish Caribbean: The Greater Antilles, 1493–1550*. Baton Rouge: Louisiana State University Press, 2021.

Altman, Ida. "The Revolt of Enriquillo and the Historiography of Early Spanish America." *The Americas* 63, no. 4 (2007): 587–614.

Altman, Ida, and David Wheat, eds. *The Spanish Caribbean and the Atlantic World in the Long Sixteenth Century*. Lincoln: University of Nebraska Press, 2019.

Alvarez Blásquez, Xosé María. *O libro do porco: Recollido do pobo*. Vigo: Ediciones Castrelos, 1972.

Anatol, Giselle Liza. *The Things That Fly in the Night: Female Vampires in Literature of the Circum-Caribbean and African Diaspora*. New Brunswick, NJ: Rutgers University Press, 2015.

Anderson, Jennifer L. *Mahogany: The Costs of Luxury in Early America*. Cambridge, MA: Harvard University Press, 2012.

Anderson, Virginia DeJohn. *Creatures of Empire: How Domestic Animals Transformed Early America*. New York: Oxford University Press, 2004.

Andrews, Kyrstin Mallon. "Sinks for the Press: Cholera and the State Performance of Power at the Dominican Border." *Journal of Latin American and Caribbean Anthropology* 23, no. 2 (2018): 338–62.

Andújar Persinal, Carlos. *Identidad cultural y religiosidad popular*. Santo Domingo: Editora Cole, 1999.

"Aparece un bacá en el paraje Limonae, en Jarabacoa." YouTube, posted by Jarabacoavideo, January 4, 2011. https://www.youtube.com/watch?v=zq_BhkGLJvY.

Appadurai, Arjun, ed. *The Social Life of Things: Commodities in Cultural Perspective*. New York: Cambridge University Press, 1986.

Apter, Andrew, and Lauren Derby. "Introduction." In *Activating the Past: History and Memory in the Black Atlantic World*, edited by Andrew Apter and Lauren Derby, xiii–xxxiii. Newcastle upon Tyne: Cambridge Scholars Publishing, 2010.

Archetti, Eduardo P. *Guinea-Pigs: Food, Symbol and Conflict of Knowledge in Ecuador*. Translated by Valentina Napolitano and Peter Worsley. Oxford: Berg, 1997.

Arluke, Arnold, and Clinton Sanders, eds. *Between the Species: Readings in Human-Animal Relations*. Boston: Pearson A & B, 2009.

Arnold, A. James, ed. *Monsters, Tricksters, and Sacred Cows: Animal Tales and American Identities*. Charlottesville: University of Virginia Press, 1996.

Arthur, Charles, and Michael Dash, eds. *Libète: A Haiti Anthology*. Princeton, NJ: Markus Wiener, 1999.

Arzeno Rodríguez, Luis. *Enrique Blanco, héroe o forajido?* Santo Domingo: Publicaciones América, 1980.

Asma, Stephen T. *On Monsters: An Unnatural History of Our Worst Fears*. Oxford: Oxford University Press, 2009.

Asmann, Parker. "Drug Ring Exposes Massive Money Laundering in Dominican Republic." *InSight Crime*, August 11, 2020. https://insightcrime.org/news/brief/dominican-republic-massive-money-laundering/.

Associated Press. "Two Ex-MLB Players Accused in Dominican Republic Drug-Trafficking Investigation." *Los Angeles Times*, August 20, 2019.

"Aterrador un baca golpea hombre en casa endemoniada PERSONAJES CON EL CHICO SANDY." YouTube, posted by el chico sandy, February 1, 2020. https://youtu.be/DyhZ7SYmNxE.

Austerlitz, Paul. *Merengue: Dominican Music and Dominican Identity*. Philadelphia: Temple University Press, 1997.

Austin, Anastasia, and Douwe den Held. "The Dominican Republic: The Caribbean's Cocaine Hub." *Insight Crime*, September 7, 2022. https://insightcrime.org/investigations/dominican-republic-caribbean-cocaine-hub/.

Austin, J. L. "Performative Utterances." In J. L. Austin, *Philosophical Papers*, edited by J. O. Urmson and G. J. Warnock, 220–40. Oxford: Oxford University Press, 1979.

Averill, Gage. *A Day for the Hunter, a Day for the Prey: Popular Music and Power in Haiti*. Chicago: University of Chicago Press, 1997.

Ávila Suero, Víctor. *Barreras: Estudio etnográfico de una comunidad rural dominicana*. Santo Domingo: Editorial CENAPEC, 1988.

Babcock, Barbara. "Introduction." In *The Reversible World: Symbolic Inversion in Art and Society,* edited by Barbara Babcock, 13–38. Ithaca, NY: Cornell University Press, 1978,

Bakhtin, Mikhail M. *Rabelais and His World*. Translated by Hélène Iswolsky. Cambridge, MA: MIT Press, 1971.

Balaguer, Joaquín. *La isla al revés: Haití y el destino dominicano*. Santo Domingo: Fundación José Antonio Caro, 1983.

Barber, Karin. "How Man Makes God in West Africa: Yoruba Attitudes Towards the *Orisa*." *Africa* 51, no. 3 (1981): 724–45.

Barboza, David. "Goliath of the Hog World: Fast Rise of Smithfield Foods Makes Regulators Wary." *New York Times*, April 7, 2000.

Barcia Paz, Manuel. *Seeds of Insurrection: Domination and Resistance on Western Cuban Plantations, 1808–1848*. Baton Rouge: Louisiana State University Press, 2008.

Baretta, Silvio R. Duncan, and John Markoff. "Civilization and Barbarism: Cattle Frontiers in Latin America." *Comparative Studies in Society and History* 20, no. 4 (1978): 587–620.

Barndt, Deborah. "On the Move for Food: Three Women Behind the Tomato's Journey." In *Food and Culture: A Reader*, edited by Carole Counihan and Penny Van Esterik, 472–84. New York: Routledge, 2015.

Barnet, Miguel. *Biography of a Runaway Slave*. Translated by W. Nick Hill. Willimantic, CT: Curbstone Press, 1994.

Bataille, Georges, and Allan Stoekl. *Visions of Excess: Selected Writings, 1927–1939*. Minneapolis: University of Minnesota Press, 1985.

Baud, Michiel. "'Constitutionally White': The Forging of a National Identity in the Dominican Republic." In *Ethnicity in the Caribbean: Essays in Honor of Harry*

Hoetink, edited by G. Oostindie, 121–51. Amsterdam: Amsterdam University Press, 2011.

Baud, Michiel. *Historia de un sueño: Los ferrocarriles públicos en la República Dominicana, 1880–1930.* Santo Domingo: Fundación Cultural Dominicana, 1993.

Baud, Michiel. "State-Building and Borderlands." *Fronteras: Towards a Borderless Latin America,* edited by Pitou van Dijck, Arij Ouweneel, and Annelis Zoomers, 41–79. Amsterdam: CEDLA, 2000.

Baud, Michiel. "Una frontera para cruzar: La sociedad rural a través de la frontera dominico-haitiana (1870–1930)." *Estudios Sociales* 26, no. 94 (1993): 5–28.

Baud, Michiel. "Una frontera—refugio: Dominicanos y haitianos contra el estado (1870–1930)." *Estudios Sociales* 26, no. 92 (1993): 39–64.

Baud, Michiel, and Willem Van Schendel. "Toward a Comparative History of Borderlands." *Journal of World History* 8, no. 2 (1997): 211–42.

Bauman, Richard. "Performance." In *A Companion to Folklore,* edited by Regina F. Bendix and Galit Hasan-Rokem, 94–118. Malden, MA: Wiley Blackwell, 2012.

Bauman, Richard. "Performance and Honor in 13th-Century Iceland." *Journal of American Folklore* 99, no. 392 (1986): 131–50.

Bauman, Richard. *Story, Performance, and Event: Contextual Studies of Oral Narrative.* Cambridge: Cambridge University Press, 1986.

Bauman, Richard. "Verbal Art as Performance." *American Anthropologist* 77, no. 2 (1975): 290–311.

Bautista, Domingo, and Wilson Mejía. *Si me permiten hablar: La historia de Palma Sola.* Santo Domingo: Editora de la Universidad Autónoma de Santo Domingo, 2006.

Baxter, Daniel. "Law Enforcement Seizes 24 Pounds of Liquid Cocaine at Logan International Airport." *Aviation Online Magazine,* February 9, 2013. http:// avstop.com/february_2013/law_enforcement_seizes_24_pounds_of_liquid _cocaine_at_logan_international_airport.htm.

Bayart, Jean-François. *The State in Africa: The Politics of the Belly.* Cambridge: Polity, 2009.

Beauvoir-Dominique, Rachel. "Underground Realms of Being: Vodoun Magic." In *Sacred Arts of Haitian Vodou,* edited by Donald Cosentino, 153–77. Los Angeles: UCLA Fowler Museum of Cultural History, 1995.

Beck, Jane. *To Windward of the Land: The Occult World of Alexander Charles.* Bloomington: Indiana University Press, 1979.

Beck, Jane. "West Indian Sea Magic." *Folklore* 88, no. 2 (1977): 194–202.

Beckles, Hilary. "Black Masculinity in Caribbean Slavery." In *Interrogating Caribbean Masculinities: Theoretical and Empirical Analyses,* edited by Rhoda E. Reddock, 225–43. Kingston: University of the West Indies Press, 2004.

Beckman, Ericka. "What's Left of Macondo?" *Dissent,* April 23, 2014. https://www .dissentmagazine.org/blog/whats-left-of-macondo.

Beckwith, Martha Warren. *Black Roadways: A Study of Jamaican Folk Life.* New York: Negro Universities Press, 1969.

Beier, Ulli. "Dog Magic of Yoruba Hunters." In *The Hunter Thinks the Monkey Is Not Wise—the Monkey Is Wise, but He Has His Own Logic: A Selection of Essays*, edited by Wole Ogundele, 77–80. Bayreuth: Bayreuth University, 2001.

Beier, Ulli. "The Yoruba Attitude Toward Dogs." In *The Hunter Thinks the Monkey Is Not Wise—the Monkey Is Wise, but He Has His Own Logic: A Selection of Essays*, edited by Wole Ogundele, 69–76. Bayreuth: Bayreuth University, 2001.

Beinart, William, Karen Middleton, and Simon Pooley, eds. *Wild Things: Nature and the Social Imagination*. Cambridge: White Horse Press, 2013.

Bell, Madison Smartt. "Twenty Dollars." In *Haiti Noir*, edited by Edwidge Danticat, 88–114. New York: Akashic, 2011.

Bendix, Regina, and Galit Hasan-Rokem, eds. *A Companion to Folklore*. Malden, MA: Wiley-Blackwell, 2012.

Benítez-Rojo, Antonio. *The Repeating Island: The Caribbean and the Postmodern Perspective*. Translated by James E. Maraniss. Durham, NC: Duke University Press, 1996.

Benjamin, Walter. "On the Mimetic Faculty." In *Reflections: Essays, Aphorisms, Autobiographical Writings*, edited by Peter Demetz, translated by Edmund Jephcott, 333–36. New York: Harcourt Brace Jovanovich, 1979.

Benjamin, Walter. "The Paris of the Second Empire in Baudelaire." In *Selected Writings*, Vol. 3, *1938–1940*, 75–135. Translated by Howard E. Wels. Cambridge, MA: Belknap Press of Harvard University Press, 2008.

Benjamin, Walter. "Some Motifs in Baudelaire." In *Charles Baudelaire: A Lyric Poet in the Era of High Capitalism*, 107–54. London: Verso, 1976.

Benjamin, Walter. *The Storyteller: Tales out of Loneliness*. Edited and translated by Sam Dolbear, Esther Leslie, and Sebastian Truskolaski. New York: Verso, 2016.

Bennett, Jane. *Vibrant Matter: A Political Ecology of Things*. Durham, NC: Duke University Press, 2010.

Bennett, Joshua. *Being Property Once Myself: Blackness and the End of Man*. Cambridge, MA: Harvard University Press, 2020.

Bentley, William Holman. *Dictionary and Grammar of the Kongo Language*. London: Baptist Missionary Society, 1887.

Berger, John. "Why Look at Animals?" In *The Animals Reader: The Essential Classic and Contemporary Writings*, edited by Linda Kalof and Amy J. Fitzgerald, 251–61. London: Bloomsbury Academic, 2014.

Bernardo y Estrada, Rodrigo de. *Manual de agrimensura cubana según el sistema especial que rige en la isla: Contiene una explicación por orden alfabético de las principales voces facultativas, el modo de operar sobre el terreno y los autos acordados, reales órdenes y reglamentos que tienen relación con la facultad*. N.p.: Sagua la Grande Imprenta de la Hoja Económica, 1854.

Bettega, Amilcar, and Pilar Altinier. *Barrera*. Tenerife: Baile del Sol, Ediciones S.L., 2021.

Bettelheim, Judith, ed. *Cuban Festivals: A Century of Afro-Cuban Culture*. Princeton, NJ: Markus Wiener, 2000.

Bettelheim, Judith, ed. *Cuban Festivals: An Illustrated Anthology*. New York: Garland, 1993.

Bettelheim, Judith. "Jonkonnu and Other Christmas Masquerades." In *Caribbean Festival Arts: Each and Every Bit of Difference*, edited by John W. Nunley and Judith Bettelheim, 39–84. Saint Louis, MO: Saint Louis Art Museum, 1988.

Bettelheim, Judith. "Palo Monte Mayombe and Its Influence on Contemporary Cuban Art." *African Arts* 34, no. 2 (2001): 36–49, 94–96.

Bettelheim, Judith, and Lauren Derby. "Olivorio Altars and *Espiritismo*." In *Transcultural Pilgrim: Three Decades of Work by José Bedia*, edited by Judith Bettelheim and Janet Catherine Berlo, 141–46. Los Angeles: UCLA Fowler Museum of Cultural History, 2012.

Bettelheim, Judith, John Nunley, and Barbara Bridges. "Caribbean Festival Arts: An Introduction." In John W. Nunley, Judith Bettelheim, et al., *Caribbean Festival Arts: Each and Every Bit of Difference*, 31–38. Saint Louis, MO: Saint Louis Art Museum, 1988.

Billows, Harry Clyde, and Harold Beckwith. *Palm Oil and Kernels: The "Consols of the West Coast"; An Exposition of the Palm Oil Industry, Its Romantic Development and Commercial Possibilities*. Liverpool: Birchhall, 1913.

Bishko, Charles Julian. "The Peninsular Background of Latin American Cattle Ranching." *Hispanic American Historical Review* 32, no. 4 (1952): 491–515.

Blachette, L.-J., F.-S. Zoega, and J. de Fontenelle. *A Manual of the Art of Making and Refining Sugar from Beets, Including the Cultivation of the Plant, and the Various Improvements in the Manufacture*. Boston: Marsh, Capen and Lyon, 1836.

Blakley, Christopher Michael. *Empire of Brutality: Enslaved People and Animals in the Atlantic World*. Baton Rouge: Louisiana State University Press, 2023.

Blakley, Christopher Michael. "'To Get a Cargo of Flesh, Bone, and Blood': Animals in the Slave Trade in West Africa." *International Review of Environmental History* 5, no. 1 (2019): 85–111.

Blanco, María, and Esther Peeren. "Introduction: Conceptualizing Spectralities." In *The Spectralities Reader: Ghosts and Haunting in Contemporary Cultural Theory*, edited by María Blanco and Esther Peeren, 1–28. New York: Bloomsbury Academic, 2013.

Blier, Suzanne Preston. *African Vodun: Art, Psychology, and Power*. Chicago: University of Chicago Press, 1995.

Block, Kristen. "Healing Waters of the Caribbean: Affliction and Hope in Creole Discourses on Water Cures." Paper presented at the annual meeting of the History of Science Society, Utrecht, 2019.

Bockie, Simon. *Death and the Invisible Powers: The World of Kongo Belief*. Bloomington: Indiana University Press, 1993.

Bogaert, Harold Olsen. "Descripción de tipos cerámicos de Cueva Collantes Distrito Nacional." *Boletín del Museo del Hombre Dominicano*, no. 18 (1983): 91–110.

Bonó, Pedro Francisco. "El montero." In *Lengua y folklore de Santo Domingo*, edited by Emilio Rodríguez Demorizi, 308. Santiago, Dominican Republic: UCMM, 1975.

Bonó, Pedro Francisco. "In the Army Camp at Bermejo." In *The Dominican Republic Reader*, edited by Eric Paul Roorda, Lauren Derby, and Raymundo González, 149–53. Durham, NC: Duke University Press, 2014.

Bosch, Juan. *La Mañosa: Novela*. 1936. Santo Domingo: Alfa y Omega, 1979.

Bosch Carcuro, Matías, ed. *Masacre de 1937, 80 años después: Reconstruyendo la memoria*. Santo Domingo: Fundación Juan Bosch, 2018.

Bottemiller, Helena. "Codex Adopts Ractopamine Limits for Beef and Pork." *Food Safety News*, July 6, 2012.

Bourdieu, Pierre. *The Logic of Practice*. Translated by Richard Nice. Stanford, CA: Stanford University Press, 1990.

Bourdieu, Pierre. *Outline of a Theory of Practice*. Translated by Richard Nice. Cambridge: Cambridge University Press, 1977.

Bourgois, Philippe I. *In Search of Respect: Selling Crack in El Barrio*. Cambridge: Cambridge University Press, 1996.

Bourguignon, Erika. "The Persistence of Folk Belief: Some Notes on Cannibalism and Zombis in Haiti." *Journal of American Folklore* 72, no. 283 (1959): 36–46.

Bradford, Anita Casavantes, and Raúl Fernández. "Cuba's Second Golden Age of Popular Music, 1989–2005." In *Oxford Research Encyclopedia of Latin American History*, edited by Ángela Vergara. New York: Oxford University Press, 2016.

Bragadir, Nathalie. "Contested Topographies: Border Passing in Colonial Hispaniola." PhD diss., Department of Comparative Literature, New York University, 2014.

Bragadir, Nathalie. "Shifting Territories: The Production of Space on Eighteenth Century Hispaniola." In *Transnational Hispaniola: New Directions in Haitian and Dominican Studies*, edited by April J. Mayes and Kiran Jayaram, 23–43. Gainesville: University of Florida Press, 2017.

Brandt, Keri. "A Language of Their Own: An Interactionist Approach to Human-Horse Communication." *Society and Animals* 12, no. 4 (2004): 299–316.

Brantz, Dorothee, ed. "Introduction." In *Beastly Natures: Animals, Humans, and the Study of History*, edited by Dorothee Brantz, 1–16. Charlottesville: University of Virginia Press, 2010.

Brendbekken, Marit. "Beyond Vodou and Anthroposophy in the Dominican-Haitian Borderlands." *Social Analysis* 46, no. 3 (2002): 31–74.

Brendbekken, Marit. *Hablando con la mata: Estudio antropológico de la interdependencia entre "la vida social de las plantas" y la construcción de la identidad campesina en el área fronteriza de la República Dominicana*. Santo Domingo: Instituto de Medicina Dominicana, 1998.

Brennan, Denise. *What's Love Got to Do with It? Transnational Desires and Sex Tourism in the Dominican Republic*. Durham, NC: Duke University Press, 2004.

Breslaw, Elaine G., ed. *Witches of the Atlantic World: A Historical Reader and Primary Sourcebook.* New York: New York University Press, 2000.

Brotherton, David. "Dominican Republic: The Deportees." *NACLA*, September 25, 2007. https://nacla.org/article/dominican-republic-deportees.

Brown, David H. *The Light Inside: Abakuá Society Arts and Cuban Cultural History.* Washington, DC: Smithsonian Institution Press, 2003.

Brown, David H. *Santería Enthroned: Art, Ritual, and Innovation in an Afro-Cuban Religion.* Chicago: University of Chicago Press, 2003.

Brown, Karen McCarthy. "Making *Wanga*: Reality Constructions and the Magical Manipulations of Power." In *Transparency and Conspiracy: Ethnographies of Suspicion in the New World Order*, edited by Harry G. West and Todd Sanders, 233–57. Durham, NC: Duke University Press, 2003.

Brown, Karen McCarthy. *Mama Lola: A Vodou Priestess in Brooklyn.* Berkeley: University of California Press, 1991.

Brown, Vincent. *The Reaper's Garden: Death and Power in the World of Atlantic Slavery.* Cambridge, MA: Harvard University Press, 2008.

Brunk, Samuel, and Ben Fallaw, eds. *Heroes and Hero Cults in Latin America.* Austin: University of Texas Press, 2006.

Bulamah, Rodrigo. "From Marrons to Kreyòl: Human-Animal Relations in Early Caribbean." In *Global Plantations in the Modern World: Sovereignties, Ecologies, Afterlives*, edited by Colette Le Petitcorps, Marta Macedo, and Irene Peano, 35–58. Cham: Palgrave Macmillan, 2023.

Bulamah, Rodrigo. "*Lòk*: Pandemics and (Im)mobility in Northern Haiti." *Global Perspectives* 2, no. 1 (2021): 29–39.

Bulamah, Rodrigo. "Pode um porco falar? Doença, sistemas e sacrifício no Caribe." *Horizontes Antropológicos* 26, no. 57 (2020): 57–92.

Bulamah, Rodrigo. *Ruínas circulares: Uma antropologia da história no norte do Haiti.* Rio de Janeiro: Papéis Selvagens Edições, 2024.

Burke, Timothy. *Lifebuoy Men, Lux Women: Commodification, Consumption, and Cleanliness in Modern Zimbabwe.* Durham, NC: Duke University Press, 1996.

Burnard, Trevor G., and John D. Garrigus. *The Plantation Machine: Atlantic Capitalism in French Saint-Domingue and British Jamaica.* Philadelphia: University of Pennsylvania Press, 2016.

Burnett, D. Graham. *Masters of All They Surveyed: Exploration, Geography, and a British El Dorado.* Chicago: University of Chicago Press, 2000.

Burton, Richard D. E. "Names and Naming in Afro-Caribbean Cultures." *New West Indian Guide* 73, nos. 1–2 (1999): 35–58.

Burton, Richard Francis. *A Mission to Gelele, King of Dahome.* New York: Praeger, 1966.

"Buxton Baccoos Keep Up Attacks on Family." *Sunday Chronicle* (Guyana), August 28, 1966.

Bynum, Caroline Walker. *Metamorphosis and Identity.* New York: Zone Books, 2001.

Cabral, Héctor Incháustegui. *Informe sobre el sacrificio de cerdos*. Santo Domingo: Secretario de Estado de Agricultura, Ministerio de Agricultura, April 19, 1979.

Cabral, Manuel del. *Compadre Mon*. 1940. Santo Domingo: Banco de Reservas de la República Dominicana, 2001.

Cabrera, Lydia. *Afro-Cuban Tales: Cuentos Negros de Cuba*. Translated by Alberto Hernández-Chiroldes and Lauren Yoder. Lincoln: University of Nebraska Press, 2004.

Cabrera, Lydia. *El monte*. Havana: Editorial Letras Cubanas, 2006.

Cabrera, Lydia. *La sociedad secreta Abakuá: Narrada por viejos adeptos*. Colección de Chicherekú. Miami: Ediciones C.R., 1970.

Cabrera, Lydia. *Reglas de Congo/Palo Monte Mayombe*. Miami: Peninsular Print, 1979.

Cadeau, Sabine. *More Than a Massacre: Racial Violence and Citizenship in the Haitian–Dominican Borderlands*. Cambridge: Cambridge University Press, 2022.

Calder, Bruce J. *The Impact of Intervention: The Dominican Republic During the U.S. Occupation of 1916–1924*. Austin: University of Texas Press, 1984.

Calvo, Pedrito. "El cochino." *Cuba Hits Envidia*, Vol. 1. Música Tropical, 2008.

Candea, Matei. "'I Fell in Love with Carlos the Meerkat': Engagement and Detachment in Human–Animal Relations." *American Ethnologist* 37, no. 2 (2010): 241–58.

Canessa, Andrew. *Intimate Indigeneities*. Durham, NC: Duke University Press, 2012.

Carney, Judith Ann, and Richard Nicholas Rosomoff. *In the Shadow of Slavery: Africa's Botanical Legacy in the Atlantic World*. Berkeley: University of California Press, 2009.

Carpentier, Alejo. *The Kingdom of This World*. Translated by Pablo Medina. New York: Farrar, Straus and Giroux, 2017.

Caruth, Cathy. "Unclaimed Experience: Trauma and the Possibility of History." *Yale French Studies*, no. 79 (1991): 181–92.

Casas, Bartolomé de las. *A Short Account of the Destruction of the Indies*. La Vergne, TN: Neeland Media, 2019.

Cassá, Roberto. "Rebelión de los capitanes: Un movimiento popular en un espacio local." In *Historia general del pueblo dominicano*, vol. 2, edited by Roberto Cassá and Raymundo González, 461–510. Santo Domingo: Academia Dominicana de Historia, 2018.

Castillo Bueno, María de los Reyes. *Reyíta: The Life of a Black Cuban Woman in the Twentieth Century*. Edited by Daisy Rubiera Castillo. Translated by Anne McLean. Durham, NC: Duke University Press, 2000.

Catalogue d'objets d'art . . . , meubles, belle tenture en cuir de Cordoue. Paris: Hachette Livre, 1873.

Certeau, Michel de. *Heterologies: Discourse on the Other*. Translated by Brian Massumi. Minneapolis: University of Minnesota Press, 1986.

Certeau, Michel de. *The Practice of Everyday Life*. Translated by Steven Rendall. Berkeley: University of California Press, 1984.

Cestero, Tulio M. *La sangre: Una vida bajo la tiranía*. Havana: Casa de las Américas, 1978.

Chakrabarty, Dipesh. "Minority Histories, Subaltern Pasts." In *Provincializing Europe*, 97–114. Princeton, NJ: Princeton University Press, 2018.

Chamoiseau, Patrick. *Slave Old Man: A Novel*. Translated by Linda Coverdale. New York: New Press, 2018.

Chariandy, David. *Soucouyant*. Vancouver: Arsenal Pulp, 2007.

Charlier, Philippe. *Zombies: An Anthropological Investigation of the Living Dead*. Translated by Richard J. Gray. Gainesville: University Press of Florida, 2015.

Chasteen, John Charles. *Heroes on Horseback: A Life and Times of the Last Gaucho Caudillos*. Albuquerque: University of New Mexico Press, 1995.

Chéry, André Vilaire. *Le chien comme métaphore en Haïti: Analyse d'un corpus de proverbes et de textes littéraires haïtiens*. Port-au-Prince: Ethnos, 2004.

Chiquita Banana's Recipe Book. New York: United Fruit Company, 1950.

Chochotte, Marvin. "Making Peasants *Chèf*: The *Tonton Makout* Militia and the Moral Politics of Terror in the Haitian Countryside During the Dictatorship of François Duvalier, 1957–1971." *Comparative Studies in Society and History* 61, no. 4 (2019): 925–53.

"Choncholí Se Va Pa'l Monte." YouTube, posted by Familia Valera Miranda—Topic, November 7, 2014. https://www.youtube.com/watch?v=aX1zsxlSSGY.

CIA Special Report. "The Twelve Years." In *The Dominican Republic Reader*, edited by Eric Paul Roorda, Lauren Derby, and Raymundo González, 362–64. Durham, NC: Duke University Press, 2014.

Clarke, Austin. *Pig Tails 'n' Breadfruit: A Barbadian Memoir*. Kingston: Ian Randle, 1999.

Clastres, Pierre. *Society Against the State: Essays in Political Anthropology*. Translated by Robert Hurley and Abe Stein. New York: Zone Books, 1987.

Cohen, Jeffrey Jerome. "Monster Culture (Seven Theses)." In *The Monster Theory Reader*, edited by Jeffrey Andrew Weinstock, 3–25. Minnesota: University of Minnesota Press, 2020.

Cohen, Jeffrey Jerome, ed. *Monster Theory: Reading Culture*. Minneapolis: University of Minnesota Press, 1996.

Cohn, Norman. *Europe's Inner Demons: An Enquiry Inspired by the Great Witch-Hunt*. New York: New American Library, 1977.

Coleman, Jon T. *Vicious: Wolves and Men in America*. New Haven, CT: Yale University Press, 2004.

Collado, Lipe. *El tíguere dominicano*. Santo Domingo: Ed. El Mundo, 1992.

Comaroff, John L., and Jean Comaroff. "Goodly Beasts, Beastly Goods: Cattle and Commodities in a South African Context." *American Ethnologist* 17, no. 2 (1990): 195–216.

Comaroff, John L., and Jean Comaroff. "Occult Economies and the Violence of Abstraction: Notes from the South African Postcolony." *American Ethnologist* 26, no. 2 (1999): 279–303.

Conde, Narciso. "R. Dominicana. Haitiano, fobia y poder." Lahaine.org, July 27, 2015. https://www.lahaine.org/mm_ss_mundo.php/haitiano-fobia-y-poder.

Connell, R. W. *Masculinities*. Berkeley: University of California Press, 1995.

Connerton, Paul. *The Spirit of Mourning: History, Memory and the Body*. Cambridge: Cambridge University Press, 2011.

Connolly, Brian, and Marisa Fuentes. "Introduction: From Archives of Slavery to Liberated Futures?" *History of the Present* 6, no. 2 (2016): 105–16.

Contreras, Randol. *The Stickup Kids: Race, Drugs, Violence, and the American Dream*. Berkeley: University of California Press, 2013.

Cooper, Carolyn. "Erotic Maroonage: Embodying Emancipation in Jamaican Dancehall Culture." In *Caribbean Popular Culture: Power, Politics and Performance*, edited by Yanique Hume and Aaron Kamugisha, 79–86. Kingston: Ian Randle, 2016.

Cooper Owens, Deirdre. *Medical Bondage: Race, Gender, and the Origins of American Gynecology*. Athens: University of Georgia Press, 2017.

Cordero Michel, Emilio, and José Abreu Cardet. *Homenaje a Emilio Cordero Michel*. Santo Domingo: Academia Dominicana de la Historia, 2004.

Cosentino, Donald, ed. *In Extremis: Death and Life in Twenty-First-Century Haitian Art*. Los Angeles: Fowler Museum of Cultural History at UCLA, 2012.

Cosentino, Donald, ed. *Sacred Arts of Haitian Vodou*. Los Angeles: Fowler Museum of Cultural History at UCLA, 1998.

Costa, Emília Viotti da. *The Brazilian Empire: Myths and Histories*. Chapel Hill: University of North Carolina Press, 2000.

Courlander, Harold. "The Cat, the Dog and Death." In *The Piece of Fire, and Other Haitian Tales*. New York: Harcourt, Brace and World, 1964.

Courlander, Harold. *The Drum and the Hoe: Life and Lore of the Haitian People*. Berkeley: University of California Press, 1973.

Craft, Renée Alexander. *When the Devil Knocks: The Congo Tradition and the Politics of Blackness in Twentieth-Century Panama*. Columbus: Ohio State University Press, 2015.

Crain, Mary M. "Poetics and Politics in the Ecuadorian Andes: Women's Narratives of Death and Devil Possession." *American Ethnologist* 18, no. 1 (1991): 67–89.

Crassweller, Robert D. *Trujillo: The Life and Times of a Caribbean Dictator*. New York: Macmillan, 1966.

Crawford, Sharika D. *The Last Turtlemen of the Caribbean: Waterscapes of Labor, Conservation, and Boundary Making*. Chapel Hill: University of North Carolina Press, 2021.

Crespo Vargas, Pablo L. "Inquisición y artes mágicas en Santo Domingo: 1620–1657." *Clío* 92, no. 205 (2023): 337–64.

Crosby, Alfred W. *The Columbian Exchange: Biological and Cultural Consequences of 1492*. Westport, CT: Greenwood, 1972.

Crosby, Alfred W. *Germs, Seeds and Animals: Studies in Ecological History.* Armonk, NY: M. E. Sharpe, 1994.

Crosson, J. Brent. *Experiments with Power: Obeah and the Remaking of Religion in Trinidad.* Chicago: University of Chicago Press, 2020.

Crosson, J. Brent. "What Obeah Does Do: Healing, Harm, and the Limits of Religion." *Journal of Africana Religions* 3, no. 2 (2015): 151–76.

Crowley, John E. "Sugar Machines: Picturing Industrialized Slavery." *American Historical Review* 121, no. 2 (2016): 403–36.

Cruz Duran, José Edilberto. "Análisis de las consecuencias económico-sociales de la peste porcina Africana en la República Dominicana en el año 1978." Undergraduate thesis, University of Guadalajara, Mexico, 1979.

Csordas, Thomas J. "Embodiment as a Paradigm for Anthropology." *Ethos* 18, no. 1 (1990): 5–47.

Cuba. *Ley de caza de Cuba de enero 22, de 1909.* Havana: Rambla y Bouza, 1909.

Cuba Hits Envidia—Vol. 1. CD. RYQZ, 2008.

Cunha, Olívia Maria Gomes da, and H. U. E. Thoden van Velzen. "Through Maroon Worlds: A Conversation with Bonno Thoden van Velzen." *Canadian Journal of Latin American and Caribbean Studies* 41, no. 2 (2016): 254–78.

Curtis, Isaac. "Masterless People: Maroons, Pirates, and Commoners." In *The Caribbean: A History of the Region and Its Peoples,* edited by Stephan Palmié and Francisco A. Scarano, 149–62. Chicago: University of Chicago Press, 2011.

Cvetkovich, Ann. *An Archive of Feelings: Trauma, Sexuality, and Lesbian Public Cultures.* Durham, NC: Duke University Press, 2003.

Dallas, Robert Charles. *The History of the Maroons, from Their Origin to the Establishment of Their Chief Tribe at Sierra Leone, Including the Expedition to Cuba for the Purpose of Procuring Spanish Chasseurs and the State of the Island of Jamaica for the Last Ten Years with a Succinct History of the Island Previous to That Period,* vol. 2. London: T. N. Longman and O. Rees, 1803.

Dalmas, Antoine. *Histoire de la Révolution de Saint-Domingue,* vol. 1. London: Forgotten Books, 2022.

DaMatta, Roberto. *Carnivals, Rogues, and Heroes: An Interpretation of the Brazilian Dilemma.* Translated by John Drury. Notre Dame, IN: University of Notre Dame Press, 1991.

Damirón, Rafael. *De nuestro sur remoto, conferencia leída en el Ateneo Dominicano.* Ciudad Trujillo: Publicaciones de la Secretaría de Estado de Educación y Bellas Artes, 1938.

Danticat, Edwidge. *Claire of the Sea Light.* New York: Alfred A. Knopf, 2013.

Danticat, Edwidge, ed. *Haiti Noir.* New York: Akashic, 2011.

David, Anniarys. "Los apodos más famosos de los peloteros dominicanos." Conectate.com.do, March 10, 2022. https://www.conectate.com.do/articulo/apodos-peloteros-dominicanos/.

D'Avignon, Robyn. *A Ritual Geology: Gold and Subterranean Knowledge in Savanna West Africa.* Durham, NC: Duke University Press, 2022.

Davis, Martha Ellen. "Afro-Dominican Religious Brotherhoods: Structure, Ritual, and Music." PhD diss., Department of Ethnomusicology, University of Illinois at Urbana-Champaign, 1976.

Davis, Martha Ellen, dir. *The Dominican Southwest: Crossroads of Quisqueya and Center of the World.* Video. Ethnica, 2004.

Davis, Martha Ellen. "*La Montería:* The Hunt for Wild Pigs and Goats." In *The Dominican Republic Reader,* edited by Eric Paul Roorda, Lauren Derby, and Raymundo González, 446–49. Durham, NC: Duke University Press, 2014.

Davis, Martha Ellen. *La otra ciencia: El vodú dominicano como religión y medicina populares.* Santo Domingo: Editora Universitaria, UASD, 1987.

Davis, Martha Ellen. *La ruta hacia Liborio: Mesianismo en el sur profundo dominicano.* Santo Domingo: Secretaría de Estado de Cultura, 2004.

Davis, Wade. *Passage of Darkness: The Ethnobiology of the Haitian Zombie.* Chapel Hill: University of North Carolina Press, 1988.

Dawdy, Shannon Lee. "La 'Comida Mambisa': Food, Farming, and Cuban Identity, 1839–1999." *New West Indian Guide* 76, nos. 1–2 (2002): 47–80.

Dayan, Colin. *Haiti, History, and the Gods.* Berkeley: University of California Press, 1995.

Dayan, Colin. *The Law Is a White Dog: How Legal Rituals Make and Unmake Persons.* Princeton, NJ: Princeton University Press, 2011.

Dayan, Joan. "Vodoun, or the Voice of the Gods." In *Sacred Possessions: Vodou, Santería, Obeah, and the Caribbean,* edited by Margarite Fernández Olmos and Lizabeth Paravisini-Gebert, 13–36. New Brunswick, NJ: Rutgers University Press, 1997.

Deans-Smith, Susan. "Creating the Colonial Subject: Casta Paintings, Collectors, and Critics in Eighteenth-Century Mexico and Spain." *Colonial Latin American Review* 14, no. 2 (2005): 169–204.

De Ferranti, David, Guillermo E. Perry, William Foster, Daniel Lederman, and Alberto Valdés. *Beyond the City: The Rural Contribution to Development.* Washington, DC: World Bank, 2005.

Deive, Carlos Esteban. *Antología de la flora y fauna de Santo Domingo en cronistas y viajeros: Siglos XV–XX.* Santo Domingo: Colección Bibliófilos, 2002.

Deive, Carlos Esteban. *La esclavitud del negro en Santo Domingo, 1492–1844.* Santo Domingo: Museo del Hombre Dominicano, 1980.

Deive, Carlos Esteban. *La mala vida: Delincuencia y picaresca en la colonia española de Santo Domingo.* Santo Domingo: Fundación Cultural Dominicana, 1988.

Deive, Carlos Esteban. *Los cimarrones del Maniel de Neiba: Historia y etnografía.* Santo Domingo: Banco Central de la República Dominicana, 1985.

Deive, Carlos Esteban. *Los guerrilleros negros: Esclavos fugitivos y cimarrones en Santo Domingo.* Santo Domingo: Fundación Cultural Dominicana, 1997.

Deive, Carlos Esteban. *Tangomangos: Contrabando y piratería en Santo Domingo, 1522–1606.* Santo Domingo: Fundación Cultural Dominicana, 1996.

Deive, Carlos Esteban. *Vodú y magia en Santo Domingo.* Santo Domingo: Museo del Hombre Dominicano, 1979.

DeLoughrey, Elizabeth. "Yam, Roots, and Rot: Allegories of the Provision Grounds." *Small Axe*, no. 34 (2011): 58–75.

DeLoughrey, Elizabeth, Renée K. Gosson, and George B. Handley, eds. *Caribbean Literature and the Environment: Between Nature and Culture.* Charlottesville: University of Virginia Press, 2005.

DeLoughrey, Elizabeth, and George Handley, eds. *Postcolonial Ecologies: Literatures of the Environment.* New York: Oxford University Press, 2011.

Del Pilar Sánchez, Sebastián. "Bosch forma escuela durante polémica con el MPL." *Últimas Noticias,* May 8, 2020.

Del Rosario, Pedro, and Julio Morrobel. *Ocupación y pobreza rural en la República Dominicana.* Santo Domingo: Instituto Dominicano de Investigaciones Agropecuarios e forestales, 2018. https://wp.sodiaf.org.do/publicaciones/wp -content/uploads/2023/02/OCUPACION_POBREZA_RURAL_R_D.pdf.

Del Toro, Guillermo. "Foreword: The Ecstasy of St. Arthur." In Arthur Machen, *The White People and Other Weird Stories*, vii–x. New York: Penguin, 2011.

Demorizi, Emilio Rodríguez. *Sociedades, cofradías, escuelas, gremios y otras corporaciones dominicanas.* Santo Domingo: Editora Educativa Dominicana, 1975.

Dent, Alexander Sebastian. *River of Tears: Country Music, Memory, and Modernity in Brazil.* Durham, NC: Duke University Press, 2009.

Depestre, René. *Hadriana in All My Dreams.* Translated by Kaiama L. Glover. Brooklyn, NY: Akashic, 2017.

Derby, Lauren. "Beyond Fugitive Speech: Rumor and Affect in Caribbean History." *Small Axe: A Journal of Criticism* 18, no. 2 (2014): 123–40.

Derby, Lauren. *The Dictator's Seduction: Politics and the Popular Imagination in the Era of Trujillo.* Durham, NC: Duke University Press, 2009.

Derby, Lauren. "Doña Pico's Story and the Long History of the Haitian-Dominican Border." *Revue d'Histoire Haïtienne*, no. 4 (2025): 71–94.

Derby, Lauren. "Gringo Chickens with Worms: Food and Nationalism in the Dominican Republic." In *Close Encounters of Empire*, edited by Gilbert M. Joseph, Catherine C. LeGrand, and Ricardo D. Salvatore, 451–94. Durham, NC: Duke University Press, 1998.

Derby, Lauren. "Haitians in the Dominican Republic: Race, Politics, and Neoliberalism." In *Afro-Descendants, Identity, and the Struggle for Development in the Americas*, edited by Bernd Reiter and Kimberly Eison Simmons, 51–66. Lansing: Michigan State University Press, 2012.

Derby, Lauren. "Haitians, Magic, and Money: Raza and Society in the Haitian-Dominican Borderlands, 1900 to 1937." *Comparative Studies in Society and History* 36, no. 3 (1994): 488–526.

Derby, Lauren. "Imperial Idols: French and United States Revenants in Haitian Vodou." *History of Religions* 54, no. 4 (2015): 394–422.

Derby, Lauren. "Imperial Secrets: Vampires and Nationhood in Puerto Rico." In *The Religion of Fools? Superstition Past and Present*, edited by Steven A. Smith and Alan Knight, supplement, *Past and Present* (2008): 290–312.

Derby, Lauren. "Stealing the Citadel: Icons of Nationhood and Memories of Theft in Haitian Narratives of *Kout Kouto*." *New West Indian Guide* 98, nos. 1–2 (2024): 1–39.

Derby, Lauren. "Trujillo, the Goat: Of Beasts, Men, and Politics in the Dominican Republic." In *Centering Animals in Latin American History*, edited by Martha Few and Zeb Tortorici, 302–28. Durham, NC: Duke University Press, 2013.

Derby, Lauren. "Zemis and Zombies: Amerindian Healing Legacies on Hispaniola." In *Medicine and Healing in the Age of Slavery*, edited by Sean Morey Smith and Christopher D. E. Willoughby, 21–43. Baton Rouge: Louisiana State University Press, 2021.

Derby, Lauren, and Richard Turits. *Terreurs de frontière: Le massacre des haïtiens en République Dominicaine en 1937*. Edited by Watson Denis. Port-au-Prince: Centre Challenges, 2021.

Derby, Lauren, and Marion Werner. "The Devil Wears Dockers: Devil Pacts, Trade Zones, and Rural-Urban Ties in the Dominican Republic." *New West Indian Guide* 87, nos. 3–4 (2013): 294–321.

Deren, Maya. *Divine Horsemen: The Living Gods of Haiti*. New Paltz, NY: McPherson, 1983.

Derrida, Jacques. *The Animal That Therefore I Am*. Edited by Marie-Louise Mallet. Translated by David Wills. New York: Fordham University Press, 2008.

Derrida, Jacques. *Specters of Marx: The State of the Debt, the Work of Mourning, and the New International*. Translated by Peggy Kamuf. New York: Routledge, 1994.

Descartes, René. "From the Letters of 1646 and 1649." In *The Animals Reader: The Essential Classic and Contemporary Writings*, edited by Linda Kalof and Amy J. Fitzgerald, 59–62. London: Bloomsbury Academic, 2014.

Descola, Philippe. *Beyond Nature and Culture*. Translated by Janet Lloyd. Chicago: University of Chicago Press, 2013.

Descola, Philippe. *In the Society of Nature: A Native Ecology in Amazonia*. Translated by Nora Scott. Cambridge: Cambridge University Press, 1994.

Descourtilz, M. E. *Flore pittoresque et médicale des Antilles, ou histoire naturelle des plantes usuelles des colonies françaises, anglaises, espagnoles et portugaises*, vol. 7. France: Chez l'Editeur, 1833.

Descourtilz, M. E. *Voyages d'un naturaliste, et ses observations: Faites sur les trois règnes de la nature, dans plusieurs ports de mer français, en Espagne, au continent de l'Amérique septentrionale, à Saint-Yago de Cuba, et à St.-Domingue, où l'auteur devenu le prisonnier de 40,000 noirs révoltés, et par suite mis en liberté par une colonne de l'armée française, donne des détails circonstanciés sur l'expédition du Général Leclerc*. 3 vols. Paris: Dufart Père, 1809.

Des Prés, François. *Children of Yayoute: Folk Tales of Haiti*. New York: Universe Books, 1994.

Diamond, Jared. *Collapse: How Societies Choose to Fail or Succeed*. New York: Viking, 2005.

Díaz, Junot. *The Brief Wondrous Life of Oscar Wao.* New York: Riverhead Books, 2007.

Díaz, Junot. "The Ghosts of Gloria Lara." *New Yorker*, November 6, 2023, 52–62.

Díaz Quiñones, Arcadio. "De cómo y cuándo bregar." In *El arte de bregar: Ensayos*, 13–18. San Juan: Ediciones Callejón, 2000.

"Dicen 'Bacá' atemoriza residentes en Oviedo." YouTube, posted by El Nacional, September 3, 2018. https://www.youtube.com/watch?v=f7CwWWA8m8E.

Diederich, Bernard. "The Creole Pig Disaster: Swine Fever Ironies." In *Libète: A Haiti Anthology*, edited by Charles Arthur and Michael Dash, 104–5. Princeton, NJ: Markus Wiener, 1999.

Dietler, Michael, and Brian Hayden, eds. *Feasts: Archaeological and Ethnographic Perspectives on Food, Politics, and Power.* Washington, DC: Smithsonian Institution Press, 2001.

Dimock, Wai Chee. *Through Other Continents: American Literature Across Deep Time.* Princeton, NJ: Princeton University Press, 2009.

Dirksen, Rebecca. *After the Dance, the Drums Are Heavy: Carnival, Politics, and Musical Engagement in Haiti.* New York: Oxford University Press, 2020.

Dobal, Carlos. "Los lechones o diablos cojuelos de Santiago." *Boletín del Museo del Hombre Domincano*, no. 19 (1984): 59–68.

"Dominican Republic Emerges as Drug Trafficking Center of the Caribbean." *HuffPost*, January 23, 2013. https://www.huffpost.com/entry/dominican -republic-emerge_n_2533210.

Donoghue, John. "Indentured Servitude in the 17th Century English Atlantic: A Brief Survey of the Literature." *History Compass* 11, no. 10 (2013): 893–902.

Dooren, Thom van, and Deborah Bird Rose. "Lively Ethnography: Storying Animist Worlds." *Environmental Humanities* 8, no. 1 (2016): 77–94.

Doris, David T. *Vigilant Things: On Thieves, Yoruba Anti-Aesthetics, and the Strange Fates of Ordinary Objects in Nigeria.* Seattle: University of Washington Press, 2011.

Douglas, Mary. "Animals in Lele Religious Symbolism." *Africa: Journal of the International African Institute* 27, no. 1 (1957): 46–58.

Douglas, Mary. "Deciphering a Meal." In *Implicit Meanings: Selected Essays in Anthropology*, 249–75. London: Routledge, 1999.

Douglas, Mary. *Natural Symbols: Explorations in Cosmology.* New York: Vintage Books, 1970.

Douglas, Mary. *Purity and Danger: An Analysis of Concepts of Pollution and Taboo.* New York: Praeger, 1966.

Drewal, Margaret Thompson, and Henry John Drewal. "More Powerful Than Each Other: An Egbado Classification of Egungun." *African Arts* 11, no. 3 (1978): 28–39, 98–99.

Duara, Prasenjit. "Linear History and the Nation-State." In *Rescuing History from the Nation: Questioning Narratives of Modern China*, 17–50. Chicago: University of Chicago Press, 1997.

Dubois, Laurent. *Avengers of the New World: The Story of the Haitian Revolution.* Cambridge, MA: Belknap Press of Harvard University Press, 2004.

Dubois, Laurent, and Richard Lee Turits. *Freedom Roots: Histories from the Caribbean*. Chapel Hill: University of North Carolina Press, 2019.

Dulin, John. "Vulnerable Minds, Bodily Thoughts, and Sensory Spirits: Local Theory of Mind and Spiritual Experience in Ghana." *Journal of the Royal Anthropological Institute* (2020): 61–76.

Dumett, Raymond E. *El Dorado in West Africa: The Gold-Mining Frontier, African Labor, and Colonial Capitalism in the Gold Coast, 1875–1900*. Athens: Ohio University Press, 1998.

Dundes, Alan. "Structuralism and Folklore." In *The Meaning of Folklore: The Analytical Essays of Alan Dundes*, edited by Simon J. Bronner, 123–53. Logan: Utah State University Press, 2007.

Dundes, Alan. *The Vampire: A Casebook*. Madison: University of Wisconsin Press, 1998.

Dunham, Katherine. *Island Possessed*. Chicago: University of Chicago Press, 1994.

Dunn, Peter N. "Spanish Picaresque Fiction as a Problem of Genre." *Dispositio* 15, no. 39 (1990): 1–15.

Durán, Rubén, dir. *Cimarrón Spirit: Afro-Dominican Maroon Culture*. DVD. Cab 95 Films/Cosmic Light Productions, 2015.

Duranti, Alessandro, and Charles Goodwin, eds. *Rethinking Context: Language as an Interactive Phenomenon*. Cambridge: Cambridge University Press, 1992.

Durland, William Davies. "The Forests of the Dominican Republic." *Geographical Review* 12, no. 2 (1922): 206–22.

Eagle, Marc. "The Early Slave Trade to Spanish America: Caribbean Pathways, 1530–1580." In *The Spanish Caribbean and the Atlantic World in the Long Sixteenth Century*, edited by Ida Altman and David Wheat, 139–62. Lincoln: University of Nebraska Press, 2019.

Earle, Rebecca. *The Body of the Conquistador: Food, Race and the Colonial Experience in Spanish America, 1492–1700*. Cambridge: Cambridge University Press, 2012.

Ebanks, R. "The Maroons of Jamaica: An African Response to Colonial Oppression in the Western Diaspora, ad 1500–1750." *Sankofa: The Legon Journal of Archaelogical and Historical Studies*, no. 2 (1976): 79–85.

Ebert, Allan. "Porkbarreling Pigs in Haiti: North American 'Swine Aid' an Economic Disaster for Haitian Peasants." *Multinational Monitor*, December 1985. https://www.multinationalmonitor.org/hyper/issues/1985/12/ebert-porkbarrel.html.

Echenique, Maria Elva. "Documenting Realities of Oppression: The Latin American Genre of Testimonio in Literature and Film." Paper presented at the annual conference of the Pacific Ancient and Modern Language Association, Pasadena, CA, 2016.

Edelman, Marc. "Landlords and the Devil: Class, Ethnic, and Gender Dimensions of Central American Peasant Narratives." *Cultural Anthropology* 9, no. 1 (1994): 58–93.

Edwards, Bryan. *The History, Civil and Commercial, of the British Colonies in the West Indies*. London: Printed for John Stockdale, Piccadilly, 1807.

Edwards, Bryan, and the Governor and Assembly of Jamaica. *The Proceedings of the Governor and Assembly of Jamaica, in Regard to the Maroon Negroes.* Cambridge: Cambridge University Press, 2013.

Eisenstadt, S. N., and L. Roniger. *Patrons, Clients and Friends: Interpersonal Relations and the Structure of Trust in Society.* Cambridge: Cambridge University Press, 1984.

Eller, Anne. "To Cap-Haïten, with My Family: Dominican Passport Petitions, 1862–1863." In *Transnational Hispaniola: New Directions in Haitian and Dominican Studies,* edited by April J. Mayes and Kiran C. Jayaram, 67–77. Gainesville: University Press of Florida, 2018.

Eller, Anne. "Raining Blood: Spiritual Power, Gendered Violence, and Anticolonial Lives in the Nineteenth-Century Dominican Borderlands." *Hispanic American Historical Review* 99, no. 3 (2019): 431–65.

Eller, Anne. "Rumors of Slavery: Defending Emancipation in a Hostile Caribbean." *American Historical Review* 122, no. 3 (2017): 653–79.

Eller, Anne. *We Dream Together: Dominican Independence, Haiti, and the Fight for Caribbean Freedom.* Durham, NC: Duke University Press, 2016.

"El metro lleva costo de RD$24,000 millones." *Hoy: Guardianes de La Verdad.* January 20, 2009.

Erikson, Philippe. "Myth and Material Culture: Matis Blowguns, Palm Trees, and Ancestor Spirits." In *Beyond the Visible and the Material: The Amerindianization of Society in the Work of Peter Rivière,* edited by Neil L. Whitehead and Laura M. Rival, 101–21. Oxford: Oxford University Press, 2001.

Evans, Rhonda, Deann K. Gauthier, and Craig J. Forsyth. "Dogfighting: Symbolic Expression and Validation of Masculinity." In *The Animals Reader: The Essential Classic and Contemporary Writings,* edited by Linda Kalof and Amy J. Fitzgerald, 219–36. Oxford: Berg, 2007.

Evans, W. J. *The Sugar-Planter's Manual: Being a Treatise on the Art of Obtaining Sugar from the Sugar-Cane.* Philadelphia: Lea and Blanchard, 1848.

Evans-Pritchard, E. E. "Customs and Beliefs Relating to Twins Among the Nilotic Nuer." *Uganda Journal* 3 (1935): 230–38.

Evans-Pritchard, E. E. *Kinship and Marriage Among the Nuer.* Oxford: Clarendon Press, 1960.

Evans-Pritchard, E. E. *The Nuer: A Description of the Modes of Livelihood and Political Institutions of a Nilotic People.* Oxford: Clarendon Press, 1940.

Evans-Pritchard, E. E. "The Sacrificial Role of Cattle Among the Nuer." *Africa: Journal of the International African Institute* 23, no. 3 (1953): 181–98.

Ewing-Chow, Daphne. "Five Overlooked Facts About Caribbean Food Insecurity." *Forbes,* February 20, 2019.

"Existen o no existen los Bacá." YouTube, posted by Mañanero tv, September 6, 2017. https://www.youtube.com/watch?v=3nRcusCXeU8.

Exquemelin, A. O. *The Buccaneers of America.* Translated by Alexis Brown. Baltimore: Penguin Books, 1969.

Exquemelin, A. O. *The History of the Buccaneers of America: Containing Detailed Accounts of Those Bold and Daring Freebooters; Chiefly Along the Spanish Main, in the West Indies, and in the Great South Sea, Succeeding the Civil Wars in England.* Boston: Benjamin B. Mussey, 1853.

Fabian, Johannes. *Power and Performance: Ethnographic Explorations Through Proverbial Wisdom and Theater in Shaba, Zaire.* Madison: University of Wisconsin Press, 1990.

Fabre-Vassas, Claudine. *The Singular Beast: Jews, Christians, and the Pig.* Translated by Carol Volk. New York: Columbia University Press, 1997.

Famine Early Warning System Network. "Central American and Caribbean Acute Food Insecurity Classification." Accessed May 8, 2024. https://fews.net/data/acute-food-insecurity.

Fanger, Claire, ed. *Conjuring Spirits: Texts and Traditions of Medieval Ritual Magic.* University Park: Pennsylvania State University Press, 1998.

Fardon, Richard. *Between God, the Dead and the Wild: Chamba Interpretations of Religion and Ritual.* Edinburgh: University Press for the International African Institute, 1990.

Farmer, Paul. *AIDS and Accusation: Haiti and the Geography of Blame.* Berkeley: University of California Press, 2006.

Farmer, Paul. "Bad Blood, Spoiled Milk: Bodily Fluids as Moral Barometers in Rural Haiti." *American Ethnologist* 15, no. 1 (1988): 62–83.

Farmer, Paul. "Sending Sickness: Sorcery, Politics, and Changing Concepts of AIDS in Rural Haiti." *Medical Anthropological Quarterly* 4, no. 1 (1990): 6–27.

Farmer, Paul. "Swine Aid." In *The Haiti Files: Decoding the Crisis*, edited by James Ridgeway, 130–33. Washington, DC: Essential Books, 1994.

Farrell, Joseph. "Walcott's *Omeros*: The Classical Epic in a Postmodern World." *South Atlantic Quarterly* 96, no. 2 (1997): 247–73.

Fausto, Carlos. "Feasting on People: Eating Animals and Humans in Amazonia." *Current Anthropology* 48, no. 4 (2007): 497–530.

Ferme, Mariane C. *The Underneath of Things: Violence, History, and the Everyday in Sierra Leone.* Berkeley: University of California Press, 2001.

Fernandez, James W., ed. *Beyond Metaphor: The Theory of Tropes in Anthropology.* Stanford, CA: Stanford University Press, 1991.

Fernandez, James W. "The Mission of Metaphor in Expressive Culture." In *Persuasions and Performances: The Play of Tropes in Culture*, 28–72. Bloomington: Indiana University Press, 1986.

Fernández de Oviedo y Valdés, Gonzalo. *Historia general y natural de las Indias, islas y tierra-firme del mar Océano.* 8 vols. Asunción, Paraguay: Editorial Guaranía, 1944.

Fernández de Zafra, Rafael. "El terror de los esclavos: El dogo o mastín de Cuba." *Leer de Perros* (blog), June 7, 2014. https://leerdeperros.blogspot.com/2014/06/el-terror-de-los-esclavos-el-dogo-o.html.

Fernández Olmos, Margarite, and Lizabeth Paravisini-Gebert. *Creole Religions of the Caribbean: An Introduction from Vodou and Santería to Obeah and Espiritismo.* New York: New York University Press, 2011.

Fernández Olmos, Margarite, and Lizabeth Paravisini-Gebert, eds. *Sacred Possessions: Vodou, Santería, Obeah, and the Caribbean.* New Brunswick, NJ: Rutgers University Press, 1997.

Ferrer, Ada. *Freedom's Mirror: Cuba and Haiti in the Age of Revolution.* New York: Cambridge University Press, 2014.

Ferrer, Ada. "Haiti, Free Soil, and Antislavery in the Revolutionary Atlantic." *American Historical Review* 117, no. 1 (2012): 40–66.

Ferrer, Ada. *Insurgent Cuba: Race, Nation, and Revolution, 1868–1898.* Chapel Hill: University of North Carolina Press, 1999.

Ferry, Stephen. *I Am Rich Potosí: The Mountain That Eats Men.* New York: Monacelli, 1999.

Few, Martha, and Zeb Tortorici, eds. *Centering Animals in Latin American History.* Durham, NC: Duke University Press, 2013.

Fieser, Ezra. "The Caribbean Drug Kingpin Turned Porn Star." *Time,* August 18, 2010. https://time.com/archive/6950722/the-caribbean-drug-kingpin-turned -porn-star/.

Fieser, Ezra. "A Graft Machine's Collapse Sows Chaos in the Caribbean." *Bloomberg,* June 12, 2017. https://www.bloomberg.com/news/features/2017-06-12 /odebrecht-corruption-machine-s-collapse-sows-chaos-in-the-dominican -republic.

Filan, Kenaz. *Vodou Money Magic: The Way to Prosperity Through the Blessings of the Lwa.* Rochester, VT: Destiny Books, 2010.

Finch, Aisha. *Rethinking Slave Rebellion in Cuba: La Escalera and the Insurgencies of 1841–1844.* Chapel Hill: University of North Carolina Press, 2014.

Finnegan, Ruth H. *The Oral and Beyond: Doing Things with Words in Africa.* Oxford: James Currey, 2007.

Flores-Sasso, Virginia, and Esteban Prieto-Vicioso. "Cofradías de esclavos negros, morenos y mulatos libres en la Catedral de Santo Domingo, Primada de América." *Anuario de Historia de la Iglesia,* no. 30 (2021): 335–62.

Food and Drink in History. Marlborough: Adam Matthew Digital, 2019. https:// www.foodanddrink.amdigital.co.uk/.

Forde, Maarit. "Introduction." In *Passages and Afterworlds: Anthropological Perspectives on Death in the Caribbean,* edited by Maarit Forde and Yanique Hume, 1–27. Durham, NC: Duke University Press, 2018.

Forde, Maarit. "The Moral Economy of Spiritual Work: Money and Rituals in Trinidad and Tobago." In *Obeah and Other Powers,* edited by Diana Paton and Maarit Forde, 198–219. Durham, NC: Duke University Press, 2020.

Forde, Maarit, and Yanique Hume, eds. *Passages and Afterworlds: Anthropological Perspectives on Death in the Caribbean.* Durham, NC: Duke University Press, 2018.

Fouchard, Jean. *The Haitian Maroons: Liberty or Death*. New York: E. W. Blyden, 1981.

Frankfurter, David. *Evil Incarnate: Rumors of Demonic Conspiracy and Ritual Abuse in History*. Princeton, NJ: Princeton University Press, 2006.

Franklin, James. *The Present State of Hayti (Saint Domingo): With Remarks on Its Agriculture, Commerce, Laws, Religion, Finances and Population*. London: J. Murray, 1828.

Freeland, Cynthia. "Natural Evil in the Horror Film: Alfred Hitchcock's *The Birds*." In *The Changing Face of Evil in Film and Television*, edited by Martin F. Norden, 55–69. Amsterdam: Rodopi, 2007.

Freud, Sigmund. *Introductory Lectures on Psycho-Analysis*. London: Hogarth, 1963.

Freud, Sigmund. *Jokes and Their Relation to the Unconscious*. New York: W. W. Norton, 1960.

Freud, Sigmund. *Totem and Taboo: Some Points of Agreement Between the Mental Lives of Savages and Neurotics*. London: Routledge & Kegan Paul, 1960.

Freud, Sigmund. "The Uncanny." In *The Standard Edition of the Complete Psychological Works of Sigmund Freud*, vol. 17, 219–52. London: Hogarth, 1919.

Frías V., Francisco. *Historia general*, vols. 2 and 3. Santiago de Chile: Nascimento, 1963.

Fricker, Miranda. *Epistemic Injustice: Power and the Ethics of Knowing*. Oxford: Oxford University Press, 2007.

Fuchs, Barbara. *Knowing Fictions: Picaresque Reading in the Early Modern Hispanic World*. Philadelphia: University of Pennsylvania Press, 2020.

Fuchs, Barbara. "Suspended Judgments: Skepticism and the Pact of Fictionality in Cervantes's Picaresque Novellas." *Modern Language Quarterly* 76, no. 4 (2015): 447–63.

Fudge, Erica. "A Left-Handed Blow: Writing the History of Animals." In *Representing Animals: Theories of Contemporary Culture*, edited by Nigel Rothels, 3–18. Bloomington: Indiana University Press.

Fuente, Ariel de la. *Children of Facundo: Caudillo and Gaucho Insurgency During the Argentine State-Formation Process (La Rioja, 1853–1870)*. Durham, NC: Duke University Press, 2000.

Fuentes, Marisa J. *Dispossessed Lives: Enslaved Women, Violence, and the Archive*. Philadelphia: University of Pennsylvania Press, 2016.

Fuller, Norma. "The Social Constitution of Gender Identity Among Peruvian Males." In *Changing Men and Masculinities in Latin America*, edited by Matthew C. Guttman, 134–52. Durham, NC: Duke University Press, 2020.

Fumagalli, Maria Cristina. *On the Edge: Writing the Border Between Haiti and the Dominican Republic*. Liverpool: Liverpool University Press, 2015.

Funes Monzote, Reinaldo. "Cultura ganadera en la historia de Cuba: Una aproximación." *Catauro: Revista Cubana de Antropología* 13, no. 25 (2012): 6–28.

Funes Monzote, Reinaldo. *From Rainforest to Cane Field in Cuba: An Environmental History Since 1492*. Translated by Alex Martin. Chapel Hill: University of North Carolina Press, 2008.

Gaillard, Roger. *Charlemagne Péralte le caco*. Port-au-Prince: R. Gaillard, 1982.

Gaillard, Roger. *La guérilla de Batraville: 1919–1934*. Port-au-Prince: Impr. Le Natal, 1983.

Gallas, Daniel. "Brazil's Odebrecht Corruption Scandal Explained." BBC News, April 17, 2019.

"Gallos: Tony García presidirá coliseo Bonetti Burgos." *Listín Diario*, March 10, 2014, https://listindiario.com/el-deporte/2014/03/10/313718/tony-garcia -presidira-coliseo-bonetti-burgos.html.

Gan, Elaine, Heather Swanson, Nils Bubandt, and Anna Tsing. "Introduction: Haunted Landscapes of the Anthropocene." In *Arts of Living on a Damaged Planet: Ghosts of the Anthropocene, Monsters of the Anthropocene*, edited by Elaine Gan et al., 1–15. Minneapolis: University of Minnesota Press, 2017.

Garcia, Saudi. "Environmental Maroonage: Perspectives on Place, Space and Ecological Resistance in Hispaniola's Black Ecologies." Paper presented at the annual meeting of the Latin American Studies Association, May 5, 2022.

Garcia Arévalo, M. A. "The Bat and the Owl: Nocturnal Images of Death." In *Taíno: Pre-Columbian Art and Culture from the Caribbean*, edited by Fatima Bercht, 112–23. New York: El Museo del Barrio and Monacelli, 1997.

Garcia Arévalo, M. A. "El murciélago en la mitologia y el arte taino." *Boletín del Museo del Hombre Dominicano*, no. 19 (1984): 45–55.

García-Cartagena, Manuel. *Bacá*. Santo Domingo: n.p., 2007.

García Garagarza, León. "The Year the People Turned Into Cattle: The End of the World in New Spain, 1558." In *Centering Animals in Latin American History*, edited by Martha Few and Zeb Tortorici, 31–61. Durham, NC: Duke University Press, 2020.

García-Peña, Lorgia. *The Borders of Dominicanidad Race, Nation and Archives of Contradiction*. Durham, NC: Duke University Press, 2016.

Garrido, Víctor. *En la ruta de mi vida, 1886–1966*. Santo Domingo: Impresora Arte y Cine, 1970.

Garrido, Víctor. *Espigas históricas*. Santo Domingo: Impresora Arte y Cine, 1972.

Garrido de Boggs, Edna. *Reseña histórica del folklore dominicano*. Santo Domingo: Editora Búho, 2006.

Garrigus, John. *Before Haiti: Race and Citizenship in French Saint-Domingue*. New York: Palgrave Macmillan, 2006.

Garrigus, John. "'Like an Epidemic One Could Only Stop with the Most Violent Remedies': African Poisons Versus Livestock Disease in Saint Domingue, 1750–88." *William and Mary Quarterly* 78, no. 4 (2021): 617–52.

Garrigus, John. *A Secret Among the Blacks: Slave Resistance Before the Haitian Revolution*. Cambridge, MA: Harvard University Press, 2023.

Garry, Stephanie. "Crossing Rivers—and Cultural Bounds—in the Dominican Republic." Partners in Health, May 23, 2013. https://www.pih.org/article /crossing-borders.

Garth, Hanna, ed. *Food and Identity in the Caribbean*. London: Bloomsbury Academic, 2013.

Gascón, Margarita. "The Military of Santo Domingo, 1720–1764." *Hispanic American Historical Review* 73, no. 3 (1993): 431–52.

Gates, Henry Louis. "Introduction." In *The Classic Slave Narratives*, 1–14. New York: Signet Classics, 2012.

Gates, Henry Louis, ed. *The Signifying Monkey: A Theory of African-American Literary Criticism*. New York: Oxford University Press, 2014.

Gautreaux-Piñero, Bonaparte. "Lo de Haití." *Hoy*, November 16, 2022. https://hoy
.com.do/lo-de-haiti/?fbclid=IwY2xjawJBloZleHRuA2FlbQIxMAABHcQfo
zPtY8ciKnbMqhZaeFFJdYaZJxg-MRjNwYEDfsYaKDq3HSZojgDIYw_aem
_RPJwOoW_SwA9QtWr6ng89Q.

Geary, Patrick J. *Phantoms of Remembrance: Memory and Oblivion at the End of the First Millennium*. Princeton, NJ: Princeton University Press, 1994.

Geertz, Clifford. "Deep Play: Notes on the Balinese Cockfight." *Daedalus* 134, no. 4 (2005): 56–86.

Geggus, David. "Atrocity, Race, and Region in the Early Haitian Revolution: The Fond d'Icaque Rising." In *Oxford Research Encyclopedia of Latin American History*, edited by Ángela Vergara. New York: Oxford University Press. Published online April 26, 2018.

Geggus, David, ed. *The Haitian Revolution: A Documentary History*. Indianapolis: Hackett, 2014.

Gerbi, Antonello. *Nature in the New World: From Christopher Columbus to Gonzalo Fernández de Oviedo*. Translated by Jeremy Moyle. Pittsburgh: University of Pittsburgh Press, 1985.

Geschiere, Peter. *The Modernity of Witchcraft: Politics and the Occult in Postcolonial Africa*. Charlottesville: University of Virginia Press, 1997.

Geurts, Kathryn Linn. *Culture and the Senses: Bodily Ways of Knowing in an African Community*. Berkeley: University of California Press, 2002.

Ginzburg, Carlo. "Clues: Roots of an Evidential Paradigm." In *Clues, Myths, and the Historical Method*, translated by John and Anne C. Tedeschi, 96–125. Baltimore: Johns Hopkins University Press, 1992.

Girard, René. *Violence and the Sacred*. Translated by Patrick Gregory. Baltimore: Johns Hopkins University Press, 1977.

Gleijeses, Piero. *The Dominican Crisis: The 1965 Constitutionalist Revolt and American Intervention*. Translated by Lawrence Lipson. Baltimore: Johns Hopkins University Press, 1978.

Glissant, Édouard. "For Opacity." In *Poetics of Relation*, 189–94. Translated by Betsy Wing. Ann Arbor: University of Michigan Press, 1979.

Glover, Adam. "Todo a Relajo: Jorge Mañach and Metaphysical Rebellion." *Inter-American Journal of Philosophy* 4, 1 (2103): 21–34.

Goffman, Erving. *Forms of Talk*. Philadelphia: University of Pennsylvania Press, 1981.

Goffman, Erving. *Frame Analysis. An Essay on the Organization of Experience.* Cambridge, MA: Harvard University Press, 1974.

Goffman, Erving. "The Nature of Deference and Demeanor." In *Interaction Ritual: Essays on Face-to-Face Behavior*, 47–96. New York: Pantheon, 1967.

Goffman, Erving. *The Presentation of Self in Everyday Life.* Garden City, NY: Doubleday, 1959.

Goffman, Erving. *Relations in Public: Microstudies of the Public Order.* New York: Basic Books, 1971.

Goffman, Erving. *Stigma.* New York: Simon and Schuster, 2009.

Goffman, Erving. *Strategic Interaction.* Philadelphia: University of Pennsylvania Press, 1969.

Gómez, Pablo. *The Experiential Caribbean: Creating Knowledge and Healing in the Early Modern Atlantic.* Chapel Hill: University of North Carolina Press, 2017.

Gonzalez, Clara. "Sancocho (Meat and Root Vegetables Stew)." Dominican Cooking, December 21, 2001. https://www.dominicancooking.com/sancocho.

Gonzalez, Johnhenry. *Maroon Nation: A History of Revolutionary Haiti.* New Haven, CT: Yale University Press, 2019.

González, Raymundo. "Campesinos monteros en Santo Domingo colonial: Dispersión rural en la sociedad esclavista." In *Sometidos a esclavitud: Los africanos y sus descendientes en el Caribe Hispano*, edited by Consuelo Naranjo Orovio, 225–51. Santa Marta, Colombia: Editorial Unimagdalena, 2021.

González, Raymundo. *De esclavos a campesinos: Vida rural en Santo Domingo colonial.* Santo Domingo: Archivo General de la Nación, 2011.

González, Raymundo. "El comegente, una rebelión campesina al final del período colonial." In *Homenaje a Emilio Cordero Michel*, edited by Emilio Cordero Michel and José Abreu Cardet, 175–234. Santo Domingo: Academia Dominicana de la Historia, 2004.

González, Raymundo. "Hunting and the Free Peasantry in the Dominican Republic." In *Oxford Research Encyclopedia of Latin American History*, edited by Ángela Vergara. New York: Oxford University Press. Published online 2021.

González, Raymundo. "Monterías y campesinos monteros." In *Historia general del pueblo dominicano*, vol. 2, edited by Roberto Cassá and Raymundo González de Peña, 511–58. Santo Domingo: Academia Dominicana de la Historia, 2013.

González Echevarría, Roberto. "Biografía de un cimarrón and the Novel of the Cuban Revolution." In *The Voice of the Masters: Writing and Authority in Modern Latin American Literature*, 110–23. Austin: University of Texas Press, 1985.

González Llana, M. "Isla de Santo Domingo." In *Relaciones geográficas de Santo Domingo*, edited by Emilio Rodríguez Demorizi, 249–70. Santo Domingo: Editora Taller, 1977.

Goodman, Glenda. "Elegant Instruments of Imperial Influence: Joseph Brant's Barrel Organ at Grand River." Paper presented at the conference "Material Culture Studies and Early American History," *William and Mary Quarterly* and Early Modern Studies Institute, Huntington Library, Pasadena, December 11, 2021.

Gordillo, Gastón. "The Breath of the Devils: Memories and Places of an Experience of Terror." *American Anthropologist* 29, no. 1 (2002): 33–57.

Gordillo, Gastón. *Landscapes of Devils: Tensions of Place and Memory in the Argentinian Chaco*. Durham, NC: Duke University Press, 2004.

Gordon, Avery. *Ghostly Matters: Haunting and the Sociological Imagination*. Minneapolis: University of Minnesota Press, 1997.

Gordon, Leah, Madison Smartt Bell, Donald Cosentino, Richard Fleming, Katherine Smith, and Myron Beasley. *Kanaval: Vodou, Politics and Revolution on the Streets of Haiti*. London: Soul Jazz, 2010.

Gordon, Leah, and Eddie Hutton-Mills, dirs. *Kanaval: A People's History of Haiti in Six Chapters*. Tigerlily Productions, 2022.

Gordon, Leah, and Anne Parisio, dir. *A Pig's Tale*. London: Parisio Productions, 1997.

Goss, Linda, and Marian Barnes, eds. *Talk That Talk: An Anthology of African-American Storytelling*. New York: Simon and Schuster, 1989.

Gosse, Philip Henry. *A Naturalist's Sojourn in Jamaica*. London: Longman, Brown, Green and Longmans, 1851.

Gottlieb, Alma. *The Afterlife Is Where We Come from: The Culture of Infancy in West Africa*. Chicago: University of Chicago Press, 2004.

Gottlieb, Alma. "Dog: Ally or Traitor? Mythology, Cosmology, and Society Among the Beng of Ivory Coast." *American Ethnologist* 13, no. 3 (1986): 477–88.

Gould, Jeffrey L. *To Lead as Equals: Rural Protest and Political Consciousness in Chinandega, Nicaragua, 1912–1979*. Chapel Hill: University of North Carolina Press, 1990.

Govindrajan, Radhika. *Animal Intimacies: Interspecies Relatedness in India's Central Himalayas*. Chicago: University of Chicago Press, 2008.

Greenblatt, Stephen. "Filthy Rites." *Daedalus* 111, no. 3 (1982): 1–16.

Greene, Ann Norton. *Horses at Work: Harnessing Power in Industrial America*. Cambridge, MA: Harvard University Press, 2008.

Gregory, Steven. *The Devil Behind the Mirror: Globalization and Politics in the Dominican Republic*. Berkeley: University of California Press, 2007.

Guarnizo, Luis E. "Los Dominicanyorks: The Making of a Binational Society." *Annals of the American Academy of Political and Social Science* 533, no. 1 (1994): 70–86.

Gugolati, Maica. "La Djablesse: Between Martinique, Trinidad (and Tobago), and Its Pan-Caribbean Dimension." *Women, Gender, and Families of Color* 6, no. 2 (2018): 151–80.

Guha, Ranajit. *The Small Voice of History: Collected Essays*. Edited by Partha Chatterjee. Ranikhet: Permanent Black, 2009.

Guillén, Claudio. "Toward a Definition of the Picaresque." In *Literature as System: Essays Toward the Theory of Literary History*, 71–106. Princeton, NJ: Princeton University Press, 2015.

Guisti-Cordero, Juan. "Beyond Sugar Revolutions: Rethinking the Spanish Caribbean in the Seventeenth and Eighteenth Centuries." In *Empirical Futures: Anthropologists and Historians Engage the Work of Sidney Mintz*, edited by George Baca, Aisha Khan, and Stephan Palmié, 58–83. Chapel Hill: University of North Carolina Press, 2009.

Guisti-Cordero, Juan. "Sugar and Livestock: Contraband Networks in Hispaniola and the Continental Caribbean in the Eighteenth Century." *Revista Brasileira do Caribe* 15, no. 29 (2014): 13–41.

Gutiérrez Escudero, Antonio. "Contrabando en el Caribe: Comercio ilícito entre franceses y españoles en Santo Domingo." *Estudios de Historia Social y Económica de América* 1 (1985): 71–90.

Gutiérrez Escudero, Antonio. "El hato ganadero y la ganadería en Santo Domingo durante el siglo XVIII." In *Historia general del pueblo dominicano*, vol. 2, edited by Roberto Cassá and Raymundo González, 343–96. Santo Domingo: Academia Dominicana de la Historia, 2013.

Hagler, Anderson. "Exhuming the Nahualli: Shapeshifting, Idolatry, and Orthodoxy in Colonial Mexico." *The Americas* 78, no. 2 (2021): 197–228.

"Haiti Rumors Woman Transforming into Snake." *Teleimage Valerio St. Louis Haiti News*, September 1, 2006.

Haraway, Donna J. *The Companion Species Manifesto: Dogs, People, and Significant Otherness*. Chicago: Prickly Paradigm, 2003.

Haraway, Donna J. *Primate Visions: Gender, Race, and Nature in the World of Modern Science*. London: Routledge, 1989.

Haraway, Donna J. *When Species Meet*. Minneapolis: University of Minnesota Press, 2008.

Hartlyn, Jonathan. *The Struggle for Democratic Politics in the Dominican Republic*. Chapel Hill: University of North Carolina Press, 1998.

Hartman, Saidiya. "The Dead Book Revisited." *History of the Present* 6, no. 2 (2016): 208–15.

Hartman, Saidiya. *Lose Your Mother: A Journey Along the Atlantic Slave Route*. New York: Farrar, Straus and Giroux, 2007.

Hazard, Samuel. *Santo Domingo, Past and Present: With a Glance at Hayti*. Santo Domingo: Editora de Santo Domingo, 1974.

Hebdige, Dick. *Hiding in the Light: On Images and Things*. London: Routledge, 1988.

Heinl, Robert Debs, and Nancy Gordon Heinl. *Written in Blood: The Story of the Haitian People, 1492–1995*. Boston: Houghton Mifflin, 1978.

Hémardinquer, Jean-Jacques. "The Family Pig of the Ancien Régime: Myth or Fact?" In *Food and Drink in History*, edited by Robert Forster and Orest Ranum, 50–72. Baltimore: Johns Hopkins University Press, 1974.

Herbert, Eugenia W. *Red Gold of Africa*. Madison: University of Wisconsin Press, 1984.

Hernández González, Manuel. *El sur dominicano (1680–1795)*, Vol. 1, *El área capitalina*. Santa Cruz de Tenerife: Idea, 2008.

Hernández González, Manuel. *El sur dominicano (1680–1795)*, Vol. 2, *El sureste*. Santa Cruz de Tenerife: Idea, 2008.

Hernández González, Manuel. *La colonización de la frontera dominicana 1680–1795*. Santo Domingo: Archivo General de la Nación, 2006.

Herrera y Tordesillas, Antonio de. *Historia general de los hechos de los castellanos en las islas i tierra firme del mar oceano*. Madrid: Impr. Real de N. Rodriguez Franco, 1726.

Herskovits, Melville J. *Life in a Haitian Valley*. New York: A. A. Knopf, 1937.

Hertz, Robert. *Death and the Right Hand*. Translated by Rodney Needham and Claudia Needham. Aberdeen: Cohen and West, 1960.

Hess, Amanda. "The End Is Near. What's Your Hurry?" *New York Times*, February 6, 2022.

Heywood, Linda M., ed. *Central Africans and Cultural Transformations in the American Diaspora*. New York: Cambridge University Press, 2002.

Heywood, Linda M., and John K. Thornton. *Central Africans, Atlantic Creoles, and the Foundation of the Americas, 1585–1660*. New York: Cambridge University Press, 2007.

Hintzen, Amelia. *De la masacre a la sentencia 168-13: Apuntes para la historia de la segregación de los haitianos y sus descendientes en la República Dominicana*. Santo Domingo: Fundación Juan Bosch, 2017.

Hippert, Christine. *Not Even a Grain of Rice: Buying Food on Credit in the Dominican Republic*. Lanham, MD: Lexington Books, 2020.

Hirsch, Marianne, and Leo Spitzer. "Testimonial Objects: Memory, Gender, and Transmission." *Poetics Today* 27, no. 2 (2006): 353–83.

"A History of Dominican Music in the United States: Narrative: 1910s and 1920s: The Early Presence of Dominican Music." CUNY Dominican Studies Institute. Accessed March 8, 2022. http://dominicanmusicusa.com/narratives/1910s-1920s-the-early-presence-of-dominican-music/5.

Hobsbawm, E. J. *Primitive Rebels: Studies in Archaic Forms of Social Movement in the 19th and 20th Centuries*. Manchester: Manchester University Press, 1959.

Hoermann, Raphael. "'A Very Hell of Horrors'? The Haitian Revolution and the Early Transatlantic Haitian Gothic." *Slavery and Abolition* 37, no. 1 (2016): 183–205.

Hogan, Edmund. *History of the Irish Wolfdog*. N.p.: Read Books, 2013.

"Hog-Raising in Cuba." *Journal of the Royal Society of Arts* 64, no. 3334 (1916): 802–3.

Holland, Sharon P., Marcia Ochoa, and Kyla Wazana Tompkins. "On the Visceral." *GLQ* 20, no. 4 (2014): 391–406.

Holt, Thomas C. "Marking: Race, Race-Making, and the Writing of History." *American Historical Review* 100, no. 1 (1995): 1–20.

Honychurch, Lennox. *In the Forests of Freedom: The Fighting Maroons of Dominica.* London: Papillote Press, 2017.

hooks, bell. "Eating the Other: Desire and Resistance." In *Black Looks: Race and Representation*, 33–52. Boston: South End Press, 1992.

Horkheimer, Max, and Theodor W. Adorno. "On the Theory of Ghosts." In *Dialectic of Enlightenment*, 178–79. Translated by John Cumming. New York: Continuum, 1994.

Horn, Maja. *Masculinity After Trujillo: The Politics of Gender in Dominican Literature.* Gainesville: University Press of Florida, 2014.

Hurbon, Laënnec. "The Bizoton Affair." *Haiti: An Island Luminous.* Accessed August 24, 2024. https://islandluminous.fiu.edu/part05-slide10.html.

Hurbon, Laënnec. *Le barbare imaginaire.* Paris: Les Editions du Cerf, 1988.

Hurbon, Laënnec. *Voodoo: Search for the Spirit.* Translated by Lory Frankel. New York: H. N. Abrams, 1995.

Hurston, Zora Neale. *Tell My Horse.* Philadelphia: J. B. Lippincott, 1938.

Hutchinson, Sharon. "The Cattle of Money and the Cattle of Girls Among the Nuer, 1930–83." *American Ethnologist* 19, no. 2 (1992): 294–316.

Hutchinson, Sydney. "Entangled Rhythms on a Conflicted Island: Digging Up the Buried Histories of Dominican Folk Music." *Revista Resonancias* 20, no. 39 (2016): 139–54.

Hutchinson, Sydney. "'A Limp with Rhythm': Convergent Choreographies in Black Atlantic Time." *Yearbook for Traditional Music*, no. 44 (2012): 87–108.

Hutchinson, Sydney. *Tigers of a Different Stripe: Performing Gender in Dominican Music.* Chicago: University of Chicago Press, 2016.

Hyatt, Harry Middleton. *Hoodoo—Conjuration—Witchcraft—Rootwork: Beliefs Accepted by Many Negroes and White Persons, These Being Orally Recorded Among Blacks and Whites.* Memoirs of the Alma Egan Hyatt Foundation. Hannibal, MO: Western Publishing, 1970.

Hyde, Lewis. *Trickster Makes This World: Mischief, Myth, and Art.* New York: Farrar, Straus and Giroux, 1998.

"ICE Deportations: Gender, Age, and Country of Citizenship." Transactional Records Access Clearinghouse, Syracuse University. Accessed March 11, 2022. https://trac.syr.edu/immigration/reports/350/.

Incháustegui, Arístides. *El disco en República Dominicana.* Santo Domingo: n.p., 1988.

Ingold, Tim. *The Appropriation of Nature: Essays on Human Ecology and Social Relations.* Iowa City: University of Iowa Press, 1987.

Ingold, Tim. "On Reindeer and Men." *Man* 9, no. 4 (1974): 523–38.

Ingold, Tim. *The Perception of the Environment: Essays on Livelihood, Dwelling and Skill.* London: Routledge, 2011.

Inoa, Orlando. *Diccionario de dominicanismos.* Santo Domingo: Editorial Letra Gráfica, 2010.

Ito, Robert. "In 'Star Trek Beyond' or on TV: Half-Vulcan. Half-Human. All Role Model." *New York Times*, October 2, 2016.

Jackson, Michael. *Paths Toward a Clearing: Radical Empiricism and Ethnographic Inquiry*. Bloomington: Indiana University Press, 1989.

Jackson, Zakiyyah Iman. *Becoming Human: Matter and Meaning in an Antiblack World*. New York: New York University Press, 2020.

Jacobs, Nancy J. "The Great Bophuthatswana Donkey Massacre: Discourse on the Ass and the Politics of Class and Grass." *American Historical Review* 106, no. 2 (2001): 485–507.

Jacobs, Shayna. "Major Drug Trafficker Who Ran Two Heroin Rings in NYC from Dominican Republic After Being Deported Extradited to U.S." *New York Daily News*, August 29, 2019.

Jäger, Hans-Wolf. "Is Little Red Riding Hood Wearing a Liberty Cap? On Presumable Connotations in Tieck and in Grimm." In *Little Red Riding Hood: A Casebook*, edited by Alan Dundes, 89–120. Madison: University of Wisconsin Press, 1989.

James, Daniel. *Doña María's Story: Life History, Memory, and Political Identity*. Durham, NC: Duke University Press, 2000.

James, Daniel. *Resistance and Integration: Peronism and the Argentine Working Class, 1946–1976*. Cambridge: Cambridge University Press, 1988.

James, Joel, José Millet, and Alexis Alarcón. *El vodú en Cuba*. Santiago de Cuba: Editorial Oriente, 1998.

Jansen, Silke. "Los sonidos del merengue: Variatión lingüística e identidad en la música nacional dominicana." *Revista internacional de lingüística iberoamericana: RILI* 15, no. 2, 30 (2017): 145–60.

Jarvis, Michael. *In the Eye of All Trade: Bermuda, Bermudians, and the Maritime Atlantic World, 1680–1783*. Chapel Hill: University of North Carolina Press, 2010.

Jiménez, R. Emilio. *Al amor del bohío (tradiciones y costumbres dominicanas)*. Santo Domingo: V. Montalvo, 1927.

"Johnny Ventura con Anthony Rios (Video 1982)—Caña Brava—Merengue Clasico." YouTube, posted by Elgalan718, October 11, 2010. https://www.youtube .com/watch?v=mJU9yqYi6sM.

Johnson, John J. "The Introduction of the Horse into the Western Hemisphere." *Hispanic American Historical Review* 23, no. 4 (1943): 587–610.

Johnson, Paul Christopher, ed. *Spirited Things: The Work of "Possession" in Afro-Atlantic Religions*. Chicago: University of Chicago Press, 2014.

Johnson, Sara E. *Encyclopédie Noire: The Making of Moreau de Saint-Méry's Intellectual World*. Chapel Hill: University of North Carolina Press, 2023.

Johnson, Sara E. *The Fear of French Negroes: Transcolonial Collaboration in the Revolutionary Americas*. Berkeley: University of California Press, 2012.

Johnson, Sara E. "'You Should Give Them Blacks to Eat': Waging Inter-American Wars of Torture and Terror." *American Quarterly* 61, no. 1 (2009): 65–92.

Johnson, Walter. "On Agency." *Journal of Social History* 37, no. 1 (2003): 113–24.

Johnstone, Barbara. *Stories, Community, and Place: Narratives from Middle America*. Bloomington: Indiana University Press, 1990.

Joiris, Daou V. "Baba Pygmy Hunting Rituals in Southern Cameroon How to Walk Side by Side with the Elephant." *Civilisations* 41, nos. 1–2 (1993): 51–81.

Jones, Geoffrey. *Renewing Unilever*. Oxford: Oxford University Press, 2005.

"José Figueroa Acosta Arrested: Feds Catch Alleged Puerto Rico Drug Lord After 10 Year Hunt." *Huffington Post*, July 28, 2010.

Joseph, Raymond A. *For Whom the Dogs Spy: Haiti; From the Duvalier Dictatorships to the Earthquake, Four Presidents, and Beyond*. New York: Arcade, 2014.

Joseph, Richard. *Democracy and Prebendal Politics in Nigeria: The Rise and Fall of the Second Republic*. Cambridge: Cambridge University Press, 1988.

Kahn, Jeffrey S. "Smugglers, Migrants, and Demons: Cosmographies of Mobility in the Northern Caribbean." *American Ethnologist* 46, no. 4 (2019): 470–81.

Karnowski, Steve. "A Population of Hard to Eradicate 'Super Pigs' in Canada Is Threatening to Invade the US." *Los Angeles Times*, November 23, 2023.

Karush, Matthew B. "Populism, Melodrama, and the Market: The Mass Cultural Origins of Peronism." In *The New Cultural History of Peronism*, edited by Matthew B. Karush and Oscar Chamosa, 21–52. Durham, NC: Duke University Press, 2010.

Karush, Matthew B., and Oscar Chamosa, eds. *The New Cultural History of Peronism: Power and Identity in Mid-Twentieth-Century Argentina*. Durham, NC: Duke University Press, 2010.

Kelley, M. J., Dana Leipold, Elaine Chao, and Woelf Dietrich. *Interspecies*. Hawkes Bay, New Zealand: Kōsa Press, 2016.

Kences, James E. "The Horses and Horse Trades of Colonial Boston." In *New England's Creatures: 1400–1900*, edited by Peter Benes and Jane Montague Benes, 73–84. Boston: Boston University Press, 1995.

Kettler, Andrew. "The Miasmic Theft of Modernity: Sulfuric Aromata and Early Modern Empires." *Venti* 2, no. 2 (2023). https://www.venti-journal.com /andrew-kettler.

Kettler, Andrew. *The Smell of Slavery: Olfactory Racism and the Atlantic World*. New York: Cambridge University Press, 2020.

Kimhi, Ayal. "International Remittances, Domestic Remittances, and Income Inequality in the Dominican Republic." *Research in Applied Economics*, no. 12 (2010). https://doi.org/10.5296/rae.v12i3.16235.

Kinser, Sam. *Carnival, American Style: Mardi Gras at New Orleans and Mobile*. Chicago: University of Chicago Press, 1990.

Kivland, Chelsey L. *Street Sovereigns: Young Men and the Makeshift State in Urban Haiti*. Ithaca, NY: Cornell University Press, 2020.

Klein, Naomi. *The Shock Doctrine: The Rise of Disaster Capitalism*. New York: Metropolitan Books/Henry Holt, 2007.

Knight, John. *Waiting for Wolves in Japan: An Anthropological Study of People-Wildlife Relations*. New York: Oxford University Press, 2003.

Ko, Aph. *Racism as Zoological Witchcraft: A Guide to Getting Out*. Brooklyn, NY: Lantern Books, 2019.

Köhler, Axel. "Half-Man, Half-Elephant: Shapeshifting Among the Baka of Congo." In *Natural Enemies: People-Wildlife Conflicts in Anthropological Perspective*, edited by John Knight, 58–85. London: Routledge, 2001.

Kohn, Eduardo. "How Dogs Dream: Amazonian Natures and the Politics of Transspecies Engagement." *American Ethnologist* 34, no. 1 (2007): 3–24.

Kohn, Eduardo. *How Forests Think: Toward an Anthropology Beyond the Human*. Berkeley: University of California Press, 2013.

Koselleck, Reinhart. "Terror and Dream: Methodological Remarks on the Experience of Time During the Third Reich." In *Futures Past*, 213–30. Translated by Keith Tribe. New York: Columbia University Press, 2004.

Kramer, Andrew E., and Maria Varenikova. "At Ukraines' Gravesites, a Spring Ritual Hints at Renewal." *New York Times*, April 24, 2023.

Krohn-Hansen, C. *Jobless Growth in the Dominican Republic: Disorganization, Precarity, and Livelihoods*. Stanford, CA: Stanford University Press, 2022.

Krohn-Hansen, C. "Magic, Money and Alterity Among Dominicans." *Social Anthropology* 3, no. 2 (1995): 129–46.

Krohn-Hansen, C. "Masculinity and the Political Among Dominicans." In *Machos, Mistresses, Madonnas: Contesting the Power of Latin American Gender Imagery*, edited by Marit Melhuus and Kristi Anne Stølen, 108–33. New York: Verso, 1996.

Krohn-Hansen, C. *Political Authoritarianism in the Dominican Republic*. New York: Palgrave Macmillan, 2009.

Krohn-Hansen, C. "A Tomb for Columbus in Santo Domingo: Political Cosmology, Population and Racial Frontiers." *Social Anthropology* 9, no. 2 (2001): 165–92.

Krug, Jessica A. *Fugitive Modernities: Kisama and the Politics of Freedom*. Durham, NC: Duke University Press, 2018.

Kuffner, Emily. *Fictions of Containment in the Spanish Female Picaresque: Architectural Space and Prostitution in the Early Modern Mediterranean*. Amsterdam: Amsterdam University Press, 2019.

Labat, Jean-Baptiste. *The Memoirs of Père Labat, 1693–1705*. Translated by John Eaden. London: F. Cass, 1970.

Labat, Jean-Baptiste. *Nouveaux voyages aux isles de l'Amérique*. Paris: T. Le Gras, 1722.

Labat, Jean-Baptiste. *Voyages aux isles de l'Amérique (Antilles) 1693–1705*. Paris: Éditions Duchartre, 1931.

Labourt, José. *Sana, sana, culito de rana*. Santo Domingo: Editora Taller, 1982.

Labov, William. "The Transformation of Experience in Narrative Syntax." In *Language in the Inner City: Studies in the Black English Vernacular*, 354–96. Philadelphia: University of Pennsylvania Press, 1972.

Labov, William, and Joshua Waletzky. "Narrative Analysis: Oral Versions of Personal Experience." *Journal of Narrative and Life History* 7, nos. 1–4 (1997): 3–38.

Lachatañeré, Rómulo. *¡¡Oh mío Yemaya!! Cuentos y cantos negros*. Havana: Editorial de Ciencias Sociales, 1992.

Laclau, Ernesto. *On Populist Reason*. London: Verso, 2005.

"La corrupción sin castigo": Casos denunciados en los medios de comunicación, 2000–2013. Santo Domingo: Universidad Autónoma de Santo Domingo, 2014.

"'La Cruz de Palo Bonito' por Miriam Cruz: El Merengue según Mateo." YouTube, posted by Ministerio de Cultura República Dominicana, June 14, 2018. https://www.youtube.com/watch?v=qJae7Lw2MVo.

La frontera: Prioridad en la agenda nacional del siglo XXI. Santo Domingo: Secretaría de Estado de las Fuerzas Armadas, 2004.

Laguerre, Michel. *The Military and Society in Haiti*. Houndmills, UK: Macmillan, 1993.

Laguerre, Michel. *Voodoo and Politics in Haiti*. London: Palgrave Macmillan, 1989.

Lambert, David. "Master-Horse-Slave: Mobility, Race and Power in the British West Indies, c. 1780–1838." *Slavery and Abolition* 36, no. 4 (2015): 618–41.

Lancaster, Roger N. *Life Is Hard: Machismo, Danger, and the Intimacy of Power in Nicaragua*. Berkeley: University of California Press, 1992.

Landers, Jane. *Atlantic Creoles in the Age of Revolutions*. Cambridge, MA: Harvard University Press, 2010.

Landers, Jane. "The Central African Presence in Spanish Maroon Communities." In *Central Africans and Cultural Transformations in the American Diaspora*, edited by Linda M. Heywood, 227–41. Cambridge: Cambridge University Press, 2002.

Lane, Kris E. *Pillaging the Empire: Piracy in the Americas, 1500–1750*. Armonk, NY: M. E. Sharpe, 1998.

Large, Josaphat-Robert. "Rosanna." In *Haiti Noir*, edited by Edwidge Danticat, 155–78. New York: Akashic, 2011.

Larkin, Brian. "The Politics and Poetics of Infrastructure." *Annual Review of Anthropology* 42 (2013): 327–43.

La Rosa Corzo, Gabino. *Runaway Slave Settlements in Cuba: Resistance and Repression*. Translated by Mary Todd. Chapel Hill: University of North Carolina Press, 2003.

Lauria, Anthony. "'Respeto,' 'Relajo' and Inter-Personal Relations in Puerto Rico." *Anthropological Quarterly* 37, no. 2 (1964): 53–67.

Lauro, Sarah Juliet. *The Transatlantic Zombie: Slavery, Rebellion, and Living Death*. New Brunswick, NJ: Rutgers University Press, 2015.

Lawrence, Denise L. "Menstrual Politics: Women and Pigs in Rural Portugal." In *Blood Magic: The Anthropology of Menstruation*, edited by Thomas Buckley and Alma Gottlieb, 113–36. Berkeley: University of California Press, 2020.

Leach, Edmund. "Anthropological Aspects of Language: Animal Categories and Verbal Abuse." *Anthrozoös* 2, no. 3 (1989): 151–65.

Leach, Edmund. *New Directions in the Study of Language*, edited by Eric H. Lenneberg. Cambridge, MA: MIT Press, 1964.

LeGrand, Catherine. "Living in Macondo: Economy and Culture in a United Fruit Company Banana Enclave in Colombia." In *Close Encounters of Empire:*

Writing the Cultural History of U.S.-Latin American Relations, edited by Gilbert M. Joseph, Catherine LeGrand, and Ricardo Donato Salvatore, 333–68. Durham, NC: Duke University Press, 1998.

Le Roy Ladurie, Emmanuel. "Carnivals in History." *Thesis Eleven* 3, no. 1 (1981): 52–59.

Lescallier, Daniel. "Itinerario desde el río masacre a Santo Domingo, por Santiago, La Vega y Cotuí." In *Viajeros de Francia en Santo Domingo*, edited by Emilo Rodríguez Demorizi, 61–73. Santo Domingo: Editora del Caribe, 1979.

Lescallier, Daniel. "Itinerario desde Santo Domingo a Cap Français y desde esta ciudad hasta el limite de San Rafael pasando por Azua y San Juan 75 leguas y 1/2." In *Viajeros de Francia en Santo Domingo*, edited by Emilo Rodríguez Demorizi, 47–59. Santo Domingo: Editora del Caribe, 1979.

Lescallier, Daniel. "Nociones sobre los principales lugares de la colonia Española por un ingeniero francés que la visitó en 1764." In *Viajeros de Francia en Santo Domingo*, edited by Emilio Rodríguez Demorizi, 9–31. Santo Domingo: Editora del Caribe, 1979.

Leverenz, David. "The Last Real Man in America: From Natty Bumppo to Batman." *American Literary History* 3, no. 4 (Winter 1991): 753–81.

Lévi-Strauss, Claude. *The Raw and the Cooked*, vol. 1. London: Jonathan Cape, 1969.

Lewis, Laura A. *Hall of Mirrors: Power, Witchcraft, and Caste in Colonial Mexico*. Durham, NC: Duke University Press, 2003.

Liberato, Ana S. Q. *Joaquín Balaguer, Memory, and Diaspora: The Lasting Political Legacies of an American Protégé*. Lanham, MD: Lexington Books, 2013.

Lightfoot, Natasha. *Troubling Freedom: Antigua and the Aftermath of British Emancipation*. Durham, NC: Duke University Press, 2015.

Ligon, Richard. *A True and Exact History of the Island of Barbados*. Edited by Karen Ordahl Kupperman. Indianapolis, IN: Hackett, 2011.

Limón, José Eduardo. "Carne, Carnales, and the Carnivalesque." In *Dancing with the Devil: Society and Cultural Poetics in Mexican-American South Texas*, 123–40. Madison: University of Wisconsin Press, 1994.

Linebaugh, Peter. *The London Hanged: Crime and Civil Society in the Eighteenth Century*. London: Allen Lane, 1991.

Livingston, Julie, and Jasbir K. Puar. "Introduction." Special issue: "Interspecies." *Social Text* 29, no. 1 (2011): 3–14.

Lizardo Barinas, Fradique. "Tres aspectos de los 'diablos cajuelos' en Santo Domingo." *Boletín del Museo del Hombre Dominicano* (1973): 85–91.

Lobban, Richard A. "Pigs and Their Prohibition." *International Journal of Middle East Studies* 26, no. 1 (1994): 57–75.

Loichot, Valérie. *Water Graves: The Art of the Unritual in the Greater Caribbean*. Charlottesville: University of Virginia Press, 2020.

Lomax, Alan. *Alan Lomax in Haiti*. CD. Harte Recordings, 2009.

Lomnitz-Adler, Claudio. *Death and the Idea of Mexico*. Brooklyn, NY: Zone Books, 2005.

Long, Edward. *The History of Jamaica: Or, General Survey of the Antient and Modern State of That Island: With Reflections on Its Situation, Settlements, Inhabitants, Climate, Products, Commerce, Laws, and Government.* London: T. Lowndes, 1774.

Longinović, Tomislav Z. *Vampire Nation: Violence as Cultural Imaginary.* Durham, NC: Duke University Press, 2011.

López y Sebastián, Lorenzo E., and Justo L. del Río Moreno. "La ganadería vacuna en la isla Española (1508–1587)." *Revista Complutense de Historia de América*, no. 25 (1999): 11–49.

"Los extraños apodos de aspirantes políticos." *Listín Diario*, January 21, 2020.

Louis, Liliane Nérette. *When Night Falls, Kric! Krac! Haitian Folktales.* Edited by Frederick J. Hay. Englewood, CO: Libraries Unlimited, 1999.

Lundahl, Mats. *The Haitian Economy: Man, Land and Markets.* Oxford: Routledge, 2015.

Lundahl, Mats, and Jan Lundius. *Peasants and Religion: A Socioeconomic Study of Dios Olivorio and the Palma Sola Religion in the Dominican Republic.* London: Taylor and Francis, 2012.

Lundius, Jan. *The Great Power of God in San Juan Valley: Syncretism and Messianism in the Dominican Republic.* Lund, Sweden: Religionshistoriska avdelningen, Lunds University, 1995.

MacGaffey, Wyatt. *Art and Healing of the Bakongo, Commented by Themselves: Minkisi from the Laman Collection.* Stockholm: Folkens Museum-Etnografiska, 1991.

MacGaffey, Wyatt. "Complexity, Astonishment and Power: The Visual Vocabulary of Kongo Minkisi." *Journal of Southern African Studies* 14, no. 2 (1988): 188–203.

MacGaffey, Wyatt. "Ethnography and the Closing of the Frontier in Lower Congo, 1885–1921." *Africa* 56, no. 3 (1986): 263–79.

MacGaffey, Wyatt. *Kongo Political Culture: The Conceptual Challenge of the Particular.* Bloomington: Indiana University Press, 2000.

MacGaffey, Wyatt. "The Personhood of Ritual Objects: Kongo 'Minkisi.'" *Etnofoor* 3, no. 1 (1990): 45–61.

MacGaffey, Wyatt. *Religion and Society in Central Africa: The BaKongo of Lower Zaire.* Chicago: University of Chicago Press, 1986.

MacGaffey, Wyatt. "Twins, Simbi Spirits, and Lwas in Kongo and Haiti." In *Central Africans and Cultural Transformations in the American Diaspora*, edited by Linda M. Heywood, 211–26. New York: Cambridge University Press, 2002.

MacGaffey, Wyatt, and Michael D. Harris. *Astonishment and Power.* Washington, DC: Smithsonian Institution Press, 1993.

Machen, Arthur. *The White People and Other Weird Stories.* New York: Penguin, 2011.

Malamud, Randy. "Zoo Spectatorship." In *The Animals Reader: The Essential Classic and Contemporary Writings*, edited by Linda Kalof and Amy Fitzgerald, 219–36. Oxford: Berg, 2007.

Malcolmson, Robert W., and Stephanos Mastoris. *The English Pig: A History*. London: Hambledon, 1998.

Mañach, Jorge. *Indagación del choteo*. Havana: La Verónica, 1940.

Mancall, Peter C. *Nature and Culture in the Early Modern Atlantic*. Philadelphia: University of Pennsylvania Press, 2017.

Mancall, Peter C. "Pigs for Historians: *Changes in the Land* and Beyond." *William and Mary Quarterly* 67, no. 2 (2010): 347–75.

Mandelblatt, Bertie. "Pen-Keeping." *History Workshop Journal* 72, no. 1 (2011): 310–14.

Maríñez, Sophie. *Spirals in the Caribbean: Representing Violence and Connection in Haiti and the Dominican Republic*. Philadelphia: University of Pennsylvania Press, 2024.

Marple, Olivia. "Machismo, Femicide, and Sex Tourism: An Overview of Women's Rights in the Dominican Republic." Council on Hemispheric Affairs, June 4, 2015. https://coha.org/machismo-femicide-and-sex-tourism-an-overview-of -womens-rights-in-the-dominican-republic/.

Márquez, Luis. "'Los primeros caballos que pisaron América.'" *Hoy Digital*, September 24, 2016. https://hoy.com.do/los-primeros-caballos-que-pisaron -america-3-de-3/.

Marrero Aristy, Ramón. *Over: Novela*. 1939. Santo Domingo: Taller, 1976.

Marshall, Emily Zobel. *Anansi's Journey: A Tale of Jamaican Cultural Resistance*. Kingston: University of the West Indies Press, 2012.

Martínez, Lusitania. *Palma Sola: Opresión y esperanza (su geografía mítica y social)*. Santo Domingo: Ediciones CEDEE, 1991.

Martínez, Orlando. "Why Not, Dr. Balaguer?" In *The Dominican Republic Reader*, edited by Eric Paul Roorda, Lauren Derby, and Raymundo González, 365–67. Durham, NC: Duke University Press, 2014.

Martínez, Regino. "La victoria del cimarrón." *Estudios Sociales* 19, no. 64 (June 1986): 53–62.

Marvin, Garry. *Wolf*. London: Reaktion, 2012.

Marvin, Garry. "Wolves in Sheep's (and Others') Clothing." In *Beastly Natures: Animals, Humans, and the Study of History*, edited by Dorothee Brantz, 59–80. Charlottesville: University of Virginia Press, 2010.

Marx, Karl. "The Fetishism of Commodities and the Secret Thereof." In *Capital*, vol. 1. https://www.marxists.org/archive/marx/works/1867-c1/ch01 .htm.

Marx, Karl, and Friedrich Engels. *The Marx-Engels Reader*. Edited by Robert C. Tucker. New York: W. W. Norton, 1978.

Marx, Leo. *The Machine in the Garden: Technology and the Pastoral Ideal in America*. New York: Oxford University Press, 1964.

Massey, Douglas S., Mary J. Fischer, and Chiara Capoferro. "International Migration and Gender in Latin America: A Comparative Analysis." *International Migration* 44, no. 5 (2006): 63–91.

Massumi, Brian. "The Future Birth of the Affective Fact: The Political Ontology of Threat." In *The Affect Theory Reader*, edited by Gregory J. Seigworth and Melissa Gregg, 52–70. Durham, NC: Duke University Press, 2020.

Mateo, Andrés. "The 'Eat Alones' of the Liberation Party." In *The Dominican Republic Reader: History, Culture, Politics*, edited by Eric Paul Roorda, Lauren Derby, and Raymundo González, eds., 373–75. Durham, NC: Duke University Press, 2014.

Matibag, Eugenio. *Haitian-Dominican Counterpoint*. New York: Palgrave, 2003.

Matos de la Rosa, Luis Enrique. *San Juan de la Maguana: Una introducción a su historia de cara al futuro*. Santo Domingo: Dirección General de la Feria del Libro, 2007.

Matos Espinosa, Juan Francisco. "Caza de venados y puercos cimarrones en Los Haitises." *Noticiario Barahona* (blog), July 13, 2012. web.archive.org /web/20210602195107/http://www.noticiariobarahona.com/2012/07/caza-de -venados-y-puercos-cimarrones-en.html.

Mauss, Marcel. *The Gift: Forms and Functions of Exchange in Archaic Societies*. New York: W. W. Norton, 1967.

Mayes, April J. *The Mulatto Republic: Class, Race, and Dominican National Identity*. Gainesville: University Press of Florida, 2014.

Mayes, April J., and Kiran C. Jayaram. *Transnational Hispaniola: New Directions in Haitian and Dominican Studies*. Gainesville: University Press of Florida, 2018.

Mazzarella, William. *The Mana of Mass Society*. Chicago: University of Chicago Press, 2017.

Mazzarella, William. *Shoveling Smoke: Advertising and Globalization in Contemporary India*. Durham, NC: Duke University Press, 2003.

McAfee, Kathy. *Storm Signals: Structural Adjustment and Development Alternatives in the Caribbean*. Boston: South End Press, 1991.

McAlister, Elizabeth. "From Slave Revolt to a Blood Pact with Satan: The Evangelical Rewriting of Haitian History." *Studies in Religion/Sciences Religieuses* 41, no. 2 (2012): 187–215.

McAlister, Elizabeth. "The Jew in the Haitian Imagination: A Popular History of Anti-Judaism and Proto-Racism." In *Race, Nation, and Religion in the Americas*, edited by Henry Goldschmidt and Elizabeth McAlister, 79–99. New York: Oxford University Press, 2004.

McAlister, Elizabeth. "The Militarization of Prayer in America: White and Native American Spiritual Warfare." *Journal of Religious and Political Practice: Prayer and Politics* 2, no. 1 (2016): 114–30.

McAlister, Elizabeth. "Possessing the Land for Jesus." In *Spirited Things: The Work of "Possession" in Afro-Atlantic Religions*, edited by Paul C. Johnson, 177–205. Chicago: University of Chicago Press, 2014.

McAlister, Elizabeth. *Rara!: Vodou, Power, and Performance in Haiti and Its Diaspora*. Berkeley: University of California Press, 2002.

McAlister, Elizabeth. "Slaves, Cannibals, and Infected Hyper-Whites: The Race and Religion of Zombies." *Anthropological Quarterly* 85, no. 2 (2012): 457–86.

McAlister, Elizabeth. "A Sorcerer's Bottle: The Visual Art of Magic in Haiti." In *Sacred Arts of Haitian Vodou*, edited by Donald Cosentino, 305–22. Los Angeles: UCLA Fowler Museum of Cultural History, 1995.

McCreery, David. "Debt Peonage." In *Encyclopedia of Latin American History and Culture*, edited by Jay Kinsbruner and Erick D. Langer, 756–59. New York: Gale, 2008.

McHugh, Susan. *Dog*. London: Reaktion, 2004.

McNaughton, Patrick R. *The Mande Blacksmiths: Knowledge, Power, and Art in West Africa*. Bloomington: Indiana University Press, 1988.

McPherson, Alan. *The Invaded: How Latin Americans and Their Allies Fought and Ended U.S. Occupations*. New York: Oxford University Press, 2013.

Medina, Danilo. "Dominican Republic Emerged as Drug Trafficking Center of the Caribbean." *HuffPost*, January 23, 2013.

Melillo, Edward D. "The First Green Revolution: Debt Peonage and the Making of the Nitrogen Fertilizer Trade, 1840–1930." *American Historical Review* 117, no. 4 (2012): 1028–60.

Melville, Elinor G. K. *A Plague of Sheep: Environmental Consequences of the Conquest of Mexico*. Cambridge: Cambridge University Press, 1994.

Menchú, Rigoberta. *I, Rigoberta Menchú: An Indian Woman in Guatemala*. Edited by Elisabeth Burgos-Debray. Translated by Ann Wright. London: Verso, 1984.

Métraux, Alfred. *Voodoo in Haiti*. Translated by Hugo Charteris. New York: Schocken, 1972.

Meyer, Birgit. "Religion and Materiality: Food, 'Fetish' and Other Matters." In *Stepping Back and Looking Ahead: Twelve Years of Studying Religious Contact at the Käte Hamburger Kolleg Bochum*, edited by Maren Freudenberg, Frederik Elwert, Tim Karis, Martin Radermacher, and Jens Schlamelcher, 267–301. London: Brill, 2023.

Milin, Gaël. *Les chiens de Dieu: La représentation du loup-garou en Occident, XIe–XIXe siècles*. Brest: Centre de Recherche Bretonne et Celtique, Université de Bretagne Occidentale, 1993.

Miller, Daniel. "Coca-Cola: A Black Sweet Drink from Trinidad." In *The Cultural Politics of Food and Eating: A Reader*, edited by James L. Watson and Melissa L. Caldwell, 54–69. Malden, MA: Blackwell, 2005.

Miller, Ivor. *Voice of the Leopard: African Secret Societies and Cuba*. Jackson: University Press of Mississippi, 2009.

Miller, Joseph Calder. "Introduction: Listening for the African Past." In *The African Past Speaks: Essays on Oral Tradition and History*, edited by Joseph Calder Miller, 1–59. Hamden, CO: Archon, 1980.

Mintz, Sidney. *Caribbean Transformations*. Chicago: Aldine, 2015.

Mintz, Sidney. "Slavery and the Rise of Peasantries." *Historical Reflections* 6, no. 1 (1979): 213–53.

Mintz, Sidney. *Sweetness and Power: The Place of Sugar in Modern History.* New York: Viking, 1985.

Mintz, Sidney, and Douglas Hall. *The Origins of the Jamaican Internal Marketing System.* Papers in Caribbean Anthropology 47. New Haven, CT: Yale University Department of Anthropology, 1960.

Mir, Pedro. *Cuando amaban las tierras comuneras.* Mexico City: Siglo XXI Editores, 1978.

Mira Caballos, Esteban. "Justo del Río Moreno, *Caballos y equipos españoles en la conquista y colonización de América* (siglo XVI)." *Revista ECOS UASD* 2, no. 3 (1994): 242–43.

Mitchell, Timothy. *Blood Sport: A Social History of Spanish Bullfighting.* With an essay and bibliography by Rosario Cambria. Philadelphia: University of Pennsylvania Press, 1991.

Mizelle, Brett. *Pig.* London: Reaktion, 2011.

Mobley, Christina. "The Mystery of the 'Mondongue' Midwife in Saint Domingue: Cannibalism, Infanticide and the Manufacture of Myth." Unpublished manuscript, n.d.

Mol, Annemarie. *Eating in Theory.* Durham, NC: Duke University Press, 2011.

Moore, Sophie. "Chronic Carriers: Creole Pigs, Postplantation Politics, and Disturbing Agrarian Ontologies in Haiti." In *Coloniality, Ontology, and the Question of the Posthuman,* edited by Mark Jackson, 81–99. London: Routledge, 2018.

Mora Oviedo, Hostos Guaroa. *Bánica: Apuntes para su historia.* Santo Domingo: n.p., 2004.

Morban Laucer, F. "Características de los dientes de grupos raciales prehistoricos y su presencia actual." *Boletín del Museo del Hombre Dominicano,* no. 20 (1987): 17–45.

Morban Laucer, F. "Fauna extinguida de la Hispaniola." *Boletín del Museo del Hombre Dominicano,* no. 19 (1984): 27–42.

Moreau de Saint-Méry, M. L. E. "The Border Maroons of Saint Domingue, Le Maniel." In *Maroon Societies: Rebel Slave Communities in the Americas,* edited by Richard Price, 135–42. Baltimore: Johns Hopkins University Press, 1996.

Moreau de Saint-Méry, M. L. E. *Description topographique, physique, civile, politique et historique de la partie espagnole de l'isle Saint-Domingue.* Philadelphia: Imprimé par L'auteur, 1796.

Moreau de Saint-Méry, M. L. E. *Description topographique, physique, civile, politique et historique de la partie française de l'isle Saint Domingue.* 2 vols. Paris: Société de l'histoire des colonies françaises, 1958.

Moreau de Saint-Méry, M. L. E. *Vue de l'entrée du Gouffre au dessus des sources des eaux therminales de Banica.* 1875. Digital Library of the Caribbean. https://www.dloc.com/CA00500300/00001/citation.

Moreno Fraginals, Manuel. *El ingenio: Complejo económico social cubano del azúcar*, vol I. Havana: Editorial de Ciencias Sociales, 1978.

Morgan, Philip D. "Slaves and Livestock in Eighteenth-Century Jamaica: Vineyard Pen, 1750–1751." *William and Mary Quarterly* 52, no. 1 (1995): 47–76.

Moscoso Puello, Francisco E. *Cañas y bueyes: Novela*. 1936. Santo Domingo: Letragráfica, 2015.

Moscoso Puello, Francisco. "From Paris to Santo Domingo." In *The Dominican Republic Reader*, edited by Eric Paul Roorda, Lauren Derby, and Raymundo González, 195–200. Durham, NC: Duke University Press, 2014.

Moya, E. Antonio de. "Power Games and Totalitarian Masculinity in the Dominican Republic." In *Caribbean Masculinities: Working Papers*, edited by Rafael L. Ramírez, Víctor Iván García Toro, and Ineke Cunningham, 105–46. San Juan, Puerto Rico: HIV/AIDS Research and Education Center, University of Puerto Rico, 2002.

Moya, E. Antonio de. "Power Games and Totalitarian Masculinity in the Dominican Republic." In *Interrogating Caribbean Masculinities: Theoretical and Empirical Analyses*, edited by Rhoda Reddock, 68–104. Kingston: University of the West Indies Press, 2004.

Moya Pons, Frank. *Después de Colón: Trabajo, sociedad y política en la economía del oro*. Madrid: Alianza, 1987.

Moya Pons, Frank. *Empresarios en conflicto: Políticas de industrialización y sustitución de importaciones en la República Dominicana*. Santo Domingo: Fondo para el Avance de las Ciencias Sociales, 1992.

Moya Pons, Frank. *La otra historia dominicana*. Santo Domingo: Librería La Trinitaria, 2008.

Mubitana, Kafungulwa. "Wiko Masquerades." *African Arts* 4, no. 3 (1971): 58–62.

Mullin, Molly H. "Mirrors and Windows: Sociocultural Studies of Human-Animal Relationships." *Annual Review of Anthropology* 28 (1999): 201–24.

Musgrave-Portilla, L. Marie. "The Nahualli or Transforming Wizard in Pre- and Postconquest Mesoamerica." *Journal of Latin American Lore* 8, no. 1 (1982): 3–62.

Musharbash, Yasmine. "Introduction: Monsters, Anthropology, and Monster Studies." In *Monster Anthropology in Australasia and Beyond*, edited by Yasmine Musharbash and Geir Henning Presterudstuen, 1–24. New York: Palgrave Macmillan, 2014.

Mychajliw, Alexis. "On the Extinction (and Survival) of Caribbean Mammals." *Behind the Paper* (blog), SpringerNature Research Communities, November 6, 2017. https://communities.springernature.com/posts/22332-on-the-extinction-and-survival-of-caribbean-mammals.

Myers, Megan Jeanette, and Edward Paulino, eds. *The Border of Lights Reader: Bearing Witness to Genocide in the Dominican Republic*. Amherst, MA: Amherst College Press, 2021.

Nance, Susan, ed. *The Historical Animal.* Syracuse, NY: Syracuse University Press, 2015.

Narconon. "Cocaine and Other Drugs in the Dominican Republic." Accessed March 15, 2025. https://www.narconon.org/drug-information/dominican -republic-cocaine.html.

Nash, June. *We Eat the Mines and the Mines Eat Us: Dependency and Exploitation in Bolivian Tin Mines.* New York: Columbia University Press, 1993.

Navaro-Yashin, Yael. *The Make-Believe Space: Affective Geography in a Postwar Polity.* Durham, NC: Duke University Press, 2012.

Nessler, Graham T. *An Islandwide Struggle for Freedom: Revolution, Emancipation, and Reenslavement in Hispaniola, 1789–1809.* Chapel Hill: University of North Carolina Press, 2016.

Neufeld, Stephen. "Animal Perspectives: Nonhuman Creatures' Roles in Modern Latin America." In *Oxford Research Encyclopedia of Latin American History,* edited by Ángela Vergara. New York: Oxford University Press, 2022.

Ney Suero, Luis. "Hallan muerto a encargado junta distrital en Bánica de Elías Piña." Barrigaverde.net, March 29, 2022. http://www.barrigaverde.net/?q =node/5103.

Nicholls, Robert. *The Jumbies' Playing Ground: Old World Influences on Afro-Creole Masquerades in the Eastern Caribbean.* Jackson: University Press of Mississippi, 2012.

Northern Manhattan Coalition for Immigrant Rights. "Deportado, Dominicano, y Humano: The Realities of Dominican Deportations and Related Policy Recommendations." 2009. https://www.law.nyu.edu/sites/default /files/upload_documents/Deportado%20Dominicano%20y%20Humano .pdf.

Norton, Marcy. "The Chicken or the *Iegue*: Human-Animal Relationships and the Columbian Exchange." *American Historical Review* 120, no. 1 (2015): 28–60.

Norton, Marcy. "Going to the Birds: Animals as Things and Beings in Early Modernity." In *Early Modern Things,* edited by Paula Findlen, 51–81. New York: Routledge, 2021.

Norton, Marcy. "Subaltern Technologies and Early Modernity in the Atlantic World." *Colonial Latin American Review* 26, no. 1 (2017): 18–38.

Norton, Marcy. *The Tame and the Wild: People and Animals After 1492.* Cambridge, MA: Harvard University Press, 2023.

Nunley, John W., and Judith Bettelheim, eds. *Caribbean Festival Arts: Each and Every Bit of Difference.* Saint Louis, MO: Saint Louis Art Museum, 1988.

Ochoa, Todd Ramón. *Society of the Dead: Quita Manaquita and Palo Praise in Cuba.* Berkeley: University of California, 2010.

"Odebrecht Scandal in the Dominican Republic Refuses to Go Away." Esendom, April 1, 2022. https://esendom.com/notis/2018/6/13/odebrecht-scandal-in-the -dominican-republic-refuses-to-go-away.

Ogborn, Miles. *The Freedom of Speech: Talk and Slavery in the Anglo-Caribbean World*. Chicago: University of Chicago Press, 2019.

Ohnuki-Tierney, Emiko. *Rice as Self: Japanese Identities Through Time*. Princeton, NJ: Princeton University Press, 1993.

Ohnuki-Tierney, Emiko. "We Eat Each Other's Food to Nourish Our Body: The Global and the Local as Mutually Constituent Forces." In *Food in Global History*, edited by Raymond Grew, 250–82. New York: Routledge, 1999.

Oliver, José R. *Caciques and Cemí Idols: The Web Spun by Taíno Rulers Between Hispaniola and Puerto Rico*. Tuscaloosa: University of Alabama Press, 2009.

Orovio, Helio. *El carnaval habanero: Su música y sus comparsas*. Havana: Ediciones Extramuros, 2005.

Ortiz, Fernando. *Cuban Counterpoint: Tobacco and Sugar*. Translated by Harriet De Onís. Durham, NC: Duke University Press, 1995.

Ortiz, Fernando. *Los bailes y el teatro de los negros en el folklore de Cuba*. Havana: Editorial Letras Cubanas, 1981.

Ortiz, Fernando. *Los instrumentos de la música Afrocubana*. 5 vols. Havana: El Ministerio de Cultura y Educación, 1952.

Ortiz, Fernando. *Los negros curros*. Havana: Editorial de Ciencias Sociales, 1986.

Ortiz, Fernando. *Nuevo cateauro de cubanismos*. Havana: Editorial de Ciencias Sociales, 1974.

Ortner, Sherry B. "Is Female to Male as Nature Is to Culture?" *Feminist Studies* 1, no. 2 (1972): 5–31.

Otten, Charlotte F., ed. *A Lycanthropy Reader: Werewolves in Western Culture*. Syracuse, NY: Syracuse University Press, 1986.

Pacini Hernandez, Deborah. *Bachata: A Social History of a Dominican Popular Music*. Philadelphia: Temple University Press, 1995.

Padilla, Mark. *Caribbean Pleasure Industry: Tourism, Sexuality, and AIDS in the Dominican Republic*. Chicago: University of Chicago Press, 2007.

Padron, Francisco Morales. "Los caballos de la conquista." In *Libro de homenaje a Aurelio Miró Quesada Sosa*, edited by Estuardo Nuñex, 633–46. Lima: Taller Gráf. P.L. Villanueva, 1987.

Pagán Perdomo, Dato. *Sir Robert H. Schomburgk, notas críticas a su obra etnológica en Santo Domingo*. Santo Domingo: Museum del Hombre, Academia de Ciencias de la República Dominicana, 1985.

Paik, A. Naomi. *Rightlessness: Testimony and Redress in U.S. Prison Camps Since World War II*. Chapel Hill: University of North Carolina Press, 2016.

Palmer, Ernest Charles. "Land Use and Landscape Change Along the Dominican-Haitian Borderlands." PhD diss., Department of Geography, University of Florida, Gainesville, 1976.

Palmié, Stephan. "Other Powers: Tylor's Principle, Father Williams's Temptations, and the Power of Banality." In *Obeah and Other Powers: The Politics of Caribbean Religion and Healing*, edited by Diana Paton and Maarit Forde, 316–40. Durham, NC: Duke University Press, 2012.

Palmié, Stephan. "Thinking with *Ngangas*: Reflections on Embodiment and the Limits of 'Objectively Necessary Appearances.'" *Comparative Studies in Society and History* 48, no. 4 (2006): 852–86.

Palmié, Stephan. *Wizards and Scientists: Explorations in Afro-Cuban Modernity and Tradition*. Durham, NC: Duke University Press, 2002.

Paravisini-Gebert, Lizabeth. "'Extinct Through Human Causes': Human Predation and the Extinction of the Caribbean Monk Seal." Unpublished manuscript, 2022.

Parés, Luis Nicolau, and Roger Sansi-Roca, eds. *Sorcery in the Black Atlantic*. Chicago: University of Chicago Press, 2011.

Park, Robert E., Ernest W. Burgess, and Roderick D. McKenzie. *The City*. Chicago: University of Chicago Press, 1925.

Parrinder, Geoffrey. "Activities of African Witches." In *Witches of the Atlantic World: A Historical Reader and Primary Sourcebook*, edited by Elaine G. Breslaw, 145–52. New York: New York University Press, 2000.

Parry, Jonathan P., and Maurice Bloch, eds. *Money and the Morality of Exchange*. Cambridge: Cambridge University Press, 1989.

Parry, Tyler D., and Charlton W. Yingling. "Slave Hounds and Abolition in the Americas." *Past and Present* 246, no. 1 (2020): 69–108.

Parsons, James J. "The Acorn-Hog Economy of the Oak Woodlands of Southwestern Spain." *Geographical Review* 52, no. 2 (1962): 211–35.

Passerini, Luisa. *Fascism in Popular Memory: The Cultural Experience of the Turin Working Class*. Translated by Robert Lumley and Jude Bloomfield. Cambridge: Cambridge University Press, 1987.

Patai, Daphne. "Whose Truth? Iconicity and Accuracy in the World of Testimonial Literature." In *The Rigoberta Menchú Controversy*, edited by Arturo Arias, 270–87. Minneapolis: University of Minnesota Press, 2001.

Patín Maceo, Manuel A. *Dominicanismos*. Ciudad Trujillo: Librería Dominicana, 1947.

Paton, Diana. *The Cultural Politics of Obeah: Religion, Colonialism and Modernity in the Caribbean World*. Cambridge: Cambridge University Press, 2015.

Paton, Diana, and Maarit Forde, eds. *Obeah and Other Powers: The Politics of Caribbean Religion and Healing*. Durham, NC: Duke University Press, 2012.

"Pat Robertson Says Haiti Paying for 'Pact with the Devil.'" CNN.com, January 13, 2013.

Patterson, Orlando. *Slavery and Social Death: A Comparative Study*. Cambridge, MA: Harvard University Press, 1982.

Paul, Edmond. "Pa Wowo (The Dance Steps of Wowo)." In *Kanaval: Vodou, Politics and Revolution on the Streets of Haiti*, edited by Leah Gordon et al., 78–85. London: Soul Jazz, 2010.

Paul, Tawny. *The Poverty of Disaster: Debt and Insecurity in Eighteenth-Century Britain*. New York: Cambridge University Press, 2019.

Paulino, Edward. *Dividing Hispaniola: The Dominican Republic's Border Campaign Against Haiti, 1930–1961*. Pittsburgh: University of Pittsburgh Press, 2016.

Pearson, Susan J., and Mary Weismantel. "Does 'the Animal' Exist? Toward a Theory of Social Life with Animals." In *Beastly Natures*, edited by Dorothee Brantz, 17–37. Charlottesville: University of Virginia Press, 2010.

Pedersen, Morten Axel. *Not Quite Shamans: Spirit Worlds and Political Lives in Northern Mongolia*. Ithaca, NY: Cornell University Press, 2011.

Peguero, Valentina. *The Militarization of Culture in the Dominican Republic, from the Captains General to General Trujillo*. Lincoln: University of Nebraska Press, 2004.

Peluffo, Ana. "Heroic Masculinities and the War of the Pacific." In *Power, Culture, and Violence in the Andes*, edited by Christine Hunefeldt and Misha Kokotovic, 85–96. Brighton: Sussex Academic Press, 2009.

Pels, Peter. "The Spirit of Matter: On Fetish, Rarity, Fact and Fancy." In *Border Fetishisms: Material Objects in Unstable Spaces*, edited by Patricia Spyer, 91–121. London: Routledge, 1998.

Peña Batlle, Manuel Arturo. *Orígenes del estado haitiano*. Santo Domingo: Ediciones Librería La Trinitaria, 2004.

Pérez, Elizabeth. *Religion in the Kitchen: Cooking, Talking, and the Making of Black Atlantic Religions*. New York: New York University Press, 2016.

Pérez, Juan Bautista. *Geografía y sociedad*. Santo Domingo: Editora del Caribe, 1972.

Pérez, Tony. "El pueblo de los apodos." *Acento*, January 18, 2018. https://acento .com.do/opinion/pueblo-los-apodos-8527489.html.

Pérez y Pérez, Rafael Leonidas. *Algunas de las creencias y supersticiones de un pueblo fronterizo: Duvergé (Contribución a su estudio)*. Santo Domingo: n.p., 2000.

Perks, Robert, and Alistair Thomson, eds. *The Oral History Reader*. New York: Routledge, 1998.

Pešoutová, Jana. *Indigenous Ancestors and Healing Landscapes: Cultural Memory and Intercultural Communication in the Dominican Republic and Cuba*. Leiden: Sidestone Press, 2019.

Pestana, Carla Gardina. *The English Conquest of Jamaica: Oliver Cromwell's Bid for Empire*. Cambridge, MA: Belknap Press of Harvard University Press, 2017.

Peter, Foges. "Porfirio Rubirosa: The Most Interesting Man in the World." *Thrillist*, May 15, 2014. https://www.thrillist.com/authors/peter-foges.

Phillips, Sarah. "The Pig in Medieval Iconography." In *Pigs and Humans: 10,000 Years of Interaction*, edited by Umberto Albarella, Keith Dobney, Anton Ervynck, and Peter Rowley-Conwy, 373–87. New York: Oxford University Press, 2007.

Philoctète, René. *Massacre River*. Translated by Linda Coverdale. New York: New Directions, 2005.

Pichardo, José María. *Tierra adentro*. Santo Domingo: Archivo General de la Nación, 2010.

Pietz, William. "The Problem of the Fetish, I." *Res: Anthropology and Aesthetics*, no. 9 (1985): 5–17.

Pietz, William. "The Spirit of Civilization: Blood Sacrifice and Monetary Debt." *Res: Anthropology and Aesthetics*, no. 28 (1995): 23–38.

Pimentel Paulino, Alicides. "Motes, apodos y sobrenombres." *El Nuevo Diario* (Dominican Republic), October 16, 2018. https://elnuevodiario.com.do/motes-apodos-y-sobrenombres/?amp=1.

Pineda, Jorge. "Dominican Republic Arrests Officials in Odebrecht Bribery Probe." Reuters, May 29, 2017. https://www.reuters.com/article/idUSKBN18P1S7/.

Pintor, José, Milbert Pérez, Franklin Romero, Fausto Mata, Zdenka Kalina, Tony Pascual, Patricia Banks, et al. *Sanky Panky*. CD. Premium Latin Music, 2008.

Pires, Rogério Brittes W., Stuart Earle Strange, and Marcelo Moura Mello. "The *Bakru* Speaks: Money-Making Demons and Racial Stereotypes in Guyana and Suriname." *New West Indian Guide* 92, nos. 1–2 (2018): 1–34.

Pluchon, Pierre. *Vaudou, sorciers, empoisonneurs: De Saint-Domingue à Haïti*. Paris: Éditions Karthala, 1987.

Ponce Vázquez, Juan José. *Islanders and Empire: Smuggling and Political Defiance in Hispaniola, 1580–1690*. New York: Cambridge University Press, 2020.

Porcher, Jocelyne. "Animal Work." In *The Oxford Handbook of Animal Studies*, edited by Linda Kalof, 302–18. New York: Oxford University Press, 2017.

Portelli, Alessandro. *The Death of Luigi Trastulli, and Other Stories: Form and Meaning in Oral History*. Albany: State University of New York Press, 1991.

Pratten, David. *The Man-Leopard Murders: History and Society in Colonial Nigeria*. Bloomington: Indiana University Press, 2007.

Prestol Castillo, Freddy. *Pablo Mamá*. Santo Domingo: Editora Taller, 1985.

Prestol Castillo, Freddy. *You Can Cross the Massacre on Foot*. Translated by Margaret Randall. Durham, NC: Duke University Press, 2019.

Price, Richard. "Fishing Rites and Recipes in a Martiniquan Village." *Caribbean Studies* 6, no. 1 (1966): 3–24.

Price, Richard, ed. *Maroon Societies: Rebel Slave Communities in the Americas*. Baltimore: Johns Hopkins University Press, 1996.

Puckett, Newbell Niles. *Folk Beliefs of the Southern Negro*. Montclair, NJ: Patterson Smith, 1968.

Putnam, Lara. "Rites of Power and Rumors of Race: The Circulation of Supernatural Knowledge in the Greater Caribbean, 1890–1940." In *Obeah and Other Powers*, edited by Diana Paton and Maarit Forde, 243–67. Durham, NC: Duke University Press, 2020.

"Quirogas Garcia 'El tíguere Dominicano.'" YouTube, posted by Quirogas garcia, August 29, 2009. https://www.youtube.com/watch?v=njm_ovuGiro&t=160s.

Radcliffe-Brown, A. R. "On Joking Relationships." *Africa: Journal of the International African Institute* 13, no. 3 (1940): 195–210.

Radcliffe-Brown, A. R. "On Social Structure." In *The Social Anthropology of Radcliffe-Brown*, edited by Adam Kuper, 25–41. London: Routledge and Kegan Paul, 1977.

Rainsford, Marcus. *An Historical Account of the Black Empire of Hayti*. Edited by Paul Youngquist and Grégory Pierrot. Durham, NC: Duke University Press, 2013.

Rainsford, Marcus. *An Historical Account of the Black Empire of Hayti: Comprehending a View of the Principal Transactions in the Revolution of Saint Domingo; with its Antient and Modern State*. London: Cundee, 1805.

Ramírez, Dixa. *Colonial Phantoms: Belonging and Refusal in the Dominican Americas, from the 19th Century to the Present*. New York: New York University Press, 2018.

Ramírez, Rafael L. *What It Means to Be a Man: Reflections on Puerto Rican Masculinity*. Translated by Rosa E. Casper. New Brunswick, NJ: Rutgers University Press, 1999.

Ramírez, Rafael L., Víctor Iván García Toro, and Ineke Cunningham, eds. *Caribbean Masculinities: Working Papers*. San Juan: HIV/AIDS Research and Education Center, University of Puerto Rico, 2002.

Ramírez-D'Oleo, Dixa. "Insolence, Indolence and the Ayitian Free Black." *Interventions* 24, no. 7 (2022): 1011–28.

Ramírez López, Irio Leonel. "Díos Olivorio Mateo: The Living God." In *The Dominican Republic Reader*, edited by Eric Paul Roorda, Lauren Derby, and Raymundo González, 411–14. Durham, NC: Duke University Press, 2014.

Ramos, Alejandro Paulino, and Aquiles Castro. *Diccionario de cultura y folklore Dominicano*. Santo Domingo: ABC Editorial, 2005.

Ramsey, Kate. *The Spirits and the Law: Vodou and Power in Haiti*. Chicago: University of Chicago Press, 2011.

Rappaport, Roy A. *Pigs for the Ancestors: Ritual in the Ecology of a New Guinea People*. New Haven, CT: Yale University Press, 1984.

Rarey, Matthew Francis. "Assemblage, Occlusion, and the Art of Survival in the Black Atlantic." *African Arts* 51, no. 4 (2018): 20–33.

Raynolds, Laura T. "Harnessing Women's Work: Restructuring Agricultural and Industrial Labor Forces in the Dominican Republic." *Economic Geography* 74, no. 2 (1998): 149–69.

Raynolds, Laura T. "The Organic Agro-Export Boom in the Dominican Republic: Maintaining Tradition or Fostering Transformation?" *Latin American Research Review* 43, no. 1 (2008): 161–84.

Reader, W. J. *Unilever: A Short History*. London: Information Division, Unilever House, 1960.

Reddock, Rhoda, ed. *Interrogating Caribbean Masculinities: Theoretical and Empirical Analyses*. Kingston: University of the West Indies Press, 2004.

Rediker, Marcus. *Outlaws of the Atlantic: Sailors, Pirates, and Motley Crews in the Age of Sail*. London: Verso, 2014.

Reiss, Tom. *The Black Count: Glory, Revolution, Betrayal, and the Real Count of Monte Cristo*. New York: Broadway Books, 2012.

Rémy, Catherine. "The Animal Issue in Xenotransplantation: Controversies in France and the United States." *History and Philosophy of the Life Sciences* 31, nos. 3–4 (2009): 405–28.

Renda, Mary A. *Taking Haiti: Military Occupation and the Culture of U.S. Imperialism, 1915–1940*. Chapel Hill: University of North Carolina Press, 2001.

Renton, Kathryn. *Feral Empire: Horse and Human in the Early Modern Iberian World*. New York: Cambridge University Press, 2024.

Rey, Terry. "Kongolese Catholic Influences on Haitian Popular Catholicism: A Sociocultural Exploration." In *Central Africans and Cultural Transformations in the American Diaspora*, edited by Linda M. Heywood, 265–85. New York: Cambridge University Press, 2002.

Rey, Terry. *The Priest and the Prophetess: Abbé Ouvière, Romaine Rivière, and the Revolutionary Atlantic World*. New York: Oxford University Press, 2017.

Reyes, Gerardo. "Narco se convierte leyenda para los dominicanos." *El Nuevo Herald*, April 10, 2024. https://www.elnuevoherald.com/noticias/america -latina/article2007792.html.

Rice, Michael. *The Power of the Bull*. London: Routledge, 1998.

Richman, Karen E. *Migration and Vodou*. Gainesville: University Press of Florida, 2005.

Richman, Karen E. "A More Powerful Sorcerer: Conversion, Capital, and Haitian Transnational Migration." *New West Indian Guide* 82, nos. 1–2 (2008): 3–45.

Richman, Karen E. "Mortuary Rites and Social Dramas in Léogâne, Haiti." In *Passages and Afterworlds*, edited by Yanique Hume and Maarit Forde, 139–56. Durham, NC: Duke University Press, 2020.

Richman, Karen E. "Possession and Attachment: Notes on Moral Ritual Communication Among Haitian Descent Groups." In *Spirited Things: The Work of Possession in Afro-Atlantic Religions*, edited by Paul Christopher Johnson, 207–24. Chicago: University of Chicago Press, 2014.

Richman, Karen E. "Religion at the Epicenter: Agency and Affiliation in Léogâne After the Earthquake." *Studies in Religion/Sciences Religieuses* 41, no. 2 (2012): 148–65.

Richman, Karen E. "The Vodou State and the Protestant Nation: Haiti in the Long Twentieth Century." In *Obeah and Other Powers: The Politics of Caribbean Religion and Healing*, edited by Diana Paton and Maarit Forde, 268–87. Durham, NC: Duke University Press, 2012.

Ricoeur, Paul. *Memory, History, Forgetting*. Translated by Kathleen Blamey and David Pellauer. Chicago: University of Chicago Press, 2004.

Ricoeur, Paul. "Memory—History—Forgetting." In *The Collective Memory Reader*, edited by Jeffrey K. Olick, Vered Vinitzky-Seroussi, and Daniel Levy, 475–80. New York: Oxford University Press, 2011.

Ridore, Lemaire. "Yahweh." In Leah Gordon et al., *Kanaval: Vodou, Politics and Revolution on the Streets of Haiti*, 134–37. London: Soul Jazz, 2010.

Rigaud, Milo. *Secrets of Voodoo*. Translated by Robert B. Cross. San Francisco: City Lights, 1985.

Rigaud, Milo. *Vè-vè : Diagrammes rituels du voudou*. New York: French and European Publications, 1974.

Río Moreno, Justo Lucas del. *Ganadería, plantaciones y comercio azucarero antillano: Siglos XVI y XVII*. Santo Domingo: Academia Dominicana de la Historia, 2012.

Río Moreno, Justo Lucas del. *Guerreros y ganaderos I: Caballos y équidos españoles en la conquista y colonización de América*. Sevilla: Caja Rural Provincial de Sevilla, 1992.

Ripley, Geo. *Imágenes de posesión: Vudú dominicano*. Santo Domingo: Cocolo Editorial, 2022.

Ritvo, Harriet. *The Animal Estate: The English and Other Creatures in the Victorian Age*. Cambridge, MA: Harvard University Press, 1987.

Rivero Glean, Manuel, and Gerardo Chávez Spínola. *Cátauro de seres míticos y legendarios en Cuba*. Havana: Centro de Investigación y Desarrollo de la Cultura Cubana Juan Marinello, 2005.

Roach, Joseph. *Cities of the Dead: Circum-Atlantic Performance*. New York: Columbia University Press, 2021.

Roberts, A. F. "'Perfect' Lions, 'Perfect' Leaders.'" *Journal des Africanistes* 53, no. 1–2 (1983): 93–105.

Roberts, A. F. "The Place of Iron in African Cosmologies." In *Striking Iron: The Art of African Blacksmiths*, edited by Allen F. Roberts, Tom Joyce, and Marla Burns, 52–71. Los Angeles: Fowler Museum of Cultural History at UCLA, 2019.

Roberts, Michael. *Food Law in the United States*. Cambridge: Cambridge University Press, 2016.

Robins, Jonathan E. *Oil Palm: A Global History*. Chapel Hill: University of North Carolina Press, 2021.

Rocha, Gabriel de Avilez. "Maroons in the Montes: Toward a Political Ecology of Marronage in the Sixteenth-Century Caribbean." In *Early Modern Black Diaspora Studies: A Critical Anthology*, edited by Cassander L. Smith, Nicholas R. Jones, and Miles P. Grier, 15–35. Cham, Switzerland: Palgrave Macmillan, 2018.

Rodríguez Demorizi, Emilio. *Enciclopedia dominicana del caballo*. Ciudad Trujillo: Editora Montalvo, 1960.

Rodríguez Demorizi, Emilio. *Lengua y folklore de Santo Domingo*. Santiago, Dominican Republic: UCMM, 1975.

Rodríguez Demorizi, Emilio. *Viajeros de Francia en Santo Domingo*. Santo Domingo: Editora del Caribe, 1979.

Rohlehr, Gordon. "The Calypsonian as Artist: Freedom and Responsibility." In *Caribbean Popular Culture: Power, Politics and Performance*, edited by Yanique Hume and Aaron Kamugisha, 87–106. Kingston: Ian Randle, 2016.

Rohlehr, Gordon. "I Lawa: The Construction of Masculinity in Trinidad and Tobago Calypso." In *Interrogating Caribbean Masculinities: Theoretical and Empirical Analyses*, edited by Rhoda E. Reddock, 326–403. Kingston: University of the West Indies Press, 2004.

Román, Reinaldo L. *Governing Spirits: Religion, Miracles, and Spectacles in Cuba and Puerto Rico, 1898–1956.* Chapel Hill: University of North Carolina Press, 2007.

Roorda, Eric Paul. *The Dictator Next Door: The Good Neighbor Policy and the Trujillo Regime in the Dominican Republic, 1930–1945.* Durham, NC: Duke University Press, 1998.

Roorda, Eric Paul. "The Murder of the Mirabal Sisters in the Dominican Republic." In *Oxford Research Encyclopedia of Latin American History,* edited by Ángela Vergara. New York: Oxford University Press, 2019.

Roorda, Eric Paul, Lauren Derby, and Raymundo González, eds. *The Dominican Republic Reader: History, Culture, Politics.* Durham, NC: Duke University Press, 2014.

"The Roots of *La Sentencia*: An Interview with Rachel Nolan." *Jacobin,* June 20, 2015. https://jacobin.com/2015/06/dominican-republic-haiti-immigration-harpers.

Rosen, Lauren Coyle. *Fires of Gold: Law, Spirit, and Sacrificial Labor in Ghana.* Oakland: University of California Press, 2020.

Rotberg, Robert I. "Vodun and the Politics of Haiti." In *The African Diaspora: Interpretive Essays,* edited by Martin L. Kilson and Robert I. Rotberg, 342–65. Cambridge, MA: Harvard University Press, 1976.

The Rough Guide to Merengue and Bachata. CD. World Music Network, 2001.

Rouse, John E. *The Criollo.* Norman: University of Oklahoma Press, 1977.

Routon, Kenneth. "Conjuring the Past: Slavery and the Historical Imagination in Cuba." *American Ethnologist* 35, no. 4 (2008): 632–49.

Routon, Kenneth. *Hidden Powers of State in the Cuban Imagination.* Gainesville: University Press of Florida, 2010.

Ruiz, Frankie. "Soy un lobo domesticado." *Soloista . . . pero no solo.* Rodven Records, 1988.

Rupert, Linda Marguerite. *Creolization and Contraband: Curaçao in the Early Modern Atlantic World.* Athens: University of Georgia Press, 2012.

Safa, Helen. "Female-Headed Households and Poverty in Latin America: A Comparison of Cuba, Puerto Rico, and the Dominican Republic." In *Women's Activism in Latin America and the Caribbean, Engendering Social Justice, Democratizing Citizenship,* edited by Elizabeth Maier and Nathalie Lebon, 60–75. New Brunswick, NJ: Rutgers University Press, 2019.

Salvatore, Ricardo Donato. *Wandering Paysanos: State Order and Subaltern Experience in Buenos Aires During the Rosas Era.* Durham, NC: Duke University Press, 2003.

Sánchez, Rafael. "Channel-Surfing: Media, Mediumship, and State Authority in the María Lionza Possession Cult (Venezuela)." In *Religion and Media,* edited by Hent de Vries and Samuel Weber, 388–434. Stanford, CA: Stanford University Press, 2001.

Sánchez Botija, C. "Peste porcina africana: Nuevos desarrollos." *Revue Scientifique et Technique (International Office of Epizootics)* 1, no. 4 (1982): 991–1094.

Sánchez Mora, Alexander. "El Cadejos sí existe: Aportes folclorísticos a la lexicografía." *Káñina* 36, no. 1 (2012): 215–21.

Sánchez Valverde, Antonio. *Idea del valor de la isla española*. Ciudad Trujillo: Editora Montalvo, 1947.

Sánchez Valverde, Antonio. "The Idea of Value on Hispaniola." In *The Dominican Republic Reader: History, Culture, Politics*, edited by Eric Roorda, Lauren Derby, and Raymundo González, 88–92. Durham, NC: Duke University Press, 2014.

Sanders, Clinton R. "Actions Speak Louder Than Words: Close Relationships Between Humans and Nonhuman Animals." *Symbolic Interaction* 26, no. 3 (2003): 405–26.

Sanders, Todd, and Harry G. West. "Power Revealed and Concealed in the New World Order." In *Transparency and Conspiracy: Ethnographies of Suspicion in the New World Order*, edited by Harry G. West and Todd Sanders, 1–37. Durham, NC: Duke University Press, 2003.

Santner, Eric L. *Stranded Objects: Mourning, Memory, and Film in Postwar Germany*. Ithaca, NY: Cornell University Press, 1990.

Santos-Granero, Fernando. "Introduction: Amerindian Constructional Views of the World." In *The Occult Life of Things: Native Amazonian Theories of Materiality and Personhood*, edited by Fernando Santos-Granero, 1–30. Tucson: University of Arizona Press, 2009.

Santos-Granero, Fernando, ed. *The Occult Life of Things: Native Amazonian Theories of Materiality and Personhood*. Tucson: University of Arizona Press, 2009.

Santos-Granero, Fernando. "The Virtuous Manioc and the Horny Barbasco: Sublime and Grotesque Modes of Transformation in the Origin of Yanesha Plant Life." *Journal of Ethnobiology* 31, no. 1 (2011): 44–71.

Santos-Granero, Fernando, and Frederica Barclay. "Bundles, Stampers, and Flying Gringos: Native Perceptions of Capitalist Violence in Peruvian Amazonia." *Journal of Latin American and Caribbean Anthropology* 16, no. 1 (2011): 143–67.

Sarg, Freddy. "Comment on élève et on tue le cochon en Alsace Bossue." *Revue des Sciences Sociales de la France de l'Est Strasbourg* 9 (1980): 293–98.

Sartorius, David. *Ever Faithful: Race, Loyalty, and the Ends of Empire in Spanish Cuba*. Durham, NC: Duke University Press, 2013.

Sartorius, David. "Transitory Trust: Falsified Passports, Circulars, and Other Speculations in Nineteenth-Century Cuba." *Journal of Social History* 55, no. 1 (2021): 7–26.

Savage, John. "Slave Poison/Slave Medicine: The Persistence of Obeah in Early Nineteenth-Century Martinique." In *Obeah and Other Powers*, edited by Diana Paton and Maarit Forde, 149–71. Durham, NC: Duke University Press, 2020.

Savino, Giovanni, dir. *La comarca fija de Liborio (The Real Comarca of Liborio)— Disappearing Religious Popular Music from the Dominican Republic*. DVD and CD. Magnetic Art Productions, 2008.

Savino, Giovanni, dir. *The Culture of Palo—Palo Music and Oral Traditions from the Dominican Republic*. DVD. EarthCDs, 2005.

Savino, Giovanni, dir. *Misterios—A Journey in the Complex and Mysterious World of Vudú, Filmed in New York, Haiti, and the Dominican Republic*. DVD. EarthCDs, 2005.

Scarano, Francisco A. "The *Jíbaro* Masquerade and the Subaltern Politics of Creole Identity Formation in Puerto Rico, 1745–1823." *American Historical Review* 101, no. 5 (1996): 1398–431.

Schama, Simon. *Landscape and Memory*. New York: Alfred A. Knopf, 1995.

Schefer, Charles, and H. Cordier, eds. *Recueil de voyages et de documents pour servir à l'histoire de la géographie depuis le XIIIe jusqu'à la fin du XVIe siècle, vol. IV. Discours de la navigation de Jean et Raoul Parmentier*. Amsterdam: Philo Press, 1882.

Schendel, Willem van, and Itty Abraham, eds. *Illicit Flows and Criminal Things: States, Borders, and the Other Side of Globalization*. Bloomington: Indiana University Press, 2005.

Scheper-Hughes, Nancy. *Death Without Weeping: The Violence of Everyday Life in Brazil*. Berkeley: University of California Press, 1992.

Schudson, Michael. *Advertising, the Uneasy Persuasion: Its Dubious Impact on American Society*. New York: Basic Books, 1984.

Scott, James C. *The Art of Not Being Governed: An Anarchist History of Upland Southeast Asia*. New Haven, CT: Yale University Press, 2009.

Scott, James C. *Domination and the Arts of Resistance: Hidden Transcripts*. New Haven, CT: Yale University Press, 1990.

Scott, James C. *The Moral Economy of the Peasant: Rebellion and Subsistence in Southeast Asia*. New Haven, CT: Yale University Press, 1976.

Scott, Julius Sherrard. *The Common Wind: Afro-American Currents in the Age of the Haitian Revolution*. London: Verso, 2018.

Scott, Rebecca J. "Reclaiming Gregoria's Mule: The Meanings of Freedom in the Arimao and Caunao Valleys, Cienfuegos, Cuba, 1880–1899." *Past and Present* 170, no. 1 (2001): 181–216.

Scott, Rebecca J. *Slave Emancipation in Cuba: The Transition to Free Labor, 1860–1899*. Princeton, NJ: Princeton University Press, 1985.

Seabrook, William. *The Magic Island*. New York: Dover, 2016.

Seigworth, Gregory J., and Melissa Gregg. "An Inventory of Shimmers." In *The Affect Theory Reader*, edited by Melissa Gregg and Gregory J. Seigworth, 1–28. Durham, NC: Duke University Press, 2010.

Serpell, James. *In the Company of Animals: A Study of Human-Animal Relationships*. Oxford: Blackwell, 1986.

Shalhoub-Kevorkian, Nadera. "The Occupation of the Senses: The Prosthetic and Aesthetic of State Terror." *British Journal of Criminology* 57, no. 6 (2017): 1279–300.

Shanklin, Eugenia. "Sustenance and Symbol: Anthropological Studies of Domesticated Animals." *Annual Review of Anthropology* 14 (1985): 375–403.

Shapiro, Kenneth. "Understanding Dogs Through Kinesthetic Empathy, Social Construction, and History." *Anthrozoos* 3, no. 3 (1990): 184–95.

Sharpe, Christina Elizabeth. *In the Wake: On Blackness and Being*. Durham, NC: Duke University Press, 2016.

Sharpe, Jenny. *Immaterial Archives: An African Diaspora Poetics of Loss*. Evanston, IL: Northwestern University Press, 2020.

Shaw, Rosalind. *Memories of the Slave Trade: Ritual and the Historical Imagination in Sierra Leone*. Chicago: University of Chicago Press, 2002.

Sheller, Mimi. *Consuming the Caribbean: From Arawaks to Zombies*. London: Routledge, 2003.

Sheller, Mimi. "Sword-Bearing Citizens." In *Citizenship from Below: Erotic Agency and Caribbean Freedom*, 142–65. Durham, NC: Duke University Press, 2012.

Shepherd, Verene. *Livestock, Sugar and Slavery: Contested Terrain in Colonial Jamaica*. Kingston: Ian Randle, 2009.

Shipton, Parker MacDonald. *Bitter Money: Cultural Economy and Some African Meanings of Forbidden Commodities*. Washington, DC: American Anthropological Association, 1989.

Shipton, Parker MacDonald. *The Nature of Entrustment: Intimacy, Exchange, and the Sacred in Africa*. New Haven, CT: Yale University Press, 2007.

"Shooting and Hunting in Florida." *North American and United States Gazette* 72, nos. 2–3 (1854).

Silié, Rubén. *Economía, esclavitud y población: Ensayo de interpretación histórica del Santo Domingo español en el siglo XVIII*. Santo Domingo: Academia Dominicana de la Historia, 2009.

Silié, Rubén. "The Hato and the Conuco: The Emergence of Creole Culture." In *Dominican Cultures: The Making of a Caribbean Society*, edited by Sheridan Wigginton and Bernardo Vega, 409–12. Translated by Christine Ayorinde. Princeton, NJ: Markus Wiener, 2009.

Silverstein, Michael. "The Secret Life of Texts." In *Natural Histories of Discourse*, edited by Michael Silverstein and Greg Urban, 81–105. Chicago: University of Chicago Press, 1996.

Silverstein, Michael, and Greg Urban, eds. *Natural Histories of Discourse*. Chicago: University of Chicago Press, 1996.

Simmel, Georg. "The Sociology of Secrecy and of Secret Societies." *American Journal of Sociology* 11, no. 4 (1906): 441–98.

Simmel, Georg. "The Stranger." In *The Sociology of Georg Simmel*, 402–408. Translated by Kurt H. Wolff. Glencoe, IL: Free Press, 1950.

Simpkins, Kate, Juniper Johnson, and Dannie Brice. "The Makandal Text Network." Early Caribbean Digital Archive, 2019. https://ecda.northeastern.edu/makandal-exhibit-introduction.

Simpson, G. E. "Haitian Magic." *Social Forces* 19, no. 1 (1940): 95–100.

Simpson, G. E. "Loup Garou and Loa Tales from Northern Haiti." *Journal of American Folklore* 55, no. 218 (1942): 219–27.

Simpson, G. E. "Magical Practices in Northern Haiti." *Journal of American Folklore* 67, no. 266 (1954): 395–403.

Sloane, Hans. *A Voyage to the Islands Madera, Barbados, Nieves, S. Christophers and Jamaica: With the Natural History of the Herbs and Trees, Four-Footed Beasts, Fishes, Birds, Insects, Reptiles, &c. of the Last of Those Islands; to Which Is Prefix'd, an Introduction, Wherein Is an Account of the Inhabitants, Air, Waters, Diseases, Trade, &c. of That Place, with Some Relations Concerning the Neighbouring Continent, and Islands of America. Illustrated with Figures of the Things Described, Which Have Not Been Heretofore Engraved.* London: Printed by B.M. for the author, 1707.

Sluyter, Andrew. *Black Ranching Frontiers: African Cattle Herders of the Atlantic World, 1500–1900.* New Haven, CT: Yale University Press, 2012.

Smith, Jay M. *Monsters of the Gévaudan: The Making of a Beast.* Cambridge, MA: Harvard University Press, 2011.

Smith, Jonathan Z. "I Am a Parrot (Red)." *History of Religions* 11, no. 4 (1972): 391–413.

Smith, Katherine. "Atis Rezistans: Gede and the Art of Vagabondaj." In *Obeah and Other Powers: The Politics of Caribbean Religion and Healing*, edited by Diana Paton and Maarit Forde, 121–48. Durham, NC: Duke University Press, 2012.

Smith, Katherine. "Dialoging with the Urban Dead in Haiti." *Southern Quarterly* 47, no. 4 (2010): 61–90.

Smith, Katherine. "Genealogies of Gede." In *In Extremis: Death and Life in 21st-Century Haitian Art*, edited by Donald Cosentino, 84–99. Los Angeles: Fowler Museum of Cultural History at UCLA, 2012.

Smith, Katherine. "Lansetkòd: Memory, Mimicry, Masculinity." In *Kanaval: Vodou, Politics and Revolution on the Streets of Haiti*, edited by Leah Gordon et al., 71–106. London: Soul Jazz, 2010.

Smith, Katherine. "Le Monde Invisible: Art, Death and Vodou in Urban Haiti." Unpublished manuscript.

Smith, Katherine, and Jerry Philogene. *Myrlande Constant: The Work of Radiance.* Los Angeles: UCLA Fowler Museum of Cultural History, 2023.

Smith, Mark M. *A Sensory History Manifesto.* University Park: Pennsylvania State University Press, 2021.

Smith, M. G. *Kinship and Community in Carriacou.* New Haven, CT: Yale University Press, 1962.

Smith, Raymond T. *Kinship and Class in the West Indies: A Genealogical Study of Jamaica and Guyana.* Cambridge: Cambridge University Press, 1988.

Smith, Raymond T. *The Matrifocal Family: Power, Pluralism, and Politics.* New York: Routledge, 1996.

Somers, Margaret R. "The Narrative Constitution of Identity: A Relational and Network Approach." *Theory and Society* 23, no. 5 (1994): 605–49.

Soto David, Moises de, and Juan Pérez Terrero. "Un hallazgo arqueológico: Armas y objetos del negro cimarrón." *Boletín del Museo del Hombre Dominicano*, no. 22 (1989): 83–93.

"Soup Joumou." Haitian Recipes. Accessed February 3, 2025. https://haitian -recipes.com/soup-joumou/.

Sousa, Lisa. *The Woman Who Turned Into a Jaguar, and Other Narratives of Native Women in Archives of Colonial Mexico*. Stanford, CA: Stanford University Press, 2017.

Sprinker, Michael, ed. *Ghostly Demarcations: A Symposium on Jacques Derrida's "Specters of Marx."* London: Verso, 1999.

Spyer, Patricia, ed. *Border Fetishisms: Material Objects in Unstable Spaces*. New York: Routledge, 1998.

"A Stand Against Statelessness: Haitian-Dominicans and Refugees Protest Against Statelessness in the Dominican Republic." Council on Hemispheric Affairs. July 23, 2013. https://coha.org/a-stand-against-statelessness-haitian-dominicans -and-refugees-protest-against-statelessness-in-the-dominican-republic/.

State Sugar Council. "Dominican, Cut the Cane!" In *The Dominican Republic Reader*, edited by Eric Roorda, Lauren Derby, and Raymundo González, 368. Durham, NC: Duke University Press, 2014.

Stefanelli, Eugenia. *Country Fact Sheet on Food and Agriculture Policy Trends— Dominican Republic*. Rome: FAO, 2016. https://www.fao.org/publications/card /en/c/a5a54669-8a75-4c3b-b704-45ef4586eb6f/.

Stevens, Alta Mae. "Manje in Haitian Culture: The Symbolic Significance of Manje in Haitian Culture." *Journal of Haitian Studies* 1, no. 1 (1995): 75–88.

Stewart, Kathleen. *Ordinary Affects*. Durham, NC: Duke University Press, 2007.

Stewart, Pamela J., and Andrew Strathern. *Witchcraft, Sorcery, Rumors, and Gossip*. Cambridge: Cambridge University Press, 2003.

St. John, Spenser. *Hayti: Or, The Black Republic*. London: Smith, Elder, 1889.

Stoler, Ann Laura. *Along the Archival Grain: Epistemic Anxieties and Colonial Common Sense*. Princeton, NJ: Princeton University Press, 2009.

Stoler, Ann Laura, ed. *Imperial Debris: On Ruins and Ruination*. Durham, NC: Duke University Press, 2013.

Stoler, Ann Laura. "'In Cold Blood': Hierarchies of Credibility and the Politics of Colonial Narratives." *Representations* 37, no. 1 (1992): 151–89.

Stoler, Ann Laura. "Introduction: 'The Rot Remains.'" In *Imperial Debris: On Ruins and Ruination*, edited by Ann Laura Stoler, 1–36. Durham, NC: Duke University Press, 2013.

Stoller, Paul. *Embodying Colonial Memories: Spirit Possession, Power, and the Hauka in West Africa*. New York: Routledge, 1995.

Stoller, Paul. *The Taste of Ethnographic Things: The Senses in Anthropology*. Philadelphia: University of Pennsylvania Press, 1989.

Stone, Erin. "America's First Slave Revolt: Indians and African Slaves in Española, 1500–1534." *Ethnohistory* 60, no. 2 (2013): 195–217.

Stone, Erin. "War and Rescate: The Sixteenth-Century Circum-Caribbean Indigenous Slave Trade." In *The Spanish Caribbean and the Atlantic World in the Long Sixteenth Century*, edited by Ida Altman and David Wheat, 47–68. Nebraska: University of Nebraska Press, 2019.

"The Strange Economic Miracle of the Dominican Republic." *Dominican Today*, January 18, 2020. https://dominicantoday.com/dr/economy/2020/01/18/the -strange-economic-miracle-of-the-dominican-republic/.

Strathern, Marilyn. "Eating (and Feeding)." *Cambridge Journal of Anthropology* 30, no. 2 (2012): 1–14.

Strathern, Marilyn. *The Gender of the Gift: Problems with Women and Problems with Society in Melanesia*. Berkeley: University of California Press, 1988.

Street, John M. "Feral Animals in Hispaniola." *Geographical Review* 52, no. 3 (1962): 400–406.

Striffler, Steve, and Mark Moberg, eds. *Banana Wars: Power, Production, and History in the Americas*. Durham, NC: Duke University Press, 2003.

Strongman, Roberto. "Transcorporeality in Vodou." *Journal of Haitian Studies* 14, no. 2 (2008): 4–29.

Suárez, Lucía M. *The Tears of Hispaniola: Haitian and Dominican Diaspora Memory*. Gainesville: University of Florida Press, 2006.

Sundaram, Jomo Kwame, and Anis Chowdhury. "Agricultural Trade Liberalization Undermined Food Security—World." ReliefWeb, May 21, 2018. https:// reliefweb.int/report/world/agricultural-trade-liberalization-undermined -food-security.

Suprema Corte de Justicia, República Dominicana. *Boletín judicial*. Ciudad Trujillo: República Dominicana, 1928.

Taussig, Michael. *Defacement: Public Secrecy and the Labor of the Negative*. Stanford, CA: Stanford University Press, 1999.

Taussig, Michael. *The Devil and Commodity Fetishism in South America*. Chapel Hill: University of North Carolina Press, 1980.

Taussig, Michael. "History as Sorcery." *Representations*, no. 7 (1984): 87–109.

Taussig, Michael. *Mimesis and Alterity: A Particular History of the Senses*. New York: Routledge, 1993.

Taussig, Michael. *Shamanism, Colonialism, and the Wild Man: A Study in Terror and Healing*. Chicago: University of Chicago Press, 1987.

Taussig, Michael. "What Color Is the Sacred?" *Critical Inquiry* 33, no. 1 (2006): 28–51.

Taylor, Charles. "To Follow a Rule . . ." In *Bourdieu: Critical Perspectives*, edited by Pierre Bourdieu, Craig J. Calhoun, Edward LiPuma, and Moishe Postone, 45–60. Chicago: University of Chicago Press, 1993.

Tejeda Ortíz, Dagoberto. *El carnaval dominicano: Antecedentes, tendencias y perspectivas*. Santo Domingo: Instituto Panamericano de Geografía e Historia, Sección Nacional de Dominicana, 2008.

Tejera, Emiliano. "Public Enemies: The Revolutionary and the Pig." In *The Dominican Republic Reader*, edited by Eric Roorda, Lauren Derby, and Raymundo González, 201–4. Durham, NC: Duke University Press, 2014.

Terrall, Mary. "Heroic Narratives of Quest and Discovery." *Configurations* 6, no. 2 (1998): 223–42.

Thicknesse, Philip. *Memoirs and Anecdotes of Philip Thicknesse: Late Lieutenant Governor of Land Guard Fort, and Unfortunately Father to George Touchet, Baron Audley*. Dublin: Printed by Graisberry and Campbell for William Jones M., 1790.

Thoby-Marcelin, Philippe. *The Beast of the Haitian Hills*. Translated by Peter C. Rhodes. New York: Rinehart, 1946.

Thompson, E. P. "The Moral Economy of the English Crowd in the Eighteenth Century." *Past and Present* 50, no. 1 (1971): 76–136.

Thompson, Krista A. *Shine: The Visual Economy of Light in African Diasporic Aesthetic Practice*. Durham, NC: Duke University Press, 2015.

Thompson, Robert Farris. *Flash of the Spirit: African and Afro-American Art and Philosophy*. New York: Random House, 1983.

Thompson, Robert Farris. *The Four Moments of the Sun: Kongo Art in Two Worlds*. Washington, DC: National Gallery of Art, 1981.

Thompson, Robert Farris. "From the Isle Beneath the Sea: Haiti's Africanizing Vodou Art." In *Sacred Arts of Haitian Vodou*, edited by Donald Cosentino, 91–119. Los Angeles: UCLA Fowler Museum of Cultural History, 1995.

Thomson, Alistair. "Indexing and Interpreting Emotion: Joy and Shame in Oral History." *Oral History Australia Journal*, no. 41 (2019): 1–11.

Thornton, Brendan Jamal. *Negotiating Respect: Pentecostalism, Masculinity, and the Politics of Spiritual Authority in the Dominican Republic*. Gainesville: University Press of Florida, 2016.

Thornton, John. *Africa and Africans in the Making of the Atlantic World, 1400–1800*. New York: Cambridge University Press, 1998.

Thylefors, Markel. "Poverty and Sorcery in Haiti." PhD diss., Dept. of Social Anthropology, Göteborg University, 2002.

"Timeline: The History of Smithfield Foods." *Virginian Pilot*, May 29, 2013. https://www.pilotonline.com/2013/05/29/timeline-the-history-of-smithfield-foods/Acquisitions.

Todorov, Tzvetan. *The Conquest of America: The Question of the Other*. Norman: University of Oklahoma Press, 1999.

Tompkins, Kyla Wazana. *Racial Indigestion: Eating Bodies in the 19th Century*. New York: New York University Press, 2012.

Torre, Oscar de la. "The Well That Wept Blood." *American Historical Review* 127, no. 4 (2023): 1635–58.

Tortorici, Zeb. "Visceral Archives of the Body: Consuming the Dead, Digesting the Divine." *GLQ: A Journal of Lesbian and Gay Studies* 20, no. 4 (2014): 407–37.

Tráfico de seres humanos y migraciones: Un análisis desde la perspectiva de los derechos humanos; Conferencia internacional "Tráfico de seres humanos y migraciones." Madrid: Iepala Editorial, 2005.

Trio Matamoros. *35 canciones desde Cuba con amor.* CD. Vintage Music, 2012.

Trouillot, Évelyne. *The Infamous Rosalie.* Translated by Marjorie Attignol Salvodon. Lincoln: University of Nebraska Press, 2020.

Trouillot, Michel-Rolph. "Culture on the Edges: Creolization in the Plantation Context." In *Trouillot Remixed: The Michel-Rolph Trouillot Reader,* edited by Yarimar Bonilla, Greg Beckett, and Mayanthi L. Fernando, 194–214. Durham, NC: Duke University Press, 2021.

Trouillot, Michel-Rolph. *Silencing the Past: Power and the Production of History.* Boston: Beacon, 1995.

Tsing, Anna. "Unruly Edges: Mushrooms as Companion Species." *Environmental Humanities* 1, no. 1 (2012): 141–54.

Tsing, Anna, Jennifer Deger, Alder Keleman Saxena, and Feifei Zhou, eds. *The Feral Atlas.* Stanford, CA: Stanford University Press, 2021.

Tsing, Anna, Heather Swanson, Elaine Gan, and Nils Bubandt, eds. *Arts of Living on a Damaged Planet.* Minneapolis: University of Minnesota Press, 2017.

Turits, Richard Lee. *Foundations of Despotism: Peasants, the Trujillo Regime, and Modernity in Dominican History.* Stanford, CA: Stanford University Press, 2003.

Turits, Richard Lee. "Slavery and the Pursuit of Freedom in 16th-Century Santo Domingo." In *Oxford Research Encyclopedia of Latin American History,* edited by Ángela Vergara. New York: Oxford University Press, 2019.

Turits, Richard Lee. "A World Destroyed, a Nation Imposed: The 1937 Haitian Massacre in the Dominican Republic." *Hispanic American Historical Review* 82, no. 3 (2002): 589–635.

Turits, Richard Lee, and Lauren Derby. "Haitian-Dominican History and the 1937 Haitian Massacre." In *The Border of Lights Reader: Bearing Witness to Genocide in the Dominican Republic,* edited by Megan Jeanette Myers and Edward Paulino, 43–53. Amherst, MA: Amherst College Press, 2021.

Turnbull, David. *Travels in the West: Cuba; with Notices of Porto Rico, and the Slave Trade.* London: Longman, 1840.

Turner, Patricia A. *I Heard It Through the Grapevine: Rumor in African-American Culture.* Berkeley: University of California Press, 1993.

Turner, Terence. "Commentary: Ethno-Ethnohistory; Myth and History in Native South American Representations of Contact with Western Society." In *Rethinking History and Myth: Indigenous South American Perspectives on the Past,* edited by Jonathan David Hill, 235–81. Urbana: University of Illinois Press, 1988.

Turner, Terence. "'We Are Parrots,' 'Twins Are Birds': Play of Tropes as Operational Structure." In *Beyond Metaphor: The Theory of Tropes in Anthropology,* edited by James W. Fernandez, 121–58. Stanford, CA: Stanford University Press, 1991,

Turner, Victor W. *The Ritual Process: Structure and Anti-Structure*. Ithaca, NY: Cornell University Press, 1977.

Tussac, F.-R. de. *Flore des Antilles ou Histoire générale botanique, rurale, et économique des végétaux indigènes des Antilles, et des exotiques qu'on est parvenu à y naturaliser*, vol. 1. Paris: L'Auteur, 1808.

Tutino, John. "From Involution to Revolution in Mexico: Liberal Development, Patriarchy, and Social Violence in the Central Highlands, 1870–1915." *History Compass* 6, no. 3 (2008): 796–842.

Twiss, Richard. *Travels Through Portugal and Spain, in 1772–1773*. London: Robinson, 1775.

Ubiñas Renville, Juan Guaroa. *Historias y leyendas afro-dominicanas*. Santo Domingo: Manatí, 2003.

Ubiñas Renville, Juan Guaroa. *Mitos, creencias y leyendas dominicanas*. Santo Domingo: Ediciones Librería la Trinitaria, 2000.

Ubiñas Renville, Juan Guaroa. *Pedro Bululú: La africanidad en el imaginario dominicano*. Santo Domingo: n.p., 2015.

Ulrickson, Maria Cecilia. "'Esclavos que fueron' in Santo Domingo, 1768–1844." PhD diss., Department of History, Notre Dame University, 2018.

United Nations High Commissioner for Refugees. "Freedom in the World 2008—Dominican Republic." Refworld, July 2, 2008. https://www.refworld.org/docid/487ca20555.html.

Upham, Nathan S. "Past and Present of Insular Caribbean Mammals: Understanding Holocene Extinctions to Inform Modern Biodiversity Conservation." *Journal of Mammalogy* 98, no. 4 (2017): 913–17.

Valerio Holguín, Fernando. "Oda al Mangú." *Acento*, February 10, 2022. https://acento.com.do/opinion/oda-al-mangu-9031623.html.

Valoy, Cuco, con la Nueva Tribu. "Anaisa." Anaisa/Swing Latino, 1990.

Van Berkel, Adriaan. *The Voyages of Adriaan van Berkel to Guiana: Amerindian-Dutch Relationships in 17th-Century Guyana*. Edited by Martijn van den Bel, Lodewijk Hulsman, and Lodewijk Wagenaar. Leiden: Sidestone Press, 2014.

Van Bockhaven, Vicky. "Leopard-Men of the Congo in Literature and Popular Imagination." *Tydskrif vir Letterkunde* 46, no. 1 (2017): 79–94.

Van Deusen, Nancy E. *Global Indios: The Indigenous Struggle for Justice in Sixteenth-Century Spain*. Durham, NC: Duke University Press, 2015.

Vanhee, Hein. "Central African Popular Christianity and the Making of Haitian Vodou Religion." In *Central Africans and Cultural Transformations in the American Diaspora*, edited by Linda M. Haywood, 243–64. New York: Cambridge University Press, 2002.

Vargas, Tahira. *De la casa a la calle: Estudio de la familia y la vecindad en un barrio de Santo Domingo*. Santo Domingo: Editora Búho, 1998.

Vargas, Tahira. "Everyday Life in a Poor Barrio." In *The Dominican Republic Reader: History, Culture, Politics*, edited by Eric Roorda, Lauren Derby, and Raymundo González, 450–55. Durham, NC: Duke University Press, 2014.

Vargas Llosa, Mario. *The Feast of the Goat*. Translated by Edith Grossman. New York: Farrar, Straus and Giroux, 2001.

Varner, John Grier, and Jeannette Johnson Varner. *Dogs of the Conquest*. Norman: University of Oklahoma Press, 1983.

Vaughan, Umi. "*Timba Brava*: Maroon Music in Cuba." In *Caribbean Popular Culture: Power, Politics and Performance*, edited by Yanique Hume and Aaron Kamugisha, 667–92. Kingston: Ian Randle, 2016.

Vega, Bernardo, and Emilio Cordero Michel, eds. *Asuntos dominicanos en archivos ingleses*. Santo Domingo: Fundación Cultural Dominicana, 1993.

Vega, Bernardo, and Carlos Esteban Deive. "Topónimos dominicanos vinculados a esclavos y a Africa. (Toponymes dominicains liés aux esclaves et à l'Afrique)." *Boletín del Museo del Hombre Dominicano*, no. 14 (1980): 147–64.

Vega, Wenceslao B. "Elías Piña y el origen de su denominación." *Diario Libre*, October 20, 2019.

Veloz Maggiolo, Marcio, Rímoli O. Renato, and Fernando Luna Calderón. "Investigaciones arqueológicas en Cueva Collantes." *Boletín del Museo del Hombre Dominicano*, no. 18 (1983): 73–90.

Velten, Hannah. *Cow*. London: Reaktion, 2007.

Vergara, Germán. "Animals in Latin American History." In *Oxford Research Encyclopedia of Latin American History*, edited by Ángela Vergara. New York: Oxford University Press. Published online, 2018.

Vidal, Silvia, and Neil L. Whitehead. "Dark Shamans and the Shamanic State: Sorcery and Witchcraft as Political Process in Guyana and the Venezuelan Amazon." In *In Darkness and Secrecy*, edited by Neil L. Whitehead and Robin Wright, 60–90. Durham, NC: Duke University Press, 2004.

Viveiros de Castro, Eduardo. "Cosmological Deixis and Amerindian Perspectivism." *Journal of the Royal Anthropological Institute* 4, no. 3 (1998): 469–88.

Viveiros de Castro, Eduardo. *From the Enemy's Point of View: Humanity and Divinity in an Amazonian Society*. Translated by Catherine V. Howard. Chicago: University of Chicago Press, 2020.

Wachtel, Nathan. *Gods and Vampires: Return to Chipaya*. Translated by Carol Volk. Chicago: University of Chicago Press, 1994.

Wade, Peter. *Blackness and Race Mixture: The Dynamics of Racial Identity in Colombia*. Baltimore: Johns Hopkins University Press, 1993.

Wald, Susan. "Gulf and Western's 'Slave Labor Camp' in Dominican Republic." *Intercontinental Press* 16, no. 42 (1978): 12–32.

Walker, Andrew. "Strains of Unity: Emancipation, Property, and the Post-Revolutionary State in Haitian Santo Domingo, 1822–1844." PhD diss., Department of History, University of Michigan, 2018.

Walton, William. *Present State of the Spanish Colonies; Including a Particular Report of Hispañola, or the Spanish Part of Santo Domingo; with a General Survey of the Settlements on the South Continent of America.* London: Printed for Longman, Hurst, Rees and Orme, 1810.

Wareing, John. "'Violently Taken Away or Cheatingly Duckoyed': The Illicit Recruitment in London of Indentured Servants for the American Colonies, 1645–1718." *London Journal* 26, no. 2 (2001): 1–22.

Wasch, Adam. "Children Left Behind: The Effect of Major League Baseball on Education in the Dominican Republic." *Texas Review of Entertainment and Sports Law* 11, no. 1 (2009): 99–128.

Weaver, Karol K. *Medical Revolutionaries: The Enslaved Healers of Eighteenth-Century Saint Domingue.* Urbana: University of Illinois Press, 2006.

Weheliye, Alexander G. *Habeas Viscus: Racializing Assemblages, Biopolitics, and Black Feminist Theories of the Human.* Durham, NC: Duke University Press, 2014.

Weiner, Annette B. *Inalienable Possessions: The Paradox of Keeping-While-Giving.* Berkeley: University of California Press, 1992.

Weisberger, Mindy. "Humans Doomed Caribbean's 'Lost World' of Ancient Mammals." Livescience.com, July 11, 2017. https://www.livescience.com/60870-caribbean-lost-world-ancient-mammals.html.

Weismantel, Mary J. *Cholas and Pishtacos: Stories of Race and Sex in the Andes.* Chicago: University of Chicago Press, 2001.

Weismantel, Mary J. *Food, Gender, and Poverty in the Ecuadorian Andes.* Philadelphia: University of Pennsylvania Press, 1988.

Weismantel, Mary J. "White Cannibals: Fantasies of Racial Violence in the Andes." *Identities* 4, no. 1 (1997): 9–43.

Werner, Marion. *Global Displacements: The Making of Uneven Development in the Caribbean.* Sussex: John Wiley and Sons, 2015.

Werner, Marion. "Placing the State in the Contemporary Food Regime: Uneven Regulatory Development in the Dominican Republic." *Journal of Peasant Studies* 48, no. 1 (2021): 137–58.

West, Harry G. *Ethnographic Sorcery.* Chicago: University of Chicago Press, 2007.

West, Harry G., and Todd Sanders, eds. *Transparency and Conspiracy: Ethnographies of Suspicion in the New World Order.* Durham, NC: Duke University Press, 2003.

Wheat, David. *Atlantic Africa and the Spanish Caribbean, 1570–1640.* Chapel Hill: University of North Carolina Press, 2016.

White, Hayden. "The Forms of Wildness: Archaeology of an Idea." In *Tropics of Discourse: Essays in Cultural Criticism*, 150–83. Baltimore: Johns Hopkins University Press, 1978.

White, Luise. *Speaking with Vampires: Rumor and History in Colonial Africa.* Berkeley: University of California Press, 2000.

White, Luise. "'They Could Make Their Victims Dull': Genders and Genres, Fantasies and Cures in Colonial Southern Uganda." *American Historical Review* 100, no. 5 (1995): 1379–402.

Whitehead, Neil L. "Afterword: The Taste of Death." In *Terror and Violence: Imagination and the Unimaginable-*, edited by Andrew Strathern, Pamela J. Stewart, and Neil L. Whitehead, 231–38. London: Pluto Press, 2006.

Whitehead, Neil L. "Conclusion: Loving, Being, Killing Animals." In *Centering Animals in Latin American History*, edited by Martha Few and Zeb Tortorici, 329–46. Durham, NC: Duke University Press, 2020.

Whitehead, Neil L. *Dark Shamans: Kanaimà and the Poetics of Violent Death*. Durham, NC: Duke University Press, 2002.

Whitehead, Neil L. *Of Cannibals and Kings: Primal Anthropology in the Americas*. University Park: Pennsylvania State University Press, 2011.

Whitehead, Neil L., and Sverker Finnström, "Introduction: Virtual War and Magical Death." In *Virtual War and Magical Death: Technologies and Imaginaries for Terror and Killing*, edited by Neil L. Whitehead and Sverker Finnström, 1–25. Durham, NC: Duke University Press, 2013.

Whitehead, Neil L., and Robin Wright, eds. *In Darkness and Secrecy: The Anthropology of Assault Sorcery and Witchcraft in Amazonia*. Durham, NC: Duke University Press, 2004.

Whitten, Norman E., and Arlene Torres, eds. *Blackness in Latin America and the Caribbean: Social Dynamics and Cultural Transformations*. 2 vols. Bloomington: Indiana University Press, 1998.

Wilentz, Amy. *Farewell, Fred Voodoo: A Letter from Haiti*. New York: Simon and Schuster, 2013.

Wilk, Richard. "The Extractive Economy: An Early Phase of the Globalization of Diet." *Review (Fernand Braudel Center for the Study of Economies, Historical Systems, and Civilizations)* 27, no. 4 (2004): 285–306.

Willerslev, Rane. *Soul Hunters: Hunting, Animism, and Personhood Among the Siberian Yukaghirs*. Berkeley: University of California Press, 2007.

Williams, Raymond. *The Country and the City*. New York: Oxford University Press, 1973.

Williams-Forson, Psyche A. *Building Houses out of Chicken Legs: Black Women, Food, and Power*. Chapel Hill: University of North Carolina Press, 2006.

Wilson, Charles. *The History of Unilever: A Study in Economic Growth and Social Change*. London: Cassell, 1970.

Wilson, Peter J. *Crab Antics: The Social Anthropology of English-Speaking Negro Societies of the Caribbean*. New Haven, CT: Yale University Press, 1973.

Wilson, Peter J. "Reputation and Respectability: A Suggestion for Caribbean Ethnology." *Man* 4, no. 1 (1969): 70–84.

Wilson, Samuel M. *Hispaniola: Caribbean Chiefdoms in the Age of Columbus*. Tuscaloosa: University of Alabama Press, 1990.

Wipper, Audrey. "The Partnership: The Horse-Rider Relationship in Eventing." *Symbolic Interaction* 23, no. 1 (2000): 47–70.

Wolseth, Jon. *Life on the Malecón: Children and Youth on the Streets of Santo Domingo*. New Brunswick, NJ: Rutgers University Press, 2015.

Woodard, Vincent. *The Delectable Negro: Human Consumption and Homoeroticism Within U.S. Slave Culture.* Edited by Justin A. Joyce and Dwight A. McBride. New York: New York University Press, 2014.

Wooding, Bridget. "Haitian Immigrants and Their Descendants in the Dominican Republic." In *Oxford Research Encyclopedia of Latin American History,* edited by Ángela Vergara. New York: Oxford University Press. Published online, 2018.

Wong, Dwayne. *Jumbie Tales.* N.p.: CreateSpace, 2015.

World Bank. "The World Bank in Dominican Republic." Accessed March 6, 2022. https://www.worldbank.org/en/country/dominicanrepublic.

Wright, Irene Aloha. *The Early History of Cuba, 1492–1586.* New York: Macmillan, 1916.

Wucker, Michele. *Why the Cocks Fight: Dominicans, Haitians, and the Struggle for Hispaniola.* New York: Hill and Wang, 1999.

Wynter, Sylvia. "Novel and History, Plot and Plantation." *Savacou* 5 (1971): 95–102.

Valoy, Cuco. *Anaisa/Swing Latino.* 1990.

Yingling, Charlton. "The Maroons of Santo Domingo in the Age of Revolutions: Adaptation and Evasion, 1783–1800." *History Workshop Journal,* no. 79 (2015): 25–51.

Yingling, Charlton, and Tyler Parry. "The Canine Terror." *Jacobin,* May 19, 2016. https://jacobin.com/2016/05/dogs-bloodhounds-slavery-police-brutality -racism.

Yoder, April. *Pitching Democracy: Baseball and Politics in the Dominican Republic.* Austin: University of Texas Press, 2023.

Zeledón C., Elías. *Leyendas ticas de la tierra, los animales, las cosas, la religión y magia.* San José: Editorial Costa Rica, 1994.

Zeuske, Michael. "Hidden Markers, Open Secrets: On Naming, Race-Marking, and Race-Making in Cuba." *New West Indian Guide* 76, nos. 3–4 (2002): 211–41.

Zuckerman, Jocelyn C. *Planet Palm: How Palm Oil Ended Up in Everything—and Endangered the World.* New York: New Press, 2021.

INDEX

Page numbers in italics indicate illustrations.

www.ingramcontent.com/pod-product-compliance
Lightning Source LLC
Chambersburg PA
CBHW032342280326
41935CB00008B/423